JEWISH IDENTITY
IN EARLY RABBINIC WRITINGS

ARBEITEN ZUR GESCHICHTE DES ANTIKEN JUDENTUMS UND DES URCHRISTENTUMS

HERAUSGEGEBEN VON

Martin Hengel (Tübingen), Peter Schäfer (Berlin),
Pieter W. van der Horst (Utrecht), Martin Goodman (Oxford),
Daniël R. Schwartz (Jerusalem)

XXIII

JEWISH IDENTITY
IN EARLY RABBINIC WRITINGS

BY

SACHA STERN

E.J. BRILL
LEIDEN · NEW YORK · KÖLN
1994

Library of Congress Cataloging-in-Publication Data

Stern, Sacha.
   Jewish identity in early rabbinic writings/ by Sacha Stern.
      p.   cm. — (Arbeiten zur Geschichte des antiken Judentums und des Urchristentums, ISSN 0169-734X ; [Bd.] 23)
   Rev. version of the author's thesis (D.Phil.)—Jews' College.
   Includes bibliographical references and index.
   ISBN 9004100121 (alk. paper)
      1. Jews in rabbinical literature.   2. Jews—Identity.   3. Gentiles in rabbinical literature.   4. Rabbinical literature—History and criticism.   5. Judaism—Relations.   I. Title.   II. Series.
   BM509.J48S73   1994
   296.1'2—dc20
                                                                       94-14802
                                                                       CIP

Die Deutsche Bibliothek - CIP-Einheitsaufnahme

Stern, Sacha:
Jewish identity in early rabbinic writings / by Sacha Stern. - Leiden ; New York ; Köln : Brill, 1994
   (Arbeiten zur Geschichte des antiken Judentums und des Urchristentums ; 23)
   Zugl.: Diss.
   ISBN 90-04-10012-1
NE:GT

ISSN   0169-734X
ISBN   90 04 10012 1

CONTENTS

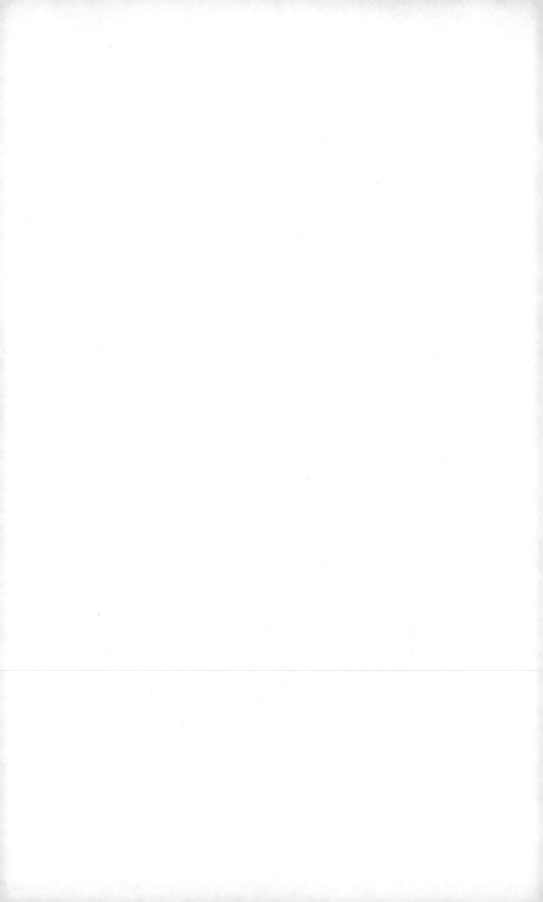

ACKNOWLEDGMENTS

Foremost acknowledgments are due to the Harold Hyam Wingate Foundation, without whose generous financial assistance (1988–91) my D.Phil. thesis, of which this book is a revised version, could never have been written. I am also grateful to the Craven Foundation (1988–91) and to Jews' College for a research fellowship (1990–1).

The thesis itself was written under the supervision of Martin Goodman, who encouraged me to engage in this work and who has continued assisting me in every possible manner. I am most grateful for his support and friendship. Essential advice was also provided by Lin Foxhall, Jadran Mimica, my examiners Geza Vermes and Jonathan Webber, and two anonymous readers. I am also grateful to Allen Abramson, Sue Gessler, Debbie Golden, Irving Jacobs, Esra Kahn (Jews' College library), Francis Landy, Maryon McDonald, John Matthews, Fergus Millar, Oonagh O'Brien, Alison Salvesen, Yaacov Schonberg, Joseph Spitzer, Giuseppe Veltri, and Tamra Wright; and finally, to my wife and relatives for their constant assistance, patience and support.

This book is dedicated to the memory of my mother, *z.l.*

ABBREVIATIONS

Bible
Gen.   Genesis
Ex.   Exodus
Lev.   Leviticus
Num.   Numbers
Deut.   Deuteronomy
Est.   Esther
Eccl.   Ecclesiastes
Song   Song of Songs
Lam.   Lamentations
Dan.   Daniel

Talmudic sources
M.   Mishna
T.   Tosefta ed. Zuckermandel (L: ed. Lieberman, cited only when
                  text or reference differs significantly from Zuckermandel).
Y.   Yerushalmi (Palestinian Talmud)
B.   Bavli (Babylonian Talmud)

Each of these initials is followed with the name of the tractate, abbreviated as follows:
Arakh.   Arakhin
AZ   Avoda Zara
BB   Bava Batra
Bekh.   Bekhorot
Ber.   Berakhot
BK   Bava Kamma
BM   Bava Metzia
Eruv.   Eruvin
Git.   Gittin
Hag.   Hagiga
Hor.   Horayot
Hul.   Hullin
Ker.   Keritot
Ket.   Ketubot
Kid.   Kiddushin
Mak.   Makkot
Meg.   Megila
Men.   Menahot
MK   Moed Katan
Naz.   Nazir
Ned.   Nedarim
Pes.   Pesahim
RH   Rosh HaShana
Sanh.   Sanhedrin
Shab.   Shabbat
Shek.   Shekalim
Shevi.   Sheviit
Shevu.   Shevuot
Sot.   Sota

Suk.	Sukka
Taan.	Ta'anit
Yev.	Yevamot
YT	Yom Tov (Tosefta)
Zev.	Zevaḥim
Avot dRN	Avot deRabbi Natan (recension A, unless otherwise stated).
Dik.Sof.	R. Rabbinovicz, *Dikdukei Sofrim (Variae Lectiones in Mischnam et in Talmud Babylonicum)*, New York: M.P. Press Inc., 1976 (2 vols.).

Midrashim

Eliyahu	Tanna deVei Eliyahu (Rabba and Zuta), ed. Friedman.
Mekh.	Mekhilta deRabbi Yishmael.
Mekh. dRShbY	Mekhilta deRabbi Shimon b. Yohai.
PdRE	Pirkei deRabbi Eliezer.
PdRE ed.Higger	M. Higger, "Pirkei deRabbi Eliezer", in *Horeb* 10, New York 1948, esp. pp. 188–91 (ch.28).
Pes.dRK.	Pesikta deRav Kahana.
Pes.R.	Pesikta Rabbati.
Tanh.	Midrash Tanhuma.
Tanh.B.	Midrash Tanhuma ed. S. Buber.
pet.	petihta (introduction).
R.	Rabba (e.g.: Genesis Rabba)
Z.	Zuta
Eisenstein (ed.)	J.D. Eisenstein, *Otzar Midrashim*, New York: E. Grossman, 1915 (2 vols.).
Wertheimer (ed.)	S.A. Wertheimer, *Battei Midrashot*, (2nd ed.: A.J. Wertheimer), Jerusalem: Ktab Yad Wasepher, 1953 (2 vols.). Midrash Shir haShirim: *Midrash Shir haShirim* (ed. J.Ch. Wertheimer, 1981).

Journals

AJS Review	Association for Jewish Studies—Review.
HUCA	Hebrew Union College Annual.
JJS	Journal of Jewish Studies.
JQR	Jewish Quartely Review.
JSJ	Journal for the Study of Judaism.

Miscellaneous

R.	Rabbi/Rabban/Rav
b.	ben/bar

NOTE ON TRANSLITERATION

Hebrew and Aramaic words have been transliterated according to the rules listed in the *Encyclopedia Judaica*, vol. 1 (index volume), p. 90. For reasons of convenience I have adopted its 'general' transliteration rules, not its 'scientific' ones. For the sake of clarity, however, I have transliterated *tzade* as "*tz*".

INTRODUCTION

1. THE TOPIC

Definition

This study is concerned with identity in its widest sense: namely, the *perception and experience of a person's self* in all its lived dimensions. 'Jewish identity', as understood in this work, represents therefore the perception by a Jew of his self specifically *as Jewish*.

'Jewish identity' is usually associated in modern scholarship, more restrictively, with the famous question of "who is a Jew?"—i.e., who is perceived to belong to the group called 'Jewish'. This question has already been studied at some depth with reference to the early rabbinic period,[1] and I shall address it myself in a chapter of this work (chapter III). However, Jewish identity is much more than a question of Halakhic (legal) or ethnic[2] status. The experience of being Jewish pervades indeed the plenum of lived experience, in all its physical, social, and cultural dimensions. A study of Jewish identity (or of 'Jewishness') entails, therefore, establishing what constitutes the *general* experience of being Jewish, or 'what it is like to be a Jew'.

I propose to examine Jewish identity, in this wider sense, as it was experienced in Late Antiquity by the authors of early rabbinic sources.

A contemporary concern

The theme of Jewish identity has haunted the minds of many contemporary Jewish thinkers, which accounts, perhaps, for my own motivation to explore it. Yet we may wonder to what extent this modern obsession would have been shared by Jews of the early rabbinic period. There is no Talmudic tractate on Jewish identity; nor is there even a word, Hebrew or Aramaic, to refer explicitly to this notion. The evidence I have gleaned, in preparing this study, represents a

---

[1] E.g. by L.H. Schiffman, *Who was a Jew?*, Ktav: New Jersey, 1985.

[2] Throughout this work I use the terms 'ethnic' and 'ethnicity' as referring not to a social group of objective, common biological descent, but rather to one that shares a common culture and a general, subjective feeling of mutual 'belonging' (usually on the grounds of a putative common biological descent, but allowing also for the possibility of new-comers and/or 'converts').

most disparate corpus of intimations, side-lines, and out-of-context quotations which do not correspond as a whole to any sustained, systematic piece of rabbinic writing.

The choice of this topic, and the imposition of a modern concern upon an ancient body of literature, may thus appear artificial or anachronistic, but it is inherent to any historical inquiry; as I shall argue in the coming pages, the subjective standpoint of the historian is the motivational force behind any historical interpretation. The fact that the authors of rabbinic sources did not conceptualize the notion of Jewish identity or study it in its own right—though not, in itself, without significance[3]—does not imply that they had no experience at all of being Jewish. As we shall see, their writings are replete with references to their 'Jewishness', which is to say, to their distinctive features as 'Israel'. Thus, my search for Jewish identity in rabbinic writings, though perhaps incongruous in early rabbinic terms, is both justifiable and legitimate.

2. ANTHROPOLOGICAL ISSUES

In the course of my study a number of theoretical issues about the nature of identity will unavoidably arise. Many of these have been dealt with by anthropologists and sociologists, particularly in the last twenty years, when interest in identity and ethnic studies has remarkably accrued. The dialectical interdependency between self and other (see chapter I), the boundaries between 'us' and 'them' (see chapters III and IV), ethnic identity and religious identity (see section II.4), the strategies involved in the manipulation and protection of identity (e.g. against the threat of assimilation—see chapter IV), are all familiar themes which will be encountered and discussed at various stages in this work. A number of themes, however, are relevant to the whole thrust of my study, and require therefore immediate attention. I shall begin with an attempt to define the subjective 'self'.

Collectivity and individuation

Commonsense would dictate that the self—the subject of identity— corresponds to the individual person; thus, that Jewish identity was experienced separately and *individually* by each rabbi. However,

---

[3] I shall return to this important observation in the conclusion to this work.

anthropologists have realised for some time that not all cultures conceive of the empirical individual as a separate, autonomous entity. Following the lead of Durkheim, it has been argued that in Australian Aboriginal culture the individual perceives himself as merging with the landscape and the Ancestors in an unbroken continuum, in sharp contrast with our accepted Western distinction between the individual and the outside world. In some North American cultures the individual sees himself as an organic constituent of his totemic clan; he is thus inseparable from his collective group and has no autonomous personhood of his own.[4] In such societies self-identity as we know it would be inconceivable, since the individual is not distinguished conceptually from the social group he belongs to. Subjective self-identity would have to be allocated somehow to the social group as a whole, as a collective act of social identification and of differentiation from other, collective social groups.[5]

The extent of individuation in early rabbinic sources would deserve a separate study of its own. It would seem, on the one hand, that the notion of autonomous individual personhood is taken for granted in the Halakhic system of the *Mishna*, as each individual is assessed as a free agent, responsible for his own actions and interacting as an independent entity with other people.[6] On the other hand, individual and collectivity are in some respects confused: as we shall see, the

---

[4] See Marcel Mauss, "A category of the human mind: the notion of person, the notion of self" (1935, rev. 1950), in M. Carrithers, S. Collins, S. Lukes (eds.), *The Category of the Person*, Cambridge: CUP, 1985. This theory has been much developed by Louis Dumont in his work on Indian society: see *Homo Hierarchicus*, London: Weidenfeld & Nicholson, 1970; and "The Individual as Impediment to Sociological Comparison and Indian History", in *Religion, Politics and History in India: Collected Papers in Indian Society*, The Hague: Mouton, 1970.

[5] For a modern attempt, from a Western scientific view-point, to account for the possibility of a non-individuated collectivity, see Dana Zohar, *The Quantum Self*, London: Bloomsbury, 1990. Zohar argues that according to quantum mechanical theory, under certain conditions ('wave-like', as opposed to 'particle-like') the notion of individuation becomes untenable, both at a microcosmic level (in that matter can no longer be regarded as a cluster of particles, but rather as a wave-ridden whole), and at a macrocosmic level (including for instance that of human consciousness). In these conditions self-identity profoundly differs from our classical, Newtonian conceptualisation of it: it is no longer the preserve of a disjointed individual, but rather participation in a universal state of unity and empathy. (Unfortunately, and against her better judgement, Zohar remains committed to an intellectualistic confusion between the self and *mental* consciousness, which I shall criticise below—to the extent, for instance, that in ch. 13 she reduces the act of pot-making to a purely mental activity).

[6] See E.E. Urbach, *The Sages, their concepts and beliefs*, (trans. I. Abrahams), Cambridge (Mass.): Harvard Univ. Press, 1975, p. 217, quoting *M.Sanh.* 4,5 as further evidence to this effect.

theoretical individual Jew is referred to as 'an Israel', exactly the same term as is used for the Jewish people as a whole.[7] This suggests that the identity of 'Israel', in rabbinic writings, was attributed to the Jewish nation as a whole, and that Jewish identity was perceived by rabbinic writers not as the experience of individual Jews, but rather as a collective experience, the experience of 'Israel'.

The distinction between primitive collectivism and modern, individuated 'personhood' is clearly not as straightforward as earlier anthropologists originally suggested. Recent studies have reinstated individuality, alongside collectivism, as a notion universal to all cultures.[8] A blend of individuation and collectivism is likely to be found, similarly, in early rabbinic writings; suffice it to say that to their authors, 'personal identity' may have been conceptualised and experienced far more collectively than we may have first allowed.

Mind, body, and the self

Having assessed the *external* boundaries of the self, his *internal* constitution must also be given some attention. In the Cartesian philosophical tradition, still dominant in contemporary Western thought, the seat of the subjective self is located exclusively within his *mental* consciousness. The experience of the self is deemed to be based entirely on intellection and imagination, as epitomized in the seminal contention: *cogito ergo sum*.

It would be rash, however, to accept this notion of the self as definitive. The Cartesian worldview has been correctly challenged by modern philosophers such as Merleau-Ponty, who argue that other elements of the human person, particularly the body, may be just as important constituents of his subjective self. Merleau-Ponty suggests that the body, in human experience, is in fact a *participating part* of the subjective self, rather than (as in the Cartesian worldview) an object distinct

---

[7] In the latter sense, the singular noun 'Israel' is always treated as a plural. See section I.2.A.

[8] See G. Lienhardt, "Self: public, private. Some African representations", in M. Carrithers *et al.*, op.cit. See also M. Jackson, *Paths towards a clearing: Radical empiricism and ethnographic inquiry*, Bloomington and Indianapolis: Indiana University Press, 1989: the Kuranko of Sierra Leone refer to the person as *morgo*, i.e. the empirical individual "that is recognized in all societies", but the derivative concept of *morgoye* does not refer to personhood or personality, nor does it suggest "notions of personal identity, distinctive individual character, or autonomous moral being"; instead it denotes "proper social relationships" with wider society and indeed with the wider world; this explains how individuals can identify themselves as *being* (in the most literal sense) their clan and their totem (pp. 106–8). The importance of individuality among the Kuranko is given emphasis, on the other hand, in chs. 2–3 of the same work...

from the self and external to it; consequently, the subjective *ego* consists at once, ontologically, of a mental and a bodily experience.[9]

Evidence would suggest that the authors of early rabbinic sources experience their self in a similarly 'holistic' manner. In *Avot* 3,1, it appears quite clearly that the subjective self identifies with his body as much as with his soul:

> Where are you from?—from a putrid drop (of semen). Whither are you going?—to a place of dust, worms, and maggots. Before whom are you destined to give account (of your deeds)?—before the King of Kings of Kings, the Almighty.[10]

"You", in this passage, corresponds to the earthly body as much as to the soul. We may also note that in rabbinic writings, the Hebrew word *guf* can mean the 'body' (as opposed to the 'soul': see *B.Sanh.* 91a) but also the 'person', the 'self'.[11]

In a recent study on Jewish self-identity, Jacob Neusner has restricted himself to the semantic meaning of one word: 'Israel' (e.g. as a family, a chosen people, a nation, etc.). As a result, the experience of self-identity is misleadingly reduced in his work to a purely semantic or *nomenclatural* activity, hence to an essentially intellectualistic and 'disembodied' experience.[12] The 'holistic' approach which I am advocating, by contrast, is far more compatible with early rabbinic perceptions of self and of self-identity; it will necessitate our understanding of the central role of *bodily praxis* (e.g. the performance of the commandments) in the constitution of the rabbinic identity of 'Israel' (see chapter II).

---

[9] See Maurice Merleau-Ponty, *Phenomenology of Perception*, trans. C. Smith, London: Routledge & Kegan Paul, 1962.

[10] *M. Avot* 3,1; *Y.Sot.* 2,2; *Lev.R.* 18,1; quoted by Urbach, *op.cit.*, pp. 224–5.

[11] As in *M.Avot* 4,6; *B.Kid.* 20a, etc.; see M. Jastrow, *A dictionary of the Targumim, the Talmud Babli and Yerushalmi, and the Midrashic literature*, New York: Judaica Press, 1971, s.v. *guf* II). Urbach (pp. 214–254) argues at length that the Platonic split between mind and body, quite common in Late Antique thought (including Philo and Christianity), is not to be found in the Bible, and hardly in early rabbinic writings. Urbach concedes that mind and body are distinguished in the sources as different, even as separate entities; but the self is not identified as a soul imprisoned in the body and striving to escape it.

[12] J. Neusner, *Judaism and its Social Metaphors: Israel in the History of Jewish Thought*, Cambridge: Cambridge University Press, 1989. Similarly, his interpretation of the Mishnaic 'Israel' as a mere *theoretical* abstraction (representing, he argues, a flight from the unhappy historical circumstances of 70CE: pp. 166ff; ch. 11; etc.), ignores the *concrete praxis* which the *Mishna*, in connection with 'Israel', continually refers to and assumes (even if much of the *Mishna* remains admittedly 'Utopian'; see below pp. 128–30). On Neusner's approach to historical change, see below in this introduction.

Phenomenology and self-identity

In this respect I follow an existing trend in contemporary anthropological theory which may be labelled 'phenomenological', as it owes
much, indeed, to the philosophical school of phenomenology.[13]
Phenomenology, as a method of inquiry, has been found most effective
at capturing and elucidating the subjective experience of human
existence in all its naive reality. I believe, however, that it lends itself
particularly well to the study of identity. This is because phenomenology draws particular attention to the notion of 'ontology', by which
I mean the crude, existential experience of 'being'.[14] I would suggest
that the experience of Jewish identity must be seen itself as '*an* ontology',
namely as the experience of a particular aspect of one's 'being', i.e.
'being Jewish'. Towards the end of this work, I will thus consider
Jewish identity as an 'ontological' experience, a way of 'being-in-the-
world' (a notion developed by Merleau-Ponty), in its holistic array
of conceptual, bodily and social manifestations.[15]

---

[13] As well as to the related school of existentialism. Jackson (*op.cit.*), for instance,
makes frequent use of the works of J.P. Sartre and Merleau-Ponty.

[14] My use of the term 'ontology' ('ontological', 'ontologically'—especially in section
V.2) follows that of R.D. Laing, whose example, in applying existentialism to psychiatry,
I emulate to some extent in my own field:

"Despite the philosophical use of 'ontology' . . . I have used the term in its present
empirical sense because it appears to be the best adverbial or adjectival (and I add:
substantive) derivative of 'being'." (R.D. Laing, *The Divided Self: an existential study in
sanity and madness*, London: Penguin Books, 1965, p. 39, footnote).

With the ever widening application of phenomenological ideas to the arts and
the social sciences, the term 'ontology' has become somewhat abused. It is used
extensively, for instance, by B. Kapferer, *Legends of People, Myths of State: violence, intolerance
and political culture in Sri Lanka and Australia*, Washington & London: Smithsonian
Institution Press, 1988. He treats 'ontology' as "constitutive principles of being", as
a "meaning" with a "logic", and as a "constitutive or positioning force" (which is
however inseparable from the reality of experience and simultaneous with it, and
which can only emerge through its engagement in the context of specific historical
action) (p. 220f., n. 5). He reluctantly admits that 'ontology' is to him a substitute
for the old structuralist notion of 'deep structure' or 'root paradigm' (*ib.*); this is
confirmed later on in his work (pp. 79–84) where ontology is opposed to 'ideology',
the former being "prereflective", "beneath the level of conscious reflection" (p. 84),
and potential, as opposed to ideology which is actual.

I maintain, on the other hand, that 'ontology' is an *immediate, actual* experience
of being, which should not be associated with any notion of potential, of 'depth'
or of 'root' experience (which the term 'ontogenesis' could perhaps convey). Ontology
is not constitutive of anything else, nor is it a causal force; it is not "*pre*reflective",
but a present and tangible lived experience.

[15] Section V.2. The specific experience of 'being', as distinguished from the whole
plenum of human experience, may have been somewhat overemphasized by existentialist philosophy; nonetheless, it is sound to posit that it is universally shared,

Strangely, this fundamental characteristic of identity has been taken too often for granted. Much attention has been given by social scientists to the cultural (artistic, religious, linguistic, etc.) and political *uses* of ethnic identity in human societies;[16] but few have ventured to describe what the phenomenological experience of 'being ethnic' actually consists of. It would appear that even twenty years after the seminal work of Fredrik Barth, the systematic, anthropological study of ethnic identity is only still in its inception.[17]

Objectivity and radical empiricism

In the course of this work it has become clear to me that one cannot study or understand a 'raw', ontological experience, without being subjected to it oneself. Many anthropologists today would concur with this realisation, and would apply it to the whole activity of ethnographic inquiry. Objectivity and scientific detachment is an impossible myth which, in the post-structural era, no longer fascinates historians and social scientists; subjectivity is now recognized not only as unavoidable, but indeed as *epistemologically indispensable*. This gives way to a new empirical methodology, which Jackson calls 'radical empiricism' and sums up as follows:

---

to some extent, by the whole of mankind. The notion of existence or of 'being there' may find implicit expression in rabbinic sayings: for instance, that "against your will you were created, against your will you *live*" (*M.Avot* 4, end.), or Hillel's claim that "if I am here, all is here" (*Avot dRN* 12,11; *B.Suk.* 53a). 'Being Jewish', again, is an experience which rabbinic writings demonstrably express, as will become evident throughout this study.

[16] As in A. Cohen, *Custom and Politics in Urban Africa*, London: Routledge, Kegan & Paul, 1969; A.P. Royce, *Ethnic Identity: Strategies of Diversity*, Bloomington and Indianapolis: Indiana University Press, 1982. The 'invention of ethnic identity' has also become a popular theme in anthropological, sociological and historical studies (for instance, on modern nationalisms, A.D. Smith, *The ethnic revival*, Cambridge: CUP, 1981). I shall not address this theme in this work, as it is impossible to trace, on the basis of early rabbinic writings, the *origins* of the rabbinic notion of Jewish identity (as I argue later in this introduction).

[17] The work of F. Barth, published in 1969, will be discussed and criticised at the end of chs. III and IV. The same applies to the field of Ancient Jewish studies. Besides the work of Neusner (above mentioned), I can only refer to the pioneering work of E.P. Sanders, A.I. Baumgarten, & A. Mendelson (eds.), *Jewish and Christian Self-Definition, vol. II: Aspects of Judaism in the Graeco-Roman Period*, Philadelphia: Fortress Press and London: SCM Press, 1981 (which gives however little attention to the evidence of early rabbinic writings). This volume deals with many general aspects of Judaism in the 2nd century but fails to address the question of identity in a directly relevant manner; again, the notion of Jewish identity (or "self-definition") is taken

Our habit of excluding the lived experience of the observer from the field of the observed on the grounds that it is a 'regrettable disturbance' is, as George Devereux shows, a stratagem for alleviating anxiety, not a rule of scientific method. A radically empirical method *includes* the experience of the observer and defines the experimental field as one of interactions and intersubjectivity. Accordingly, we make ourselves experimental subjects and treat our experiences as primary data. Experience, in this sense, becomes a mode of experimentation, of testing and exploring the ways in which our experiences conjoin or connect us with others, rather than the ways they set us apart.[18]

This approach rests on the assumption of a "continuity of experience across cultures and through time, the psychic[19] unity of our species" (*ib.* p. 5), which is indeed the foundation of any attempt to understand and 'make sense' of other people. It would be wrong, no doubt, to obliterate the historical and/or ethnological differences which make us 'other' from the authors of rabbinic sources—thus defeating the whole purpose of our inquiry. My study demands thus at once a recognition of their 'otherness' and the acceptance of our trans-historical, intersubjective continuity without which all understanding would become impossible.

Therefore, a genuinely phenomenological understanding of the early rabbinic experience of Jewish identity requires a concomitant inquiry into our own. I have done so throughout my study, and would invite anyone, engaged in the same field, to do the same. People who know me may recognize in the introvert stance of rabbinic sources, which I analyze in detail at the end of this work, an empathetic reflection

---

completely for granted, and not satisfactorily defined.

[18] *Op.cit.*, p. 4; he quotes an article by R. Rosaldo, whose understanding of the Illongot experience of bereavement was profoundly altered when he succeeded in relating it to his own experience.

[19] The human species is not only *psychically* united—thus sharing similar emotional and mental experiences—but also, and most obviously so, *bodily* united. This point is made quite forcefully by J. Blacking, in J. Blacking (ed.), *The Anthropology of the Body*, London: Academic Press, 1977, p. 5f:

"... the observer's body may serve as a diagnostic tool. My knowledge is both generated and restricted by the perceptions and cognitive processes of my society, but through my body I can sometimes understand more than I know through my or another's society, because I have more experience than society labels. It should therefore be our task, as anthropologists, to experience other's bodies through our own bodies and to learn more about some of the somatic states that we can understand but about which we know little beyond the inadequate verbal descriptions of our society. I suggest we can and ought to be rational about our feelings, and that conscious subjectivity can be scientifically productive".

of my own personality. Moreover, my own standpoint, as an Orthodox Jew of the 20th century—who perceives himself, therefore, as a follower of early rabbinic teachings—may have proved essential to my understanding of early rabbinic sources. I would stress that I have adhered throughout my research to rigorous standards of historical methodology, proceeding empirically from the evidence of the sources and refraining from imposing any pre-conceived assumption upon them. I am only stating, as a radical empiricist, that my—and my readers'—*understanding* of these sources will necessarily depend upon an intersubjective process, of which we shall remain aware throughout the unfolding of this work.[20]

3. Approaches to Rabbinic Writings

Early rabbinic writings: tradition and redaction

This study is restricted to the evidence of 'early', i.e. late Antique, rabbinic writings. I will not refer to more or less contemporary non-rabbinic Jewish writings (such as Philo and Josephus), as it appears that they belonged to decisively different literary and cultural traditions.

The nature of early rabbinic writings and their value as historical sources must first be clarified. What do we mean by 'early rabbinic writings', and who are the authors of these texts as we now have them? These questions are still hotly debated, for instance, between P. Schäfer and Ch. Milikowsky in recent issues of the *Journal of Jewish Studies*, and the outcome remains far from clear.[21]

I can do no more, in this introduction, than to state the position which I have adopted in this work. 'Early rabbinic writings' consist of a body of writings, principally known as the *Talmud* and the *Midrash*, which were produced, ostensibly by 'rabbis', in Palestine and in

---

[20] Empathy does not necessarily undermine the validity or 'truth' of ethnographic analysis: see again Jackson *op.cit.*, ch. 11.

[21] Peter Schäfer, "Research into rabbinic literature: an attempt to define the *status quaestionis*", in *JJS* 37(2), 1986, pp. 139–152; Ch. Milikowsky, "The *status quaestionis* of research in rabbinic literature", in *JJS* 39(2), 1988, pp. 201–211; P. Schäfer, "Once again the *status quaestionis* of research in rabbinic literature: an answer to Chaim Milikowsky", in *JJS* 40(1), 1989, pp. 89–94. Without any inconsistency, my own position wavers between both views, as I shall presently explain. Unlike Schäfer or Milikowsky, I do not believe that further research into manuscript traditions will ever yield reliable and definitive answers to these questions, not least because extant manuscripts post-date, by and large, the first millennium of this era, i.e. the formative period in the production of early rabbinic literature.

Babylonia in the course of the first millennium of the common era. The authorities which they quote by name (the 'rabbis') belong exclusively to the first half of this period.

The process which led to the production of these writings remains most elusive, but it clearly involved on the one hand *compilation* and *redaction*, either oral or written, of earlier traditional sources; and on the other hand, oral or written *transmission* of these raw materials and (in the latter stage) of the redacted works. There is no evidence that there ever was, at any point in time, a clear-cut switch from oral to written modes of redaction and transmission. Nor, in my opinion, is there any evidence that there ever was a clear distinction between redaction and transmission; it is fairly clear, at least, that there never was a stage at which redaction came to a standstill and transmission of redacted works began.[22] Early rabbinic writings were compiled and edited in a gradual, cumulative manner, and are therefore in essence undatable and undated: "'open texts', which elude temporal and redactional fixation".[23]

Nevertheless, it is fair to assume that at some point in time, redacted works began to emerge and to be treated, if only by name, as single identifiable entities. Thus, the *Talmud* itself treats the *Mishna*, if not as a finished product, at least as an identifiable work around which its argumentation can revolve. In this respect it may be possible to assign approximate dates to these redacted works, even if the continuous process of multilayer redaction did not entirely cease thereafter, and even if we find that variations between different manuscript traditions and early printed editions can be quite considerable.[24]

---

[22] Indeed, J.N. Epstein, *Mavo leNusaḥ haMishna*, Jerusalem: Magnes Press, 1964 (2 vols.), has shown the extent to which the text of the *Mishna*, though putatively redacted in the early 3rd century, was constantly revised in the subsequent Amoraic period. This could lead to emendations in recensions of the actual text: for instance, the comments of *B.Pes.* 116a (in contrast with *Y.Pes.* 10,3) on *M.Pes.* 10,4 led to a variant recension of the latter in some manuscripts and in the *Rif* (see *Dik.Sof.*). In this sense, the transmitters of the redacted *Mishna* were themselves engaged in a process of 're-redaction', so that Schäfer argues (1989, pp. 90–1) that the 'zero-point' between redaction and transmission becomes historically fictitious.

[23] Schäfer (1986), p. 150. Milikowsky stresses (pp. 208–9) in particular the *oral* nature of the formative process of early rabbinic literature, and criticises Schäfer (1986) for speaking of a "dynamic manuscript tradition" (p. 151), whilst ignoring that the oral tradition is no less, if not more, dynamic and susceptible to change.

[24] In this point I concur with Milikowsky, who argues that variations between extant manuscript versions of a 'same' work are only mild, thus pointing to some redactional identity, possibly even to some common redactional origin. But I do not agree that recensional variations are only due to the hazards of transmission and

The dating of early rabbinic writings

Comparative analysis, and the study of interdependency between various sources, has led to the wide acceptance that some works emerged at an earlier date than others. It is generally thought that each work was redacted around the time of the latest rabbinic figures which it quotes, as the latter's sayings are rarely distorted by anachronisms. Most works appear to have been redacted in the late Roman, early Byzantine period, as they hardly refer to major events of mediaeval history such as the Arab conquest of the 7th century.

The *Mishna, Tosefta, Mekhilta, Sifra, Sifre,* and *Targum Onkelos* are thought to have been initially redacted in the 3rd century; the *Palestinian (Yerushalmi) Talmud, Genesis* and *Leviticus Rabba* appear to have taken shape in the 5th century; the *Babylonian (Bavli) Talmud,* other *Targumim* (*Jonathan, Ps-Jonathan* and *Yerushalmi*) might have emerged in the 7th century, whilst some other *Midrashim* did not come into being until the later mediaeval period.[25] Most works, except for the *Babylonian Talmud* and some of the later *Targumim,* appear to have been redacted in 'Palestine', i.e. Galilee and its adjoining areas.

The dating of individual sayings

The significance of these approximate, conjectural dates is however limited, for it is clear that even the latest works to have been redacted draw much of their material from earlier sources, not extant in writing, which may go back as early as the Tannaitic period (1st-3rd cent.CE). This might be inferred, aside from linguistic and contextual considerations, from the mere fact that rabbinic writings attribute most of their teachings to rabbinic figures living from the 1st to the 3rd centuries CE (called *Tannaim*) and from the 3rd to the 6th centuries CE (called *Amoraim*).

Whilst many have accepted these attributions at face value, and

---

censorial tampering (on the latter, see my remarks in p. 9 and p. 17), and not also to some subsequent redactional activity; nor does a broadly-based, common redactional origin necessarily imply the existence of a *single* authoritative *Urtext* (see Schäfer (1989) p. 90).

[25] In this I differ with Schäfer (1986, p. 142), who maintains that dates of final redaction are *totally* unknown. *Final* redaction may be unknown, but it is clear to most scholars that as identifiable works, albeit perhaps unfinished, their emergence can be *tentatively* 'chronologized' in the way I have outlined. See H.L. Strack & G. Stemberger, *Introduction to the Talmud and Midrash,* Edinburgh: T. & T. Clark, 1991; M.D. Herr, in *Encyclopedia Judaica,* s.v. *Midrash,* vol. 11, pp. 1511-2.

have used them as tools for the original dating of our sources, most scholars would agree today that they are not sufficiently reliable for historical purposes. Neusner and his school have expressed much scepticism in this context, stressing as they do the fluidity and hazards of oral traditions, and the traceable historical development in the traditions concerning rabbis of the Tannaitic period.[26] We also have internal evidence that sayings were at times fictitiously—and deliberately—ascribed to earlier rabbis.[27] Moreover, the attribution of a saying to a particular rabbi does not necessarily mean that the latter was its *original* author; no doubt, much of what the rabbis said reflected their predecessors' teachings rather than their own creative thinking.[28] So, although there is no reason to doubt that many attributions are in fact reliable, we have no objective way of distinguishing them from 'false' attributions; moreover, we cannot know to what extent an attribution is indicative of the date in which the saying was *originally* produced.

The 'synchronic' approach

The realisation that early rabbinic sources are largely undatable has led a number of scholars, especially in recent years, to reject a purely 'historical', i.e. *diachronic* analysis of rabbinic writings. They argue, indeed, that since individual sayings and teachings cannot be reliably dated, rabbinic sources cannot be used as historical evidence for the formation and historical development of early rabbinic Judaism, without yielding excessively speculative conclusions. But although the origins of individual, early rabbinic sayings remain obscure, they argue that rabbinic writings can at least inform the historian of the state of rabbinic Judaism at the time when they were redacted into the present

---

[26] For references, see D. Kraemer, "On the reliability of attributions in the Babylonian Talmud", in *HUCA* 60, 1989, pp. 175–190.

[27] Either for literary convenience, or in order to invest them with greater authority; see L. Jacobs, "How much of the Babylonian Talmud is pseudepigraphic?", in *JJS* 28, 1977, pp. 46–59. A most striking example is found in *B.Eruv.* 51a, where Rabba attributed an anonymous Tannaitic text to R. Yose so as to invest it with further authority.

[28] We are still far from understanding the procedure of rabbinic attribution, its function, its meaning and its historical significance. This topic would deserve systematic study, perhaps of an anthropological kind, but I doubt that we shall ever be in a position of *proving* the historical reliability of any particular attribution. See now my article, "Attribution and Authorship in the Babylonian Talmud", in *JJS* 45.1, Spring 1994, pp. 28–51.

form. Thus, rabbinic writings should be treated as original, redacted entities rather than as compilations of earlier, traditional sayings. This approach may be termed '*synchronic*', as it restricts its analysis to fixed points in historical time, the putative times of final redaction of rabbinic works.[29]

Whilst this approach may be satisfactory for the purposes of literary analysis (to which scholars like Goldberg restrict themselves), its value to the ancient historian is however slim. Because it does not account for chronological development, this approach tends to ignore the socio-historical process which eventually brought rabbinic writings into existence. Moreover, as Schäfer argues, the dating of the synchronic points in time which this approach implicitly refers to is often doubtful. This is especially the case if one studies, like Urbach, many or all the early rabbinic writings as a single synchronic whole; this is to assume that they all belong to the same historical setting, whereas there is actually no evidence that early rabbinic works were redacted in the same place and at the same time, nor indeed that in any point in time in the mediaeval period, our sources as extant today ever constituted as a whole the preserve of any single section of Jewish society.

But this global, synchronic approach is not devoid of all historical significance. The fact that the *Mishna* and other Tannaitic teachings, for instance, may have been redacted some time in the early-mid 3rd century, does not mean that in historical terms they only 'belonged' to the rabbinic Judaism of that period. As we have seen, the *Talmudim* testify that the rabbis of the post-Tannaitic period, in Palestine and in Babylonia alike, were constantly engaged in the correction and re-formulation of the *Mishna* and other Tannaitic teachings.[30] This suggests that the centrality of the *Mishna* in Talmudic works was not merely due to some traditionalist reverence to an archaic, outdated work of the past; quite on the contrary, the *Mishna* was to the *Amoraim* a work of the present, which embodied their way of thinking, their experiences and their general world-view. The constant emendation and reformulation of these early sources, in the *Talmudim*, suggests that the *Amoraim* and Talmudic redactors treated Tannaitic sources,

---

[29] See Schäfer (1986), referring to the 'thematic' approach of E.E. Urbach (p. 141) and the 'analytical-descriptive' approach of Arnold Goldberg (p. 145).
[30] See above note 22.

to some extent, as their own.[31] In this sense, the *Mishna* as we now have it may be just as representative of the Judaism of the Amoraic or of the later Talmudic period.

The relative fluidity of early rabbinic writings, as described above, suggests in fact that by the beginning of the Geonic period, Tannaitic and Amoraic traditional teachings had come to form a partially amorphous *pool of early rabbinic traditions* which was largely shared by all, and out of which rabbinic writings had been gradually emerging. That this pool of traditions would have probably been shared by most rabbis of the period, in Babylonia as well as in Palestine, is suggested by the numerous parallels which are found across the Talmudic and *Midrashic* literature from this period. The centrality of Tannaitic and Amoraic traditions in early rabbinic writings suggests, moreover, that they were treated by their redactors as representative of their own experiences and beliefs.[32] Although many of these Tannaitic and Amoraic traditions would have become divorced, by then, from their original historical context, they can be taken to represent, in this decontextualised form, the Judaism of the rabbis of this later period.

In so far as the early rabbinic literature which we now possess represents a later configuration of this redactional pool of traditions, its synchronic study may serve to identify the Judaism which, in broad terms, was probably shared by most rabbis in this specific period.

The 'soft' diachronic approach

The global, synchronic reduction of all early rabbinic sources to a specific point in time suffers, however, from being historically over-restrictive. In an attempt to restore a sense of diachronic development in the study of early rabbinic Judaism, many historians have preferred what might be termed a 'soft' diachronic approach: for instance Neusner in his more recent works, as we shall later see. This approach concedes, on the one hand, that early rabbinic works can only be treated as whole, redacted entities, and are only reprentative of rabbinic Judaism

---

[31] This applies as much to the *Mishna*—referred by the *Babylonian Talmud* as *matnitin*, '*our* teaching'—as to other Tannaitic sources, which the *Talmud* constantly emends so as to accommodate them with its own way of thinking.

[32] This is so even if the *Talmudim* persist in quoting each saying "in the name of its sayer" (*B.Meg.* 15a), thus distinguishing for instance between Tannaitic and Amoraic sayings (the former having greater authority), and eliminating inconsistencies in the sayings attributed to a single rabbi.

as at the time of their final redaction. On the other hand, it proposes to compare different works with one another so as to trace, on the basis of their different putative dates of redaction, some form of diachronic, historical evolution between them.

This approach is based, however, on three questionable assumptions:

1. That rabbinic works can be assigned a firm and reliable date of final redaction. But Schäfer argues, against this 'soft' diachronic approach, that the process of ongoing, cumulative redaction makes it impossible to prove that a passage from one work was 'earlier', in redaction, than a similar passage found elsewhere.[33]

2. That the occurrence of new material, or of new versions of older sources, in 'later' redacted works is necessarily due to redactional innovation or emendation, and hence representative of Judaism specifically and only in this 'later' period. But as Heinemann objects,[34] this is to ignore the genuine possibility that this seemingly 'new' material, or these seemingly 'new' versions, were actually older traditions, which were only redacted at a later stage because of some hazards, perhaps, in their oral transmission. It is often impossible to tell whether a passage is the original work of its final redactor, or simply the quotation of some earlier tradition. Most of our sources remain compilations of traditional teachings, which may be *just as* representative, in historical terms, of the period in which they were *originally* produced as of the period of their *final* redaction into their present written form.

3. That redactional innovation necessarily reflects historical change. This is to ignore a number of other factors, such as literary context and literary genre, which would not have been specific to the historical context of that particular period, and which may often have affected the redactor's choice of one particular version over the next. Thus, the diachronic approach may amount to no more than the study of literary difference. This critique will be later applied (in section 4, below) to Neusner's recent work on the identity of Israel.

---

[33] Schäfer, 1986, pp. 145–51, argues with reference to *Genesis Rabba* and the *Talmud Yerushalmi*, and to the *Mishna* and the *Tosefta*, that the notion of precedence is virtually nonsensical.

[34] Joseph Heinemann, *Aggadot veToledotehen*, Jerusalem: Keter, 1974, pp. 44–5, *contra* Neusner.

Conclusion

No one approach to early rabbinic writings can satisfy the critical historian. The diachronic approach suffers, in a nutshell, from having to rely on the datings of individual rabbinic sayings and of finished, redacted works, which are generally fluid and no more than speculative. The synchronic approach denies the possibility of studying historical development and change; by restricting itself to the post-Amoraic, pre-Geonic period, when Judaism probably consisted of a pool of Tannaitic and Amoraic traditions, the historical interest of early rabbinic writings becomes considerably reduced.

And yet, if we are to conduct a historical study of our sources, a choice of approach must undoubtedly be made. Since there is no reason to favour, *a priori*, one model over the other, I would advocate a pragmatic choice on the basis of what seems most appropriate for the specific topic to be considered. In this work, I have generally adopted a global synchronic approach, though I would not negate entirely the value of an alternative, diachronic outlook. In the following pages I would like to explain why I have considered this global synchronic approach, with all its limitations, to be most suited in practical terms to the study of Jewish identity in early rabbinic writings.

4. THE HISTORICAL DIMENSION AND ITS LIMITS

A study on rabbinic Judaism cannot be divorced from its historical background. Before opting for any methodological approach, it may be useful to lay down the historical assumptions which can be made, from the outset, concerning early rabbinic Jewish identity, and which may help us to assess the potential usefulness of early rabbinic sources.

The history of Jewish identity: diversity and dynamics

I do not claim, in this work, to account for Jewish Palestinian and Babylonian society in their entirety: the Jewish identity I am studying is, specifically, no more than that of the authors of our sources. Nevertheless, it is reasonable to assume as a premise that the rabbinic experience of Jewish identity could not have remained identical and monolithic throughout the late Antique period. The diversity of this experience, and the change which it must have regularly undergone, would have been due to a number of important factors.

Firstly, we must consider that the authors of rabbinic writings, whom we might conveniently refer to as 'rabbis', comprised a wide range of people who are likely to have held, at times, significantly different experiences and different views. Particularly relevant to the study of Jewish identity is the divergence of experience which must have existed between the rabbis of Palestine and those of Babylonia, each living under different geo-political and socio-political conditions (under Roman and Persian rule respectively) and hence likely to have formed different views about Jewish identity and the Jewish nation. We also note, in rabbinic sources, controversies between different individual rabbis or between their schools, which could have had a bearing on their experience of Jewish identity.

Secondly, just as any other cultural experience, Jewish identity must have responded to historical events, and hence be subject to the vicissitudes of historical change. Major historical turning-points such as the destruction of Jerusalem and the relative loss of Jewish statehood in 70CE, the (possibly Messianic) failure and defeat of Bar-Kokhba in 135CE, the Christian conversion of Constantine in the early 4th century, and the Arab conquest of the mid 7th century, could not have failed to have made their mark on the rabbis' experience of their identity as Jews and as members of the Jewish people.

It is important to note that this diverse and evolving experience cannot be described and categorised in terms of well-defined historical periods, geographical areas, or rabbinic schools. This would amount, effectively, to reducing a complex process into a relatively 'static', segmental model, which it probably could never have been. This is because, to a large extent, the rabbis did not live in isolation from one another: travel and exchange of ideas was common, for instance, between the Palestinian and Babylonian rabbinic communities, as the Talmudic evidence testifies. This means that rabbis from different backgrounds and with different outlooks would have had ample opportunity to exert influence upon their colleagues; in this light, their experiences (e.g. of Jewish identity) would have been constantly evolving and re-assessed.

Similarly, important historical events did not prevent the rabbis from quoting teachings from earlier periods, as, again, early rabbinic sources testify. This suggests, on the one hand, the possibility of considerable continuity throughout the late Antique period, as well as between different areas and different rabbinic schools. This is not to say that the diversity of experience, which I have just outlined, was altogether blurred by rabbinic anachronistic conservatism. The point I would make is that periods, areas and schools (and even, perhaps, individual rabbis) cannot be labelled as static, independent and well-defined entities. Because of their mutual interdependence, they must have been themselves subject to constant re-adjustment and change. It is thus likely that Jewish identity was not static in its diversity, but a dynamic, ever-resilient process.

Neusner on Jewish identity

The complexity of this process does not help the modern historian in his task. Modern scholars of early rabbinic Judaism have tended, for the sake of simplicity, to ignore the 'dynamic' element of this process and focus instead on its 'diversity'. Much of Jacob Neusner's work, for instance, is based on the assumption that the early rabbinic period can be segmented into well-defined sub-periods, e.g. pre-70CE, 70–135CE, post-135CE, pre- and post-300CE, etc. This segmental, chronological scheme is justifiable as a useful working model, although it gives the false illusion of changelessness within a given period and, on the contrary, of a sudden 'quantum leap' in the year which marks the transition from one period to the next. As a historical reality, therefore, this model must be handled with some care.

In the work already quoted, Neusner identifies a chronological development in the rabbinic perception and use of the term 'Israel'—and hence, by implication, in the perception of rabbinic self-identity. He distinguishes between an earlier period, 70–300CE, where 'Israel' was only viewed, in rabbinic sources, as a taxonomic abstraction which hardly represented a social reality, and the post-Constantinian period of *circa* 300–600CE, where Neusner suggests that in reaction against Christianity, 'Israel' took on the vividness of a real social group, as a family, a chosen people, or as a nation.

I have not endorsed this model in my work, because I consider it problematic in a number of respects. First of all, we may recall the first two problems (see above) which a 'soft' diachronic approach to rabbinic sources entails. Neusner's model is based on the premiss that earlier redacted works such as the *Mishna* (including *Avot*), *Tosefta*, *Sifra* and *Sifre* can be taken to represent Judaism in its "first statement", i.e. 70–300CE (p. 44), whereas later redacted works such as the *Yerushalmi*, *Genesis* and *Leviticus Rabba* can be taken to represent Judaism in its "second statement", i.e. 300–600CE (p. 108). This entails a wide range of assumptions concerning the date of redaction of these works, let alone the date in which the traditional material which they quote was *originally* produced. One would be hard-pressed, for instance, to prove that a passage from *Genesis Rabba* (e.g. *Gen.R.* 44, 18.1, quoted by Neusner, p. 120) was not, in its inception, prior to the fatal turning point of 300CE.

Secondly—and this relates to the 'third' problem of the soft diachronic approach (see above)—the *generic* nature of Neusner's sources cannot be overlooked. The evidence which Neusner draws for his first (70–300CE) period consists exclusively of Halakhic material from the *Mishna*, the *Tosefta*, and Halakhic *Midrashim*. His second period (300–600CE), on the other hand, is documented exclusively with Aggadic[35] material from the *Yerushalmi*, *Genesis* and *Leviticus Rabba*, which, admittedly, were not redacted before this period. This leads Neusner to the illusion that the earlier concept of 'Israel' was only abstract and taxonomic, and that 'Israel' came to be perceived as a concrete reality only in the post-Constantinian period. In actual fact, this 'change' may not reflect a historical development, as Neusner concludes, but rather a literary, generic difference between his sources: indeed, Halakhic sources are most likely, as legal works, to refer to 'Israel' as a 'theoretical' category rather than as actual, lived reality; whereas Aggadic passages would be most likely, by nature, to relate to Israel as concretely experienced in lived reality.[36]

The fact that Aggadic works appear not to have been redacted before 300CE may suggest that *aggada* was less important than *halakha* in this period, but it would be absurd to conclude that *aggada*, and hence the Aggadic concept of 'Israel', did not exist in this period. The virtual absence of references in the *Mishna* to 'Israel' as a real people does not imply that the authors of the *Mishna* were unaware of this notion. In this respect, Neusner relies on a fallacious argument *a silentio*. Resort to such an argument proceeds from the relative limitations of our available sources (especially prior to 300CE), as I shall now explain.

---

[35] 'Non-legal', which includes stories, homilies, and ethical teachings. On *halakha* and *aggada*, see E. Schürer, *The History of the Jewish People in the Age of Jesus Christ (175 B.C.- A.D. 135)*, revised and edited by G. Vermes & F. Millar, 4 vols., Edinburgh: T. & T. Clark, 1973–87, vol. II, pp. 337–355 and n. 27.

[36] In section I.2.A I will refer to a semantic distinction between the *Halakhic*, taxonomic use of 'Israel' as an individual person, and its *Aggadic* use referring to the Jewish people as a whole. This generic difference appears consistently, and without ostensible historical variation, in the whole of early rabbinic literature that is extant.

The limits of rabbinic sources

The shortcomings of Neusner's account are largely due to the reticence of rabbinic sources on Jewish identity. As I have stated at the outset, rabbinic sources do not explicitly discuss the experience of being Jewish, even if it is implicit everywhere and at all times. This limitation is exacerbated by the fact that identity, as I have earlier described (section 2), is an all-embracing, ontological experience which covers all areas of one's existence. Thus, being Jewish could not be reduced to a purely legal (Halakhic) status, nor is it only a matter for Aggadic writings. Being Jewish is a multifarious and holistic experience which can only be satisfactorily described with reference to the *whole* panoply of Jewish life.

Consequently, only the widest range of literary sources could satisfactorily account for it—if, of course, it can be done at all. It would not be sufficient, for instance, to rely on purely legal texts— e.g. Halakhic passages of the *Mishna*—to account for the experience of Jewish identity in any given period. Neusner's work may demonstrate, if anything, that since most rabbinic works redacted before 300CE were essentially Halakhic in nature, not much can be said about Jewish identity—and certainly nothing comprehensive about it—in that period.

In the course of my research I have found, in general, that if one splits early rabbinic sources into chronological layers, as Neusner has attempted, insufficient evidence is left, for any given period, to assess its experience of Jewish identity in a comprehensive manner. Discrimination between sources of different (putative) time and place of redaction may lead to a number of discrete, diachronic findings: for instance, that Tannaitic and Amoraic sources differ considerably in their Halakhic view of the *Kuti*'s (Samaritan's) status as Jewish (section III.2.C); or that, not surprisingly perhaps, Palestinian sources often refer to the Romans as "the nations", whereas Babylonian sources do not (pp. 15–6); or again, that certain rabbis (for instance, R. Abbahu—p. 98, n. 94; p. 181) as well as certain redacted works (for instance, *Tanna deVei Eliyahu*—p. 2, note 4; p. 32, n. 238) may be said to have held rather idiosyncratic, unrepresentative views.

However, such piece-meal findings are limited in scope and not necessarily pertinent to the experience of Jewish identity *as a whole*. They do not necessarily indicate either a *general* diachronic development or a *general* geographic divergence in the rabbinic experience of being Jewish. Thus for practical purposes, a diachronic, piece-meal approach (such as Neusner's) is unlikely to be productive in the context of a study on Jewish identity.

On the other hand, I have found in the majority of cases that the concepts, sayings and passages which are of most relevance to the *general* experience of Jewish identity are often repeated with little or no significant variation in rabbinic works of very different putative date and provenance (e.g. the *Babylonian Talmud*, early Aggadic *Midrashim*, and later Aggadic compilations). For instance, reference to the Jewish people as 'Israel', a monolithic and collective entity, is found invariably throughout early rabbinic literature. The identification of Israel as "the righteous" and the nations as "the wicked" is found, without variation, in the *Mishna, Yerushalmi, Bavli*, and in early and later *Midrashim* (p. 8). The idea that Israel are "holy" is, again, pervasive in all our sources, Halakhic, Aggadic and even liturgical (pp. 31–2). That Israel are distinctive primarily through their study of *Torah* and performance of the *mitzvot* is found in the *Sifre*, the *Bavli*, and later *Midrashim* such as *Pesikta Rabbati* and *Eliyahu Zuta* (section II.3.A-B). The identity of the convert as 'Israel' is emphasized in all our redacted sources, ranging from the *Bavli, Mekhilta, Sifre, Ruth Rabba*, and later works like *Numbers Rabba* (8), without significant modification (pp. 89–90). The re-occurrence of such *central* notions, with sayings repeated often *verbatim* throughout the range of early rabbinic literature, undermines, in the context of this study, any attempt to produce a diachronic account of this experience.

At first sight, this may also suggest relative continuity and lack of change, in the experience of Jewish identity, between various rabbinic authorities and between the various sources.[37] Such an impression, however, should not be taken at face value. It is more than likely, as I have stated at the outset, that throughout the early rabbinic period Jewish identity was diverse and dynamic, and in a constant process

---

[37] A similar conclusion is reached by Porton in his meticulous study on the non-Jews in the *Mishna* and *Tosefta*, which mirrors in some respects my study on the Jews (Gary G. Porton, *Goyim: Gentiles and Israelites in Mishnah-Tosefta*, Atlanta: Scholars Press, 1989). He notes, in ch. 4 (pp. 125–48), that concerning sayings on non-Jews in the *Mishna* and *Tosefta*, no distinction can be made between various 'schools', settings or places (cf p.131); it is also difficult to establish a chronology among sayings in the *Mishna* and *Tosefta* on the non-Jews, since many of them are unattributed. Elsewhere, he shows that the chronological incompatibilities between the attribution of sayings in the *Mishna* and in the *Tosefta* make it impossible to identify historical evolution in rabbinic rulings referring to non-Jews (pp. 170–2).

of fluidity and change. The most that can be said, however, is that our sources do not appear to yield such an impression. This may suggest, perhaps, that Tannaitic and Amoraic traditions underwent, around the time of their redaction, some degree of 'homogenisation', leading to an illusory image of consistency and continuity in the rabbinic view of 'Israel'. If such a process of redactional 'homogenisation' did indeed take place, it would only confirm that the *synchronic* approach is more suited to the study of Jewish identity in rabbinic sources as they now stand, i.e. as indicative of the experience of Jewish identity in the redactors' period alone.

Conclusion: the historical significance of a synchronic study

Thus, although diversity and change in the early rabbinic experience of Jewish identity can be taken as axiomatic, it would appear that our sources are inadequate to convey such a historical reality. This has led me to favour, in this specific study, a synchronic approach to early rabbinic sources. Let me briefly reiterate what this approach entails.

My aim is to analyse the sources as they present themselves to us, namely, in the state of their final redaction. It is reasonable to assume that by the 7th century CE (just before the Arab conquest) most of the mainstream rabbinic sources were already redacted, more or less, as they are now extant: by which I include the *Targumim*, the *Mishna* and *Tosefta*, the *Palestinian* and *Babylonian Talmudim*, the *Midreshei halakha* (*Sifra*, *Mekhilta*, and *Sifre*), and the earlier *Midrashei aggada* (*Genesis* and *Leviticus Rabba*, *Pesikta deRav Kahana*, etc.). Some of the material included in later *Midrashim* may also have been circulating already at the time, as part of the general pool of Tannaitic and Amoraic traditions. A synchronic study of these sources[38] would aim at presenting, therefore, rabbinic Judaism as it stood in this redactional period.

A number of remarks, however, need to be made. Firstly, the relative disparity of our sources prevents us from referring to an absolutely

---

[38] I have restricted myself, in this study, to sources which *may* have been produced during the Roman (and late Roman) period. I have avoided late mediaeval (post-11th century) anthologies and compilations such as the *Yalkutim* and the *Zohar*, as well as the liturgical works (*Siddur* and *Piyyut*) of the Geonic period (7th-11th centuries), on the presumption, perhaps unjustified, that it is *less* likely that the material they use (other than what is explicitly found in early rabbinic writings) originates as far back as the Roman period.

'single' experience of Jewish identity. Disputes are frequent in our sources, and we shall see that some of the passages quoted in this work represent no more than one, early rabbinic opinion. It is significant to note, however, that even if these opinions may not always have prevailed in rulings of *halakha*, they are all represented and discussed in early rabbinic sources. Their persistence as part of the common 'pool' of redacted traditions suggests that they must have had *some* impact on rabbinic perceptions in this redactional period, and hence, that they should not be ignored as totally irrelevant.

Secondly, the relationship of this synchronic rabbinic Judaism with its contemporary historical context—say, the early 7th century Near East—is difficult for us to appreciate. This is because this Judaism depended largely on traditions which had been transmitted from earlier centuries, as early, in some cases, as the first century CE. It is difficult to know the extent to which these traditions were re-fashioned by the redactors of our sources and adapted to the historical conditions of their own times; hence, the extent to which our sources reflect the specific historical context of the early 7th century, rather than an amalgamation of many centuries of early rabbinic history under Roman and Persian rule.

Thirdly, it must be recognised that in spite of our tentative dating to the early 7th century, the date, place and identity of these 'rabbinic' figures who would have shared this pool of traditions and redacted it into our present corpus of early rabbinic literature remain somewhat elusive. To call them '*Savoraim*', '*Stammaim*', 'early *Geonim*' or 'late *Amoraim*' would not do much to solve the question of their identity. I will prefer to speak of "rabbinic sources" rather than of "rabbis", their anonymous authors and redactors. However, we should never lose sight of the fact that these writings were produced by real, historical people who embraced these teachings as representative of their own experiences. It is these real, human experiences that we are ultimately trying to unravel.

5. ADDITIONAL REMARKS

The limits of literary and of archaeological evidence

My account of Jewish identity is based on *literary* evidence alone. This may be justified on the grounds that the written word is, to the historian, the most explicit and articulate expression of a cognitive experience such as self-identity. However, as I have intimated above (section 2), the experience of identity cannot be reduced exclusively to the evidence of words. It is also experienced and expressed through non-verbal means, such as body language, social posture, and material culture, which would not necessarily need to be described in written, literary works. Music and cookery, for instance, may have constituted important features of Jewish identity in early rabbinic society; unfortunately, however, they are nowhere accounted for in rabbinic writings. Consequently, these aspects of material culture—which one expects to find in any study of ethnic identity—have been completely omitted in this work.

In view of this unfortunate limitation, it may be worth considering whether other forms of evidence, especially archaeological, would not have provided us with further insights into the material culture of the 'rabbis' in the late Antique Near East, and hence into their general experience of Jewish identity. My failure, in this work, to draw on this type of evidence in a systematic manner calls for some justification.

Although the archaeology of Jewish society in Palestine and in the Diaspora of late Antiquity is relatively well developed, we encounter first of all the difficulty of identifying, with any degree of certainty, material finds as 'belonging' to the 'rabbis' of rabbinic literature. Sites such as Beth Shearim (see pp. 242–3), and perhaps the synagogue of Ḥammath-Tiberias (p. 230, n. 209), are in this respect exceptional.

But the greater difficulty consists, secondly, in *interpreting* this form of evidence, and reading into it the experience of ethnic self-identity. How Jewish identity was mediated through material culture, even through identifiably 'Jewish symbols' such as the *menora* in pictorial representations, is a process upon which we can do no more than speculate (see appendix to chapters I–II).

This is why I fall back, almost exclusively, on literary sources and on verbal expressions of Jewish identity, with the awareness however that although they lend themselves most effectively to the study of cognitive processes in societies of the past, they represent no more than a limited aspect of a vast, holistic experience.[39]

---

[39] The archaeological discoveries which I refer to are usually epigraphic, thus again, significantly *linguistic* in nature: e.g. the inscriptions at the Rehob synagogue (p. 11, n. 69), at the En Gedi synagogue (p. 221, n. 142), and the onomastics of the Beth Shearim necropolis (pp. 242–3). See however my remarks on the mosaic of the Ḥammath-Tiberias synagogue in pp. 230, n. 209.

Surveying early rabbinic sources

Much of this study, and particularly its first two chapters, is based on an extensive survey which I have conducted throughout the majority of Talmudic and Midrashic sources that are now extant. In this process I have constantly faced the difficult task of deciding what was 'relevant' to the experience of Jewish identity. It could be argued, indeed, that the whole experience of lived reality, in all its multiple facets, is relevant to *some* extent to personal identity, and cannot be ignored in such a study. On the other hand, there would be little point in analyzing passages where the experience of identity is only subsidiary, and hence inarticulate and diffused. I have generally given attention, therefore, to the more *explicit* descriptions of the Jews and of the Jewish people. In the course of my survey I may have committed some minor omissions, but I do not think they would significantly affect my arguments.

My survey has included Halakhic sources. Although overtly theoretical, they betray a number of assumptions about the nature of the Jew (as opposed, for instance, to that of the non-Jew) which are indicative of the rabbis' conception and experience of Israel in their lived—albeit, perhaps, intellectual—reality.

I have also taken account of *Aggadot* and exegetical passages relating to 'Israel' of the pre-rabbinic, Biblical past. Neusner has remarked, indeed, that through (fictitious?) genealogical ties, rabbinic sources identify themselves with the Patriarchs and the Biblical Israelites, whilst wicked Biblical figures are identified with their current oppressors. Consequently, the rabbis *read themselves* into the Bible, in so far as the Biblical Israel is taken to reflect their own, unchanged identity.[40] The truth is that the Bible itself—as the rabbis would have read it—should be treated as a document relevant to our study, because of its formative role in the rabbis' shaping of their own experiences.

Finally, liturgical phrases should also be considered of greatest significance, as they would have been recited on a *regular* basis by the authors of our sources.

Reference to sources

Statements in my main text, followed by references to rabbinic sources in the notes, are—unless otherwise stated—translations or close

---

[40] Neusner, *op.cit.* 1989, pp. 112–131, esp. p. 112. More on this in section I.2.D.

paraphrases of explicit rabbinic statements.[41] In each note I endeavour
to refer to all parallel sources, indicating textual variations only if
significant. I have not given attention to the frequency with which
certain passages re-occur in rabbinic literature, because this may often
depend on the hazards of redaction or on the importance of the wider
literary context to which these passages belong, rather than on the
relative importance of the passage *per se*. Frequency of occurrence
in the extant sources is therefore of no statistical significance.

---

[41] For convenience, I have generally translated the phrase "the Holy Blessed be
He" as 'the Almighty'.

CHAPTER ONE

ISRAEL AND THE NATIONS
ASSUMPTIONS, IMAGES AND REPRESENTATIONS

"Dire l'autre enfin, c'est bien évidemment une facon de parler de *nous*."—
François Hartog.

1. SELF AND OTHER: CULTURAL REPRESENTATIONS

A. *The dialectics of self and other*

In his study of Herodotus' *Histories*, François Hartog shows how any
discourse about others reflects, in a mirror-like fashion, an implicit
discourse about oneself.[1] Herodotus makes sense of barbarian *nomoi*
by setting them in contrast with his own nomoi, the *nomoi* of the Greeks;
his account is predicated on an us/them polarity, to which he frequently
refers. Thus the representation of the 'other' implies a concomitant
representation of the 'us', which, even though it is implicit, the reader
should be able to discern.

Conversely, a representation of the 'us' necessitates a representation
of 'them'. By definition, the 'self' is that which is distinguished from
the 'other'. Self implies other, 'Jew' implies 'non-Jew'; the former is
only meaningful if in contradistinction with the latter. The rabbis'
experience of being specifically Jewish depends fundamentally on their
awareness of this distinction. I will begin, therefore, with its study.[2]

The opposition between Jewish and non-Jewish is not my own
hypothesis, nor is it merely implicit in rabbinic writings. Jews ('Israel')
and non-Jews ('the nations')[3] are treated explicitly as radically different

---

[1] F. Hartog, *Le miroir d'Hérodote. Essai sur la représentation de l'autre*, NRF Gallimard,
1980, especially pp. 369–71. See also E. Hall, *Inventing the Barbarian: Greek self-definition
through tragedy*, Oxford: Oxford University Press, 1989, especially p. 162; and more
generally, George Devereux, "Ethnic Identity: its Logical Foundations and its
Dysfunctions", in G. De Vos & L. Romanucci-Ross (eds.), *Ethnic Identity, Cultural
Continuity and Change*, Palo Alto, 1975, pp. 42–70 (esp. p. 48).

[2] Since the logical opposite of Jew is non-Jew, the contrast between them should
constitute our main consideration. A number of interstitial categories such as Jewish
converts, apostates, heretics and common people may also be seen, from the rabbis'
point of view, to be distinguishable from what is perceived as 'Israel'. To what extent
they share the 'otherness' of non-Jews will be discussed in chapter III.

[3] On this nomenclature, see below.

2 CHAPTER ONE

entities,[4] for instance: "among the nations there is none like (Israel)".[5]

This notion is fostered through the weekly liturgical recitation of the *havdala* ('separation', a ritual marking the end of *shabbat*), which concludes:

> (God) distinguishes between holiness and the profane, between light and darkness, between Israel and the nations, between the seventh day and the six. . . .[6]

The *Midrash* glosses that the difference between light and darkness is the same as between Israel and the nations.[7]

The non-Jew is given much attention in early rabbinic sources,[8] but especially in so far as he is contrasted with the Jew. The explicitness of this contrast is worthy of note. The following examples from the *Midrash* are quoted for their *formal* contrastive features only (the *contents* of these passages will be examined in the coming sections of this chapter):

> The nations are a seed of impurity; you are a seed of truth and holiness.[9]
> "The wise"—these are Israel; "the fools"—these are the nations.[10]
> The nations are 'strangers' before the Almighty; Israel are close to Him, His 'sons'.[11]

---

[4] Our sources are unanimous on this point, with the exception of *Tanna DeVei Eliyahu* which contains a few passages suggesting that Jews and non-Jews are essentially the same (esp. *Eliyahu R.* 10; also *ib.* 17, end; *Eliyahu Z.* 7; cf also *Eliyahu R.* 15, p. 75). This work differs from the rest of our sources in many other respects: unlike other *Midrashim*, it is clearly not the compilation of various sayings and traditions, but a uniform work stamped with a coherent character of its own. Although its author draws on many rabbinic traditions, he employs original expressions and a distinctly rhetorical and poetical style; occasionally he deviates from normative *halakha* (see *Encyclopedia Judaica* s.v. *Tanna DeVei Eliyahu*; on the controversy surrounding date and authorship, see W.G. Braude & I.J. Kapstein, *Tanna Debe Eliyyahu*, Jewish Publication Society of America, 1981, pp. 3–12). Therefore, some the views of expressed in this *Midrash* on the non-Jews may be regarded as unrepresentative (the phrase of *Eliyahu R.* 10 is however echoed in *Lev.R.* 2, 11). (Other sources do occasionally draw a *parallel* between Jews and non-Jews (e.g. *Lev.R.* 5, 7), but this does not mean that they are the *same*).

[5] *Num.R.* 10, 5.

[6] *B.Pes.* 103b.

[7] *Num.R.* 18, 7.

[8] With the exception perhaps of the *Mishna*, where the non-Jew is not a major concern (except in tractate *AZ*); in the *Tosefta*, however, the non-Jew becomes an important Halakhic theme in its own right (e.g. *T.Demai* 1, 12–23): see Porton, *op.cit.* pp. 14–22. Porton's work constitutes an indispensable—and unique—source-book on the early rabbinic image of the non-Jew.

[9] *Tanh. Naso* 7.

[10] *Tanh. Tetzave* 11.

[11] *Est.R.* 7, 13.

Israel and the nations differ in their institutions: in a variety of sources, synagogues and houses of learning are frequently contrasted with public baths,[12] theatres and circuses.[13] Their customs are also radically distinguished:

> The prepuce is repulsive . . . circumcision is great.[14]
> A solar eclipse is a bad omen for the nations, a lunar eclipse is a bad omen for Israel, for the nations have a solar calendar, and Israel have a lunar one.[15]
> When Israel eat and drink, they engage in words of *Torah* . . . but the nations . . . engage in obscenities.[16]

In some passages the notion of difference itself is spelled out in full, for instance:

> Some nations . . . do not have a writing, others do not have a language, others do not have either . . . *are Israel the same?* . . . (no:) they have both writing and language; some nations . . . do not know their fathers, others do not know their mothers, others do not know either . . . *are Israel the same?* . . . (no:) they know both their fathers and their mothers.[17]
> *See how different you are from the nations!* Among the nations, they adorn their wives and pass them on to other men etc..[18]

Finally, in a number of passages the clause relating to the non-Jews is no more than the *negation* of that relating to Israel:

> You are called "man", *the nations not.*[19]
> Israel are busy with *Torah, the nations are not.*[20]
> The Almighty brought me into His innermost chambers, *but did not bring any other nation or kingdom.*[21]
> Since Israel stood at Mount Sinai, their filth has been removed; as to the nations *who did not, their filth has not* been removed.[22]

This repetitive style, not uncommon elsewhere in rabbinic literature, takes on a specific significance in this context: it indicates that the sole function of the non-Jews (in this context at least) is to enhance

---

[12] *B.Ta'an.* 20a; *Eccl.R.* 1, 7, 5; etc.
[13] *B.Meg.* 6a; *Eccl.R. ib.*, etc.
[14] *M.Ned.* 3, 10; *T.Ned.* 2, 4–7; etc.
[15] *T.Suk.* 2,6; *B.Suk.* 29a; *Mekh. Bo* 1; *Ex.R.* 15.
[16] *B.Meg.* 12b; *Est.R.* 3, 13.
[17] *Song R.* 6, 8.
[18] *Sifra Kedoshim* 11, 18 (my emphasis). Cf *Tanh. Balak* 14; *Tanh. Re'eh* 6.
[19] *B.Yev.* 61a.
[20] *B.Meg.* 15b.
[22] *Eliyahu R.* 7.
[22] *B.AZ* 22b.

the identity of the Jews through a dialectical process of contrastive negation.

B. *The other as a cultural construct*

The passages I have quoted already suggest that the rabbinic image of the non-Jews is xenophobic in the extreme. Indeed, rabbinic sources assume, as we shall see in the course of this study, that non-Jews are intrinsically wicked and dedicated to murder, sexual offences and idolatry (see section I.3.A). They suggest, besides, that whereas the Jews are akin to angels, non-Jews are akin to animals (section I.4.A). Much of this material has been quoted by antisemitic writers of the early modern period—not least, by Eisenmenger in his *Entdecktes Judenthum*[23]—with the sole purpose of vilifying the Jews and their religion. Whilst I do not wish to engage in value-judgements, whether critical or apologetic,[24] about early rabbinic Judaism, I would loathe to convey the same, antisemitic impression in my own work. A few remarks, therefore, are called for.

It must be stressed, first of all, that 'racial' prejudice of this kind—which, incidentally, Eisenmenger displays himself, at the very least,

---

[23] Johann Andreas Eisenmenger, *Entdecktes Judenthum*, Koenigsberg 1711, 2 vols. Most of the rabbinic sources referred to in that work are late mediaeval/early modern. Of particular interest are vol. 1, chs. 14–15 (pp. 568–630, on rabbinic views of Jews and of non-Jews), ch. 16 (pp. 631–728, on the nomenclature of non-Jews and its significance), ch. 17 (pp. 728–803, on the nomenclature of Rome, i.e. the Roman empire and Christendom), ch. 18 (esp. pp. 803–20, on the 70 nations), and vol. 2, chs. 11–2 (pp. 574–646, on rabbinic views concerning Jewish/non-Jewish relations). Whilst his quotation of original sources is generally reliable, his translation and interpretation of them not always are. Eisenmenger makes no effort to hide his anti-Jewish stance and motives.

[24] In way of apologetics, we may note that unlike other forms of 'racism', the early rabbinic view of Israel as superior to the non-Jews was almost never called upon to vindicate the use of violence or exploitation. On the rabbinic attitude towards the ownership of non-Jewish slaves, see section III.2.B. The ill-reputed statement of R.Shimon b.Yohai who exclaimed: "Kill the non-Jew, even the best among them!" (*Mekh. Vayehi* 1, *Y.Kid.* 4, 11, *Sofrim* 15, 10; printed editions are commonly distorted by censorship), is most exceptional and probably idiosyncratic (see M.M. Kasher, *Torah Shelemah*, vol. 9 (tome 10: *Va'era*), New York: American Biblical Encyclopedia Society, 1945, p. 91 n. 59, and appendix 19). According to *T.AZ* 8, 5, he who kills a non-Jew is exempt from punishment (cf also *M.BK* 4, 6), but it is emphasized in *B.Sanh.* 57a (cf also *B.AZ* 26a) that this does not imply that one may kill him in the first place. According to *B.Sanh.* 57a and *B.AZ* 13b, however, if a non-Jew fell in pit he should be left there to die (see below p. 109). *T.BK* 10, 15 and *B.Sanh.ib.* rule that stealing from a non-Jew is worse than from a Jew, since it leads to the desecration of the Almighty's name. Thus, the practical significance of this rabbinic 'racism' was considerably restricted.

to the same degree—was common currency in the Late Antique Near Eastern world. Rabbinic prejudice towards non-Jews may be compared with contemporary non-Jewish (and later, Christian) prejudice towards the Jews,[25] Greek prejudice towards Oriental peoples,[26] and so forth.[27] It should be noted that by the Middle Ages, Talmudic scholars unanimously ruled that this negative image of the non-Jew pertained specifically to the pagans of Antiquity and was no longer applicable.[28]

In broader terms, the rabbinic perception of the non-Jews represents no more than a cultural tradition. In their empirical experience, the authors of our sources *may* well have had a different awareness of the non-Jews, whom they would have encountered in their daily transactions and among whom many of them may have lived.[29] They *may* well have recognized that in reality, their cultural image of the non-Jew did not always obtain. Nevertheless, they chose to ignore empirical observation and to refer instead to the authority of earlier rabbinic teachings and traditions.[30] In the context of their process of self-identification, this fictitious, stereotypical image of the non-Jew was to them of far greater relevance.[31]

Fictitious images of the ethnic other are just as rife in modern Western culture, and take the same priority over the evidence of empirical observation. We may refer, for instance, to Roland Barthes' study

---

[25] See for instance Schürer, *op.cit.*, vol. III, pp. 150–3.

[26] See for instance Javier Teixidor, "Interpretations and Misinterpretations of the East in Hellenistic Times", in Per Bilde, Troels Engberg-Pedersen, Lise Hannestad, and Jan Zahle (eds.), *Religion and Religious Practice in the Seleucid Kingdom*, Aarhus University Press, 1990, pp. 66–78.

[27] Gary Porton, in his study on the image of non-Jews in the *Mishna* and *Tosefta*, argues that disparaging attitudes towards the ethnic 'other' are actually a universal feature of human culture: *op.cit.*, pp. 238–9 and 298–9, quoting a number of sociologists as well as anthropologist Rodney Needham, *Primordial Characters*, Charlottesville, 1978, p. 5.

[28] See Jacob Katz, *Exclusiveness and Tolerance—Studies in Jewish-Gentile relations in Medieval and Modern Times*, London: OUP, 1961.

[29] See section IV.1.A-B; M.D. Goodman, *State and Society in Roman Galilee AD 132–212*, New Jersey: Rowman and Allanheld, 1983, pp. 41–53; G.G. Porton, *op.cit.* pp. 18–20 & 29 (quoting for instance *T.Eruv.* 5, 18–9). In the present state of research it is impossible, unfortunately, to quantify the extent of Jewish and non-Jewish intermingling in Late Antique Near Eastern society.

[30] On the rabbinic ability to ignore certain aspects of empirical reality, which I think is common to all cultures, see section III.5.B.

[31] Porton argues (*op.cit.* pp. 289–90) that had the rabbis lived in total isolation, they might still have conceived of a purely theoretical non-Jew, in contrast with which they could have identified. On similar lines, Merleau-Ponty (*op.cit.* p. 360) has argued that even the most solipsist self assumes the existence of an other, without which his solitude itself cannot be experienced.

of a French advertisement poster for *'Panzani'* pasta[32]. This poster, dating from around the mid 1960's, represents an open shopping bag containing packets of pasta and fresh vegetables, and carries the caption: *"A l'italienne de luxe"*. Barthes argues that the picture is designed to further the aims of the caption, namely to emphasize the 'Italian' nature of this make of pasta. The tomatoes and peppers (Mediterranean vegetables), the tricoloured hues (yellow, green, red), and the 'Italian' assonance of the name *'Panzani'*, all signify Italy or rather 'Italianicity'. Yet this Italianicity

> is a specifically "French" knowledge (an Italian would barely perceive the connotation of the name, no more probably than he would the Italianicity of tomato and pepper), based on a familiarity with certain tourist stereotypes (p. 34).

Barthes concludes that "Italianicity is not Italy, it is the condensed essence of everything that could be Italian, from spaghetti to painting". It belongs, he argues, to the domain of ideology, "which cannot but be single for a given society and history" (pp. 48–9). Thus Italianicity is not Italy, but a cultural construct belonging to what Barthes calls "French knowledge" or "ideology". Nevertheless, French people treat this stereotype, by and large, as a straightforward reality—hence the effectiveness of this poster.

The rabbinic view of the non-Jews must be seen in the same manner. Though stereotypical and conceivably—with reference to empirical historical data—'unreal', this view represents the way the authors of our sources traditionally conceived of the non-Jewish others. It formed, therefore, an integral part of their subjective, real-lived experiences, and particularly, by way of self-and-other dialectics, of their self-identity[33].

---

[32] R. Barthes, *Image, Music, Text*, (ed. and transl. S. Heath), Glasgow: Fontana 1977, pp. 32–51, with black and white illustration.

[33] As a purely cultural construct, however, it is not devoid of inconsistencies. For instance, the assumption in the *Babylonian Talmud* that the non-Jews are wicked (see section I.3.A) is also directed, more specifically, against the Arabs and the Romans (see also pp. 16–7), but not against the Persians. Except for the terse comment that they are fated for Gehenna (*B.Ber.* 8b), the Talmudic view of the Persians is remarkably benign: they are at worst ridiculous and gluttonous (cf *B.Meg.* 11a; *B.Kid.* 72a), and at best polite and worthy of emulation (*B.Ber. ib.*; 46b.). Persian law is proverbially arbitrary and misguided (*B.Shevu.* 34b; *B.BK* 58b), and the Persian taxation system is in one passage criticised (*B.AZ* 2b). In general, however, their rule is milder than the Romans', which is why the Almighty sent the Jews in exile to Babylon (*B.Git.* 17a; *B.Pes.* 87b; on the historical background, see R. Brody, "Judaism in the Sassanian

2. JEWS AND NON-JEWS: COLLECTIVITY, POLARITY AND INTERDEPENDENCE

The image of Israel and the nations which we have begun to examine is based on the assumption that both groups constitute homogenous, monolithic wholes. As we shall see in later sections, the *whole* of Israel are described indiscriminately as righteous and angelic, just as the *whole* of 'the nations' are wicked and akin to animals.[34] Before proceeding to these central themes, I would like to examine the extent to which our sources see Israel and the nations as indivisible, homogenous collectivities. I begin this section with a survey of the nomenclature which is employed with reference to Jews and non-Jews throughout early rabbinic writings.

A. *Jews and non-Jews: nomenclature*

The non-Jew (singular)
The non-Jew is referred to by the following names:[35]
Goy: meaning 'non-Jew', but literally 'nation'; it is actually derived from the plural *goyim* meaning 'nations' and hence 'non-Jews' (see below).
Nokhri: meaning 'foreigner'.[36] *Aḥer* ('other') is also found, though far less common.[37]

Empire: a case study in religious coexistence", in S. Shaked & A. Netzer (eds.), *Irano-Judaica II*, Jerusalem: Ben-Zvi Institute, 1990). The Persians are praised for the virtue of modesty, which is usually attributed to Israel (see, with references, p. 226, n. 175). The discreet conduct of Jacob in Mesopotamia (*Gen.* 31:4) is even quoted to illustrate Median/Persian customs (*B.Ber.* 8b; *Gen.R.* 74,2; *Eccl.R.* 7,23,1; *Tanh. Hukkat* 6)! It may be, therefore, that our sources distinguish the "Persians" *qua Persians* from the "non-Jews", even though, in actual reality, Persians happen to be simultaneously non-Jewish. This confirms Barthes' contention that the image of another ethnic group bears little relationship with empirical reality: as 'Italianicity' and 'non-Jewishness', 'Persian-ness' is actually no more than an abstraction.

[34] On 'righteous non-Jews', see my remarks in p. 30. On 'wicked' Jews, see sections III.2-3. Broadly speaking, these exceptions are presented as marginal in our sources, and do not affect the general, rabbinic image of the non-Jews and Israel.

[35] There is no equivalent, in rabbinic literature, to the term 'non-Jew'; *eino Yehudi* ('non-Jew') does not appear until the later Middle Ages.

[36] In *B.Sanh.* 54a, the *Talmud* explains that in a certain context *nokhri* may refer to a sinful Jew, but only as a euphemism (*lishna ma'alya*).

[37] *T.Sot.* 7,22. Also *Mekh. Nezikin* 4; *Sifra Kedoshim perek* 4,12; *ib. perek* 9,11. Cf also *Ruth R.8* (*aheret*), and *B.Sanh.* 26b (*aḥer*, according to the interpretation of *Tosafot ad loc.*).

The non-Jews (plural)

In the plural, the non-Jews can be referred to as the *wicked (reshaim)*,[38] in contrast with Israel who are the righteous (*tzadikim*).[39]

Far more commonly, however, the non-Jews are called the *nations*, with the following terms:

goyim (nations); *ummot haOlam* (the nations of the world); *ummot, ammamim* (nations—the latter are rarer).

Although Israel are also considered to be a nation,[40] "the nations" invariably refers to all '*other*', non-Jewish nations. The exclusion of Israel from the category of "the nations" may be related to the notion, often referred to in rabbinic sources, that there are 70 non-Jewish nations in the world,[41] which correspond, in turn, to the 70 languages which split up at the time of the Tower of Babel.[42] Israel, however, are not included among the 70,[43] probably because they were the only nation which came into being some time *after* the tower of Babel. The uniqueness of the nation of Israel, in contrast with the other nations, is stressed in a number of sources.[44] According to the *Babylonian Talmud*, whereas the 70 sacrificial oxen offered in the Temple during the festival of *Sukkot* correspond to the 70 nations, the single ox which is offered on the consecutive festival of *Shemini Atzeret* symbolizes the 'unique nation' (*umma yehida*), which is Israel.[45] Passages such as these may explain why Israel is not included in the term "the nations".

---

[38] *B.Sanh.* 105a; *Num.R.* 15,9 (*Tanh.B. Beha'alotekha* 11); *Num.R.* 20,21; *Tanh.Re'eh* 13. More ambiguously perhaps, *M.Ned.* 3,10.

[39] E.g. *Y.Taan.* 1,1; *Gen.R.* 41,1 (= *Num.R.* 3,1); *Num.R.* 2,13; *Song.R.* 2,2,6; *Tanh. Vayera* 5; *Midrash Tehillim* 75,5. However, a distinction—albeit fine—is drawn in *Sifre Deut.* 47 between Israel and the *tzadikim*.

[40] Israel is *the* nation *par excellence*: *Num.R.* 21,23.

[41] For instance, *B.Suk.* 55b. In *Pes.R.* 9,2, they are metaphorically referred to as 70 wolves. A different number is suggested in *Song R.* 6,8, quoted above, according to which there are a total of 180 nations: 40 have their own language but not their own writing, 40 have a writing but no language, and 100 have neither (Israel, not counted among them, have both). Although these nations are nowhere systematically listed, in a famous exegetical passage the descendants of Noah (found in *Gen.* ch.10) are identified with each of the nations of which they are the ancestors: *Y.Meg.* 1,9; *Gen.R.* 37,1; *B.Yoma* 10a. On the 70 nations as descendants of Noah, see also *Midrash Tehillim* 9.

[42] 70 languages: *M.Sot.* 7,5, etc. The correspondence between languages and nations, implied already in the Biblical account of the tower of Babel, is explicitly stated in *Targum Ps-Jonathan ad Gen.* 11:7–8, and *PdRE* 24.

[43] See *PdRE* 24.

[44] See *Num.R.* 3,6.

[45] *B.Suk.* 55b.

The non-Jews: censorial substitutions

With the exception perhaps of the term "the wicked", terms referring to non-Jews do not appear to be chosen according to context; indeed, they are generally interchangeable.[46] Variability among editions is often due, however, to censorial interference which occurred in the mediaeval and early modern period. Other terms for 'non-Jews' were commonly substituted in our sources by censors, as I shall now list. Since these terms do not mean, primarily, the 'non-Jews', they can lead at times to some confusion. Censorial substitutions can be corrected on the basis of context and of variant readings.

Oved avoda zara, or its acronym *AAZ*, meaning 'worshipper of *avoda zara*,[47] or 'pagan'. Also *oved kokhavim u-mazalot*, or its acronym *AKUM*, meaning 'worshipper of stars and constellations', and other variants such as *oved gillulim* and *oved elilim*, meaning something like 'worshipper of pagan gods'. It is usually demonstrable, and generally accepted, that these terms were not original but introduced by censors.[48]

Min ('heretic'). This term refers primarily to Jewish heretics, and by extension, to Christians (Jewish and non-Jewish).[49]

Kuti (Samaritan). This substitution is particularly confusing, as the Halakhic distinction between non-Jew and *Kuti* is all important.[50]

Tzeduki (Sadducee) is also occasionally substituted for 'non-Jew',[51] with the same confusing result.

"Romans", "Edomites".[52] Also "Egyptians"; "Canaanites"; etc. (various individual nations, often relegated to the Biblical past).

---

[46] Compare for instance *M.Terumot* 1,1 (ed. *Makhon haTalmud haYisre'eli*), which reads *nokhri*, with the parallel version in *T. Terumot* 1,15, which reads *goy*.

[47] "Foreign worship", which corresponds specifically to idol worship and more generally to what we call 'paganism'. This term will be more fully discussed in pp. 196-7.

[48] Indeed, of all terms denoting 'paganism' (or 'idolatry') in early rabbinic writings, only *avoda zara* appears to have been original. The term *avodat kokhavim u-mazalot* (with the same acronym, *AKUM*) is nowhere attested in the earlier editions and manuscripts (H.L. Strack, *Introduction to the Talmud and Midrash*, Philadelphia: Jewish Publishing Society, 1931, p. 262 n. 66); likewise, the term *avodat elilim* (see, for instance, H.J. Kassovsky, *Otzar Leshon haMishna*, Frankfurt a.- M. 1927, vol. 1, p. 173 n., referring to the *Mishna* and *Tosefta*).

[49] See section III.3.B.

[50] Many sections of *Tosefta*, for instance, are concerned with this distinction (e.g. *T. Peah* 4,1). See section III.2.C.

[51] *B.Ned.* 49b; the parallel version in *B.Ber.* 55a reads *matronita* (a non-Jewish woman of importance). See section III.3.C.

[52] However, the Romans and Edomites are commonly confused with the non-Jews. See our remarks in pp. 15-7.

The Jews

The Jews are referred to in considerably fewer terms. *Yehudi* (Jew)
is less common than *Yisrael* (Israel). Both terms are relatively well defined
in their usage; they are but rarely interchanged.[53] The Biblical *Ivri*
(Hebrew) is virtually non-existent in rabbinic literature.[54]

Yehudi

This term is first attested, and frequently used, in the book of *Esther*.
It is occasionally found in rabbinic writings, but only in the following
contexts:

1. In the exegesis of the book of *Esther*,[55] where we also find the
term *yahadut* (Jewishness, or Jewish religion).[56] In this context our sources
interpret *yehudi* as meaning 'confessor' (of the true religion)[57] or 'singled
out' (i.e. who has singled out God as the only One).[58] On the other
hand the verbal form *hityahed* (to convert to Judaism), found in *Est.*
8:17, is almost never used in rabbinic literature.[59]

2. In conversation with non-Jews, where the Jews identify themselves
as *Yehudim*,[60] and likewise the non-Jews call them by that name.[61] It
is important to note that the non-Jews have no other term by which
to refer to the Jews; to them, 'Israel' appears to be unknown. The
significance of this point will be discussed at a later stage.[62]

3. In casual conversation;[63] often with reference to specific indi-

---

[53] See *Y.Maaser Sheni* 4,6 (*Yehudai*) and its parallel version in *B.Ber.* 56b ("son of
an Israel").

[54] E.g. *Pes.R.* 23,8, R. Akiva talking to Turnus Rufus. Also, *Mekh. Bahodesh* 1, probably
as a word-play with *Aravi. Ivri* in *M.Git.* 9,7 means 'Hebrew-speaker'. See, in general,
Solomon Zeitlin, "The names Hebrew, Jew and Israel", in *JQR* 43, 1952-3, pp.
365–79.

[55] E.g. *B.Meg.* 13a: 'Jewish (*yehudi*) food'. Cf Jastrow s.v. *yehudi*.

[56] *Est.R.* 7,11 (*hapax*).

[57] *B.Meg.* 13a. The term *yehudi* is indeed associated with martyrdom: *Y.Sheviit* 4,2;
Ex.R. 42,9. This may be, however, because non-Jews call the Jews by that name
(see below).

[58] *Est.R.* 6,2.

[59] It is found exceptionally in *Midrash Yelamdenu* (ed. Wertheimer) *Kedoshim* (p. 171),
concerning Abraham.

[60] *B.Ned.* 49b; *Gen.R.* 76,8; *Eccl.R.* 1,8,4 and 9,1,3. Cf also note 20 above.

[61] *Sifre Deut.* 354; *Y.Ber.* 9,1; *Y.Sanh.* 2,6; *B.Sanh.* 64a; *Eccl.R.* 10,5; *Tanh. Shoftim*
10. A convert recalls talking about the *Yehudai* in his non-Jewish days: *B.AZ* 70a.
This usage applies to all nationalities, to Persians (e.g. Queen Ifra Hormiz: *B.Taan.*
24b; *B.Nida* 20b) as well as to the Romans of Rome (*Y.Sheviit* 4,2).

[62] Pp. 222–3.

[63] *Y.Shek.* 5,2 (by malicious Israelites); *Y.Sot.* 1,3, *Y.BM* 2,5, *B.Taan.* 22a, *Eccl.R.*
1,8,4 (in casual speech); *B.Hag.* 9b (in a popular saying).

viduals (or groups of individuals).[64] This usage is restricted to common parlance,[65] and is rarely found as a *literary* or Halakhic designation of the Jew;[66] the only significant Halakhic occurrence of this term is in the rather unusual expression *dat Yehudit* (law of a Jewess).[67]

Israel

The term *Yisrael*, or Israel, as I shall refer to it, is far more common and indeed pervasive in the whole of rabbinic literature. It is always in singular form.[68]

In a Halakhic context, 'Israel' represents the Halakhic category of the individual Jewish person. It is treated as a singular,[69] and found pervasively in the *Mishna* and *Tosefta*.

As an Aggadic term, 'Israel' refers to the Jewish people in its totality; it is thus a *collective singular*, which is normally treated as a plural (for instance, in the phrase "Israel *are* dear"[70]), but occasionally also as a singular.[71] The implications of this collective usage will now be examined.

---

[64] *Y.Ber.* 2,4 (a *Yehudi* was ploughing—elsewhere, in *Lam.R.* 1,51, he is called a 'man'); *Deut.R.* 2,16 (a *Yehudi* was travelling aboard a non-Jewish boat); *Gen.R.* 10,17 and parallels (the *Yehudai* of Caesarea); *Midrash Mishlei* 31,15 (the daughter of Pharaoh became *Yehudit*).

[65] As in *Targum Ps-Jonathan* and *Targum Yerushalmi* on *Gen.* 49:8, and *Gen.R. ad loc.* (98,6).

[66] See however *B.Pes.* 113b ("any *Yehudi* who has no wife etc."; also *B.Yev.* 62b); *B.Pes.* 8b ("a hole between the houses of a *Yehudi* and an 'Aramean'"). The "uncircumcised *Yehudi*" of *B.Pes.* 94b is a censorial interpolation, as the word *Yehudi* is not found in manuscripts, nor in the parallel text in *B.Pes.* 69a (cf *Dik.Sof. ad* 94b.). Yet it is perhaps not insignificant that many of these exceptions are found in *B.Pes.*, and we may surmise that this particular tractate was subjected to some censorial tampering. The passage on the *Yehudi* who has no wife may have been substituted for the original 'man' so as not to offend Christian celibate monks and priests.

[67] Found in *M.Ket.* 7,6. On the restricted meaning of this expression, see p. 246.

[68] Unlike the term *Yehudi*. The plural form *Yisre'elim* is occasionally found in the *Mishna*, *Tosefta* and *Sifre*: e.g. *M.Eruv.* 6,1; *M.AZ* 4,11. However, Israel Feintuch in *Mesorot veNus'haot baTalmud*, Ramat-Gan: Bar-Ilan University Press, 1985, pp. 187–90, demonstrates on the basis of manuscript readings and early editions that this plural form *Yisre'elim* is probably not authentic.

[69] In Halakhic passages it is rarely treated as a plural; see however *Y.Hala* 4,7; and paragraphs 12 and 26 of the mosaic inscription in the Rehob synagogue (J. Sussmann, "An Halachic inscription from the Beth-Shean valley", in *Tarbiz* 43, 1974, pp. 88–158, cf pp. 127 & 135 (Hebrew)), where *Yisrael* is treated as a plural, but in singular form.

[70] *Havivim Yisrael*: *M.Avot* 3,18, etc.

[71] The *Talmud* remarks explicitly: "all Israel are referred to (at times) in the singular" (*B.Mak.* 23b).

B. *Israel as a single body*

The solidarity of Israel is quite a familiar theme in all our sources, for instance:

> All Israel are brothers and friends.[72]
> All Israel are responsible for one another.[73]
> Israel are united in their practices: they all pray towards the same place;[74] their God is one, their *Torah* is one, their Temple is one.[75]

Furthermore, Israel can be conceived of "as one body, as one soul";[76] "all Israel are a single soul".[77] This organic unity transpires in the comparison of Israel with a lamb: in the same way as when a lamb hurts its head, all its limbs are in pain, so if one Jew is killed, all other Jews are in sorrow.[78] Organic unity is also implicit in the following passage:

> It is written: "you shall not take vengeance nor bear grudge against the children of your people" (*Lev.* 19:18). What does this resemble? A person was slicing meat, and he cut his hand with his knife. Would (that hand take revenge) and cut the other?.[79]

The conception of Israel as a single, homogenous entity may account for the relative confusion between singular and plural, which we have noted, in the Aggadic usage of the term 'Israel' (i.e., as a collective singular). Confusion of this kind also occurs in other ways: for instance, Israel can be simultaneously compared to a 'mother', which is singular, and to 'sons', which are plural.[80] Although this double simile is derived from exegesis, it could not make sense if singular and plural were not, in some sense, interchangeable with reference to Israel.

As a monolithic entity, the people of 'Israel' may serve as a reification

---

[72] *Tanh. Naso* 1.
[73] *Sifra Behukkotai perek* 7, end; *B.Sanh.* 27; *B.Shevu.* 39a; *Num.R.* 10,5. They are mutually responsible for punishment as well as for reward: *Tanh. Nitzavim* 2.
[74] *Song R.* 4,4,6.
[75] *Tanh. Korah* 5.
[76] *Mekh. dRShbY ad Ex.* 19:6.
[77] *Lev.R.* 4,6; *Midrash Yelamdenu, Kundris Aharon* (ed.Eisenstein), 38. The unity of Israel is also conveyed in the suggestion that the whole of Israel may sit, during the festival of *Sukkot*, under one single *sukka* (booth: *B.Suk.* 27b), or that the whole of Israel may partake of a single Passover lamb (*Mekh. Pis'ha* 5; *B.Pes.* 78b, and parallels).
[78] *Lev.R.* 4,6. Cf *Mekh. Bahodesh* 2. The same conclusion is drawn from a comparison between Israel and a heap of nuts: *SongR.* 6,11; *Pes.R.* 11,2.
[79] *Y.Ned.* 9,4.
[80] *Sifra Miluim* 15.

of the otherwise abstract notion of 'Jewishness' or Jewish identity. It also suggests, perhaps, that the authors of our sources do not experience their Jewish identity as individuals, but rather together as a joint, subjective collectivity.[81]

C. *The nations: plurality and ethnographic confusion*

The 70 nations

The term 'the nations' connotes, at first sight, plurality rather than homogeneity, especially as it may refer implicitly to the fragmentation of the 70 nations at the Tower of Babel. Non-Jewish plurality is occasionally described in rabbinic sources, as in this passage:

> Ten measures of wealth came down to the world: the Romans took nine, and the rest of the world took one—

and so, the text continues, Babylon took nine of the world's ten measures of poverty; Elam took nine of the measures of rusticity; the Persians took nine measures of might; Media took nine measures of lice; Egypt took nine measures of witchcraft; Arabia took nine measures of promiscuity; and the Negroes took nine measures of drunkenness.[82]

Yet the plurality of the nations is seldom addressed in our sources. It is hardly relevant to Mishnaic *halakha*[83], except for references to the Biblical prohibitions of marrying converts from among the Ammonites, Moabites, Edomites and Egyptians. The *Mishna* rules, however, that these prohibitions are no longer applicable, since Sennacherib conflated the 70 nations so as to render them all—the Jews, of course, excepted[84]—completely undistinguishable:

> Are the Ammonites and the Moabites where they used to be? Long ago Sennacherib, king of Assyria, came up and confused *all the nations*, as it is said: "I have removed the bounds of the peoples . . ." (*Isaiah* 10:13).[85]

---

[81] See my remarks in the introduction (section 2).

[82] The text also refers to the wisdom of the land of Israel, the beauty of Jerusalem, etc.: *B.Kid.* 49b. See another version in *Est.R.* 1,17, and a similar text in *Avot dRN* 28,1.

[83] *M.Yev.* 8,3. On the absence of references to non-Jewish ethnic diversity in the *Mishna* and *Tosefta*, see Porton, *op.cit.* p. 289.

[84] As we have seen, Israel is not counted among the 70 nations, and the survival of its distinct identity is taken for granted in our sources. A passage in *B.Yev.* 16b–17a would suggest however that the ten 'lost' tribes of the kingdom of Israel, whom Sennacherib sent into exile, have been blended together with the other nations.

[85] This saying, attributed to R. Yehoshua, clearly refers to all the nations (as I

Now that the division of the nations at Babel has been reversed, the
Mishna considers the nations as an amorphous 'melting-pot', an undifferentiated, homogenous collectivity.

The rabbis and their neighbours
Rabbinic sources are not ethnographically inclined. Their attention
is drawn somewhat to the Persians, the Arabs and the Romans, but
no more.[86] Remarkably, they appear to ignore their immediate
neighbours, the non-Jewish peoples amongst whom they lived—there
is no reference, in rabbinic sources, to 'Syrians'[87] or to 'Babylonians'.[88]
The attention given to Persians, Arabs and Romans reflects, I would

---

have emphasized in the text), although the specific case under discussion concerned
an Ammonite. R. Gamliel disagrees with R. Yehoshua concerning Ammonites (who
unlike other nations, he argues, have returned to their original homeland); but the
Mishna concludes in favour R. Yehoshua: *M.Yadayim* 4,4; *T.Yadayim* 2,17; *B.Ber.* 28a.
In *T.Kid.* 5,4, R. Akiva quotes the principle that Sennacherib blurred all the nations
as *halakha*, the accepted view. Similarly, in *B.Yoma* 54a, this principle is treated as
the accepted view; elsewhere in the *Bavli* (e.g. *B.Kid.*, ch.4) the nationis of the Ammonites
etc. are only referred to as theoretical categories. According to a later *Midrash*, likewise,
all nations are related to each other: *Est.R.* 7,4.
    The case of the Egyptians is however exceptional, as R. Yehoshua agrees with
R. Gamliel in *T.Yadayim* 2,18 that they did return to their original homeland.
Consequently, present-day Egyptians are considered by R. Yehuda Minyamin as
authentic descendants of the Egyptian nation: *Sifre Deut.* 253; *Y.Yev.* 8,2; *B.Yev.* 76b
(*ib.* 78a; *B. Sot.* 9a); although in *T.Kid.* 5,4, R. Akiva disagrees (in *Y.Yev.* 8,2 R. Akiva
also disagrees with R. Yehuda Minyamin, but on a totally different issue).
    As to whether the Libyans are a nation distinguished from the Egyptians, *Y.Shab.*
5,1 concludes with a remark to which we shall return (p. 37): "all types of mules
constitute one species".
    [86] References to Persians, Arabs and Romans abound. As to other nations, I have
only found the following sporadic—and rather uninformative—references: the *Kushiim*
(Ethiopians or negroes: *Gen.R.* 60,2; *ib.*73,10), the *Kasdiim* (Chaldeans, belonging in
all likelihood to the Biblical past: *Y.Taan.* 3,4; *B.Suk.* 52b; *Est.R.* 1,17; *Pes.R.* 17,6),
the Palmyrenes (*B.Shab.* 21b; *ib.* 31a; regarding their eligibility to conversion: *Y.Kid.*4,1;
B.Yev. 16a-17a; *B.Nida* 56b; *Lam.R.* 2,4, end).
    [87] This term might have been used with reference to non-Jewish Palestinian peoples.
Josephus calls the non-Jews of Caesarea "Syrians" (but then in the same passage:
"Greeks"); indeed, he remarks that they considered troops raised in Syria to be their
own flesh and blood: *BJ* 2,266-8.
    [88] On the 'Arameans', see below. The term *Bavlai* (Babylonians) refers to the *Jews*
of Babylonia, particularly to the rabbis, and not to Babylonian non-Jews: e.g.
B.Hul. 45a ("our Babylonian colleagues"); *B.Ket.* 75a, *Avot dRN* 12,12 ("foolish
Babylonian(s)!"—with reference to rabbis). The charge in *B.Taan.* 9b that Babylonians
are liars appears to be directed against the Jews. It is said, however, that the 'language
of Babylonia'—Aramaic—is close to the language of the *Torah*, which is why the
Jews were sent there in exile (*B.Pes.* 87b), and the observation that the Babylonians
eat raw meat because of their corrupt minds may be directed towards indigenous
non-Jews (*Y.Peah* 8,4).

surmise, the central political role which they held in the Late Roman Levant: Persian and Roman empires controlling either side of the Fertile Crescent, and Arab tribes controlling its semi-desertic fringe.[89] But the ability of our sources to ignore the existence of other peoples, even their immediate neighbours, suggests their lack of interest towards non-Jewish ethnic diversity, which may be related to the assumption that all non-Jews are confused and blurred into a single, homogenous collectivity.

Romans and non-Jews

Ethnographic blurring occurs especially between the Romans and other non-Jews. This is not simply due to the generalisation of Roman citizenship to all free subjects of the empire in 212CE: firstly, the rabbis never suggest that by the same token, they themselves could be considered 'Roman'; secondly, in most rabbinic writings the term 'Roman' refers exclusively to the representatives of the Roman Empire, namely soldiers, officials, and the imperial ruling class; not all non-Jews, therefore, can be referred to as being 'Roman'.[90]

Yet in Palestinian sources we find that the term 'the nations' is often used with actual reference to Roman imperial troops and officials: thus it is 'the nations' who destroyed the Temple;[91] they martyred

---

[89] It should be noted, however, that we find no mention in our sources of the powerful confederate tribes such as the Ghassan and the Lakhm who may have played a crucial part in the political and military history of the 6th century Levant (see I. Shahid, *Byzantium and the Arabs in the fourth century*, Washington 1984; B. Isaac, *Limits of Empire: the Roman Army in the East*, Oxford: Clarendon Press, 1990, ch.5). There is only one obscure reference to Arab rule in *B. Shab.* 11a ("better under Yishmael than under the non-Jew"); see B. Septimus, "Better under Edom than under Ishmael: the history of a saying", in *Zion*, 47, 1982 (Hebrew).

[90] In the *Babylonian Talmud*, "Romans" refers exclusively to soldiers, officials, or inhabitants of the city of Rome (except perhaps for *B. Ket.* 61b). In the *Palestinian Talmud*, "Romans" is mainly found as a reference to soldiers (see M. Sokoloff, *A Dictionary of Jewish Palestinian Aramaic of the Byzantine Period*, Ramat-Gan: Bar-Ilan Univ. Press, 1990, pp. 519–20, s.v. *Romii*): *Y.Shab.* 6,9; *Y.Eruv.* 3,5; *Y.BK* 3,1; *ib.* 8,1; *Y.Ber.* 9,1; *Y.Taan.* 4,5; and to the ruling class: *Y.Terumot* 8, end.

Gen.R. is well aware of the cosmopolitanism of the late imperial legions: thus, it remarks that since Roman troops are recruited from all the nations of the world (*Gen. R.* 42,4; *ib.* 76,6; *ib.* 88,6)—including the barbarians—Roman rule amounts to the rule of all 70 nations (*Song R.* 2,8,2). However this alone cannot account for the confusion of the nations with the Romans, which I shall now examine.

[91] *Mekh. Shira* 10.

Rabbi Akiva and his colleagues,[92] murder the Jews,[93] persecute them[94] and pass evil decrees against them.[95] It is the 'non-Jews' who impose customs, taxes and *annonae* on the Jews,[96] and again the 'non-Jews' who offer to appoint them as *hegemones, duces and eparchoi*.[97] That these passages blame the rabbis' immediate non-Jewish neighbours for the excesses of the Roman ruling power, failing to identify them as an ethnically distinct group, shows the extent to which the categories of 'Romans' and 'non-Jews' are, in Palestinian sources, confused.

Similarly, the *image* of the Romans and of the non-Jews appears to coincide. More than any other nation, the Romans embody the wickedness of the non-Jews. They are prone to theft,[98] murder.[99] homosexuality,[100] adultery,[101] and *avoda zara*,[102] which, we shall see, are all generally ascribed to the non-Jews. Esau, identified as the Biblical ancestor and forerunner of Rome,[103] is similarly described in the *Midrash* as a thief, a murderer, and as promiscuous and devoted to *avoda zara*.[104]

---

[92] *B.RH* 23a, in the name of the Palestinian sage R. Yoḥanan (whereas *B.Ber.* 61b refers to 'the wicked kingdom'). To my knowledge this confusion is not found elsewhere in Babylonian sources.

[93] *Mekh. Beshallaḥ, pet.; Tanh. Beshallaḥ* 5.

[94] *Eliyahu R.* 5.

[95] *Ruth R., pet.* 3. In all these passages the context clearly indicates that the reference is actually to Rome.

[96] *Y.Sheviit* 4,3; *ib.* 5, end; *Y.AZ* 4,10; *Y.Git.* 5,10.

[97] *Num.R.* 2,4; *Tanh. Bamidbar; Song R.* 7,1,2; *Pes.R.* 21. I have no evidence to suggest that in all these passages, the term 'non-Jews' is actually a mediaeval censorial substitution for 'Romans', and thus not a confusion committed by the rabbis of Late Antiquity. Moreover, in one passage (*Ruth R. ib.*) the terms 'Esau' (Rome) and 'non-Jews', referring both to Rome, are used simultaneously and side by side, which suggests that this text has not been tampered with.

[98] *Gen.R.* 44,15; *ib.* 17; *ib.* 65,1. Rome is greedy for money: *B.Pes.* 118b; *Gen.R.* 78,12.

[99] *Mekh. Baḥodesh* 5; *Sifre Deut.* 343; *Num.R.* 14,10; see also *Gen.R.* 63,8 & 13. The Romans kill and crucify the Jews: *Mekh. Beshallaḥ pet.; ib. Shira* 10. The only reason why they do not completely exterminate the Jewish people (besides the fact that it would be impossible) is that they do not want to be called 'the murderous kingdom': *B.Pes.* 87b; *B.AZ* 10b.

[100] *Gen.R.* 63,10; cf *B.Git.* 58a, quoted below section I.5.C.

[101] *Gen.R.* 99,2; *Num.R.* 11,1.

[102] Cf *Midrash Ḥaserot Viyeterot* 59. They have rejected the Almighty: *Pes.R.* 14,15.

[103] See p. 19.

[104] *Gen.R.* 63; 65; 75; 76; 78 (*passim*). Also *Mekh. Vayehi* 2; *Ex.R.* 21,1; *B.Git.* 57b; *Lam.R., pet.2; Pes.dRK* 15,5. Cf M. Hadas-Lebel, "Jacob et Esaü ou Israel et Rome dans le Talmud et le Midrash", in *Revue de l'histoire des religions*, 201, 1984, pp. 369–392, especially pp. 379–83; M. Hadas-Lebel, *Jérusalem contre Rome*, Paris: Cerf, 1990; Louis H. Feldman, "Some observations on Rabbinic reactions to Roman rule in third century Palestine", in *HUCA* 1992, pp. 39–81, esp. pp. 67–76. Ishmael, the ancestor of the Arabs, is similarly accused in *T.Sot.* 6,6 and *Gen.R.* 53,15 of murder, idolatry, and forbidden relations.

Rome is commonly referred to as the "wicked kingdom":[105] like the non-Jews, the Romans are, *par excellence*, the 'wicked'. Confused as they are with the non-Jews, the Romans tend to lack the ethnic distinctiveness which the Arabs and Persians occasionally maintain.

Arameans

Another example of ethnographic blurring is in the widespread usage of the term 'Arameans'. Because of its phonetic affinity, in Hebrew and in Aramaic, with the term 'Romans', it appears in some editions as a censorial substitution for the latter,[106] or in some places in a hybrid form (*Aromiim*).[107] The term 'Arameans' is also substituted, in the some editions, for 'non-Jews' in general.[108]

But aside from these cases of censorial interference, the usage of 'Aramean' as meaning 'non-Jew' may be found in apparently original, unadulterated passages.[109] This occurs, for instance, in a number of Halakhic statements.[110] This usage may be due to the fact that most

---

[105] E.g. *B.Ber.* 61b; *B.Shab.* 16a; *B.Pes.* 118b; *B.Git.* 57b; etc. Rome is also called the "guilty kingdom" (e.g. *Mekh. Vayehi* 1; *ib. Vayyassa* 5; *B.AZ* 2b) or "guilty Rome" (*Mekh. Bahodesh* 9).

[106] For instance, in the Basel edition (and subsequent editions) of the *Babylonian Talmud* in *B.RH* 23a and *B.Hul.* 56b (*Dik.Sof.*). In some cases 'Arameans' is an obvious substitute for 'Romans': *Y.Sheviit* 4,2 and *Y.Sanh.* 3,5 (on an event which took place in Rome), *Gen.R.* 63,7 (the descendants of Esau, i.e. Rome), *Eccl.R.* 7,11 (imperial agents); cf *Y.Meg.* 1,9 (a *burgani* translated the Bible from the Greek into *Aramit*—perhaps a substitution for *Romit*, i.e. 'Latin'). *B.BK* 59a (ms. Hamburg, etc.) distinguishes between an 'Aramean' palm tree and a 'Persian' palm tree; but Maimonides, in his paraphrase of this passage, refers to the former as 'Roman' (*Code of Law: the Book of Torts*, H. Klein (trans.), New Haven: Yale University Press, 1954, "Damage by Chattel", 4,14). In some editions of B. Sanh. 12a *Arammi* is substituted for *Edomi* (by graphic analogy), which is also Rome (cf *Dik.Sof.*). See Jastrow, p. 123, s.v. *Arammi*.

[107] *B.Git.* 17a: their rule is less desirable than the Persians'.

[108] *B.Pes.* 3b; *B.Hul.* 97a (*Dik.Sof.*).

[109] See Sokoloff, op.cit., p. 76, s.v. *Arammii*.

[110] *M.Meg.* 4,9; *M. Sanh.* 9,6; *Targum Ps-Jonathan ad Lev.* 25:47; *Sifra ad loc.* This usage is less common in the *Palestinian Talmud*; but see *Y.Yev.* 2,6 and *Y.Kid.* 3,12 (in parallel versions in *Gen.R.* 7,2 and *Eccl.R.* 7,23,4, the term 'non-Jew' is used instead). On the other hand, this usage is quite common in the *Babylonian Talmud: B.Ber.* 8b; *B.Shab.* 129a; *B.Shab.* 139a; *B.Pes.* 8b; *B.Pes.* 112b; *B.Pes.* 113a; *B.BB* 21a; *B.AZ* 30a; *ib.* 31b–32a; *B.Sanh.* 94a; *B.Men.* 42a; probably *B.Yev.* 45b and *B.Hul.* 111b. The choice of this term in *B.AZ* 30a (and by extension perhaps, in 31b–32a) may be dictated for poetical reasons, because of its similarity with the term *armalta* (widow) which appears in the same context (in 30a—although the reverse may be argued, that the reference to a widow is brought about for poetical reasons, because of its similarity with the term *arama'a*). 'Aramean' as non-Jew is also found in an Aggadic passage in *Avot dRN* 16,2. A derivative word, *aramiuta*, is used in the sense of 'non-Jewishhood' in *M.Meg.* 4,9 and *B.AZ* 70a. The usage of *Aramai* as 'pagans' is also attested in Christian Syriac sources (Dr Alison Salvesen, personal communication),

non-Jews in Palestine and Babylonia were Aramaic-speaking; it is possible, indeed, that in some contexts 'Aramean' refers specifically to the Aramaic-speaking peoples of the Late Antique Near East.[111] But I would stress that the Arameans are never described as an ethnic group with a distinct identity of their own (as Persians and Arabs occasionally are); they are no more than unspecifiable non-Jews.[112]

This illustrates further the rabbinic indifference towards their neighbouring non-Jewish world, which is related, I would argue, to the rabbinic assumption that all the nations constitute an amorphous, undifferentiated collectivity.

D. Jacob and Esau: polarity and interdependence

The compression of the non-Jewish nations into a single, monolithic entity, the 'nations', serves the purpose of opposing a coherent—and equivalent—'other' to the single entity of 'Israel'. This results in a balanced contrast between self and other, upon which Jewish identity can be predicated.[113]

This one-to-one polarity is vividly impersonated by the Biblical figures

---

or as a translation of "Hellene" in the Syriac New Testament (S. Lieberman, *Greek in Jewish Palestine*, New York: Jewish Theological Seminary, 1965 (2nd ed.), p. 86 n. 130).

[111] The identification of 'Arameans' with all Near Eastern Aramaic-speakers is however by no means certain. Indeed, the languages which we call 'Aramaic' do not necessarily correspond to the *Aramit* mentioned in rabbinic sources. Rabbi distinguishes between *Aramit* which is spoken in Babylonia, and *Sursi* (i.e. 'Syriac') which is spoken in Syria: *B.Sot.* 49b; *B.BK* 83a. Indeed, *Aramit* is mentioned more frequently in the *Babylonian Talmud* (*B.Sot.* 33a; *B.Sanh.* 21b–22a; etc.) than in the *Palestinian Talmud* (only in *Y.Sot.* 9,13 (cf *B.Sot.* 49a and *ib.* 33a; also in *M.Shek.* 5,3 and *Sifre Deut.* 343), whereas *Sursi* is more common in the *Palestinian Talmud* (*Y.Pes.* 5,3 (= *Mekh. Bo* 3); *Y.Meg.* 1,9; *Y.Sot.* 7,2) than in the *Babylonian Talmud* (*B.Pes.* 61a). Most significantly, the *Palestinian Talmud* calls the language of Laban (in *Gen.* 31:47) *sursi*, even though Laban comes from Aram and is called (in *Gen.* 31:20) the *Arammi* (*Y.Sot. ib.*)! If we are to conclude that rabbinic sources generally refer to Western Aramaic as 'Syriac' (just as, according to Josephus *Ant.* 1,144, the Greeks call the Arameans "Syrians"?), then the term 'Arameans' may need to be restricted to the non-Jewish inhabitants of *Babylonia* alone.

[112] As evident in both *Talmudim*, e.g. *B.Kid.* 33a (R. Yohanan would stand up out of respect even for *Aramai*); *Y.AZ* 5,4 (wine imported by the *Aramaia* to Samaria).

[113] The same is found, according to Edith Hall, in classical Greek tragedy: "tragic rhetoric often treats its invented barbarians as a single category embodying the opposite of the central Hellenic values . . . The polarization of Hellenism and barbarism even presupposes that a generic bond exists not only between all Greeks, but between all non-Greeks as well" (*op.cit.* p. 161). It is indeed implied that a family relationship exists between all barbarians, who are frequently referred to as "the entire barbarian *genos*" (*ib.*).

of Jacob and Esau, the alleged ancestor of the Romans, who typify, as we have seen, the nations. Whereas in the Bible, Esau is no more than the ancestor and founder of the small kingdom of *Edom* (Idumaea), by the rabbinic period he is identified as the ancestor of the Romans[114] or as the founder of their city.[115] Rome is thus referred to as "kingdom of Esau",[116] "son of Esau",[117] "Esau",[118] "kingdom of *Edom*"[119] and "*Edom*"[120] *tout court*; the Romans themselves are said to identify with Esau.[121] Consequently, the rabbinic exegesis of the Biblical account of Esau and Jacob constitutes a web of veiled references to Rome and Israel.[122] The contrast between Jacob and Esau—the latter relying on his physical strength, the former on prayer, as implied in the verse, "the voice is Jacob's voice, and the hands are Esau's hands" (*Gen.* 27:22)[123]—is thus an embodied prefiguration of the polarized, dialectical

---

[114] *Gen.R.* 83,4 identifies Magdiel (one of Esau's descendants in *Gen.* 36:43) with *Letianus*, emperor of Rome (i.e. *Diocletianus*, according to Theodor's conjecture). *PdRE* 38 identifies Magdiel with Rome itself.

[115] According to late Midrashic sources, Rome was built by a grandson of Esau, Tzefo b.Elifaz b.Esav: *Midrash Yelamdenu* (ed.Wertheimer) *Vayyishlah* 72 (the story is narrated in full detail in *Yosifon*, ch.2). The Esau-Rome connection may have been originally at variance with the exegetical tradition which identifies the Romans with the *Kittim* (*Targum Onkelos* and *Ps-Jonathan ad Num.* 24:24), who are descendants of *Yavan* (Ionia or Greece—*Gen.* 10:4) and hence not related to the Semitic lineage.

[116] E.g. *Tanh. Ki Tissa* 1.

[117] *B.Git.* 17a.

[118] E.g. *Gen.R.* 6,3; *Ex.R.* 31, end; *Deut.R.* 1,17; *Ruth R., pet.3*; *Pes. dRK* 2,2; *Tanh. Mishpatim* 14. In *Eccl.R.* 5,6, the title 'Esau' appears to refer to the Roman emperor rather than to the Roman empire as a whole.

[119] E.g. *Eccl.R.* 1,7,9.

[120] E.g. *B.AZ* 10b (reinterpreting a Biblical verse referring to Idumaea); *Lam.R.* 1,42. It is difficult to tell how many of these are censorial substitutions. In *B.Sanh.* 12a *Edomi* is used as a code-word for 'Roman' (or, 'Roman government') (see *Dik.Sof. ad loc.*). In rare cases, the term *Edom* in rabbinic texts can still refer to the Biblical Edom, e.g. *M.Pes.* 3,1 ("Edomite wine"); but *B.Pes.* 42b interprets this as referring to the Romans—see parallel text in *B.Meg.* 6a-b). For another unusual occurrence, see *Gen.R.* 75,13.

[121] *B.AZ* 10b; *ib.* 11b (quoted below in full); *Tanh. Teruma* 3.

[122] M. Hadas-Lebel, 1984, p. 379. As we have seen in p. 16, Esau is a thief, a murderer, promiscuous and devoted to *avoda zara*; he is thus a precursor of Rome and the founder of its wickedness (the same could be said of Ishmael in rabbinic exegesis, as he is also accused of committing murder, *avoda zara*, and forbidden relations). In some cases, in fact, Esau of the Bible is explicitly confused with Rome: *Gen.R.* 78,14 (Esau talking to Jacob of his "*duces, eparchoi*, and *stratiotes*"); *ib.* 63,10 (Esau's duplicity, as a hunter, transpires in Roman cross-examination techniques; cf Hadas-Lebel p. 382). Conversely, some rabbis treat the Romans in the same way as Jacob would have treated Esau: when R. Yehuda the Patriarch wrote a letter to Emperor Antoninus, he chose a wording similar to that which Jacob used when making approaches to Esau: *Gen.R.* 75,5.

[123] According to *Gen.R.* 63; 65; 75; 76; 78 (*passim*). Also *Mekh. Vayehi* 2; *Ex.R.*

contrast between the single entities of Israel and the nations.

It must be stressed that in the same way as the Jewish people of the rabbinic period are equated in our sources with the 'Israel' of the Bible, as though they were one and the same people,[124] rabbinic literature fails to distinguish between the non-Jews of the Bible and those of their contemporary reality.[125] Israel and Rome, the avatars of Jacob and Esau, are thus current manifestations of a changeless structure, an ever-lasting reality. In this sense, the homogeneity of the nations, which mirrors that of Israel in a dialectical, contrastive way, transcends not only ethnic plurality but also the vicissitudes of historical change.

The impression that Israel and the nations are timeless and un-changing proceeds in part from the inherent conservatism of rabbinic teachings. As I have described in the introduction, oral and written traditions about Israel, the nations, and individual peoples such as the Persians, Romans, and Arabs, were transmitted by the rabbis from one generation to the next without much regard for changing historical conditions. The de-contextualisation of these sayings did not affect, to the authors of our sources, the relevance of their timeless message. Consistently, therefore, the historical evolution from Biblical non-Jews to those of present times was considered irrelevant or at least of marginal importance. The point I would make, however, is that together with ethnographic blurring, the timelessness of Israel and the nations is a further simplification which has the effect of increasing their homogenous, monolithic, polarity.

Polarity, however, does not mean radical dichotomy. Although the *Palestinian Talmud* excludes Esau from among the heirs of Isaac,[126] *Gen.R.* concedes that "although he is Esau, he is still his (Jacob's) brother".[127] According to the *Babylonian Talmud*, this brotherhood can be occasionally invoked: a delegation of rabbis once appealed to a *matronita* (Roman lady of importance) that she should bring about the cancellation of

---

21,1; *B.Git.* 57b; *Lam.R., pet.* 2; *Pes.dRK* 15,5. See Hadas-Lebel, 1984, pp. 379–83.

[124] See p. xxxviii, quoting Neusner.

[125] For instance, their religious cults are not distinguished: cf Porton (*op.cit.* pp. 4–5 & 285–8). Thus the *Mishna* refers to alien deities of the Biblical period such as *Molekh, Ashera* and *Peor* alongside contemporary pagan gods such as *Markulis*, without any distinction (*M.Sanh.* 7,6); *B.Sanh.* 64a speaks of the cult of *Peor* in contemporary incidents.

[126] Just as Ishmael is excluded from among the heirs of Abraham: *Y.Ned.* 3,8.

[127] *Gen.R.* 75,4. The term "brother" in the Scriptures can be interpreted as a reference to Esau: *Gen.R.* 34,13.

some evil decree, with the following argument: "Why do you treat us differently and issue these decrees against us? Are we not brothers, the children of the same father and of the same mother?".[128] In some cases the descendants of Esau use the same argument to their own advantage. In the days of the Messiah, Rome will invoke its brotherhood with Israel in a desperate attempt to save itself from the Almighty's judgement.[129] According to a late *Midrash*, Haman thought that Esther would not harm him if she turned out to be Jewish, because he was descended from Esau and therefore they were related.[130]

Although this brotherhood is ultimately to no avail, it conveys the notion that in spite of the opposition between Rome and Israel, there is nonetheless some affinity between them. According to a late *Midrash*, Esau and Jacob had identical looks, which suggests in fact that they were identical twins.[131] In earlier sources Esau is called an "Israel *mumar*", an apostate Jew.[132] Rome and Israel are both hated by all the nations.[133] As rival brothers, constantly struggling against one another,[134] their histories are bound up with each other and fully interdependent.[135] Self and other are diametrically opposed, but united in so far as they need each other, interdependently. Their relationship is conflictive and contradictory, but pregnant with almost intimate immediacy.

---

[128] *B.RH* 19a; *B.Taan.* 18a.
[129] *B.Pes.* 118b; cf *Ex.R.* 35,5.
[130] *Est.R.* 7,4.
[131] *Midrash Tehillim* 18,38.
[132] *B.Kid.* 18a.
[133] *Gen.R.* 63,7.
[134] Caesarea, symbolising Rome (either because of its name, which refers to Caesar, or because Caesarea was the capital of the Roman governor of Palestine since the early 1st century CE) is in perpetual rivalry with Jerusalem: when the one is full, the other is waste (*B.Pes.* 42b; *B.Meg.* 6a; on the implicit identification, in *B.Meg.*, of Tyre in *Ezek.* 26:2 as Rome, see *Gen.R.* 61, end). Solomon in his heyday matched Hadrian in his (*Gen.R.* 63,7).
[135] On the day Solomon was married to Pharaoh('s daughter), Michael came down and laid the foundations of Rome; on the day Jeroboam erected two golden calves, Remus and Romulus came and built two huts on the site of Rome; on the day Elijah departed, a king was enthroned in Rome (*Y.AZ* 1,2, and parallel in *B. Sanh.* 21b). Thus the history of Rome and of Israel develop in parallel and inter-dependently: see G. Vermes, *Post-Biblical Jewish Studies*, Leiden: Brill, 1975, p. 223.

3. THE WICKED AND THE RIGHTEOUS

A. *The non-Jews as wicked*

The non-Jews are assumed in our sources to be 'wicked'; indeed, as we have seen, they are sometimes called by this name. Non-Jewish wickedness is referred to with much passion in rabbinic writings, but not for that matter at random: it may be seen as the structural *reverse* of the righteousness of Israel, and in this sense, a highly 'logical' system of assumptions. As we shall see, the wickedness of the non-Jews is taken for granted in our sources rather than actually reported and observed: in this respect, it is a purely 'cultural', 'theoretical' construct. Nevertheless, the rabbinic image of the non-Jew takes on a reality of its own which forms the background to a number of Halakhic rulings. When put in practice, these rulings could, in turn, determine the rabbis' relationship and attitude towards the non-Jews in their lived reality.

The non-Jews are considered Halakhically 'suspect' (*hashudim*) of a number of major offenses such as murder, adultery, and *avoda zara*.[136] This means that they are assumed to be liable, at any moment and for no particular reason, to indulge in any of these practices.[137] Although rabbinic sources seldom give reasons for holding this suspicion, it forms the basis of a number of Halakhic rulings. These rulings, mainly found in tractate *Avoda Zara*,[138] constitute a most informative source on the rabbinic perception of the wickedness of the non-Jews. In this respect the non-Jews stand in contrast, implicit more often than explicit, with Israel who are, by assumption and by name, righteous and above suspicion.

Murder

Already in the *Mishna* the non-Jews are featured as a source of public danger, especially as soldiers, raiders or bandits.[139] The suspicion that a non-Jew is liable to murder at any instant gives rise to the following

---

[136] As subject to the Noahide commandments, the non-Jews are forbidden from committing such offenses. Thus, it may be said that the non-Jews are 'wicked' in that they fail to abide by universal standards of righteousness and morality—not just that they do not comply to Jewish laws. For a full discussion of the Noahide laws and their implications, see section V.1.B.

[137] See Y. Cohen, "The attitude to the Gentile in the Halakhah and in reality in the Tannaitic period", in *Immanuel* 9, 1979, pp. 33–4.

[138] In the *Mishna*, and hence in all subsequent rabbinic works.

[139] *M.Shab.* 2,5; *M.Eruv.* 3,5; *M.Taan.* 3,7; cf *Y.Terumot* 8,12.

rulings: a Jewish infant may not be circumcised by a non-Jew,[140] nor may he be left in the care of a non-Jewish nurse; a Jew may not consult a non-Jewish physician, nor may he have his hair cut by a non-Jew.[141] Non-Jewish midwives may not be used; a Jew may not have a private meeting (*yihud*) with a non-Jew, for instance in a bath-house; if they are travelling together, he may not tell the non-Jew his destination; he must walk with the non-Jew on his right—well away from his sword—and not on his left; if they are walking up or down a hill, he must make sure he is above the other.[142] Not only is it forbidden to sell all forms of weapons and potential instruments of incarceration and torture to a non-Jew,[143] but it is also forbidden to sell him a garment with fringes (*tzitzit*), lest another Jew sees him wearing it, mistakes him for a Jew, and travels together with him without taking the necessary precautions not to be murdered.[144]

We are not told to what extent these fears and assumptions are based on lived experience—there are few accounts, in our sources, of such impulsive murders ever having taken place.[145] We do hear that Jews do not normally live on their own in a non-Jewish courtyard, because of their fear of being murdered.[146] Clearly, these assumptions were sufficiently 'real' in the rabbis' minds to condition and curtail their relationships with the non-Jews. Whilst the social significance of these rulings will be discussed at a later stage,[147] it is their underlying assumption which I would like, at present, to emphasize.

Sexual offenses

The *Tosefta* assumes that women taken as captives by non-Jewish armies must have been raped, because "the majority of non-Jews are suspect of sexual offenses".[148] It is for this very purpose that they take them

---

[140] *T.AZ* 3,12.
[141] *M.AZ* 2,1–2.
[142] *T.AZ* 3,3–5, and *Y.AZ* and *B.AZ* *ad loc.*
[143] *T.AZ* 2,4.
[144] *B.Men.* 43a; see Rashi *ad. loc.*
[145] *Y.AZ* 2,2 tells us of a non-Jewish barber who used to kill scores of Jews. Another exceptional story, attributed to R. Yaakov, shows that non-Jewish murderous instincts are not solely directed against the Jews, but also against their own kith and kin: "I once saw a non-Jew tying up his father and giving him to his dog to eat" (*Sifre Deut.* 81).
[146] *B.Eruv.* 62a.
[147] Section IV.1.
[148] *Hashudim be-Arayot*: *T.Ket.* 1, end. According to *B.Ket.* 13b, "the majority of non-Jews are wanton with sexual offenses".

into captivity.[149] The *Babylonian Talmud* assumes that when a non-Jewish army passes through a city, it may have no time for making libations, but it does have time for rape.[150] A jailer revealed that he had to protect female Jewish prisoners from being attacked by (specifically) non-Jewish inmates.[151] Such assumptions—if indeed they are no more than mere assumptions—are shared not only by rabbis, at least according to the following account in the *Babylonian Talmud*: a woman appeared to have accidentally committed adultery with a man whom she mistook to be her husband; she assumed that one of the non-Jewish perfume merchants (and in another similar incident, naphtha merchants), who were then in town, must have been responsible.[152]

Non-Jews are particulary promiscuous among themselves. During the night following Orpah's departure from Ruth and Naomi and her return to Moab, she had intercourse with one hundred non-Jewish prepuces;[153] this extraordinary orgy symbolises, I think, her departure from Judaism and return to non-Jewish ways. Non-Jewish, unmarried women are assumed to have lost their virginity;[154] though we are also told that in their early years they protect their virginity by fornicating through other orifices.[155] A non-Jew is likely to have a woman even if he is officially unmarried.[156] A married non-Jew will ornate his wife and then willingly pass her on to another man.[157] He will commit adultery even in his wife's presence; therefore, a Jewish woman is forbidden to have private meetings with a non-Jew even if his wife is present.[158] Such promiscuity leads to the breakdown of marriage and of kinship structures. Thus, a non-Jew cannot certify the identity of his father, nor that he is his first-born son.[159] According to one

---

[149] *M.Terumot* 8,12.

[150] *B.Ket.* 27a. Sex is indeed more enticing than libations: *B.AZ* 69b (but according to *M.Ket.* 2,9, financial gain would take priority over their sexual desire).

[151] *B.Taan.* 22a. In this respect, non-Jewish women are no better than men: Potiphar's wife, who attempted to seduce Joseph, is considered 'modest' in comparison with other non-Jewish women: *Tanh. Vayyeshev* 6.

[152] *B.Ned.* 91a-b.

[153] *Ruth R.* 2,20. The reference to the non-Jews as 'prepuces' is obviously significant.

[154] *Y.Nida* 1,4.

[155] *Gen.R.* 60,5.

[156] *M.Ohalot* 18,7.

[157] *Sifra Kedoshim* 11,18. However according to one opinion in *B.Sanh.* 82a, non-Jews do not normally prostitute their wives.

[158] *B.AZ* 25b.

[159] *Mekh. Bo* 13; *Song R.* 6,8. Cf *B.Yev.* 98a, *B.Sanh.* 58a, and *Gen.R.* 18,5, according to which non-Jewish paternal siblings would not form an incestuous relationship. See further pp. 37–8.

opinion, in fact, non-Jewish marriage cannot be regarded as valid.[160]

It is assumed that non-Jews have homosexual relations.[161] Far more important, however, is the charge that they engage in bestiality. A non-Jew is suspect of intercourse with another person's animal, though not with his own, as he fears he may make her barren.[162] Furthermore, non-Jews are more attracted to Jewish-owned animals than to their own wives—though they would not admit this in public.[163] If they go to their friends' wives and do not find them, and happen to find instead their animals, they have intercourse with the latter too; some suggest that this happens even if the women are around.[164]

A dog is said to have participated in Orpah's orgy.[165] A non-Jew is reported to have bought a goose from the market and to have had intercourse with it.[166]

The *Babylonian Talmud* suggests that sexual aberrations are particularly common among the Arabs. They inherited nine out of ten measures of prostitution in the world:[167] Rabbi Yirmiyah of Difti saw an Arab buying a thigh bone from the (meat) market; he cut a hole into it, adequate for copulation; he copulated with it, then fried it and ate it.[168]

Again, the dividing line between mere assumption and observed reality is difficult to assess; still, we find that these perceptions give rise to a number of practical Halakhic rulings. Jewish women taken as captives are assumed to have been defiled, as indeed we have seen that they are captured for this very purpose.[169] A Jewess may not

---

[160] *B.Sanh.* 82a, in disagreement with the opinion quoted from the same passage in note 157. This opinion holds, consequently, that a Jew who has intercourse with a non-Jewess will never be guilty of adultery, since non-Jews have no *ishut* (marriage). On the other hand, all agree that they do have a valid marriage in so far as they are prohibited from committing adultery among themselves: see *B.Sanh.* 57b; *Y.Kid.* 1,1; *Gen.R.* 18,8; cf Z.W. Falk, "On the historical background of the Talmudic laws regarding Gentiles", in *Immanuel* 14, 1982, pp. 106–109.

[161] However they are decent enough not to give marriage documents to their homosexual partners: *B.Hul.* 92a-b.

[162] *Y.AZ* 2,1.

[163] *B.Git.* 38a.

[164] *B.Git.* 38a; *B.AZ* 22b.

[165] *Ruth R.ib.*

[166] He then killed it, roasted it, and ate it: *B.AZ* 22b. Cf however *B.Ber.* 57a.

[167] *B.Kid.* 49b; cf *Avot dRN* 28,1. This image of the Arabs can be compared to the late 4th-century ethnographic comments of Ammianus Marcellinus (14,4), who describes the Saracens as living without home or laws, and as keeping 'mercenary wives', hence only a 'semblance of marriage' (*species matrimonii*); Ammianus also notes the *ardor* of their sexual relations.

[168] *B.AZ* 22b.

[169] *T.Ket.* 1,9; *B.Ket.* 13b; cf *M.Ket.* 2,9.

have a private meeting (*yiḥud*) with non-Jews, "as they are suspected of forbidden relations"; an animal may not be left in a non-Jewish stable, "as they are suspected of bestiality".[170] Similarly, a red heifer cannot be bought (for purification) from a non-Jew, because it must be virgin and its owner is suspected of bestiality.[171]

With reference to bestiality, the nations and Israel are set in explicit contrast. The *Tosefta* emphasizes that "Israel are not suspected of homosexuality or bestiality".[172] The *Babylonian Talmud* implies that the non-Jewish urge for bestiality proceeds from the original sin, when the snake is said to have had intercourse with Eve, thus defiling her and all her descendants; whereas Israel were cleaned from this pollution at Mount Sinai, the non-Jews remain polluted, which is why, the *Talmud* intimates, bestiality remains intrinsic to their nature.[173] Bestiality is also related to their affinity with animals, which we shall discuss below.[174]

The nations and Israel are also contrasted, less explicitly perhaps, with reference to other forms of sexual offenses. Promiscuity is emphatically not the "Jewish way",[175] and indeed, Jewish fatherhood is always considered valid. Israel appear not to be suspected of incest, which is why a Jew may have a private meeting with his mother; private meetings with other women are, in some conditions, forbidden, but in the presence of his wife a Jew does not commit transgressions[176]— whereas, as we have seen, non-Jews commit adultery even in their wives' presence.[177]

---

[170] *M.AZ* 2,1; see *T.Kid.* 5,9.

[171] Another reason is that the non-Jews are suspected of luring the Jews into the transgression of their commandments (e.g. by making their sacrifices invalid)—*Pes.R.* 14,1.

[172] *T.Kid.* 5,9–10; *B.Kid.* 82a; nonetheless, according to *Y.Sanh.* 6,3 two men were once caught for bestiality, and two others for homosexuality (these 'men' were probably Jews, though the matter is left unclear).

[173] *B.AZ* 22b.

[174] Section I.4.A.

[175] *Eccl.R.* 1,8,4.

[176] *M.Kid.* 4,12. Israel are not suspected of having intercourse with their wives during menstruation: *Y.Yoma* 1,1. However they may be suspected of having intercourse with their wives whilst they are *sotot* (i.e., they have incurred a suspicion of adultery): *Sifre Naso* 8; this is the only passage where the term *neḥshedu* (suspected) is applied in this way to Israel.

[177] The rabbinic image of the non-Jewish other as adulterous may be compared with the perception, in Classical Greek tragedy, of the barbarian other as incestuous (and in some passages, murderous): cf E. Hall, *op. cit.* pp. 188–9.

Avoda zara

Throughout early rabbinic literature, the non-Jews are treated, by name as well as by assumption, as worshippers of *avoda zara*.[178] This assumption has far-reaching Halakhic implications, which will be discussed at length in the fourth chapter of this work. To cite a few examples, we are told that a Jewish midwife may not assist a non-Jewish woman in labour, as she is giving birth to a potential *avoda zara* worshipper.[179] It is forbidden to sell animals to a non-Jew which might be used for sacrificial purposes,[180] or to lease a house to him, where he might bring an object of *avoda zara*.[181] Candles and spices from a non-Jewish banquet may not be used (for *havdala*), as non-Jewish banquets are presumably dedicated to *avoda zara*.[182] A non-Jew may not be trusted to write a *Torah* scroll, as his intention is presumably directed towards *avoda zara*.[183]

Most distinctly, the prohibition of non-Jewish wine rests on the conviction that the non-Jews may have used it for a libation to *avoda zara*. Since non-Jews are compulsive 'libationers', if they touch Jewish wine even for a fleeting instant they are assumed to have made it a libation to *avoda zara* (and it is therefore forbidden). Halakhic sources are extremely cautious about this prohibition; its intricacies, which I shall not go into, are discussed in large sections of tractate *Avoda Zara*.[184]

The possibility that some non-Jews may be Christian rather than pagan is seldom considered in our sources, even though the latter were redacted on the whole *after* the Christianisation of the Roman Empire.[185] This curious fact deserves some explanation. It may be attributed to the rabbinic, conservative dependence on earlier rabbinic teachings, which would have predated the Christianisation of the

---

[178] E.g. *Y.Ber.* 8,6; *Ruth R. pet.* 3.

[179] *M.AZ* 2,1.

[180] *Ib.* 1,5.

[181] *Ib.* 1,9; *T.AZ* 2,9.

[182] *B.Ber.* 52b.

[183] *B.Git.* 45b.

[184] *M.AZ* 4,8–12; 5,3–6.

[185] On the proper meaning of the term *minim*, who are commonly identified as 'Christians', see section III.3.B. Modern scholars (e.g. Neusner 1989) have argued that much of early rabbinic literature (particularly in Palestinian sources) consists of a deliberate, albeit covert, polemic response to Christian theology and exegesis, in the wake of the Christianisation of the Late Roman Empire. Nonetheless, *explicit* references to Christianity are extremely rare in our sources (see Porton, *op.cit.* p. 3), and this curious fact has not been properly explained.

Levant. Alternatively, this apparent oversight may be attributed to the general, rabbinic indifference to the historical realities of the Late Roman non-Jewish world.[186] Finally, there is some evidence that the *Babylonian Talmud* considered the Christians to be worshippers of *avoda zara* and hence, effectively, undistinguishable from them.[187]

By contrast with the nations, the suspicion of *avoda zara* does not apply to the Jews. Although in Biblical times the Israelites were prone to worship *avoda zara*, in the days of Ezra *avoda zara* was eradicated from among the Jewish people.[188] The *Babylonian Talmud* may consider elsewhere the possibility of individual Jews worshipping *avoda zara*,[189] thus becoming apostates or heretics,[190] but the Jews as a whole are no longer suspected of this transgression. With reference to Mordekhai "the Jew", the Talmud states that "whoever denies *avoda zara* is called a Jew".[191] This implies that denial of *avoda zara* is *constitutive* of Jewish identity.

This notion, again, has substantial Halakhic ramifications. For in-

---

[186] See section I.2.C. It is quite possible, however, that in the Talmudic period the majority of the non-Jews in Babylonia and even in the Levant were still 'pagan', and not (yet, if ever) Christianised: see A.H.M. Jones, *The Later Roman Empire*, vol.II, Oxford: Blackwell, 1964, pp. 938–43. This may apply especially to the rural areas of Southern Syria, including perhaps those of Galilee: see J.H.G.W. Liebeschuetz, "Epigraphic evidence on the Christianisation of Syria", in J. Fitz (ed.), *Limes: Akten des 11 Internationalen Limeskongresses, Szekesfehervar*, Budapest 1978, pp. 485–505.; and *id.*, "Problems arising from the Conversion of Syria", in D. Baker (ed.), *The Church in Town and Countryside*, 1979.

[187] According to a heavily censored passage in *B.AZ* 6a and 7b, the various prohibitions on trade with non-Jews on and before their festive days would also apply to Christians (*notzrim*) from Thursdays to Sundays, and according to R. Yishmael, throughout the whole week (see *Dik. Sof.*). This ruling, which clearly treats the Christian Sunday as a festive day of *avoda zara*, is attributed to Babylonian Amoraim, namely R. Taḥlifa b. Avdimi quoting Shemuel. This leads Jacob Katz, *op.cit.* p.123, to the suggestion that this ruling could not have been accepted in Palestine, where it would have been impossible, in a Christian land, to enforce it. I do not think, however, that it would have been *impossible* for Palestinian rabbis to refrain from some commercial transactions with Christians from Thursdays to Sundays (Katz appears to have overlooked that the prohibitions on trade with Christians throughout the whole week is only according to R. Yishmael (as against the "sages" and the first *mishna* of *AZ*), a minority view which anyway would not have been accepted in practice). For an alternative to the identification of *notzrim* (in this passage) as Christians, see Lawrence Zalcman, "Christians, Nosrim, and Nebuchadnezzar's daughter", in *JQR* 81 (3–4), 1991, pp. 411–26.

[188] As vividly depicted in *B.Yoma* 69b; *B.Sanh.* 64a. See also *B.Arakh.* 32b. According to *Song R.* 7,8, *avoda zara* was eradicated in the days of Nevuchadnezzar, or according to others, of Esther. Cf *Judith* 8:18–20. See my article, "The Death of Idolatry?", in *Le'ela*, April 1993, pp. 26–8, and further in pp. 156–7.

[189] E.g. *B.Sanh.* 64a.

[190] See section III.3.

[191] A pun on the word "Jew", *Yehudi*, which is associated with the verbal form *hoda*, to confess: *B.Meg.* 13a.

stance, although an animal slaughtered by a non-Jew is not deemed to have been dedicated to *avoda zara*,[192] it is deemed so if it was slaughtered *in front* of an object of *avoda zara*; by contrast, an animal slaughtered by another Jew, *even in front of an avoda zara*, is not suspected to have been dedicated to it—the Talmud assumes, indeed, that the Jew could only have intended to annoy the animal's owner.[193]

Theft, lies and corruption
According to the *Babylonian Talmud*, land owned by a non-Jew can be presumed to have been stolen.[194] Once Jewish money falls into non-Jewish hands, there is no prospect of recovering it.[195] If a non-Jew robs an ass claiming that it is his, there is no point in taking action against him in a non-Jewish court, for non-Jews are robbers and liars, and even if the verdict is favorable this non-Jew would not comply.[196] Indeed, non-Jewish law-courts are corrupt and deceitful.[197]

Israel are not suspected of forgery[198] or of bearing false witness;[199] by contrast, a non-Jew does not keep his word;[200] he is not to be trusted or believed;[201] his words are of no Halakhic consequence whatsoever.[202] It is even debated whether one can trust a convert's

---

[192] An animal slaughtered, albeit properly, by a non-Jew, is unfit for consumption; nonetheless, it may be used for other purposes (for instance, sale to non-Jews)—which would not be possible if the non-Jew's intention had been to slaughter the animal for *avoda zara*: *T.Hul.* 1,1 and 2,15 (the same can be inferred from *M.Hul.* 1,1). Similarly a Jew may slaughter an animal for the benefit of a non-Jew, and need not assume that his intention is *avoda zara*: *M.Hul.* 2,7 (this point is disputed in the *Mishna* by R. El'azar, whose view appears to have prevailed in the *Tosefta* (*T.Hul.* 2,15), but is decisively discarded by the *Babylonian Talmud* (*B.Hul.* 13a, on the basis of *M.Hul.* 1,1)).

[193] *B.Hul.* 41a. In this ruling, however, and for obvious reasons, an apostate Jew would be treated in the same way as a non-Jew; see section III.3.A.

[194] *B.Suk.* 30a. Some Arabs once came to Pumbadita and sequestered private land: *B.BB* 168b. The Arabs are particularly noted for being thieves: *Mekh. Bahodesh* 5; *Sifre Deut.* 343; *B.BB* 36a; *Num.R.* 14,10. Bar Adi, an Arab, robbed some wine skins from R.Yitzhak: *B.AZ* 33a.

[195] *B.BK* 117a.

[196] *B.BB* 45a.

[197] *B.Git.* 28b (only when it suits them).

[198] Although some individuals may indulge in it—*B.Ket.* 36b. In *B.AZ* 70a Rava maintains that the majority of thieves (in certain areas, presumably) are Jewish, but in *B.Betza* 15a his contemporary Abaye disagrees. However, the correct reading of these passages (according to *Dik.Sof.*) is *shayarey*, i.e. 'rovers', rather than 'thieves'.

[199] *M.Sanh.* 3,5.

[200] *B.Bekh.* 13b.

[201] *T.Peah* 4,1 (non-Jewish paupers); *B.Hul.* 133b.

[202] *T.Demai* 5,2 (non-Jewish green-grocer). However, if he speaks without ulterior motive (*lefi tummo*) the non-Jew may be believed: *B.Git.* 28b; *B.Yev.* 121b.

testimony on an event which he witnessed while he was still non-Jewish.[203] As to Justina daughter of emperor Severus, who told Rabbi that she gave birth at the age of seven, the *Talmud* laconically quotes this verse: "Their mouth speaks in vain, and their right hand is one of falsehood".[204]

Righteous non-Jews

In the *Tosefta*, R. Yehoshua is attributed the view that some exceptional non-Jews are righteous (*tzadikim*) and have a share in the world to come (whilst R. Eliezer maintains that no non-Jews have any share in it).[205] Elsewhere we hear that the very existence of the nations depends on the 30 righteous non-Jews who dwell among them.[206] *Genesis Rabba* mentions Job as a righteous non-Jew.[207] A later source lists also Jethro, Rahav, Ruth and emperor Antoninus; significantly, however, they are said to have eventually converted.[208] Similarly, we hear in the *Palestinian Talmud* that the Almighty seeks for "righteous non-Jews" to *convert* and adhere to Israel.[209] It seems that to be non-Jewish and righteous is so inherently contradictory that the only viable option, for these exceptional individuals, is to convert. Which confirms the adage: exceptions prove the rule.

B. *Israel as 'the righteous'*

Israel are righteous

The righteousness of Israel stands in direct contrast with the wickedness of the nations. Israel are 'righteous' by name as well as by nature.[210] Thus the *Mishna* rules:

> All Israel have a share in the world-to-come, as it is said: 'Your people are all righteous . . .' (*Isaiah* 60:21).[211]

---

[203] *B.Ket.* 28b.

[204] *B.Nida* 45a, quoting *Psalms* 144:8&11, which refers to non-Jews. The same verse is quoted in *B.BB ib.*

[205] *T.Sanh.* 13,2; *B.Sanh.* 105a (see *Dik.Sof.*).

[206] *B.Hul.* 92a.

[207] Though others hold that Job was a Jew: *Gen.R.* 57,4; *Deut.R.* 1,4.

[208] *Eccl.R.* 5,11,1. On Antoninus' conversion, see further section I.5.C. Cf *B.AZ* 10b: although a Roman, Antoninus did not act in the way of Esau. In *B.Taan.* 29a, a Roman officer is promised a share in the world-to-come.

[209] *Y.Ber.* 2,8.

[210] See *Num.R.* 4,1; *Tanh. Bamidbar* 19.

[211] *M.Sanh.* 10,1. The *mishna* (*ib.* 10,1–4) goes on to list some Jews (and non-Jews, e.g. Balaam) who are excluded from the world-to-come, such as those who reject

The nature of this righteousness, however, is taken for granted more often than it is described.

Israel are praised in particular for their kindness (*ḥesed*),[212] their wisdom,[213] and their faith.[214] They have three virtues by which they can be identified as true descendants of Abraham[215] and of those who stood at Mount Sinai:[216] mercy,[217] modesty,[218] and acts of kindness;[219] the Gibeonite converts were not entitled to adhere to Israel (i.e. to marry with the Jewish-born) because they could not display them.[220] Israel are distinguished.[221] They are bold in facing martyrdom.[222] They are called 'peace' (*shalom*).[223]

Israel are holy

Israel are *kedoshim*,[224] 'holy'.[225] Their holiness is God-given[226] and ever-lasting.[227] In this respect they are distinct from the nations, as is suggested by the juxtapositions of the following phrases, recited weekly in the *havdala*:

> (God) distinguishes between holiness (*kodesh*) and the profane . . . between Israel and the nations.[228]

---

the *Torah*, the *apikoros*, and some infamous Biblical characters. The extent to which these marginal, apostate figures are still considered to be part of "Israel" will be discussed in chapter III. Hence, this list of exclusions does not contradict or mitigate the general statement of *M.Sanh.* 10,1.

[212] *Y.Sot.* 1,10; see *Tanh. Kedoshim* 5.

[213] *B.Eruv.* 53b; *Derekh Eretz R.* 6; *Lam.R.* 1,19; also *Eccl.R.* 8,1,3; *Tanh. Tetzave* 11; *Tanh. Kedoshim* 5.

[214] *B.Shab.* 97a.

[215] *Kalla R.* 10.

[216] *Y.Kid.* 4,1; *Midrash Tehillim* 1,2.

[217] See also *B.Betza* 32b.

[218] Literally, 'shamefulness'. My translation is based on *Kalla R.ib.*; on the correlation between shame and modesty, see also below, section V.2.A.

[219] *Deut.R.* 3,4; *Kalla R. ib.*

[220] *Y.Kid. ib.*; *Y.Sanh.* 6,7; *B.Yev.* 79a; *Num.R.* 8,4; *Midrash Tehillim* 1,2; *ib.* 17, end. Cf *Midrash Shemuel* 28. On the status of the Gibeonites, see pp. 92–3, n. 45.

[221] *Sifra Milluim* 15.

[222] *Ex.R.* 42,9.

[223] *Derekh Eretz Z., perek shalom.*

[224] *Y.Shab.* 6,9; *Y.AZ* 5,15; *B.Hul.* 7b; *Tanh. Kedoshim* 5; *Midrash Mishlei* 9.

[225] This translation can only be approximate. The most succinct definition of the root *KDSh* in Biblical and rabbinic Hebrew, which connotes as we shall see the notions of 'separation' and 'dedication', can be found in Y. Grynbaum, *Otzar haMalbim: Sefer haKarmel*, Jerusalem: Hamesorah, 1982, vol. II p. 297 (Hebrew).

[226] *T.Ber.* 3,15 (L: 3,13): "(God) sanctifies . . . Israel" (liturgy).

[227] *Lev.R.* 24,2.

[228] *B.Pes.* 103b.

The term 'holy' (*kedoshim*) implies a notion of *separateness*, as in the following passage:

> Israel are holy and separate from the nations and their abominations.[229]

It also implies abstinence and stringent practices. Because they are holy, Israel do not eat the ramification of the sciatic nerve (which is in fact permitted).[230] Because they are holy, they do not have intercourse in daytime.[231] Israel's holiness is related in general to the observance of the commandments[232]—an essential feature of Jewish identity to which we will return.[233] The name "Israel" is interpreted in one later source as meaning:

> *Yisrael*—the man who saw God (*ish-ra'a-El*)—for all his actions are directed to Him.[234]

Israel and the Almighty

Kedoshim also implies *designation*, as in the following passage: "the Almighty has 'designated' (*kiddesh*) Israel in his Name".[235]

This designation may be related to the Biblical notion that Israel are God's people, a nation of priests,[236] and that they all have divine inspiration, being 'sons of prophets'.[237] Many sources suggest, indeed, that prophecy is exclusive to Israel.[238]

Kiddushin is also the standard term for *betrothal*;[239] hence, the holiness

---

[229] *Mekh. Bahodesh* 2. Cf *Ex.R.* 31,9: Israel are forbidden to eat prohibited meat, because they are holy.

[230] *Gen.R.* 78,6.

[231] *B.Ket.* 65b; *B.Nida* 17a.

[232] At least according to *Num.R.* 17,6; *Tanh. Shelah* 15, end.

[233] In section II.3.

[234] *Eliyahu R.* 25 (27), pp. 138–9. J. Heinemann (*op.cit.*, pp.119 and 122–4) takes this passage as a specific reference to prophecy; his evidence is however scant.

[235] *Tanh. Kedoshim* 2.

[236] *Ex.* 19:6; cf *Sifre Num.* 119.

[237] *T.Pes.* 4,2 (L: 4,14); *Y.Shab.* 19,1.

[238] See J. Heinemann, *op.cit.*, pp. 119–21 and 230, n. 8, quoting *Lev.R.* 1,12, and *Seder Olam R.* 21, end. According to *Lev.R.* 1,13, *Y.Sot.* 5, and *Eccl.R.* 3,18 the nations do have prophecy, but of a lower quality than Israel's. *Eliyahu R.* 10 (beginning) presents Jew and non-Jew as equals in prophecy, but see my remarks in p. 2, note 4. On the ambiguous status of the non-Jewish prophet Balaam, and the possible use of this theme in anti-Christian polemics, see Heinemann (quoting *Sifre Deut.* 357, *Sifre Z.* 7,89, *Targum Yerushalmi ad Num.* 24:3, *Num.R.* 4,20, *Eliyahu R.* 26 (pp. 141–2), *Eliyahu Z.* 10) and E.E. Urbach, "Homilies of the Rabbis on the Prophets of the Nations and the Balaam Stories", in *Tarbiz* 25, 1955–6, pp. 272–89.

[239] In the Mishnaic tractate *Kiddushin* (on betrothal).

of Israel may come to represent not merely designation but actual betrothal to the Almighty.[240]

The holiness of Israel, both as separateness and as designation, points undoubtedly towards a special relationship with the Almighty. Israel were chosen by God because of their holiness,[241] which allows them to sanctify the Almighty in turn.[242] The special relationship between Israel and the Almighty, characterised by the intrinsic righteousness of Israel, is perhaps the most distinctive feature of Jewish identity in early rabbinic writings; we shall return to it at the end of this study.

4. ANIMALS AND ANGELS

Israel and the nations are distinguished not only in their moral behaviour, as presented in the previous section, but also in their essential nature. This transpires in the notion that the non-Jews are somewhat akin to animals, and in this respect sub-human, whereas Israel on the contrary accede to the supernal level of the angels.

A. *The non-Jews as animals*

Jews and non-Jews: animal imagery and 'superficial' affinity
The notion that the non-Jews may be akin to animals must be treated with much caution, as many passages would appear to suggest the same with reference to Israel. The *Babylonian Talmud* points out that in three respects, the *whole* of mankind are similar to animals: they eat and drink, they procreate and multiply, and they defecate.[243] The same is found in *Genesis Rabba*, with in addition that they die.[244] More specifically, our sources remark that Israel are frequently compared in *Midrashim* to the lion and to other wild animals,[245] for their might, speed, endurance, etc. Indeed, although animals are generally considered to be inferior creatures to men,[246] many of their features, such as ingenuity and simplicity, are considered worthy of praise, which

---

[240] He 'betrothed' (*kiddesh*) Israel at Mount Sinai—*Tanh. Ekev* 11; *Pes. dRK* 12,11.
[241] *Sifre Deut.* 97.
[242] *Ex.R.* 15,24.
[243] *B.Hag.* 16a; *Avot dRN* 37,2.
[244] *Gen.R.* 8,11.
[245] *B.Sot.* 11b; *Ex.R.* 1,16; etc. A list of the main animals symbolising Israel is provided, for reference, in the appendix.
[246] See E.J. Schochet, *Animal life in Jewish tradition*, New York: Ktav, 1984, p. 90 and ch. 7.

is why the *Talmud* concludes that the mention of 'animal' in the Bible is not always to be taken as derogatory.[247]

I would stress, however, that this type of animal imagery, quite common already in the Bible, is strictly *superficial* in scope as well as in significance. The analogy drawn in these passages between the Jews and the animal world is restricted, indeed, to *specific*, individual traits: might, ingenuity, etc. There is no suggestion of some general, all-inclusive affinity between the Jews and animals, which might have implied that Israel also shared the essentially inferior characteristics of the animal world.

Much the same applies in many cases to the non-Jews, which prevents us, at this stage, from inferring that our sources consider them to be generally and somehow intrinsically identical to animals. For instance, the *Midrash* states that each of the four Kingdoms (Babylon, Persia, Greece, Rome) correspond to one of the four forbidden or 'impure' animals.[248] Yet this comparison is no more than superficial: the 'impure' animals do not symbolise the vileness of the Kingdoms in so far as they are animals, but rather, in so far as they are Halakhically 'impure'.

The same *Midrash* explains, moreover, that Rome corresponds to the pig because in the same way as the pig stretches forward its hoofs when it is resting, as if to pretend that it is permitted,[249] so Rome steals and robs under the pretence of exercising justice.[250] But in describing the pig as pleading for Halakhic permissibility, the *Midrash* has the effect, if anything, of 'humanizing' the pig—not of 'animalizing' the Romans. This comparison of Rome with the pig is only superficial; its significance should not be streched further to some notion of general affinity or identity with pigs.[251]

---

[247] *B.Hul.* 5b; *Pes.dRK* 9,1. Thus, in *Eccl.R.* 3,18 Israel are compared to animals for their obedience to the Almighty and their willingness to be slaughtered in martyrdom.

[248] Listed in *Lev.* 11:4–7: the camel, the rabbit, the hare, and the pig—*Lev.R.* 13, repeated a few times (*passim*).

[249] Permitted to eat, on the grounds that its hoofs are cloven. The pig is in fact forbidden as it does not chew the cud.

[250] *Gen.R.* 65,1; *Lev.R.* 13,5. "Exercising justice" is a conjectured translation of *matza'at bima*. It would seem that the exercise of justice corresponds to the cloven hoofs, whilst greedy extortion corresponds to the pig's failure to chew the cud.

[251] The suggestion that Rome may be more intrinsically assimilated with the pig will be raised in p. 57.

General affinity: the non-Jews as animals
Some passages suggest a more general affinity between non-Jews and animals. We are told, for instance, that a non-Jewish courtyard is "like an animal stable",[252] or that a non-Jewish corpse is "like animal carrion".[253] These comparisons are not restricted to any specific, superficial feature: they refer to the non-Jewish person *as a whole*, and suggest that the latter is generally akin, in his lowliness, to animals.

General, all-inclusive associations of this kind are common with reference to dogs. The non-Jews are considered similar to dogs;[254] they are even, according to the *Mekhilta*, of lesser account than dogs.[255] Ishmael, the ancestor of the Arabs,[256] is "equal to a dog", for both he and the dog eat carrion.[257] Eating together with an uncircumcised is like eating together with a dog: for a dog is also uncircumcised.[258] R. Akiva told Turnus Rufus that he appeared to him in a dream as a dog, and with good reason: for

> what is the difference between you and dogs?—you eat and drink, and so do they, you bear fruits and multiply, and so do they, you will eventually die, and so will they.[259]

It is quite clear that these statements aim at conveying that the non-Jews share the *general* features of the animal world, and particularly the lowliness of dogs.

---

[252] *T.Eruv.* 8,1 (L: 5,19). This is not a technical Halakhic term; hence the choice of this wording must be regarded as significant. The *Babylonian Talmud* (*B.Eruv.* 62a) enunciates the same ruling in Halakhically clearer terms: "a dwelling-place of non-Jews is not called a dwelling-place".

[253] *PdRE* 28 (ed. Higger). Again, this is not a technical, Halakhic term.

[254] *Midrash Tehillim* 4,8 and 4,11. Porton (*op.cit.* p.142, also p.116 n.12) points out that a number of passages in *T.Hul.* (e.g. 9,9), as well as *T.YT* 2,6, refer to feeding or giving something "to non-Jews or to dogs". This juxtaposition may well be significant. Similarly, we find in *M.Pes.* 2,1 a reference to feeding leaven to animals or selling it to non-Jews; and in *T.Hul.* 1,1, slaughtering by a non-Jew is equated with slaughtering by an ape.

[255] *Mekh. Kaspa* 2, according to ms.Oxford and as quoted by Rashi *ad Ex.*22:30. Ms.Munich reads "slave" instead of "non-Jew", but this is incongruous and clearly a censorial emendation.

[256] *Yishme'elim* in *Gen.* 37:25 is translated by Onkelos as *Arabai*. The term 'Ishmael' meaning 'an Arab (ruler)' is also found in *B.Ber.* 56b.

[257] *Gen.R.* 45,12.

[258] *PdRE* ch. 29 (28), in the text of first editions, quoted by Gerald Friedlander (trans.), *Pirke de Rabbi Eliezer*, New York: Sepher Hermon, 1981 (1916), p. 208, n. 5. On the 'uncircumcised' as synonymous with 'non-Jews', see p. 60, note 68.

[259] *Tanh. Teruma* 3. Hadrian is implicitly identified as a dog in *Eccl.R.* 9,4.

Metaphorical similarity and actual identity

In the sources we have so far examined, the equation of non-Jews with animals or dogs is ostensibly no more than figurative or metaphorical. This may be inferred, in fact, from the use in many of these passages of terms such as *dome* ('resembles') and *nimshal* ('compared to'), which suggest an abiding *distinction* between the non-Jews and their animal counterparts. Similarly, the frequent use of the prefix *ke-*, meaning 'like',[260] should be taken to mean *similarity* rather than equivalence or actual identity, as suggested explicitly in other sources.[261] In so far as metaphorical similarity is to be distinguished from actual identity, the analogy between Jews and animals is thus relatively *weak*.

In some passages, however, qualificatory terms such as "resembles" or "like" are notably omitted. For instance, Jacob's words: "an evil beast has eaten him (Joseph)" (*Gen.* 37:33) are interpreted as referring prophetically to Potiphar's wife—which implies that the latter was referred to directly, without qualification, as an evil beast.[262] In one passage in the *Babylonian Talmud* the Persians are only "likened" to a bear:

> they eat and drink like a bear, their flesh is swollen like a bear, they grow long hair like a bear, and they are restless like a bear.[263]

But in another context they are *directly* called "bears", without qualification:

> when R. Ami saw a Persian riding he would say: "there is a wandering bear!".[264]

In the case of Potiphar's wife, the omission of qualifications such as "resembles" or "like" may be explained away as poetical, 'prophetic'

---

[260] E.g. "like a stable", "like carrion": see above.

[261] *B.Taan.* 20a (*B.Sanh.* 104a): "*like* a widow" (*Lam.* 1:1)—"but not an actual widow" ("*ke-almana*"—*velo almana mamash*). See also *B.Kid.* 54a, where "like Jerusalem" (*ki-Yerushalayim*) is distinguished from "Jerusalem". See however p. 96, n. 70.

[262] *Gen.R.* 84,19. Similarly, in a later *Midrash* quoted in *Yalkut Shimoni* 1,146: "you (Potiphar's wife) *are* a daughter of donkeys . . . and a donkey does not see" (see also *Midrash Aggada ad Ex.*8:16; J. Heinemann, *op.cit.*, pp. 124–5 and 230–1 n. 17, quoting both passages but arguing somewhat apologetically that they are definitely no more than metaphorical). However, in *Gen.R.* 87,4 Potiphar's wife is referred to as "*like* an animal".

[263] *B.Meg.* 11a; *B.Kid.* 72a; *B.AZ* 2b. The bear, second beast in Daniel's vision (*Dan.*7), is commonly identified with Media: *Gen.R.* 99,2; *Lev.R.* 13,5. The angel in charge of the Persians is called *Doviel* (from the word *dov*, i.e. bear): *B.Yoma* 77a.

[264] *B.Kid. ib.*

licence.[265] R. Ami's statement, on riding Persians, was designed no doubt to be provocative. Nevertheless, these passages have the disturbing effect of blurring the distinction, in the affinity of non-Jews with animals, between metaphorical similarity and actual identity.

"The flesh of donkeys": Halakhic implications
The distinction between metaphorical similarity and actual identity is blurred again, though in a different manner, in references to the non-Jews as donkeys and horses. Indeed, far from treating this affinity as mere, figurative metaphor, the *Babylonian Talmud* treats it as a tangible and concrete reality to the extent that it acquires *practical*, Halakhic significance.

In the *Babylonian Talmud*, most of these Halakhic rulings are based on the verse (*Ezekiel* (23:20): "their flesh is the flesh of donkeys, and their semen the semen of horses"—which refers to the Egyptians but which the Talmud applies indiscriminately to all non-Jews.[266] Thus it infers from this verse that non-Jewish semen is as worthless as horses', and therefore, that the non-Jews have no Halakhic fatherhood.[267] In a similar vein, but without reference to this verse, the *Palestinian Talmud* concludes a discussion concerning non-Jewish nationalities and lineages with the incongruous teaching: "all types of mules constitute one species".[268] That animal, sub-human status should entail lack of fatherhood and kinship may be explained in classical anthropological terms: the essential social structures of lineage and kinship are perceived

---

[265] Similarly, according to *Midrash HaGadol ad Gen.* 49:6, Jacob refers to Joseph as an "ox". This interpretation is also given by the *Targum Yerushalmi ad loc.*, but the latter uses explicitly the qualifying term *metil*, 'compared'.

[266] Strangely, however, in one place it is applied to the whole of mankind, as an indication that human flesh—Jewish as well as non-Jewish—has the same weight per volume as a donkey's flesh: *T.Arakh.* 3,2; *B.Arakh.* 19b.

[267] *B.Yev.* 98a. The Talmud argues that the invalidity of non-Jewish fatherhood does not depend on the suspicion that non-Jewish women are adulterous, but rather on the worthlessness of the non-Jewish man's semen: consequently non-Jewish twins, even if identical, are considered not to be brothers. Lack of fatherhood also means that non-Jewish paternal siblings do not form an incestuous relationship: *B.Yev.* 98a-b; *B.Sanh.* 58a; *Gen.R.* 18,5. However, non-Jewish fatherhood is considered valid regarding laws of inheritance: *B.Naz.* 61a; *B.Kid.* 17b-18a. It is disputed whether non-Jewish fatherhood and motherhood are considered valid concerning the commandment of procreation and the status of first-borns (in a situation where these non-Jews would subsequently convert): *Y.Yev.* 2,6; *B.Yev.* 62a; cf *ib.* 23a; *B.BK* 15a.

[268] *Y.Shab.* 5,1. This teaching refers ostensibly to the laws of mating, but its unaccounted juxtaposition to the question of whether Libyans are a nation distinguished from the Egyptians leaves no doubt that there is here a skilful *double entendre*.

as the distinctive, exclusive features of human society alone. From this, the non-Jews appear to be excluded.

The Halakhic significance of the affinity between non-Jews and donkeys appears elsewhere as follows:

> R. Yehuda said: it is forbidden to recite the *Shema* in front of a naked non-Jew.
> Why did he say "non-Jew"? The same applies even to an Israel!
> - In the case of an Israel, this is obviously forbidden. But in the case of a non-Jew this ruling had to be stated, because you might have thought that since it is written, "their flesh is the flesh of donkeys", *he is only like a donkey*. So we are told that their flesh is also called 'nakedness', as it is written: "And they saw their father's nakedness" (*Gen.*9:23).[269]

The suggestion that the non-Jew is "only like a donkey" is not *per se* rejected in this passage; the Talmud only reaches its conclusion on the basis of a separate and independent consideration, namely that 'nakedness' also applies to the non-Jews. In spite of the qualificatory "like" in this passage ("*like* a donkey"), the suggestion that the non-Jew may have been treated *in concrete practice* as equal to a donkey suggests far more than mere metaphorical similarity between them.

Finally, one passage in the *Babylonian Talmud* suggests that as donkeys, the *concrete physiology* of the non-Jews is different from the Jews'. Indeed, another explanation as to how Justina daughter of Severus could have given birth when she was seven of age is that "their flesh is the flesh of donkeys".[270] Here, more than anywhere else, we find that the affinity of non-Jews with donkeys may be treated as tangible and hence, as a form of *virtual identity*.

The identification, or quasi-identification of human beings (e.g. non-Jews) with animals may appear at first sight preposterous, contradictory and absurd. Anthropologists have shown, however, that it is common in various cultures and not as illogical as it may, at first sight, appear.[271] In this respect, the passages I have quoted should not be dismissed as 'not really meaning what they say'. The identification of non-Jews

---

[269] *B.Ber.* 25b.

[270] *B.Nida* 45a; passage quoted at the end of section I.3.A.

[271] It may be argued that it is no less absurd than the common modern Western view, shared even by some scientists and philosophers, that men are 'meat machines'. For a survey of the literature and a detailed discussion of the logical and ontological implications of such statements, see Jonathan Z. Smith, *Map is not Territory*, Leiden: Brill, 1978, ch.12 ("I am a Parrot (Red)", especially pp. 277–83 and n. 50; also M. Jackson, *op.cit.* ch. 7 (pp. 102–18).

with animals is a serious Talmudic statement which deserves appropriate consideration.

"The flesh of donkeys": *sexual connotations*

One final remark. In other applications of the *Ezekiel* verse, the equation of non-Jews with donkeys has particular sexual connotations. For instance, we hear in later sources that incest has been permitted to the non-Jews because they are like horses and donkeys.[272] A non-Jew who converts in order to marry a Jewess is like a donkey.[273] More distinctly, the *Babylonian Talmud* tells the story that R. Sheila was forced to account before the Persian authorities for having lashed a man who had been found guilty of intercourse with a non-Jewish woman. In his defence, he claimed that in fact the man had been found guilty of bestiality with a donkey. When his integrity was later challenged, R. Sheila maintained quite adamantly that he had not lied to the Persian authorities, for it is written: "their flesh is the flesh of donkeys".[274] Affinity with donkeys suggests, therefore, that intercourse with non-Jewish women amounts to bestiality, as we shall later discuss (p. 165); it may also explain the rabbinic claim that non-Jews are prone themselves to bestiality (p. 25).

B. *Israel as angels*

'Man'

In the *Babylonian Talmud*, the non-Jews are excluded from a number of Halakhic rulings on the exegetical basis that they are not called 'man' (*adam*); but Israel alone are 'man'.[275] In a later *Midrash*, the

---

[272] *Midrash Alpha Beitot* (ed. Wertheimer), p. 449, with a reference to the verse from *Ezekiel* (on the apparent contradiction between this statement and the Noahide laws, see section V.1.B.).

[273] *Eliyahu R.* 27, p.146.

[274] *B.Ber.* 58a. In another late *Midrash* already quoted, Joseph says to Potiphar's wife: "you are a daughter of donkeys . . . and a donkey does not see" (*Yalkut Shimoni* 1,146); it may be argued, however, that in this context affinity with donkeys refers to her lack of sight rather than to her promiscuity (see J. Heinemann *op.cit.*, pp. 124–5). More relevant may be the Talmud's remark that the blessing recited by R. Gamliel on seeing a beautiful non-Jewish woman would also have been recited on seeing a beautiful camel, donkey or horse: *Y.Ber.* 9,1; *Y.AZ* 1,9.

[275] *B.Yev.* 61a (= B.BM 114b) (i.e., that the corpse of a non-Jew does not impart impurity in a tent; see section II.1.A); *B.Ker.* 6b; *B.Sanh.* 72b (= *T.Sanh.* 11,4); cf *Sifre Z. ad Num.* 35:12. See however Morton Smith, "On the Shape of God and the Humanity of Gentiles", in J. Neusner (ed.), *Religions in Antiquity. Essays in memory of E.R. Goodenough*, Leiden: Brill, 1968, pp. 320–6, who argues that the Talmudic

nations who are called 'animal' are contrasted with Israel who are called 'man' (adam).[276]

I would like to argue, however, that more than 'man', Israel are considered to be akin to angels.

Israel and the Angels

Israel and the angels are presented in various *Midrashim* as equals.[277] Whereas each nation (of the 70) are under the jurisdiction of an angel, Israel are under the direct jurisdiction of the Almighty.[278]

In some respects Israel even surpass the angels, which is why they alone were given the *Torah* and the commandments.[279] Israel have the power to pass decrees on the worlds above:[280] for instance they fix the date of the New Year, which is then conveyed to the angels by the Almighty.[281] Israel are dearer to the Almighty than the angels, for Israel praise Him more frequently, and of their own initiative; the angels cannot sing above until Israel have begun to sing below.[282] In the future-to-come, the angels will have no access to the precinct of Israel.[283]

---

restriction of the status of *adam* exclusively to Israel is actually not consistent, as in certain cases the term *adam* is taken to indicate non-Jews: *B.BK* 38a (= *B.Sanh.* 59a; *B.AZ* 3a). Cf Y. Cohen *op.cit.* p. 34.

[276] At least according to one saying in *Eccl.R.* 3,18; another saying in the same passage, however, compares Israel with animals, as quoted above in note 5. In *M.BK* 4,6, the distinction between animal and man is parallel to the distinction between non-Jew and Jew.

[277] *Song R.* 1,2 (s.v. *yishakeni*) end, on I*Chron*.24:5. This is also suggested in an interpretation of the name 'Israel' as meaning 'who ministers (i.e. as an angel) for God': *Midrash Haserot ViYeterot* (ed. Wertheimer) 42; cf *Gen.R.* 78,3.

[278] *Deut.R.* 2,34; *PdRE* 24. Similarly, before the episode of the golden calf, God told the angel of death: "you have no business with this nation, for they are my sons"—*Lev.R.* 18,3. See however *Ex.R.* 18,2 whereby Israel (but only Israel) are protected by the angels.

[279] *Ex.R.* 30,6; *Eliyahu R.* 19, p. 116. The angels, being fully spiritual, have no appreciation of the commandment of circumcision which they regard as filthy, bloody, abominable and repulsive; but the Almighty sides with Israel and maintains that the blood of circumcision is more pleasant to Him than myrrh and frankincense: *Tanh. Vayyera* 2. As to the demons, however, the situation is less straightforward: King Solomon was certainly ill-advised to challenge Ashmedai, the lord of the demons, with the suggestion that Israel are in no way inferior to him: *B.Git.* 68b.

[280] *Song R. ib.*

[281] *Y.RH* 1,3.

[282] *Sifre Ha'azinu* 306, end; *Y.Suk.* 5,4; *B.Hul.* 91b; cf *Midrash Shir haShirim* 1,13.

[283] *Tanh. Balak* 14.

Israel as Angels

Israel are, moreover, intrinsically like angels. This applies especially to individual rabbis,[284] but also to the Jewish people as a whole.[285] According to one *Midrash*, their angelic status depends on their observance of the commandments;[286] but in the *Babylonian Talmud*, their angelic status appears to be unconditional.[287]

In a passage from the *Babylonian Talmud* already quoted, the whole of mankind is said to resemble the angels, just as they resemble animals, again in three respects: they have understanding (*bina*), an upright posture, and they speak the holy language (Hebrew).[288] Reference to Hebrew *may* indicate that this passage refers exclusively to Israel.[289] Similarly, a Midrashic saying that "man was created in the angels' image" seems to apply exclusively to Israel, as it is invoked to explain why killing a *Jewish* person is tantamount to destroying an icon of the King.[290]

Israel as Divine

The affinity of Israel with the Divine is suggested in a number of ways. It is related, first of all, to the Talmudic notion that the Divine Presence (the *Shekhina*) rests upon Israel even when they are impure:[291] consequently, "if a non-Jew slaps the jaw of a Jew, it is as though he slapped the jaw of the Divine Presence".[292] Similarly, whoever attacks (or assists) Israel is like attacking (or assisting) the Almighty.[293]

---

[284] *Y.Ber.* 5,1 (R. Yehoshua b. Levi and others, according to the governor of Caesarea); *B.Kid.* 72a (the scholars of Babylonia); *Midrash Mishlei* 9 (the masters of Talmud, whilst learning); *Midrash Shir HaShirim* 1,4 (Moses and Aharon).

[285] *B.Kid.* 70a; *Ex.R.* 15,6 (like angels); *PdRE* 22 ("sons of God", a title also held by the angels). Also *Tanh. Bamidbar* 10: their encampment in the desert was like the angels'.

[286] *Midrash Mishlei* 8,1.

[287] *B.Kid. ib.*; cf *Sifre Num.* 119, with reference to priests, but also by implication to the whole of Israel who are called in the same passage, albeit in a wider sense, 'priests' (quoted above in p. 32, n. 236). The angelic status of Israel may be contrasted with the resemblance of the Arabs to "demons of lavatories": *B.Kid.* 72a.

[288] *B.Hag.* 16a; *Avot dRN* 37,2.

[289] The parallel passage in *Gen.R.* 8,11, however, states that men resemble angels because they stand, speak, understand, and see; no mention is made of Hebrew. On the lack of significance of the Hebrew language as to the identity of Israel, see my remarks in pp. 79–80.

[290] *Ex.R.* 30,16.

[291] *B.Yoma* 56b; *Num.R.* 7,8; *Tanh. Metzora* 9.

[292] *B.Sanh.* 58b.

[293] *Mekh. Shira* 5 (= *Tanh. Beshallah* 16); *Sifre Num.* 157; *Tanh. Vayehi* 5; *Eliyahu R.* 8, p.44. Cf *Midrash Hallel* (ed. Eisenstein) on *Psalms* 113:4.

But early and later *Midrashim* go further. Israel wear the clothes of God.[294] They can be recognized as the sons of God, for, it is implied, they resemble Him.[295] The holiness of the Almighty, of the *shabbat*, and of Israel, are all one and the same.[296] Israel are like God, for they are masters over all the inhabitants of earth.[297] The Almighty Himself has called them 'God'.[298]

To conclude, rabbinic sources suggest that although the title of "man" is restricted to Israel, in some sense Israel transcend the level of humanity, and have some affinity with the angels and even with God.[299] The nations, who have an intrinsic affinity with animals, stand in radical contrast to them.

5. ISRAEL AMONG THE NATIONS AND THE WORLD

A. *The superiority of Israel*

Righteous and angelic, the superiority of Israel over the nations should be by now self-evident. Rabbinic sources do not shy from stating that Israel are the choicest of all nations,[300] the best,[301] the greatest,[302] the highest,[303] the most beloved of the Almighty.[304] One Jew outweighs all the nations put together.[305] Appropriately, every morning is recited the daily blessing "that He has not made me a non-Jew".[306]

This superiority is said, in Talmudic and other sources, to provide substantial benefits to Israel. According to the prevailing opinion, Israel are immune from the astrological influence of constellations.[307] "Israel

---

[294] Which are might: *Tanh. Va'era* 8.
[295] *Ex.R.* 46,4, in the *mashal.* On Israel as sons of the Almighty, see section V.3.A.
[296] *Eliyahu R.* 24, p.133. Cf *Avot dRN* (B) 43 (= *Midrash Minayin* (ed. Wertheimer) 2,3): Israel, the *Torah*, and the Almighty are all compared to fire. On the *shabbat*, see pp. 76–7.
[297] *Num.R.* 1,9. See section I.5.
[298] *Sifre Deut.* 355; *Tanh. Kedoshim* 5; *Pes. dRK* 12,23.
[299] The distinctive relationship between the Almighty and Israel, to which we have alluded at the end of section I.3, will be discussed in detail at the end of this study.
[300] *Midrash Tehillim* 2,12; see *Tanh. Kedoshim* 5.
[301] *B.Sanh.* 39a-b; see *B.Men.* 53a-b. Israel are grateful that their lot and their inheritance are the best: *Sifre Deut.* 53.
[302] *Num.R.* 3,1.
[303] *Song R.* 1,3,2; *Tanh. Ki Tissa* 18; *Eliyahu R.* 7.
[304] *Sifre Deut.* 97 & 344; *Tanh. Ki Tissa* 8. The Almighty prefers Israel, even though the other nations also praise Him: *Mekh. Shira* 3.
[305] *Sifre Deut.* 97; *Eliyahu R.* 5, p. 25.
[306] *T.Ber.* 7,18 (L: 6,18). Cf *B.Men.* 43b: "that He has made me Israel".
[307] This opinion is attributed to R. Yoḥanan, with whom R. Ḥanina disagrees;

are sons of kings";[308] "all Israel are worthy of kingship".[309] Israel are not fit for slavery, for "'They are My slaves (says the Almighty)', and not slaves of any other slaves".[310] A non-Jew who hits a Jew is punishable by death.[311] According to later sources, touching Israel is tantamount to sacrilege, for they are holy.[312] Israel are compared to the beach upon which the waves cannot prevail; so the nations continuously threaten Israel, but never to any avail.[313] "Israel are mighty before the nations";[314] like God, they are masters over all the inhabitants of earth.[315]

On the other hand, our sources are well aware that in actual reality, Israel's power and Divine immunity are not apparent. Israel are subjected by Rome[316] and often molested with impunity. Our sources complain about extortionate taxes, *annonae* and *angariae*,[317] much as did other subjects of the Later Roman Empire.[318] More specifically,

---

but the Talmud leans clearly in favour of the former, as it goes on to list a number of other authorities who concur with his view (Rav, Shemuel, R. Akiva, and R. Naḥman b. Yitzḥak): *B.Shab.* 156a-b (and parallel in *B.Ned.* 32a). Abraham and his descendants are prophets, not astrologers: *Gen.R.* 44,12. See also *Tanh. Shoftim* 10.

[308] A statement with Halakhic consequences, according to one opinion in *M.Shab.* 14, end; cf also *B.Shab.* 67a, ib. 111b, *B.BM* 113b.

[309] *T.Hor.* 2,8; *Y.Hor.* 3,5. According to *Num.R.* 6,1, all Jews are worthy of being kings, though not all of being sages. According to *B.Shab.* 128a, all Jews are worthy of wearing garments worth 100 maneh (again, with Halakhic consequences). This notion gives rise to the following kind of statement: "Rabbi's store-keeper was wealthier than King Shapur" (*B.Shab.* 113b).

[310] *B.Kid.* 22b; *B.BK* 116b (= *B.BM* 10a). The term "slaves" is taken to refer to the four empires (Babylon, Persia, Greece and Rome) in *Lam.R.* 5,8.

[311] *B.Sanh.* 58b—for, as we have seen, if he slaps the jaw of a Jew, it is as though he slapped the jaw of the Divine Presence.

[312] *Ex.R.* 24,3; cf *Num.R.* 2,13.

[313] *Midrash Tehillim* 2,1.

[314] *Pes.dRK* 15,10—a bold reading of *Isaiah* 1:24.

[315] *Num.R.* 1,9, quoted above.

[316] Or, in Babylonia, by Persia, though our sources may have perceived their persecution to have been less intense: according to *B.Git.* 17a and *B.Pes.* 87b, their rule is milder than the Romans'. See R. Brody, *op. cit.*

[317] On Roman taxation, see for instance *Y.Shevi.* 4,3; *ib.*5, end; *Y.Git.* 5,10; *Y.AZ* 4,10; *Lev.R.* 23,5; *B.Shab.* 33b; *Lam.R.* 3,3; *Pes. dRK* 2,2 & 23,2; also *Song R.* 2,2,5; 2,14,1. See M. Hadas-Lebel, "La fiscalité romaine dans la littérature rabbinique jusqu'à la fin du IIIème siecle", in *Revue des études juives* 143, 1984, pp. 5–29. On 'non-Jewish' taxation, see section I.2.C, note 63. Roman jurisdiction is also perverted: *Gen.R.* 63,10 (cross-examination techniques); *Deut.R.* 1,17.

[318] A.H.M. Jones, *op.cit.* pp.467–9, 819, 1053–4; nonetheless, the *Tosefta* intimates (rightly or wrongly) in *T.Ned.* 2,2 that the Jews are more heavily taxed by the Romans than the non-Jews (Porton, *op.cit.*, pp. 85–6). The complaint that wealthier Jews are impoverished by being appointed to compulsory civic offices as *archones* and *bouleutai* (*Gen.R.* 76,6) is also echoed in other provinces of the empire, see G.E.M. De Ste Croix, *The Class Struggle in the Ancient Greek World*, London: Duckworth, 1981, ch. 8.

the Romans are blamed for having destroyed the Temple[319] and for issuing decrees against Jewish religious observance.[320] Israel suffer whilst the nations are in peace.[321] Israel are pursued by the nations[322] and singled out for harsh and humiliating treatment.[323] The nations put the Jews to death in spite of having been told by the Almighty to treat them with respect.[324] This is why Jewish courts have the duty to discourage prospective converts with the following warning:

> "Do you not know that Israel at the present time are persecuted and oppressed, despised, harassed and overcome by afflictions?".[325]

There is thus a discrepancy, throughout our sources, between the description of Israel as persecuted and oppressed, and the notion that in some sense, Israel are 'really' superior to the nations and immune from their persecutions.[326] This superiority appears to represent a subjective, 'internal' truth, transcending, on some other plane, the experiences of the outside world. The *internalisation* of the experience of Jewish identity as an alternative, 'transcendental' reality is a theme to which we shall frequently return in later chapters. Presently we may surmise that as an escapist fantasy, this perception of Israel must have provided the authors of our sources with some psychological comfort, 'compensating' for the predicament which they were experiencing as Jews in the historical reality of Late Antique society.

B. *Israel in the world*

Although I suggested, in section I.2.D, that Israel and Rome were somehow interdependent, the majority of our sources stress the

---

[319] See for instance *B.Git.* 55b–58a; *Lam.R. passim*.

[320] *Mekh. Baḥodesh* 6 (with reference to the Jews "in the land of Israel", i.e. under Roman rule); *B.Ber.* 61b (decrees against *Torah* learning, with the resulting martyrdom of R. Akiva); *B.Shab.* 49a (*tefillin*); *B.RH* 19a (*shabbat* and circumcision); *B.Taan.* 18a; *B.Meila* 17a (laws of menstrual purity); cf *Song R.* 2,14,1; *Midrash Tehillim* 13,3. Esau hates circumcision: *Gen.R.* 63,13.

[321] *T.Sot.* 13,9. The ten horns, symbols of might, which had been given by the Almighty to Israel have now been transferred to the nations: *Midrash Tehillim* 75,5; *Lam.R.* 2,6.

[322] *Lev.R.* 27,5; *Eccl.R.* 3,15; *Pes.dRK* 9,4; cf *Sifre Deut.* 311; *Eliyahu R.* 5.

[323] *B.RH* 19a (= *B.Taan.* 18a); *Lam.R. pet.* 24; cf *Deut.R.* 1,16.

[324] *Mekh. Beshallaḥ, pet.*; *Tanh. Beshallaḥ* 5. Cf *B.Ket.* 111a: the Almighty made the nations swear that they would not enslave Israel excessively.

[325] *B.Yev.* 47a; *Gerim* 1,1.

[326] An attempt to rationalize this contradiction may be found in the Talmudic claim that were it not for the *Torah* which restrains the Jews, no nation would be able to resist them (*B.Betza* 25b).

centrality of Israel in the world and the unilateral dependence of the nations upon them. We are figuratively told, in a late *Midrash*, that even when Israel are scattered to the four corners of the world, they remain nonetheless in its centre.[327] The centrality of Israel manifests itself in history, and as we shall subsequently see, in their relationship with the whole world.

World history

Israel transcend the vicissitudes of world history.[328] They are permanent, whereas the nations are transient.[329] Empires go and empires come, but Israel are forever standing;[330] by adhering to the Almighty, Israel achieve this permanence.[331]

World history evolves, moreover, with Israel as its single purpose. God gave the conquerors of Israel (Babylon, Persia, Greece and Rome) world-wide dominion for the sole sake of Israel's honour[332]—lest any nation claim that the Almighty delivered His sons into the hands of a lowly empire.[333] In the late Roman period God split the world into two empires (Rome and Sassanian Persia), in order to safeguard the security of Israel.[334] Rome is gathering riches for the future benefit of the King-Messiah; therefore, when an emperor in Rome was wasting his father's treasuries, Elijah appeared to him in a dream and rebuked him thus: "your fathers gathered and you are wasting!". He did not budge until they were re-filled.[335]

---

[327] *Eliyahu R.* 5, p.25.
[328] See my remarks in p. 20.
[329] This is the theme of many *Midrashim*. According to *Song R.* 7,3,3, quoted in full below, the nations are as transient as chaff, straw and stubble; they are neither planted, sown, or firmly rooted. According to other sources, the nations are similar to husks that are not worth counting (*Num.R.* 4,1; *Tanh. Bamidbar* 19); they are like terminal patients (*Tanh. Shemini* 6; *Tanh. Mishpatim* 3; *Ex.R.* 30,22; *Lev.R.* 13,2) and beyond hope of repair (*B.RH* 23a); they are even like carrion and corpses (*PdRE* ed. Higger 28). Cf *Gen.R.* 95 (on *Gen.*46:28). In *M.BK* 4,6, the distinction between Jew and non-Jew is parallel to the distinction between a viable child and a child of premature birth (who is born first, but is doomed to die).
[330] A *Midrash* based on *Eccl.* 1:4: "Generations go and generations come, but the earth is forever standing". *Eccl.R.* 1,4, s.v. *vehaAretz*; *Tanh. Vayak'hel* 2; *Derekh Eretz Z., Perek Shalom.*
[331] *Num.R.* 12,18. According to *Lev.R.* 23,6, Israel's permanence is related to their eternal share in the world-to-come.
[332] *Mekh. Vayehi* 1.
[333] *B.Hag.* 13b.
[334] *Eliyahu R.* 20, p.114.
[335] *Gen.R.* 83,4.

The whole world

"The world could not exist without Israel".[336] It was created for the
sake of Israel,[337] and is maintained entirely through their merit.[338]
Without Israel, there would be no rain or sunrise.[339] Israel bring light
to the world.[340] All the blessings in the world are due to Israel.[341]
This is because the Almighty attends only to Israel, whence the rest
of the world draws indirect benefit.[342]

Therefore, the nations could not exist without Israel.[343] Israel atone
for the nations.[344] All the nations on earth derive their prosperity from
Israel,[345] even distant ships, sailing from Gaul to Spain.[346] But as though
it were not sufficient that Israel are the source of all blessings, the
non-Jews impose on them extortionate taxation.[347]

Beyond the immediate reality of non-Jewish persecution, of which
we are again reminded in the latter passage, our sources depict the
existence of the world and the nations as entirely dependent upon
the fate of Israel. This 'ethnocentric', highly self-centred world-view,
confirms the extent to which the authors of our sources are exclusively
concerned with their own identity. The notion that the 'others' (the
nations, the world) are subordinate to the 'self' (Israel) and owe it
their existence, suggests a dialectical relationship of self and other where
the other serves no other purpose, and has no other *raison d'être*, but
to define and enhance the essence of the self.

---

[336] *B.Taan.* 3b; *B.AZ* 10b; *Ex.R.* 38,4; *Num.R.* 2,13; *Midrash Tehillim* 2,12; *Eliyahu R.* 18, p.105. Cf *Ex.R.* 2,5: "Israel are a fence to the world".

[337] *Gen.R.* 83, end (a point with which the nations disagree); *Lev.R.* 36,4 ("Israel created the world"); *Ex.R.* 38,4; *Song R.* 2,2,3 and 7,3, end; *Gerim* 1,5. Israel were created before the world: *Gen.R.* 1,4; *Midrash Tehillim* 74,1.

[338] *Lev.R.* 23,3; *Song R.* 2,2,3. Cf *Tanh. Nitzavim* 2: through the merit of the righteous Jew.

[339] *Num.R.* 1,3; *Tanh. Teruma* 9; cf *Midrash Tehillim* 109,4.

[340] *Song R.* 1,3,2; *ib.* 4,1,2; cf *Tanh. Tetzave* 5. This is because Israel *are* light, as is recited every week in the *havdala*: "He distinguishes between . . . light and darkness, between Israel and the nations . . .": *B.Pes.* 103b; *Num.R.* 18,7.

[341] *Bishvil Yisrael*—'because' of Israel, or perhaps 'for the sake of' Israel: *Y.Shevi.* 4,3; *ib.* 5,4; *Y.Git.* 5,10; *Y.AZ* 4,10.

[342] *Sifre Deut.* 40; *Midrash Alpha Beitot* (ed. Wertheimer) p.425.

[343] *Num.R.* 2,17.

[344] *Song R.* 1,15,2 & 4; *ib.* 4,1,2.

[345] *B.Pes.* 119a explains how all the gold and silver in the world, which is now in Rome, was initially collected and hoarded by Joseph in Egypt, and was subsequently passed down from hand to hand until the Romans took it from the Greeks.

[346] I.e., at the other end of the world: *B.Yev.* 63a.

[347] *Y.Sheviit* 4,3; *ib.* 5, end; *Y.Git.* 5,10; *Y.AZ* 4,10. Cf *Tanh. Behukkotai* 2: if the nations knew that when Israel sin and are punished, they also suffer from the consequences, they would not prevent them from keeping the commandments.

C. *Non-Jewish attitudes towards Israel*

Imperial respect

Interestingly, rabbinic sources suggest that this ethnocentric perception is somehow approved of and endorsed by the non-Jews. We are told that Israel and the Almighty are recognised by all the nations, from Tyre to Carthage.[348] Some non-Jewish rulers treated the rabbis with much respect. Queen Ifra Hormiz would marvel at the wisdom of the Jews.[349] King Yazdgard I girdled R. Huna b. Natan like a priest, because, he explained, all Israel are a "nation of priests".[350] Most remarkable is the case of Emperor *Antoninus b. A-Severus*, who treated R. Yehuda the Patriarch as a friend, a colleague, and even an authority.[351] Antoninus was indeed unusual: he owned one of Joseph's three treasures,[352] and according to Palestinian sources he converted to Judaism.[353]

Roman hatred

The case of these benevolent rulers is undoubtedly exceptional.[354] The oppression of Israel by Rome is not merely a historical accident, but as we have seen (section I.2.D), a pre-ordained, structural re-occurrence of the age-long rivalry between Esau and Israel. Rome is thus *intrinsically* opposed to Israel; as R. Shimon b. Yoḥai puts it, "it is a rule (*halakha*) that Esau hates Jacob".[355]

Roman culture is interpreted in our sources as constituting an expression of this 'anti-Jewish' nature. The term *Saturnalia*, a well-known Roman festival, is reinterpreted by Hebrew analogy and with the exegetical device of *notarikon* as meaning: 'hidden hatred'. The Jews of Rome are said to call this festival (by similar analogy): 'the

---

[348] Although they call the Almighty 'God of Gods': *B.Men.* 110a.

[349] *B.Nida* 20b. A non-Jewish captor marvelled at their wisdom and their ability, wherever they go, to gain the upper hand over their masters: *B.Sanh.* 104b.

[350] *B.Zev.* 19a, quoting *Ex.*19:6.

[351] *B.Ber.* 57b; *B.AZ* 10b; also *Gen.R.* 11; *Gen.R.* 20,7; cf S. Krauss, *Antoninus und Rabbi*, Vienna 1910.

[352] *B.Pes.* 119a; the other was owned by Korah, and the third is hidden away for the righteous in the world to come.

[353] *Y.Meg.* 1,11; *ib.* 3,2; *Y.Sanh.* 10,5; *Lev.R.* 3,2; *Eccl.R.* 9,10,2; *Midrash Tehillim* 22,24.

[354] Antoninus is righteous unlike all other Roman rulers: *Mekh. Beshallah, pet.*; *B.AZ* 10b. It is only in afterlife that wicked non-Jews like Balaam and Titus acknowledge that Israel are most important (*B.Git.* 56b–57a).

[355] *Sifre Num.* 69.

grudging hatred of Esau'.[356]. The *Babylonian Talmud* describes a most extraordinary festival which is supposedly celebrated in Rome once in seventy years, for the sole purpose of expressing their hatred of Israel. In the course of this ceremony the celebrants exclaim: "the brother of our master (i.e. Jacob, brother of Esau) is an imposter . . . what did he gain from his imposture? What did he gain from his forgery?", but they conclude: "woe unto the one when the other will rise".[357]

Israel are also hated by all the nations.[358] Similarly to Roman festivals, the ceremonies (or pantomimes) which are staged in non-Jewish theatres are solely designed to make fun of the *shabbat* and the *sheviit* (Jewish Sabbatical year).[359]

Obsessive 'anti-Jewishness' confirms the rabbinic contention that to the nations, Israel is a central and overriding concern. According to one *Midrash*, the Romans scorn Israel 'every day',[360] as though it was to them an essential occupation; and another *Midrash* remarks:

> since we are forced to work for the nations, they have nothing else to do but to sit down and make plans against us.[361]

Our sources give the impression that non-Jewish culture, with its festivals and theatre shows, is entirely devoted to the expression of hatred for Israel. As 'others', the nations have no autonomous identity of their own, except for being the logical opposite of Israel and its logical opponent.

---

[356] *Y.AZ* 1,2. So is the meaning of *senator. Gen.R.* 67,8.

[357] *B.AZ* 11b.

[358] As we have seen, non-Jews and Romans are commonly confused. On non-Jewish hatred of Israel, see *Gen.R.* 63,7; *Midrash Ḥaserot Viyeterot* (ed. Wertheimer) 59 & 228; cf *B.Shevu.* 35b; *Midrash Tehillim* 103,21. *Mekh. Kaspa* 2 lays down that 'your enemy' is always a reference to the non-Jew. However in *B.Pes.* 49b the *Amei haAretz* are said to hate the rabbis more than the non-Jews hate Israel.

Hatred of Israel is ideologically motivated: "the nations want to attack the Almighty, but since they cannot, they attack us" (*Tanh. Pekudei* 4). "If we were uncircumcised or *avoda zara* worshippers or apostates, they would not hate us and persecute us—it is only because of the *Torah* which You gave us" (*Tanh. Matot* 3).

This theme may be compared to the idea, in Classical Greek literature, that the barbarian hatred of the Greeks was insoluble and perpetual: cf E. Hall (*op.cit.* pp. 195–6).

[359] *Lam.R., pet.* 17; *ib.* 3,5.

[360] *Num.R.* 11,1.

[361] *Tanh. Toldot* 5.

The Christian claim to "Israel"

As I have already stated (p. 27, n. 185), Christianity is rarely mentioned in early rabbinic writings. Yet the following passage, a relatively early *Midrash*, refers quite clearly to the Christians and suggests, again, an implicit recognition by them of the centrality of Israel.

> A parable: the straw, the chaff and the stubble were arguing with one another, each claiming that for its sake the ground had been sown. Said the wheat to them: "Wait till the threshing time comes, and we shall see for whose sake the field has been sown". When the time came and they were all brought into the threshing-floor, the farmer went out to winnow it. The chaff was scattered to the winds; the straw he took and threw on the ground; the stubble he cast into the fire; the wheat he took and piled in a heap, and all the passers-by when they saw it kissed it . . .
>
> So of the nations some say: "We are Israel, and for our sake the world was created", and others say: "We are Israel, and for our sake the world was created". Says Israel to them: "Wait till the day of the Almighty comes, and we shall see for whose sake the world was created". And so it is written: "For behold the day comes, burning as a furnace" (*Mal.* 3:19), and it is written, "You shall fan them, and the wind shall carry them away" (*Isa.* 41:16) . . . .[362]

This polemic *Midrash* refers ostensibly to the Christians (and perhaps the Samaritans) who claim to be the 'true Israel'.[363] According to this *Midrash*, it is out of recognition of the superiority of Israel, for whose sake the world was created, that the Christians desire to be identified as 'Israel'. This suggests, perhaps, that the nations have coveted and appropriated the identity of Israel because they lacked, as mere 'others', an autonomous identity in their own right. On the other hand, from a historical perspective, we may infer from this *Midrash*—as many historians, such as Neusner (1989), have assumed—that the rise of Christianity and their claim to being the 'true Israel' had the historical

---

[362] *Song R.* 7,3,3, referred to above in connection with the notion of the transience of the nations.

[363] As suggested by J. Heinemann, *op.cit.*, pp. 118 and 230, n.4. On the identity of Samaritans in rabbinic writings, see section III.2.C. For the early Christian claim of being the 'true' Israel, implicit already in *Romans* 9:6–8, I*Cor.* 10:18 and *Gal.* 5:16, see Justin Martyr, *Dialogue with Trypho*, 11. References to Christian dogma are rare in early rabbinic sources, but on a similar theme see further: *Num.R.* 14,10; *Tanh. Vayyera* 5; *Tanh. Ki Tissa* 34; *Pes.R.* 5,1, referring also to the Christian appropriation of the Scriptures; these passages will be discussed in section II.3.B. The ontological threat which the Christian appropriation of the title 'Israel' may represent to the Jews will be studied in detail in section V.1.D. (see p. 219).

effect of enhancing, through self-and-other dialectics, the rabbis' ontological awareness of 'really' being, as Jews, Israel.

Envy, desire, and fear

The passage just quoted suggests that the nations are envious of the identity of Israel. In the *Babylonian Talmud*, we hear that the non-Jews envy the beauty of the Jews.[364] Envy of Israel may also be related to sexual desire: the non-Jews prefer having sexual intercourse with Jewish-owned animals than with their own wives.[365]

Elsewhere, by contrast, we are told that the nations are afraid of Israel.[366] Were it not for the nations' secret fear of the Almighty, Israel could not have survived among them.[367] The non-Jews fear Israel because they are circumcised;[368] they fear Israel when they keep the commandments which make them holy.[369]

Conclusion

In describing the nations' attitudes towards Israel, our sources point to a strange but familiar combination of respect and resentment, of admiration and envy, of hatred and of fear. Implicit in all this is a tacit recognition, on the part of the nations, of the centrality and superiority of Israel. This recognition not only provides *psychological* comfort to the authors of our sources, as suggested above, but also legitimizes the latter's subjective perception of Israel as being, in all respects, the centre of the world. Thus although perhaps fictitious, the gaze of the non-Jewish 'other' enhances, to the authors of our sources, the reality of their own self, of their identity as Israel. Through self-and-other dialectices, the nations' view of Israel is to them not only psychologically, but also *ontologically* momentous.

---

[364] *B.Git.* 58a: the text is slightly obscure and variable according to manuscripts, but appears to say that Roman aristocrats used to have marital intercourse in front of precious amulets (?) so as to improve conception, but now they do so in front of (or with?) Jewish captives (whom they have tied to their bed-frames), so as to induce the conception of children with the same beauty. On the beauty of the Jews, see *ib.* at length and *M.Ned.* 9,10.

[365] *B.Git.* 38a.

[366] Even when Israel are in exile: *Midrash Shir HaShirim* 6,4.

[367] *B.Yoma* 69b; *Midrash Hashem BeHokhma Yissed Aretz* (ed. Eisenstein).

[368] *Tanh. Tzav* 14,end. Animals are also fearful of them for that reason.

[369] *Num.R.* 17,6 (= *Tanh. Shelah* 15, end); *Eliyahu Z.* 15. The following story shows how non-Jews can respect the Jews for their observance of the commandments: a Roman spared the life of R. Aba b. Zamina, because he had resisted him and had refused to eat forbidden (carrion) meat. "Had you eaten it", he said, "I would have killed you: Jews (must be) Jews, and Romans Romans" (*Y.Sheviit* 4,2).

CHAPTER TWO

IDENTITY, THE COMMANDMENTS, AND BODILY EXPERIENCE

"Non ci sono gli archetipi, c'è il corpo"—Umberto Eco.

Jewish identity is not confined in our sources to the realm of mental imagination. It is not an abstraction, such as a logical, theoretical contrast between self and other. The experience of Jewish identity is first and foremost a concrete reality, which is articulated not only in an intellectual context but also in a social environment and in a physical *milieu*.

The physical *milieu* of Jewish identity, of which circumcision, for instance, will prove to be a central component, may be interpreted as a medium of experience and expression, as a range of symbols which *embody* Jewish identity, and through which the mental cognition of being Jewish is experienced and conveyed. The symbolic investment of concrete reality is commonly found in Midrashic sources in the form of the *mashal*; symbols of Israel and of Jewish identity will be discussed below in an appendix.[1]

It would be wrong, however, to treat the physical body of the Jew as merely symbolic, i.e. as a vehicle serving to 'represent', symbolically or otherwise, the identity of the Jewish person: for as I have argued in my introduction, the body must be seen *itself* as an intrinsic, constitutive part of the *subjective* Jewish person.[2] I will argue in this chapter that the experience of being Jewish is as much a *'bodily'* experience as it is a mental cognition. Indeed, the Jewish body is able *itself* to realize and experience its own Jewish being without having

---

[1] Pp. 82–6.

[2] See my remarks in the introduction. For a concise critique of the symbolistic interpretation of the body and its *praxis*, see Jackson (1989), ch. 8 ("Knowledge of the body"), pp. 119–36. He argues that the symbolistic approach, employed for instance by Mary Douglas, reduces the body to the status of a sign, to an external object which only serves the individual and 'society' as a vehicle of cultural expression. This approach ignores Merleau-Ponty's observation that the body is a subjective constituent of the human person; it does not *represent* the person, or 'stand for' cultural notions through a symbolic process—it *is* in fact the person. See also P. Bourdieu, *Outline of a Theory of Practice*, (trans. R. Nice), Cambridge: CUP, 1977, pp. 87–95 and 114–124.

to 'embody' or represent a primordially mental image.

Here again, the contrast between Israel and the nations will be brought into play. We find in our sources that Israel and the non-Jews are distinguished not only in their moral but also in their physical features; the non-Jew, in his body, is repulsive (section II.1), whereas the Jewish body is exalted (section II.2). But it is the practices of Israel, the commandments (mitzvot), which I will argue are the most distinctive features of Jewish identity in the context of concrete, bodily reality.[3]

The argument in this chapter is not entirely separable from that of the first: the rabbinic description of Jewish and non-Jewish bodies constitutes, arguably, a mental 'representation' as much as a concrete and physical experience; conversely, the perception of the non-Jews as intrinsically akin to animals, and of the Jews as quasi-angelic, cannot fail to be experienced as a bodily and concrete reality. However the material I have decided to analyze in this chapter, particularly in the practice of the mitzvot, lends itself particularly well to emphasizing the bodily aspects of Jewish identity.[4]

1. NON-JEWISH IMPURITY AND THE EXPERIENCE OF REVULSION

A. Impurity[5]

The main feature of the non-Jewish body is that it is Halakhically impure. There is however some ambiguity in Tannaitic sources, which

---

[3] On Judaism and the body, see Howard Eilberg-Schwartz (ed.), *People of the Body. Jews and Judaism from an embodied perspective*, New York: SUNY Press, 1992. This volume focusses however on issues traditionally associated with the body such as food, sexuality, gender and procreation. The (bodily) practice of the mitzvot, including even circumcision, as well as the (bodily) experience of being Jewish are largely ignored (see however on the laws of menstruation and female Jewish identity, with reference to the modern period, pp. 312–6).

[4] It should be noted that a large proportion of the mitzvot, not least circumcision and Torah learning, are not meant to be performed by or on women (see M.Kid. 1,7; M.Ber. 3,3). And yet, the status of Jewish women as 'Israel' never comes into question in our sources. The nature of women's Jewish identity, which remains undoubtedly problematic in the context of early rabbinic writings, will be tentatively addressed in section V.2.D.

[5] Non-Jewish impurity has been subject to intense controversy; see (with full references to early rabbinic sources) G. Alon, *Jews, Judaism and the Classical World*, (trans. I.Abrahams), Jerusalem: Hebrew University, 1977, pp. 146–189; G.G. Porton, *op.cit.* ch. 11. The notion of impurity (tum'a) itself, to my knowledge, has not yet been defined in phenomenological terms, even though its articulation in halakha (and hence, presumably, in daily life) has been described in detail (e.g. by J. Neusner, *The idea of purity in Ancient Judaism*, Leiden: Brill, 1973). As Neusner writes, rabbinic

also rule that the non-Jew cannot contract impurity. The *Babylonian Talmud*[6] resolves this contradiction by distinguishing between scriptural law and rabbinic decree; according to the former, the non-Jews are not, objectively, impure, nor can they contract impurity; according to the latter, the non-Jews are treated, by decree, *as though* they were intrinsically impure.

According to scriptural law, the non-Jews cannot become impure, for impurity occurs only where purity can occur as well; since ritual purification is not available to non-Jews, the Talmud infers that they are not liable to impurity either.[7] This would explain the Tannaitic rulings that non-Jews do not become impure through contact with a corpse,[8] through contracting leprosy,[9] and that non-Jewish women do not become impure through menstruation or through childbirth.[10] Analogously perhaps, their clothes and homes, if 'leprous', are not impure and do not impart impurity;[11] nor does the corpse of a non-Jew.[12]

On the other hand, according to our sources, the rabbis decreed that non-Jews should be treated as impure, to the same degree as Jews who have a menstrual[13] or any other discharge of blood or semen (even though these discharges would not *actually* render them impure).[14] Consequently, their body is impure,[15] as well as their urine[16] and their

---

'impurity' is clearly not equivalent to the modern notion of 'dirt'; nor is its avoidance restricted to cultic activity in and around the Temple (as implied in *M.Demai* 2,3, impurity should be avoided in all circumstances). What 'impurity' actually means in rabbinic literature may remain somewhat elusive, but I will assume that it is at least undesirable and repulsive.

[6] Also *T.Zavim* 2,1.

[7] *B.Naz.* 61b.

[8] *T.Ahilot* 1,4; *ib.* 14,6 (*B.BB* 20a).

[9] *M.Negaim* 3,1.

[10] *Sifra Tazria* 1.

[11] *M.Negaim* 11,1 and 12,1; *Sifra Metzora* 5,5; cf *ib.* 10; *T.Negaim* 7,10.

[12] *B.Yev.* 61a: it does not render impure in a tent; it does, however, render impure through touch and through carriage. According to *M.Nida* 10,4 and *T.Nida* 9,14, it does *not* render impure through carriage either, but *B.Nida* 69b explains this as referring to a special case.

[13] Cf *B.Sanh.* 82a; *B.AZ* 36b.

[14] *T.Zavim* 2,1; *Sifra Zavim* 1; *B.Shab.* 83a; *B.Nida* 34a; cf *T.Nida* 9,14 (*B.Nida* 69b).

[15] And irreversibly so, since ritual purification is not available to them: *M.Tohorot* 7,6, *T.Tohorot* 6,11, *M.Kelim* 1,8. In *M.Pes.* 8,8 the House of Hillel appear to think that non-Jews are actually (i.e. scripturally) impure; but both *Talmudim* concur that this impurity is not actual but only the result of a rabbinic decree, whereby they are treated as liable to impurity through contact with a corpse (*Y.Pes.* 8,8; and *B.Pes.* 92a, whereby this decree is restricted to this case). Alon argues that impurity was originally, in the pre-rabbinic period, intrinsic to non-Jews (cf Biblical sources quoted in p. 187); his argument, however, has been correctly criticised by Porton.

[16] *M.Makhshirin* 2,3; *M.Nida* 4,3.

spittle;[17] this impurity is hence transmitted to their clothes and their possessions, including their homes[18] and even their lands.[19] This decree appears not to apply to non-Jewish menstrual blood-stains,[20] semen,[21] and (according to the House of Shammai) blood,[22] which remain pure as according to Scripture; the Talmud suggests an explanation for these exceptions.[23]

In practice, therefore, and aside from a few exceptions, the non-Jew is treated and considered as impure. The Halakhic distinction between scriptural law and rabbinic decree is actually of little relevance to the pragmatic, lived reality which the *Mishna* depicts. The impurity of non-Jewish things, even if only rabbinic, would restrict commercial transactions with non-Jews and exchange of food and produce. Personal impurity would restrict physical contact with non-Jews, even close-at-hand conversations: R. Yehoshua went to immerse after talking to a *matronita*, as he had been defiled by her spittle.[24] The social significance of such restrictions will be discussed in chapter IV of this study; all I wish to stress, in this chapter, is the bodily repulsiveness which the non-Jews and their impure possessions would at all times convey.

It is not known to what extent these laws were applied in the Amoraic period (from the mid 3rd century CE); but it is widely accepted that their observance was falling by then into neglect.[25] Nonetheless, the

[17] *M.Tohorot* 5,8; *M.Nida ib.*; *Y.Shek.* 8,1. Minor tractate *Gerim* 3,2, rules that the urine, couch, seat and spittle of a 'resident convert' (see pp. 95–6) are impure, even though his bread, oil, and wine are considered pure.

[18] *M.Ohalot* 18,7. Cf *B.Shab.* 127b (the home of a *matronita*). However tents, sheds, public baths, and military camps are not considered impure (*M.Ohalot* 18,10; *T.Ahilot* 18,11–12). Since this decree concerns the *personal* impurity of the non-Jews, their homes are only indirectly impure; non-Jewish homes cannot contract direct, intrinsic impurity through 'leprosy', from which they remain (together with clothes) exegetically excluded: see *Sifra Metzora* 5,5.

[19] I.e. outside the land of Israel (see Alon, pp. 184–6): *M.Ohalot* 2,3; *M.Tohorot* 4,5; *T.Para* 3,5; *T.Kelim BM* 7,1; *T.Ahilot* 17,6; *ib.* 18 *passim*; *T.Mikvaot* 6,1–4; *B.Shab.* 14a.

[20] *M.Nida* 7,3; cf *Bertinoro ad loc.*

[21] *M.Mikvaot* 8,4.

[22] *M.Nida* 4,3.

[23] *B.Nida* 34a: since contact with blood and semen is not so common, the rabbis did not decree them impure. This inconsistency would indicate that non-Jewish impurity was not scriptural but rabbinic; the rabbis needed to clarify this point, as it is forbidden to burn sheath-offerings and sacrificial meat which have incurred impurity of a rabbinic nature only.

[24] *B.Shab.* 127b; *Avot dRN (B)* 2,19; *Pirkei Derekh Eretz* (appended to *Eliyahu Z.*, ed. Friedman) 1, p. 7. The same story is told of a high priest: *T.Yoma* 4,20 (L: 3,20); *B.Yoma* 47b; *Y.Yoma* 1,1; *Lev.R.* 20,11; *Tanh. Aharei* 7; *Avot dRN (A)* 34. In other versions, it is 'Sadducees' and *Amei haAretz* who imparted impurity through spittle (*B.Nida* 33b).

[25] As assumed by M.D. Goodman, *State and Society in Roman Galilee, AD132–212,*

notion of impurity remained firmly anchored in rabbinic culture. Laws of purity continued to be studied in detail,[26] and adherence to Mishnaic purity remained at least an edifying ideal. The notion of non-Jewish impurity, even if only a rabbinic decree and of limited practical consequence, must have affected the rabbinic perception of the non-Jew and of his home, his food and all his possessions, whenever they were encountered in lived reality.

In some passages, moreover, non-Jewish impurity is presented as tangible and intrinsic rather than as merely rabbinically decreed. According to the *Palestinian Talmud*, vessels purchased from a non-Jew "have left the impurity of the non-Jew and entered the holiness of Israel", which is why Scripture commands them to be immersed.[27] According to *Midrash Tanḥuma*, the non-Jews are from an impure stock,[28] and Israel are to the nations what pure is to impure.[29] According to *Pirkei deR.Eliezer*, Abraham circumcised his household,

> for purposes of purity, namely that they should not render his food or drink impure; indeed, . . . touching an uncircumcised is like touching a corpse.[30]

In spite of these wide-ranging sources, it is difficult to define what

---

New Jersey: Rowman and Allanheld, 1983, p. 179. Evidence for the breakdown of this observance is actually unclear. It begins in the early 3rd cent., when R. Ḥiyya is said to have instructed Rav that if he could eat food in a state of purity all the year round, he should; otherwise, he should only do so for seven days a year (a reference, perhaps, to the seven festivals—*Y.Shab.* 1,3). Then Ulla (late 3rd cent.) is said to report that his colleagues in Galilee produce some food in a state of purity and that the latter is put away untouched, for the time when Elijah the Prophet will return and reveal to the rabbis whether it may be taken to Jerusalem, or whether its passage through Samaritan land would render it impure (it is possible, indeed, that the Samaritans are non-Jewish and hence impure—see pp. 103–4) (*B.Hag.* 25a; *B.Nida* 6b). This would imply that production of pure food was by then only sporadic, and not designed for regular consumption but rather for cultic purposes in Jerusalem (then defunct). However it is not until the later Middle Ages that we are explicitly told: "nowadays we are no longer careful about impurity" (*Tosafot ad B.Pes.* 115b).

[26] It may be remarked, however, that there are no extant Talmudic tractates (Palestinian or Babylonian) on the Mishnaic *Order of Purities* (with the exception of *Nida*, on menstrual purity which, for various Halakhic reasons, is still in observance today); this may indicate a relative loss of interest in this topic, even though purity is studied in detail in many other sections of the *Talmudim*. See J. Sussmann, *Sugyot to the orders Zera'im and Tohorot* (Hebrew), Doct. Diss., Jerusalem: Hebrew University, 1969.

[27] *Y.AZ* 5,15.

[28] "From a seed of impurity": *Tanh. Naso* 7.

[29] *Tanh. Hukkat* 3.

[30] *PdRE* (ed. Higger) 28. The 'corpse' is primarily a technical term, signifying the highest degree of Halakhic impurity; cf *M.Pes.* 8,8 (quoted above).

exactly the experience of impurity consists of. In the latter passage,[31] impurity is associated with the morbidity of a corpse; in general, it is contracted and experienced through bodily means, especially tactile contact and intake of food. In a few passages, impurity is described as "repulsive";[32] this notion is probably applicable, by extension, to the impurity of the non-Jew, and will be developed in detail at the end of this section.

B. *Forbidden food*

The non-Jews are closely associated with the forbidden foods which they consume. Most non-Jewish foods, indeed, and particularly their meat, are Halakhically forbidden to the Jews. Consumption of this food is deemed to affect the physical constitution of the non-Jews; moreover, that it endows their body with concrete repulsiveness.

Pork

Pork is the non-Jewish food par excellence. It is the distinctive mark of the non-Jew: an inn-keeper used to cook and serve pork so that they should not find out that he was Jewish.[33] The *Mishna* rules that eating the bread of *Kutim* is like "eating pork".[34] Elsewhere, "pork neck" is contrasted with "Jewish food".[35] A convert may not be taunted as follows: "yesterday you were worshipping *avoda zara* . . . pork is still between your teeth".[36] References to pork can be considered, in many such cases, as metonymic for forbidden foods in general.

Rabbinic sources suggest that pork, whether specific or metonymic, is repulsive to the Jews of Late Antiquity; so much so that a *Midrash* instructs its audience to refrain from pork not out of natural revulsion, but rather for the sake of fulfilling the Almighty's will:

> One should not say: "I am incapable of eating pork", but rather "I am capable of it, but what can I do?—the Almighty has forbidden it".[37]

---

[31] Also in *M.Pes.* 8,8.

[32] *Ma'is*: of an impure person: *B.Yev.* 100a; of a menstruating woman: *B.Sot.* 42a (cf *B.Shab.* 65a).

[33] *Num.R.* 20,21; *Tanh. Balak* 15. See also *Eccl.R.* 7,11: R. Meir was in an inn where Romans were sitting and eating pork.

[34] *M.Sheviit* 8,10. On the status of *Kutim* as bordering on non-Jews, see section III.2.C.

[35] *B.Meg.* 13a.

[36] *Mekh. Nezikin* 18; *Gerim* 4,3.

[37] *Sifra Kedoshim perek* 9,13. Maimonides, in *Shemona Perakim* (introduction to *Avot*), ch. 6, quotes this passage as reading "meat with milk" instead of "pork".

Revulsion towards pork is vividly depicted in the story of a Jew who failed to wash hands before eating, whereby he was wrongly identified as a non-Jew; his host gave him pork, which he ate unknowingly; when he found out, "his hair stood up—he was agitated and in a flurry".[38]

Just as pork, the live pig is considered to be repulsive. The pig has contracted nine tenths of leprosy in the world.[39] The pig is like a mobile toilet;[40] because of its stench, its mouth is like mobile dung.[41] The pig is also closely associated with the non-Jews. Whilst swine-herding is forbidden to Jews[42] and regarded by them as insulting,[43] non-Jews rear pigs[44] and even keep them as home pets.[45] As we have already seen, the pig is symbolic of Rome,[46] so much so that in many passages this symbol is implicit and taken for granted.[47] This symbol is an expression of revulsion towards the ruling Roman power, whilst suggesting at the same time a quasi-totemic identification of the Romans with the pig, who rear pig, eat pig, and are pig.[48]

---

[38] *Num.R.* 20,21; *Tanh. Balak* 15 (this *Midrash* explicates an obscure Tannaitic statement also found in *B.Yoma* 63b and *B.Hul.* 106a). Regarding non-Jewish wine, see *B.Meg.* 13b: "If a fly falls into the cup of a Jew, he removes it and drinks; whereas if Ahasuerus touches it (the cup of wine), the Jew thrusts it to the ground and will not drink it".

[39] *B.Kid.* 49b. Certain types of leprosy are explicitly described as "repulsive" (*ma'is*): *B.Bekh.* 41a, cf *ib.* 43a.

[40] *Y.Ber.* 2,3.

[41] Even after it has bathed in a river—*B.Ber.* 25a. Both toilets (*B.Shab.* 10b) and dung (*B.Shab.* 47a) are explicitly described as "repulsive" (*ma'is*).

[42] *M.BK* 7,7; cf *Y.ad loc.*; *Y.Shevi.* 7,1; *B.BK* 82b.

[43] As when R. Yehuda was accused of it by a non-Jew: *Y.Shab.* 8,1; *Y.Shek.* 3,2; *B.Ber.* 55a; *B.Ned.* 49b; *Eccl.R.* 8,1,4.

[44] E.g. in Alexandria: *M.Bekh.* 4,4. Emperor Diocletian was originally a swineherd: *Gen.R.* 63,8; *Y.Terumot* 8,end.

[45] *M.Ohalot* 18,7–8.

[46] *Lev.R.* 13, *passim*; *Gen.R.* 65,1 (quoted in section I.4.A). Also *Midrash Tehillim* 120,6; *Midrash Haserot Vi-yeterot* (ed. Wertheimer) 228. When Israel are worthy, Rome is domesticated as a pig; but when they are not, it turns into a wild boar that kills people and cattle: *Avot dRN* 34,3.

[47] *B.Pes.* 118b; *Gen.R.* 63,8. In *Gen.R.* 44, end, this symbol applies to the non-Jews in general. In *Est.R.* 4,5, Vashti is referred to as a sow, in contrast with the "holy nation".

[48] On the identity of the "Romans" and their confusion with the non-Jews, see pp. 15–7. Although I am suggesting a close, intrinsic affinity between the Romans and the pig (cf on non-Jews and animals, section I.4.A), I should point out that according to *B.Taan.* 21b the human intestine—Jewish included—is similar to the pig's, both being susceptible to the same diseases.

'Creeping things'
Another metonymy for forbidden food are "abominations and creeping
things" (*shekatzim u-remasim*), and "reptiles" (*sheratzim*)—both terms being
phonetically as well as semantically related.[49]

The *Babylonian Talmud* states explicitly that reptiles are most "repulsive" (*ma'is*) to eat,[50] and elsewhere that the non-Jews are polluted
(*mezuhamim*) because they eat 'abominations and creepies'.[51] According
to later *Midrashim*, the Almighty allowed the non-Jews to eat abominations and 'creepies', but only as a doctor allows a terminal patient
to eat whatever he wishes;[52] 'creepies' are thus a signal of their natural
morbidity. This appears to have induced a non-Jew to convert: whilst
he still kept in his house carrion, non-kosher meat, and 'abominations
and creepies', he once exclaimed: "When will I convert and be among
Israel who eat nice food?".[53]

'Creepies' affect the organic constitution of the non-Jewish person.
According to the *Babylonian Talmud*, they cause his body to engender
excessive heat, which speeds up the decomposition of substances (e.g.
semen) within it,[54] and increases his immunity to venomous substances.[55]
The non-Jew stinks of creepies and carrion meat (which is also
considered 'repulsive'[56]), as the following story illustrates. R. Akiva
was once abroad in captivity; two non-Jewish women were sent to
entice him, but he just spat and ignored them. His captor marvelled
at his restraint, and asked: "Are these women not pretty? Are they
not human like you, made by the same Creator?"; to which R. Akiva
answered: "I smelled the stench of carrion, non-kosher meat and
reptiles/pork".[57] Thus because they eat 'creepies', pork, and other
forbidden foods, the non-Jews become themselves, in their body,
physically repulsive.

---

[49] They are confused in *M.AZ* 3,6.
[50] *B.BM* 61b. Since forbidden fish are also mentioned in this context, it would
appear that 'reptiles' are a metonymy for all forbidden foods.
[51] *B.Shab.* 145b.
[52] *Tanh. Shemini* 6.
[53] *Eliyahu R.* 27, p. 146.
[54] *B.Nida* 34b.
[55] *B.AZ* 31b; this explains why non-Jews leave their alcoholic drinks uncovered,
and are not concerned that a snake may come a drop his venom into them.
[56] *B.Hul.* 116b.
[57] *Avot dRN* 16,2. The *textus receptus* reads "reptiles", whereas ms.Oxford reads "pork".
Although R. Akiva' chastity is presented as exceptional, and similarly, perhaps, his
feelings of revulsion towards sexual intercourse with 'creepy-eating' non-Jews, this
edifying story is clearly prescriptive and designed for emulation.

Human milk

In the case of non-Jewish human milk, the non-Jewish body and forbidden food converge. The *Tosefta* rules, indeed, that it is forbidden to feed from a non-Jewish woman, just as it is from an impure (i.e. forbidden) animal.[58] This parallel suggests that just as a forbidden animal, the non-Jewess is herself intrinsically 'impure';[59] the *Palestinian Talmud* refers to both as 'abominations and impurity.'[60]

We are told in the *Babylonian Talmud* that Miriam insisted that her infant brother Moses should not be nursed by a non-Jewish woman,[61] for the Almighty had instructed: "shall the mouth that is destined to talk to Me feed from an impure thing?".[62] This suggests that the repulsiveness of non-Jewish milk is more extensive than with any other forbidden food; the *oral* contact with a non-Jewish breast, which this passage emphasizes, conveys the specifically bodily, tactile revulsion which this prohibition entails.

C. *The prepuce*

The most distinctive feature of the non-Jewish male body is its prepuce—namely, that it is uncircumcised. The *Midrash* describes the prepuce as a source of shame[63]. Abraham is said to have circumcised his slaves because their prepuce made them impure, for it is "the worst of all impurities ... the worst of all blemishes",[64] and eating

---

[58] *T.Shab.* 9,22—except for life-saving purposes. According to *M.AZ* 2,1 and *T.AZ* 3,3, an infant may be fed by a non-Jewish nurse; according to *T.Nida* 2,5, he may be fed by a non-Jewess as well as by an impure animal. Since the prohibition of milk from impure animals is well established in other sources (*B.Bekh.* 6b–7a, on *M.Bekh.* 1,2; cf *Y.AZ* 2,9; *B.AZ* 35b, 39b), it is probable that these passages, which refer specifically to an infant (cf *T.Nida ib.*), are lenient because they treat the case of an infant as 'life-saving' in all circumstances.

[59] Not 'impure' in the ordinary Halakhic sense, as discussed above in II.1.A, but rather 'forbidden' by analogy with forbidden animals which are referred to in Biblical and rabbinic sources, in a different sense, as 'impure'. I do not think, on the other hand, that this analogy necessarily suggests intrinsic affinity with animals, as I have remarked with reference to *Lev.R.* 13 in p. 34.

[60] *Y.AZ* 2,1, quoting *T.Nida ib.* that an infant may feed from both, adds: "and one need not worry about abominations and impurity".

[61] In spite of the lenient ruling in *M.AZ* 2,1 (see above).

[62] *B.Sot.* 12b; *Ex.R.* 1,25.

[63] *Gen.R.* 80,8.

[64] *PdRE* (ed.Higger) 28, quoted above in p. 55. On the prepuce and impurity, see *B.Yev.* 72b, with an opinion that the uncircumcised are impure; also *Num.R.* 12,8 and *Midrash Mishlei* 30, that "the prepuce is a sign of impurity". Cf also G. Alon, *op.cit.* p.152 n.6.

together with an uncircumcised is like eating together with a dog, as a dog is also uncircumcised.[65]

The *Mishna* states explicitly that the prepuce is 'repulsive' (*me'usa*).[66] According to the *Babylonian Talmud*, uncircumcision is so *ma'is* that even an uncircumcised *Jew* is considered repulsive, whereas a non-Jew *per se* is not.[67] However uncircumcised Jews are considered to be uncommon, as I will later show (see p. 64), whereas non-Jews are assumed to be all uncircumcised,[68] to the extent that even circumcised non-Jews are called and treated as 'uncircumcised'.[69] This suggests that being, albeit by assumption, uncircumcised, the bodies of non-Jews are considered intrinsically repulsive.

D. *Revulsion and identity: a bodily experience*

To sum up: I have tried to show how the non-Jews are frequently associated with an experience of physical revulsion. Although they are never directly referred to as 'repulsive',[70] they are considered impure, which is referred to at times as repulsive; they eat repulsive food (reptiles, pork, etc.) which affects their bodily constitution; and as uncircumcised, their prepuce renders them repulsive.[71]

The experience which I have called 'revulsion' or 'repulsiveness', and its relationship with personal identity, requires perhaps some elucidation. These terms translate the Hebrew and Aramaic root *M'S*,

---

[65] *PdRE* ch. 29 (28), in the text of first editions, quoted by Friedlander *op.cit.*, p. 208, n. 5, and above, p. 35. On the "uncircumcised" as synonymous with "non-Jews", see below note 68.

[66] *M.Ned.* 3,10; *Mekh. Amalek* 1. On the contrastive exaltation of the circumcised penis, see section II.2.A and pp. 229–32.

[67] *B.Yev.* 71a (cf *ib.* 72b; *ib.* 100a); *B.Pes.* 96a; *B.Zev.* 22b.

[68] They are called *arelim*—literally, 'with a prepuce': *M.Ned. ib.* This usage is already attested in the Bible (as *T.Ned.* 2,4 points out, the Philistines are not referred to in *Judges* 14:3 as *avoda zara* worshippers, as incestuous or as murderers, but simply as "uncircumcised"), and also found in *Targum Onkelos* (*ad Lev.*25:45 & 47). This term is given formal Halakhic recognition, regarding the wording of oaths, in *M.Ned. ib.* (quoting *Jer.* 9:25, I*Sam.* 17:36, and II*Sam.* 1:20; cf *Ex.R.* 1,15; *Pes. dRK* 28,1; cf *Midrash Mishlei pet.*).

[69] *M.Ned. ib.*; *T.Ned.ib.*; cf *B.Yev.* 71a. See further section II.2.A and pp. 206–7.

[70] According to *B.Yev.* 71a (just quoted), the non-Jew *per se* "is not repulsive", which is why the *Torah* must exclude him explicitly from eating the Passover lamb, as his exclusion would not necessarily have been inferred from the prior exclusion of the uncircumcised. However, this need not mean that the non-Jew is not repulsive *at all*, only that he is *significantly less* repulsive than the uncircumcised.

[71] Also we hear that firewood from a cult of *avoda zara*—the distinctive mark of the non-Jews (see pp. 27–9)—is considered repulsive (*ma'is*): *B.Betza* 39a. An offering to *avoda zara* is impure: *B.Hul.* 13b.

which we have already encountered (especially in the *Babylonian Talmud*). In the *Babylonian Talmud*, *M'S* is used almost exclusively in passive form,[72] with reference to things towards which one experiences a spontaneous, compelling feeling of revulsion. It refers firstly and most commonly to spoiled food, whether squashed,[73] dirty,[74] or placed in the mouth and then spat out[75] (also, dirty food containers[76]); secondly, to forbidden animals[77] and to certain animal skins;[78] thirdly, to certain items of clothing;[79] and fourthly to bodily behaviour, such as bad table manners[80] and in some circumstances sexual intercourse.[81] Since these objects of revulsion are all connected with the human body (through eating, clothing, etc.), it would appear that the term *M'S* refers to repulsiveness of a specifically *bodily* nature.[82] Indeed, *M'S* is associated in the *Targum* with bodily nausea.[83]

What this bodily experience consists of may be appreciated on the basis of our own experience of revulsion.[84] Clearly it goes well beyond the level of the mind: the entire body can be shaken with revulsion, typically with a nauseous tremor or with actual nausea. It must be stressed that nausea itself does not merely 'represent' or signal a mental

---

[72] Whereas in Biblical Hebrew it is used in active form with the plain, less specific meaning of 'rejection' (e.g. I*Sam.* 15:23; in the Talmud, I have only found such a usage in *B.Yev.* 15a).

[73] *B.BM* 21b; cf *B.Shab.* 50b. Also over-sweet wine: *B.Men.* 87a.

[74] *B.Hag.* 15b (dirty with mud and dung).

[75] *B.Ber.* 50b. Also if it were placed under one's armpit: *B.Sanh.* 39a.

[76] *B.Shab.* 29b; *ib.* 59a; *B.Pes.* 20b; *ib.* 33b; *B.BK* 115b.

[77] 'Creepies' and carrion meat: see above p. 58. A mouse which fell in a barrel of beer, rendering it repulsive: *B.AZ* 68b (cf *B.Suk.* 36b). A fly which fell in one's plate: *B.Git.* 6b. Also a sick animal, a leprous animal (*B.Bekh.* 41a), a blemished animal (*B.Yoma* 63b; but cf *B.Bekh. ib.*). With reference to sacrifices, see *B.Zev.* 72a.

[78] A donkey's: *B.Hul.* 77b. A bird's, as it is pierced with holes: *B.Shab.* 118a.

[79] A wig made with someone else's hair: *B.Shab.* 64b; a menstruation cloth: *B.Shab.* 65a.

[80] *B.Kid.* 81a. A person who spits, or who kills a louse, before another person is *nimas* (repulsive) to him: *B.Hag.* 5a; *Eccl.R.* end.

[81] A woman refuses to have intercourse with her husband on the grounds that he is *ma'is* (repulsive) to her: *B.Ket.* 63b.

[82] Except in the expression *tefilato nimeset*, "his prayer is rejected" (by the Almighty): *B.Sot.* 5b; *B.Sanh.* 43b.

[83] *Targum Onkelos ad Num.* 11:20 draws an explicit equivalence between nasal vomiting and the term *M'S*.

[84] On subjective input into phenomenological analysis, particularly in the area of bodily experience, see my introduction, note 19. I would maintain that referring to our own bodily experiences in order to understand the rabbis' is not less valid than the generally accepted academic practice of using our own rational perceptions in order to understand, for instance, a Talmudic argument.

revulsion, but *is* itself a bodily form of rejection and revulsion.[85] The same may well apply to spitting: thus, R. Akiva *spat* in the presence of repulsive non-Jewish female captives. But the *Midrash* also refers to other forms of bodily revulsion: when the Jew discovered that he had accidentally eaten pork, "his hair stood up—he was agitated and in a flurry".[86] Whatever its form, the whole person is mobilised in the experience of revulsion; it acquires thereby tremendous potency.

Appropriately, the experience of revulsion is brought about through physical sensations. In the episode just quoted, it was through (accidental) eating; in the case of the live pig, as well as of R. Akiva's non-Jewish women, it was through the sensation of smell; we also find references to tactile contact, as with Abraham's slaves.

But in many cases, it seems that the mere thought of having such a sensation is sufficient to generate revulsion. For instance, the authors of the Talmud can experience revulsion at the thought of eating carrion meat, even without actually eating it.[87] Reptiles are referred to as "repulsive to eat";[88] yet it is most unlikely that rabbis ever ate reptiles in order to bring themselves to this conclusion. Clearly, it is the mere *thought* of eating reptiles which enables the Talmudic authors to perceive them as "repulsive".[89]

Nevertheless, reptiles are said to be repulsive *"to eat"*. Although mentally generated, revulsion towards reptiles is described in terms of a physical experience: they are repulsive to the Talmud only because they are *edible* and available to eat. This suggests that it is the thought of reptiles *as food* which invites the Talmudic authors to direct their *body*, specifically, towards them; it is their body, or their digestive system, which positions itself in relation to this unwanted food. Thus the repulsion of reptiles is not just an intellectual decision, but also—quite literally—a 'gut-feeling', a bodily disposition involving the whole digestive system, or in Merleau-Ponty's terms, a form of *bodily intentionality*.[90]

---

[85] Revulsion entails either 'pushing away' the repulsive object, or alternatively recoiling (oneself) away from it. Julia Kristeva (*Pouvoirs de l'horreur—essai sur l'abjection*, Paris: Editions du seuil, 1980, pp. 9–12) associates the former with nausea and the latter with fainting (which she refers to as bodily 'self-abjection').

[86] See above, p. 57.

[87] *B.Hul.* 116b. The same applies to the repulsiveness of spoiled or soiled food.

[88] *B.BM* 61b.

[89] Mental cognition also played a part in the revulsion of the accidental pork-eater: so long as he did not *know* that his food was pork, he did not feel revulsion towards it.

[90] *Op. cit.* part I, ch.III. By extrapolation, non-Jews who eat repulsive pork become

Bodily involvement of this kind, which amounts to a subjective positioning of the bodily self, may account in the same way for the repulsiveness of the prepuce. As we have seen, that all non-Jews have a prepuce is *assumed* rather than it is actually observed; and yet, this mentally imagined object is treated as *ma'us*, an object of *physical* revulsion. This is because the prepuce is a body-part which, though excluded from the circumcised Jew, has a natural place within his body-scheme.[91] Evocation of the prepuce, even if only mental, invites his body to position itself, and elicits on its part a subjective feeling of bodily rejection. It is this bodily experience which leads the prepuce to be considered 'repulsive'.

As an act of subjective rejection, 'revulsion' embodies in all contexts a dialectical relationship between the self and the 'other'. Indeed, whatever is rejected is necessarily 'other'; for its rejection is an assertion of its 'otherness' and of its radical incompatibility with the self. Through their circumcised bodies, the authors of rabbinic sources not only reject with revulsion but also *define as 'other'* the uncircumcised bodies of the non-Jews.[92] Through this bodily, constructive positioning, moreover, their own bodily self can find, confirm and reassert its own identity as Jewish.

2. The Bodily Features of Israel

A. *Circumcision*

The covenant of Israel
Circumcision is a commandment of central importance.[93] According to our sources, the Jews are glad to perform it[94] even in spite of severe

---

themselves repulsive. However, by eating pork, the non-Jews actualize its status as food-to-be-eaten; this may elicit a more intense engagement of the rabbi's body and digestive system in relation to pork, and hence to an intensified experience of revulsion towards eating it.

[91] See Merleau-Ponty *op. cit.* part I, chs. 1–3 (his term *schéma corporel* is translated by Smith as: 'body image').

[92] In a similar context Merleau-Ponty writes: "it is through my body that I understand the other, just as it is through my body that I perceive 'things'" (*op.cit.* p.186).

[93] Hence the notion that circumcision is equivalent to all the other commandments (*B.Ned.* 32a; cf *Eliyahu R.* 22), and that it protects Israel (*Tanh. Re'eh* 13; *Pes. dRK* 10,4) from exile (*Y.Sanh.* 10,5), from Gehenna (*B.Eruv.* 19a and parallels; *Ex.R.* 19,4; *Tanh. Tazria* 5; *Tanh. Re'eh* 13), and from death (Moses: *Ex.R.* 5,8).

[94] *B.Shab.* 130a (= *Midrash Tehillim* 103); *Eliyahu R.* 22. Circumcision can be an expensive ceremony: *Eccl.R.* 3,2,3; *Tanh. Tetzave* 1; *Tanh. Tazria* 5; *PdRE* 29. This

imperial persecution.[95] The non-Jews, by contrast, are said to scorn circumcision[96]—Esau among the first.[97] In many respects, indeed, circumcision can be seen as constitutive of the identity of Israel.

According to the *Mishna*, Israel are referred to as "the circumcised", just as the non-Jews are indiscriminately called and considered "uncircumcised".[98] Although a Jewish-born remains Jewish even if uncircumcised,[99] the *Talmudim* consider that a male non-Jew can only convert and become Jewish through circumcision.[100] Many Midrashic sources state that "Israel are distinguished (among the nations[101]) through circumcision"."[102] Joseph proved his identity to his brothers by showing them his circumcision.[103] Circumcision is in some sense intrinsic to Israel: Jacob was born already circumcised, whereas Esau was not.[104]

Furthermore, circumcision is referred to in all our sources as *berit mila*, the 'covenant of circumcision':[105] more than a central component of Jewish identity, it represents the exclusive covenant between the Almighty and Abraham (hence Israel). This is why, according to later sources, withdrawing from circumcision is tantamount to withdrawing from the Almighty Himself;[106] without circumcision, there can be no

---

ceremony is likened to a sacrifice: *Gen.R.* 47,7 (= *Song R.* 4,6,1; *Tanh. Vayyera* 2); *Tanh. Vayyera* 6; *PdRE* (ed.Higger) 10; *ib.* 28; *ib.* 29.

[95] *Ex.R.* 15,7; *Midrash Tehillim* 13,3. On imperial decrees against circumcision, see references in p. 44, n. 320.

[96] *Ex.R.* 19,4.

[97] *Ruth R., pet.* 3; *Eliyahu R.* 22; according to *Tanh. Lekh* 20, he decircumcised (see below).

[98] *M.Ned.* 3,10, quoted in p. 60.

[99] If he did not circumcise for medical reasons, he remains a perfectly valid Jew (*Israel ma'alya hu*): *B.Hul.* 4b. On the status of the uncircumcised (or decircumcised) apostate, see section III.3.

[100] *B.AZ* 64b-65a; *Gerim* 1,6; cf *Y.Kid.* 3,12, *B.Yev.* 46a. See section III.2.A.

[101] *Midrash Tehillim* 2,12. Without circumcision Israel would not be hated by the nations: *Tanh. Matot* 3.

[102] *Num.R.* 12,8; *Lam.R.* 2,17; *Song R.* 1,15,2; 1,15,4; 3,11,1; 4,1,2; *Pes. dRK* 15,3.

[103] *Gen.R.* 93,8.

[104] *Midrash Tehillim* 9,7. Earlier sources refer to several individuals who were born circumcised: Moses (*B.Sot.* 12a; *Lev.R.* 20,1; etc.), Jacob and Joseph (*Gen.R.* 84,6), and Melkhizedek (*Gen.R.* 43,7). Later sources present a list of 7, 10, or 13 such people (*Tanh. Noah* 5; *Tanh.B.* 6; and both *Midrash Tehillim* 9,7 and *Avot dRN* 2,5, respectively). Surprisingly, *Avot dRN* includes one non-Israelite, the infamous Balaam, among those born circumcised. This may represent an attempt to justify why he was able to secure the gift of prophecy (see above p. 32, n. 238).

[105] This 'covenant' maintains the world in existence: *M.Ned.* 3,10; *T.Ned.* 2,4–7; *B.Ned.* 32a; *Est.R.* 7,11; *Tanh. Lekh* 17.

[106] *PdRE* ed. Higger 28. By contrast, a convert who withdraws from the prepuce is withdrawing from the grave: *M.Pes.* 8,8.

success in prayer,[107] no Divine inspiration,[108] and no learning of *Torah*.[109] This suggests, as I will later argue,[110] that Jewish identity and the Almighty's covenant with Israel are inextricably bound.

Bodily experience

It should be stressed that being circumcised is essentially a bodily experience. Whereas the prepuce renders the non-Jews repulsive, we find in the *Babylonian Talmud* that circumcision transforms the body of the Jews and renders it complete.[111] One passage goes further and suggests that the "image of God" in which Adam was created was nothing but his circumcision.[112]

According various *Midrashim*, Israel are compared (in the *Song of Songs*) to grains of wheat because they are split in the middle, just as the penises of Israel are split.[113] This suggests that in some sense, as in grains of wheat, the split of circumcision runs across the whole length of the Jewish body and characterizes it in its totality.

But the bodily significance of circumcision is particularly emphasized in the *Midrash Tanḥuma*. We find there that circumcision is bodily splendor and beauty, like a sword between one's thighs,[114] or again, like a soldier's weapon[115] (indeed, it instils fear among the nations[116]). Moreover, through circumcision the name of God (*Sha-da-i*) is inscribed in the bodies of Israel: their nose is shaped as the letter Shin (hence *Sha*), their hand as the letter Dalet (*da*) and their circumcised penis

---

[107] *PdRE ib.*; cf *Song R.* 7,6; *Pes.R.* end.

[108] *Num.R.* 12,8.

[109] With reference to a non-Jew: *Ex.R.* 30,12; *Tanh. Mishpatim* 5.

[110] At the end of this chapter.

[111] *B.Ned.* 32 (= *Tanh. Lekh* 16): when Abraham circumcised, the limbs in his body became complete; his name was also changed from *Avram* to *Avraham*, in order to bring its numerical value up to 248, which corresponds to the total number of limbs in the human body.

[112] *Avot dRN* 2,5.

[113] *Song R.* 7,3,3; cf *Midrash Tehillim* 2,12 and *Pes.R.* 10,3. Israel are also compared to the fig—the prepuce is like a fig stalk, the only part of the fruit which must be discarded (*Gen.R.* 46,1); and to the nut, which has two shells (or a shell and an outer skin)—so Israel have two commandments, circumcision and *peri'a*, incision of the foreskin (*Song R.* 6,11; *Pes.R.* 11,2).

[114] *Tanh. Lekh* 18; *Tanh.B. Lekh* 22.

[115] *Tanh. Mishpatim* 5. I am reluctant to infer from here any sexual or phallic connotation, as the purpose of this "weapon" is explicitly stated in this passage as being the ability to learn *Torah*. *Torah* learning and circumcision are frequently connected, as we shall see in other passages.

[116] Also among the animals: *Tanh. Tzav* 14, end.

as the letter Yod (i).[117] This physical engraving of the name of God points again to the relationship between Jewish identity and the Almighty's proximity to Israel. Moreover, the *Tanhuma*'s emphasis on 'bodiliness' suggests that circumcision is not merely a 'symbol' of Jewish identity and related notions, but is experienced by the *Tanhuma* as one of their tangible, concrete constituents.[118]

Decircumcision: bodily transformations

The practice of decircumcision must be seen, conversely, as a bodily divestment of Jewish identity. This complex operation is described in Graeco-Roman medical text-books,[119] perhaps for the benefit, among others, of apostatizing Jews. There is some literary evidence, in earlier non-rabbinic sources, that Jews did decircumcise in order to conceal their Jewish origins.[120] Decircumcision was also known to the rabbis of Late Antiquity; it is called 'drawing down the prepuce', *moshekh orla*.[121]

Decircumcision is condemned by the *Talmudim* as a repudiation of the Covenant.[122] Infamous characters of the Bible are said in various

---

[117] *Ib*.; *Tanh. Shemini* 8; *ib. Tazria* 5. See Elliot R. Wolfson, "Circumcision and the Divine Name: a study in the transmission of esoteric doctrine", in *JQR* 78, 1987, pp. 77–85.

[118] See my remarks at the beginning of this chapter.

[119] E.g. Celsus, *De Medicina* 7,25,1 (early 1st cent.CE). For a full description of the operation, see J.P. Rubin, "Celsus' Decircumcision Operation: Medical and Historical Implications", in *Urology* July 1980, XVI:1, pp. 121–124.

[120] I*Macc*. 1:14–15; I*Corinth*. 7:18.

[121] However, the claim is made in *Midrash Shir HaShirim* 5,3 that circumcision is irreversible. The same is implied in *B.Sanh*. 39a: when Caesar invited the Jews to join him and become one big nation, R. Tanhum answered: "it is impossible for us to be like you, for we are circumcised; but be you like us, by circumcising". Similarly, Jerome assumes that decircumcision is impossible: *adv. Jovinian*. I,11 (Migne *PL* 23, p. 235), cf *ib*. 21 (p. 250); *comm. in Isa*. 52,1 (*PL* 24, p. 496). These sources may lend support to N. Rubin's contention that decircumcision is physically impossible, because the rabbinic practice of incising the foreskin (*peri'a*) does not leave enough skin for the foreskin to be restored (N. Rubin, "On drawing down the prepuce and incision of the foreskin", in *Zion* 54, 1989, pp. 105–17, Hebrew). Rubin suggests that *peri'a* was only instituted by the rabbis at the time of the Bar-Kokhba revolt; rabbinic and Christian sources which mention decircumcision would thus refer to the earlier period, when circumcision was performed without *peri'a*; the latter was instituted precisely in order to counter the growing practice of decircumcision (cf also Schürer, *op.cit*. vol. 1, p. 149, n. 28). I believe Rubin's theory is problematic, as he has no evidence, other than speculation, for such a rabbinic institution (according to *B.Yev*. 71b, *peri'a* was first performed in the days of Joshua); moreover, such an attempt to curb apostasy would be unparalleled in early rabbinic *halakha*. Furthermore, Rubin's claim that decircumcision is impossible after *peri'a* remains to be confirmed (Dr Joseph Spitzer, personal communication).

[122] *Y.Sanh*. 10,1; *B.Sanh*. 38b.

sources to have decircumcised;[123] the Israelites did so in Egypt after the death of Joseph "so as to resemble the Egyptians",[124] and so did "many in the days of Ben-Koziba" (Bar-Kokhba).[125] In afterlife, an angel decircumcises the sinners, so that they fall defenceless into Gehenna.[126]

In a Halakhic context, it is discussed whether a decircumcised Jew has the obligation (when he repents) to re-circumcise. According to the *Talmudim*, he is not bound by the scriptures to do so, but the rabbis imposed it upon him nevertheless, either as a penalty or because he may otherwise appear to be uncircumcised.[127] R. Yehuda holds however that he should not re-circumcise, as this would be too dangerous—a point which others dispute on the grounds that "many did so in the years of Ben-Koziba and still had children and did not die".[128] Jews and converts are thus depicted as risking their lives in order to circumcise, de-circumcise, and even re-circumcise—because their identity, i.e. their whole, ontological selves, depends fundamentally on such bodily transformations.

B. *External features*

General

Wherever a Jew goes, he can be recognized;[129] nowhere can he pretend he is not Jewish.[130] Israel are recognizable among the nations:[131] they are pointed at with the finger.[132] These Midrashic passages suggest

---

[123] Adam (at the time of the sin): *B.Sanh. ib.* Achan: *B.Sanh.* 44a. Esau, Jehoiakim: *Tanh. Lekh* 20.

[124] *Tanh. Shemot* 5. According to *Eccl.R.* 9,15,4, decircumcision was forced upon them by Pharaoh (cf *PdRE* 29: Pharaoh prevented them from circumcising). Elsewhere it is simply said that the Israelites "rejected circumcision", in order to become "like the Egyptians": *Ex.R.* 1,8; *Tanh. Shemot* 5; cf *Tanh.B. Shemot* 7. The distinctiveness of circumcision is such that after its rejection, the Israelites were no longer distinguishable from the Egyptians; as a result, they were almost not redeemed: *Lev.R.* 23,2; *Song R.* 2,2,2; *Pes.R.* 15,17.

[125] *Y.Shab.* 19,2; *Y.Yev.* 8,1.

[126] *B.Eruv.* 19a; *Ex.R.* 19,4; *Tanh. Lekh* 20; *ib. Tzav* 14, end; *ib. Tazria* 5; *Midrash Tehillim* 6,1.

[127] *Y.Yev.* 8,1; also *B.Yev.* 72a.

[128] *T.Shab.* 15,9; *Y. & B.Yev. ib.*; *Y.Shab.* 19,2; also *Gen.R.* 46, end.

[129] *Num.R.* 16,24. On this basis, perhaps, a criminal court can cross-examines a witness by asking him whether the murdered victim was Jewish or non-Jewish: *B.Sanh.* 40b.

[130] *Song R.* 6,11, on *Isaiah* 61:9.

[131] *Lev.R.* 23,6; *Song R.* 2,2,6.

[132] *Ex.R.* 52,5.

that the Jews have a distinctive physical appearance;[133] but what it consists of is unfortunately left unclear.

The Jews are described in the *Babylonian Talmud* as beautiful,[134] but this again is far from precise. More interesting, perhaps, is the Midrashic suggestion that the smell of Jacob was distinguishable from the smell of Esau, and similarly, that the bones of a non-Jew smell differently from those of a Jew.[135] The sense of smell enhances, as we have discussed in connection with repulsiveness, the bodily experience of being Jewish.

Hair-style

In other passages our sources refer to more specific, physical features as distinctive to the Jews. The *Midrash* says that "Israel are distinctive through circumcision, hair-style, and fringes".[136]

I shall consider the latter two in turn. Rabbinic sources suggest that non-Jewish hair-style, to start with, may differ from the Jews' for the following reasons:

1. The non-Jews shave the *corners of their head*, which is forbidden in the scriptures (*Lev.* 19:27).[137]

2. The non-Jews grow a *belurit*,[138] i.e. a hair-lock which is eventually dedicated to *avoda zara*.[139] In Egypt, the Israelites grew a *belurit* just as they were uncircumcised.[140]

3. The non-Jews cut their hair in a style called *kome* (i.e. 'hair',

---

[133] Cf also *Tanh. Shemot* 11, which discards the suggestion that Moses could have had the appearance (*demut*) of an Egyptian (even as a youth, when he had been brought up in Pharaoh's palace).

[134] Even in times of exile and destruction: *B.Git.* 58a. According to *M.Ned.* 9,10, Jewish women are beautiful, but poverty disfigures them.

[135] *Aggadat Shir HaShirim* (ed. Schechter) 1,3. Cf *Tanh.B. Toldot* 16: the odour of "the righteous" is similar to the world-to-come. In *Pes.R.* 21,3 the nations are referred to as a "bad smell"—primarily, however, as an exegetical inference from the last word of the *Song of Songs*.

[136] Frequently in *Song R.*: 1,15,2; 3,11,1; and 4,1,2. Also in *Lam.R.* 2,17; *Pes. dRK* 16,3; *Midrash Tehillim* 2,13. Hair-style: also *Num.R.* 10,3.

[137] So did at least a (non-Jewish) 'philosopher', in *Pes.R.* 23,4.

[138] E.g. the negroes (*B.Naz.* 39a); Kozbi bat Tzur, the Midianite harlot in *Num.* 25:6–15 (*B.Sanh.* 82a; *Num.R.* 20,24; *Tanh. Balak* 20); the non-Jews in general (*T.AZ* 3,6, on how to cut a non-Jew's hair whilst avoiding his *belurit*; *Pes. dRK* 28,1: "a non-Jew grows his son a *belurit* and a prepuce"). Balaam invented this practice (*Tanh. Noah* 14). The four hundred children of David's army, born from non-Jewish captives, cut their hair in *kome* style and grew a *belurit* (*B.Kid.* 76b—see further p. 160.).

[139] *M.AZ* 1,3; *B.AZ* 29a; *Deut.R.* 2,18.

[140] *Lev.R.* 23,2; *Song R.* 2,2,2; *Pes.R.* 15,17. Again, according to *Eccl.R.* 9,15,4, this was forced upon them by Pharaoh.

in Greek).[141] Reuven b. Istroboli (early 2nd cent.CE) tried to conceal his Jewish identity by cutting his hair in *kome* style, so as to approach the Roman authorities and successfully persuade them to lift their decrees against the Jews (sadly, he was eventually unmasked).[142]

Belurit and *kome* are Halakhically forbidden,[143] which, if the prohibition was observed, may have reinforced the distinctiveness of Jewish hair-style.

Fringes and clothing[144]

There is little evidence that the Jews wear identifiable clothing.[145] According to Palestinian sources, *Torah* students wear a distinctive cloak.[146]

It should be noted that there is no clear prohibition on non-Jewish clothing, as there is on *kome* and *belurit* (see section IV.2.E). Certain non-Jewish clothes might have been forbidden, however, if they were not sufficiently modest[147] or if they were made of a mixture of wool and linen.[148] R. Ada b. Ahava saw a lady wearing a *karbalta* (lit. 'crest'; probably some fancy coat) in the market-place; he ripped it off her, for he mistook her to be Jewish. When it turned out that she was not (and hence, that R. Ada had no business to castigate her), R. Ada was instructed to pay her 400 *zuz* in damages—an exorbitant

---

[141] See further pp. 187–8.

[142] *B.Me'ila* 17a.

[143] On this prohibition, see pp. 187–8. The case of Reuven b. Istroboli must have been an exceptional dispensation. The prohibition of *kome* is equated with that of shaving the corners of the head in *Deut.R.* 2,18.

[144] For a historical account on clothing, see G. Hamel, *Poverty and charity in Roman Palestine, first three centuries CE*, Berkeley and LA: Univ. of California Press, 1990, pp. 57–93.

[145] The Maharik (R. Joseph Colon, c.1420–1480), responsum 88, infers that they do not from the following two passages: 1. The story of Reuven b.Istroboli, who did not apparently need to change his clothes so as to look non-Jewish. 2. The story of a Jewish inn-keeper who used to serve pork to non-Jews and kosher meat to Jews; he identified the latter by observing whether they washed hands before eating (*Num.R.* 20,21; *Tanh. Balak* 15; quoted above in p. 57.)—which implies that to the inn-keeper, clothing was not a way of distinguishing Jews from the non-Jews. On Persian and Babylonian clothing, see J. Neusner, *Talmudic Judaism in Sassanian Babylonia*, Leiden: Brill, 1976, pp. 144–5.

[146] *Sifre Deut.* 343 end; *Mekh. dRShbY ad Ex.* 19:18; *Derekh Eretz Z.* 5,3: *Torah* scholars are distinguishable (in the market-place) in . . . and in their cloak. Cf *Gen.R.* 82,9: two pupils of R. Yehoshua changed their cloak during a persecution so as not to be recognised.

[147] The laws of modesty are discussed in section V.2.A.

[148] *Kilayim*, forbidden in *Lev.* 19:19 and *Deut.* 22:11.

sum indeed.[149] It may be precisely the extravagance of this garment which R. Ada was objecting to.

Jewish clothing may also be distinctive in the following details:

1. The *fringes* (*tzitzit*), which are attached to four-cornered garments.[150] If a non-Jew wears them, he will be mistaken for a Jew.[151] Again, Jewish identity appears to be related to the Almighty's perceived proximity to Israel, in so far as fringes are said increase the holiness of Israel[152] and to make them look as though the Divine Presence is among them;[153] if, on the other hand, a Jew fails to wear fringes, he is counted among those who are banned from Heaven (i.e. from God).[154]

2. *Black shoes*, which appear, at least in some contexts, to be distinctively non-Jewish. A man who desired to conceal his Jewish identity put on black shoes and removed the blue thread (i.e. the fringes) from his cloak.[155]

3. Since the *Talmudim* consider them to be part of clothing,[156] I will mention finally the *tefillin* (phylacteries), which are worn on the head and on the arm. According to the *Talmudim*, this is a commandment which tended to be neglected by the Jews, in stark contrast with circumcision.[157] This neglect proceeded in part from the necessity to maintain a 'clean body' whilst wearing *tefillin*, which ordinary people found difficult to sustain.[158] It is unclear whether they are thought to have neglected this commandment altogether, or whether they did wear *tefillin* during morning prayers[159] but failed to wear them right through the day, which only a few, such as Elisha-of-the-wings are said to have observed.[160]

---

[149] *B.Ber.* 20a.
[150] *Num.* 15:37–41.
[151] *B.Men.* 43a.
[152] *Sifre Num.* 116.
[153] *Midrash Tehillim* 90,16.
[154] *B.Pes.* 113b.
[155] *B.Taan.* 22a. On the other hand, in *B.Betza* 15a black shoes are taken for granted among the Jews, as it is asked whether one may blacken one's shoes on a festival. It is most likely that conditions varied in different places and periods. The *Tosafot* (*ad B.Sanh.* 74b) attempt to reconcile the 'contradiction' by interpreting the passage in *B.Taan.* as referring only to black *shoe-straps*, which were presumably not worn by Jews. On shoe-straps, and indeed on clothing in general, see further section IV.2.E.
[156] *B.Shab.* 61a. Cf *Y.Eruv.* 10,1; *B.Eruv.* 95b.
[157] *Y.Ber.* 2,3; *B.Shab.* 130a; also *Midrash Tehillim* 103; *Pes.R.* 22,5.
[158] *Y.Ber. ib.*; *B.Shab.ib.* and 49a. Cf *Pes.R.ib.*
[159] As appears to be the practice in *B.Ber.* 14b–15a.
[160] *B.Shab.* 49a, 130a, etc. Also R. Yoḥanan b. Zakkai (who did not walk four

Tefillin have much in common with other physical features of Jewish identity. Just as circumcision, *tefillin* are Israel's might and instil fear among the nations.[161] Just as fringes, whoever does not wear *tefillin* (at all?) is counted among those who are banned from Heaven.[162] Last but not least, *tefillin* constitute a powerful expression of the relationship between the Almighty and Israel, which I will describe in detail in the final chapter of this study.[163]

3. The Commandments: Experience and Praxis

So far, in this chapter, I have considered bodily Jewish identity as a static reality: what the Jewish (and non-Jewish) body consists of, its appearance and its constitution. However bodily experience is not just a matter of 'being': it is also a matter of 'doing'. As Merleau-Ponty has stressed,[164] the body experiences itself dynamically, not only through its posture but also through mobility, 'motility' and *praxis*. In this section, I propose to examine the commandments and practices of Israel as a bodily but also a *dynamic* experience of one's identity as Israel.

A. *The commandments as a whole*

As we have already seen, a number of commandments, such as circumcision, fringes and *tefillin*, are presented in our sources as constitutive of the identity of Israel. To some extent, we may surmise that *all* the commandments are experienced in such a manner. Indeed, our sources remark that "Israel are distinctive through the commandments",[165] and that the commandments distinguish them from the nations[166] in "all their actions".[167] This notion may be accounted for in a number of ways, as I shall now explain.

---

cubits without them: *B.Suk.* 28a; *Pes.R. ib.*), his pupil R. Eliezer (*ib.*; *Avot dRN* 25,3; minor tractate *Tefillin*); R. Yoḥanan (*B.Yoma* 86a; cf *B.BK* 17a); R. Zeira (*B.Meg.* 28a); and perhaps R. Sheshet who prides himself of having "performed the commandment of *tefillin*" (*B.Shab.* 118b). This practice is treated as the norm in *Y.Eruv.* 10,1, *Pes.R. ib.*, and tractate *Tefillin*. Cf L.I. Levine, *The Rabbinic Class of Roman Palestine in Late Antiquity*, New York & Jerusalem: Jewish Theological Seminary, 1989, pp. 51–2.

[161] *B.Ber.* 6a.
[162] *B.Pes.* 113b.
[163] P. 253.
[164] *Op.cit.* part I, ch.3: "The Spaciality of One's Body and Motility" (pp. 98–147).
[165] *Sifre Deut.* 43.
[166] *Sifre Num.* 99; *B.MK* 16b; *PdRE* 53.
[167] Such as ploughing, sowing, hair-cutting and shaving, and calendar reckoning:

The Almighty and Israel
Observance of the commandments is primarily a statement of obedience
to the Almighty. Rabbinic writings suggest, as we have already seen
in a number of specific cases, that the experience of Jewish identity
and that of adherence to the Almighty are closely interrelated. In
general terms, the *Midrash* states that as soon as Israel reject the yoke
of God and no longer accept His authority, they claim to have become
"like the nations".[168] Conversely, Hanania and his colleagues are praised
for "they did not change their God and their practices, but stood
fast with their Jewishness"[169]—implying that 'Jewishness' depends on
faithfulness to God and on the practice of His commandments. We
shall return to this important notion at the conclusion of this chapter.

Pervasiveness in lived reality
The rabbinic perception of the commandments as formative of Israel's
identity may also proceed from an awareness that the commandments
regulate "all their actions" and all the aspects of their lives. In objective
terms, indeed, Mishnaic law could be said to cover all areas of human
activity. But rabbinic sources themselves observe that

> the Jew is surrounded with commandments: *tefillin* on his head, *tefillin*
> on his arm, *mezuza* on his door, circumcision on his flesh, fringes on
> his cloak.[170]

The awareness that the commandments surround Israel and condition
their entire existence may explain, alone, why they are seen by our
sources as essential components of Israel's self-identity.

The constitution of the body
Since most commandments are bodily practices, they pervade especially
the *body* of the Jew. As the *Tanhuma* remarks:

Num.R. 10,3; *Pes.R.* 15,5. The commandments are an embellishment to Israel: *Song
R.* 1,15,1; 4,1,1; 7,7. Again, they make Israel holy and instil fear among the nations:
Num.R. 17,6 (= *Tanh. Shelah* 15, end); *Eliyahu Z.* 15. On the other hand, if the Jews
were to renounce the commandments, the nations would no longer hate them: *Tanh.
Matot* 3.
    [168] *Tanh. Nitzavim* 3; *Tanh.B. ib.* 7.
    [169] *Yahadutan*—a rare but significant term: *Est.R.* 7,11.
    [170] *T.Ber.* end; *Y.Ber.* end; *Sifre Deut.* 36; *B.Men.* 43b; by no coincidence, this passage
refers to *tefillin*, circumcision and fringes, which are closely related to Jewish identity
(as we have seen in the previous section). In another Talmudic passage, the
commandments are significantly symbolized with dove's wings: for, the *Talmud* explains,
in the same way as the wings protect the dove, so the commandments protect (and,

Israel are fortunate, because to each of their limbs He gave a commandment . . . to the head, the prohibition of shaving its corners . . .
and furthermore, circumcision; etc.[171]

The *Babylonian Talmud* argues that the Jewish *body* is affected by the
mere worry of observing the commandments, just as 'abominations
and creepies' affect the physical constitution of the non-Jews.[172] In
this respect, the commandments would be perceived as powerful
constituents of the Jewish body, hence of the Jewish person and of his
personal identity.

'The commandments' and Jewish identity

Yet although our sources state, as I have quoted, that "Israel are
distinctive through the commandments", not all commandments appear to be relevant to Jewish identity to the same degree. The
commandments of counting the *omer*, separating tithes, and returning
stolen property, for instance, are not explicitly associated with the
notion of Israel in our sources, and do not appear to elicit a distinct
experience of being Jewish. Although we may postulate that as Jewish
practices, they necessarily entail some awareness of being Jewish, the
silence of our sources suggests that this awareness would only be
subsidiary and of marginal importance. Only a limited number of
practices are *explicitly* related to the notion and experience of being
Israel; it is these, especially *Torah* study and the *shabbat*, that I shall
now consider in detail.[173]

I might add, *envelop*) Israel: *B.Ber.* 53b; *B.Shab.* 49a (= *ib.* 130a).

[171] *Tanh. Shemini* 8.

[172] It causes their body to engender heat: *B.Nida* 34b. Israel are referred to
metaphorically as 'negroes' (or 'Ethiopians': *Amos* 9:7), for "in the same way as negroes
are different in their skin, so Israel are different in their practices (*Sifre*: their
commandments) from all the nations": *B.MK* 16b; *PdRE* 53; *Sifre Num.* 99. This may
imply that the commandments, just as skin-colour, constitute a *physical* mark of Jewish
ethnic identity.

[173] Porton (*op.cit.*) argues quite convincingly that taken as a whole, the distinction
established throughout *Mishna* and *Tosefta* between Jews and non-Jews (for instance
concerning the laws of damages and of finance—pp. 36–7) reinforces the distinctiveness
of Israel as an ethnic group (see p. 296). He writes: "through the agricultural laws,
the rabbis attempted to draw boundaries between themselves and the non-Israelites
who lived on the Land with them . . ." (p. 201; this argument is one of the main
themes of his work). However Porton's study is too broad-based to yield any significant
conclusions: his exhaustive analysis of *all* references to non-Jews in the *Mishna* and
Tosefta only leads him to the banal conclusion that Jewish ethnicity was "no different"
to that of other cultures. I would suggest that in order to discern the *specific* features
of the rabbis' identity as Jewish, we need to restrict ourselves to practices which
are specifically and *explicitly* related to the notion of Israel and hence of Jewish identity.

B. *Torah learning*[174]

"Israel are dear", because they have been given the *Torah*.[175] "The *Torah* is our inheritance, not theirs";[176] it is the bride of Israel.[177] Indeed, the *Torah* was given only to Israel and not to the nations,[178] because— we are specifically told—the nations were unworthy of it.[179] Thus Israel's possession of the *Torah* demonstrates their *intrinsic* superiority over the nations, and simultaneously, again, their exclusive relationship with the Almighty; as is recited every day in the following blessing (before studying *Torah*): "(God) Who has chosen us from all nations and given us the *Torah*".[180]

Rabbinic sources maintain, however, that without the *Torah*, there would be no difference between Israel and the nations.[181] As explicit already in the Bible, God's election of Israel depended on their prior acceptance of the *Torah*.[182] According to the *Pesikta deR.Kahana*, Israel became a "whole nation" (*uma shelema*) only after they had received the *Torah*,[183] and only at Sinai were they given the distinctive name of 'Israel'.[184] In this sense, the *Torah* is seen as *constitutive* of the identity of Israel.[185]

A Palestinian tradition emphasizes the Oral *Torah* as being particularly distinctive of Israel. The *Palestinian Talmud* states that had

---

[174] *Torah*—literally, 'teaching'—signifies the object of rabbinic learning, namely Scriptures and rabbinic ('oral') traditions; by extension, it also refers to all the commandments which the *Torah* prescribes. *Torah learning*, however, is considered a commandment in its own right.

[175] *Avot* 3,14; *Deut.R.* 8,7.

[176] *B.Sanh.* 59a.

[177] *Ex.R.* 33,7; cf *B.RH* 4a; *B.Pes.* 49b; *B.Sanh.* 59a.

[178] *Sifre Deut.* 345; *Tanh. Shoftim* 1; cf *Mekh. Bahodesh* 9, ad *Ex.* 20:22.

[179] *Sifre Deut.* 311. On the *exclusion* of the nations from possessing the *Torah*, see pp. 209–14.

[180] *B.Ber.* 11b.

[181] *Sifra Behukkotai, perek* 8,10; *B.Meg.* 15b; *Ex.R.* 47,3; *Pes.R.* 21,16; *Eliyahu R.* 22. *Torah* is also what distinguishes Jewish from non-Jewish judges (*Ex.R.* 30,22; *Tanh. Mishpatim* 3).

[182] *Ex.* 19:5–6.

[183] *Pes. dRK* 1,2. This may be disputed by *Eliyahu R.* 15, p. 71, which states that Israel were created before the *Torah*.

[184] *Pes. dRK* 12, 23 and *Tanh.B. Va'era* 1 ("My people"); *ib. Yitro* 15 ("Israel").

[185] To the extent, perhaps, that in some passages the *Torah* and Israel appear to be confused. For instance, in a same text they can be simultaneously—and somewhat incoherently—compared to oil which does not mix with other liquids (i.e. the other nations: *Deut.R.* 7,3; *Song R.* 1,3,2; *Tanh. Tavo* 3). Israel and the *Torah* are treated as similar entities: Israel, the *Torah*, the Almighty and Jerusalem each have 70 names (*Num.R.* 14,12); Israel, the *Torah*, the Almighty and Gehenna are "compared to" fire (*Avot dRN (B)* 43; *Midrash Minian* 2,3).

the Oral *Torah* been written, there would be no difference between Israel and the nations, for the nations have also books and scriptures.[186] This statement is expanded in later sources as follows. Moses asked that the *Mishna* be given in writing, but the Almighty foresaw that the nations—i.e., probably, the Christians—would come and take the Written *Torah* (i.e. the Bible) from the Jews, translate it (or in one version: "falsify" it[187]) into Greek and claim themselves to be 'Israel'. Therefore, the *Mishna*, the *Talmud* and the *Aggada* were given orally, so as to remain exclusive to Israel and out of the nations' reach.[188] Thus it is the Oral *Torah*, specifically, which maintains the distinctiveness of Israel from the Christians and all the other nations. It was given to Israel, according to one version, for this specific purpose;[189] inaccessible to the non-Jews, the Oral *Torah* enables Israel to remain separate from them.[190] The crystallization of rabbinic 'oral' law in the Later Roman period, with the redaction of the *Mishna* and of subsequent rabbinic works,[191] could thus be seen in itself as an act of affirmation of Jewish identity on the part of rabbis living under foreign rule, and more specifically, as a conteraction to what the rabbis perceived as a Christian 'falsification' of the Jewish Scriptures.[192]

Again, the bodily or rather 'practical' nature of *Torah* learning should be given emphasis. Although to a large extent a mental and disembodied activity, *Torah* learning is undoubtedly a practice embedded in a social and material setting (the master-teacher relationship, the *beit haMidrash*— 'house of learning', etc.). It is equally a *physical* and dynamic *praxis*, since according to the *Babylonian Talmud*, *Torah* may not be studied silently (*bi-lehisha*, literally 'whispering') but it must be uttered with one's lips and with an open mouth, and laid out over one's 248 limbs

---

[186] *Y.Peah* 2,4; *Y.Hag.* 1,8, on *Hosea* 8:12, which is interpreted as follows: 'Had I written the oral *Torah*, would not it (or: Israel) have become as foreign?'.

[187] *Num.R.* 14,10.

[188] *Ex.R.* 47,1; *Num.R.* 14,10; *Tanh. Vayyera* 5; *Tanh. Ki Tissa* 34; *Pes.R.* 5,1. This *Midrash*, an expansion of the Talmudic passage just quoted (since it is based on the same interpretation of *Hosea* 8:12), may indicate, incidentally, the extent to which the *Mishna* was still regarded as an oral text in the late Roman and early mediaeval period (see p. xxiii).

[189] Whereas the purpose of the Written *Torah*, with its commandments, was to increase the merits of Israel: *Num.R.* 14,10.

[190] *Ex.R.* 47,1. On the inaccessibility of the *Torah* to the nations, see again pp. 209–14.

[191] Which may well have remained oral in their inception, as implicit above.

[192] Cf pp. 49–50.

(all the limbs of the body).[193] The *Torah* is thus a bodily and dynamic constituent of Jewish personal identity.

C. Shabbat, festivals, and other customs

Shabbat

Already in the Bible (*Ex.* 31:12–7), the *shabbat* is described as a covenant between the Almighty and Israel; but the *Mekhilta* reads into these verses, at the same time, the notion of the distinctive identity of Israel:

> "It is a sign between Me and the children of Israel" (*Ex.*31:17)—to the exclusion of the nations.[194]

Other *Midrashim* also emphasize the exclusiveness of the *shabbat* to Israel.[195]

The text of the *havdala* (recited at the end of *shabbat*), as found in the *Babylonian Talmud*, implies an intrinsic affinity between the *shabbat* and Israel:

> . . . He (God) distinguishes between holiness and the profane . . . between Israel and the nations, between the seventh day and the six days of Creation . . . .[196]

According to *Genesis Rabba*, all the days of the week were paired: the first day with the second, the third with the fourth, the fifth with the sixth. The seventh day, *shabbat*, complained to the Almighty that it had no spouse. He answered: "the Assembly of Israel is your spouse"; indeed, just as *shabbat* is the 'odd one out' in the days of the week, so Israel are distinct from all the nations.[197]

---

[193] *B.Eruv.* 53b–54a, which devotes much attention to this topic. *Torah* learning is related specifically to the mouth as being a "covenant of the mouth", just as circumcision is considered a "covenant of the flesh": *B.Ber.* 48b–49a; *Est.R.* 7,11. Cf *B.Git.* 60b; *Sefer haYetzira* (ed. Eisenstein) 6,15. *Torah* and circumcision are related in other ways: both maintain the world in existence, being both covenants between God and Israel: *Est.R.* 7,11. See also *Tanh. Mishpatim* 5, quoted above p. 65, n. 115.

[194] *Mekh. Ki Tissa* 1 (twice). The same notion is found in *Jubilees* 2:31. On this exclusion, see pp. 207–8. According *Eliyahu R.* 22, Esau rejected the *shabbat* (as well as circumcision and "all the commandments") of his own choice.

[195] Ex.R. 25,11; *Midrash Tehillim* 92,1. As with circumcision, the Jews adhere to the *shabbat* in spite of imperial persecution: *Mekh. Ki Tissa* 1; *Ex.R.* 15,7; *Midrash Tehillim* 13,3. The *shabbat* is seen by non-Jews such as Haman as an excuse for idleness (*B.Meg.* 13b; *Est.R.* 7,12); this indictment is actually common among Roman authors, e.g. Juvenal: for references, see Schürer, vol. III.1, p. 152; see below p. 80, n. 223.

[196] *B.Pes.* 103b.

[197] *Gen.R.* 11,8; *Pes.R.* 23,6. In *B.Shab.* 119 the *shabbat* is called a 'bride'.

The *shabbat* is presented moreover as constitutive of Israel, for it increases their holiness.[198] According to later sources, the holiness of *shabbat*, of Israel, and of the Almighty are one and the same.[199] This suggests that the weekly observance of *shabbat* constitutes itself a practical, dynamic experience of the identity of Israel.

The festivals

Festivals are naturally associated with the *shabbat*,[200] and we may assume that they are experienced in much the same manner. They distinguish Israel from the nations: as we are told, Israel have their own festivals and despise non-Jewish ones (*Kalendae* and *Saturnalia*);[201] Jews and non-Jews do not celebrate the same occasions.[202]

Passover may relate to Jewish identity more than any other festival, as it celebrates the Exodus and thus, the origins of the people of Israel. Porton points out that an exceptionally long passage in the *Tosefta* is devoted to the Halakhic distinction between Jews and non-Jews with reference to the prohibitions of *hametz* (leaven) on Passover; he suggests that this expresses the specifically 'ethnic' character of this festival.[203]

The calendar

Rabbinic sources emphasize that the Jews structure their week around the *shabbat*, unlike non-Jewish systems of day-reckoning,[204] and that the nations reckon the year according to the solar cycle, whilst Israel follow the lunar cycle.[205]

The calendrical system manifests, in itself, the unique identity of Israel. It is based entirely on the reckoning of new moons, a procedure known as 'the sanctification of the month' (*kiddush haHodesh*) which is solely determined by a Jewish rabbinic court;[206] thus, if the Court

---

[198] *Mekh. Ki Tissa* 1.
[199] *Eliyahu R.* 24, p.133. The following blessing, listed in *T.Ber.* 3,15 (L: 3,13), may also evoke this notion: ". . . He sanctifies the *shabbat*, Israel, and the seasons".
[200] Together they form the second order of the *Mishna* (*Moed*).
[201] *Est.R.* 7,12.
[202] Except for that of rain-fall: *Gen.R.* 13,6; *Deut.R.* 7,7.
[203] G. Porton (1988), pp. 219–20, quoting *T.Pes.* 1,17–27 (L: 2,5–15). Porton also believes that the ruling in *T.YT* 2,6 that one may cook on festivals for a Jew but not for a non-Jew (or for dogs) reinforces, in his terms, "the ethnicity of the holidays" (pp. 213–4).
[204] *Mekh. Bahodesh* 7; *Pes.R.* 23,1.
[205] *Mekh. Bo* 1; *T.Suk.* 2,6; *B.Suk.* 29a; *Gen.R.* 6,3.
[206] *M.RH* 1,1–3,1 *passim*.

declares that today is the New Year, the Almighty informs his angels
to begin the proceedings of the day, "for so His sons have decreed"—
which, the *Talmud* adds, demonstrates the unique authority of Israel,
in contrast with all other nations.[207]

Again, we find an implicit affinity between the holiness of the calendar
and that of Israel: the *Midrash* explains that unless Israel 'sanctifies'
the new moon, it is not sanctified, for the Almighty has sanctified
Israel, and Israel in turn sanctify Him.[208] Elsewhere we hear that the
sanctification of the new moons in this world is comparable to the
sanctification of Israel in the world-to-come.[209] The calendar is thus
a projection, in the realm of *praxis*, of the holiness of Israel. Maintenance
of a distinct calendar is not merely a social or ethnic 'identity-marker',
but in fact a resolute, dynamic affirmation of Israel's unique identity
as a holy people.

Food, table and general manners
In spite of the fact that the Bible explicitly associates dietary laws
with Israel's distinction from the nations,[210] references to food as
constitutive of Israel's identity are seldom in rabbinic sources and often
no more than implicit. One *Midrash* states that Israel are distinguished
from the nations in that they cannot eat meat without properly
slaughtering the animal, whereas the nations just stab it and eat it.[211]
Israel worship one God and eat one food, whereas the nations differ
in the gods they worship and the foods they eat.[212] Exile is only exile
to the Jews, for unlike the non-Jews they are forbidden to eat the
bread and drink the wine of the peoples amongst whom they are
dispersed.[213] The distinguishing feature of the non-Jewish 'foreign
resident' is that he eats carrion.[214]

---

[207] *Y.RH* 1,3.

[208] *Ex.R.* 15,24.

[209] *PdRE* 51. Cf *T.Ber.* 3,15 (L: 3,13), quoted above (note 199).

[210] *Lev.*20:24–6; *Deut.*14:2,21. Dietary laws are referred to in IV*Macc.* 4:26 as
Ioudaismos; cf *Jubilees* 22:16: "separate yourself from the nations, and eat not with
them".

[211] *Tanh. Re'eh* 6.

[212] *Sifre Deut.* 354. In this passage the distinctiveness of Israel from the nations
lies in their unparalleled *unity*, rather than in their dietary laws.

[213] *Lam.R.* 1,28. For the nations, worldly pleasures such as food are considered
essential, because they cannot look forward to a reward in the world-to-come: *Num.R.*
21,20; *Tanh. Pinhas* 13.

[214] *Sifra Behar, parasha* 5,1 and *perek* 8,1; *Y.Yev.* 8,1; *B.AZ* 64b-65a; see p. 95.

Unlike the nations, Israel wash hands[215] and say blessings before eating.[216] During the meal they talk words of *Torah* (or: they say blessings and praises), whereas non-Jews talk about obscenities (or: about illicit sexual relations).[217]

A non-Jew "eases himself" (defecates) in the middle of the road, whereas a Jew does it by the side.[218]

4. CONCLUSION

The material we have examined suggests that through the body, the authors of our sources can experience themselves as being Jewish (and the nations as being non-Jewish) in a potent, holistic manner. This bodily experience is not only static, as in the experience of being circumcised, but also dynamic and performative, as in *Torah* learning and *shabbat* observance. In certain contexts, it becomes more appropriate for us to refer to Jewish identity not as a passive 'experience' but rather as a *practice*.[219]

We have also found that what distinguishes Israel from the nations, according to our sources, consists essentially of *religious* practices and observances. Without the *Torah*, indeed, there would be no difference between Israel and the nations. It is religious observance which endows Israel with the righteousness, holiness and perhaps affinity with angels which we have described already in the previous chapter as characteristic of the identity of Israel. Language and clothing, on the other hand, which are commonly associated with ethnicity in other cultures, are not (or hardly) presented as distinctive features of Israel;[220] this

---

[215] This is how an inn-keeper could tell whether his customers were Jewish or not: *Num.R.* 20,21; *Tanh. Balak* 15.

[216] In contrast with the nations: *Pes. dRK* 28,2; *Midrash Bayyom haShemini* (ed. Eisenstein).

[217] *B.Meg.* 12b (= *Est.R.* 3,13). Version in brackets: *Song R.* end.

[218] *B.Sanh.* 104b.

[219] Yet even as a *praxis*, Jewish identity appears in our sources as a finished and ready-made experience. "Israel" is 'already there'; although a subjective and dynamic experience, it is shared collectively and transmitted from generation to generation without apparently being subject to change, adaptation or variation. The scope for creativity within this experience—as indeed with many other aspects of rabbinic tradition—remains therefore substantially limited.

[220] On *clothing*, see above. The Hebrew *language* is nowhere presented as exclusive to Israel, although according to *PdRE* 24, it was specifically allocated to them. See *B.Sota* 36b and *Gen.R.* 89, according to which Pharaoh knew all the 70 languages of the nations, but did not know Hebrew—hence Joseph's superiority.

may be due to the fact that in early rabbinic sources, the religious significance of language and clothing is remarkably limited.[221] Thus, we may wish to define the rabbinic 'Israel' as an essentially *religious* group, characterized by its religion rather than by what may be termed its 'cultural ethnicity'.

However, this interpretation is problematic on a number of accounts. Firstly, it is unclear that the modern distinction between 'ethnicity' and 'religion' can be successfully applied to the context of early rabbinic writings. Secondly, this interpretation does not account for the fact that only a select number of 'religious' practices appear to embody the experience of Jewish identity. The dietary laws, for instance, are conspicuously absent in this context: as we have seen, the observance of dietary laws is rarely depicted in our sources as a *positive* experience of being Israel.[222] We may note, by contrast, that contemporary non-Jewish sources see the dietary laws as one of the most distinctive features of the Jewish people.[223]

I would suggest therefore that it is not 'religious' observances which are, as such, characteristic of Israel, but more specifically commandments of a *covenantal* nature. Indeed, each of the main constituents of Jewish identity which we have discussed, i.e. circumcision, *Torah* learning, and *shabbat*, are referred to in our sources as a *berit*, a covenant; the calendar, *tefillin*, and the commandments 'as a whole', are also associated, implicitly, with such a notion. More than cultural or religious identity-markers, these commandments are taken to represent and

---

[221] Although Hebrew is usually referred to as "the holy tongue" (e.g. *M.Yev.* 12,6; *M.Sot.* 7,2–4; 8,1; 9,1), most of the liturgy may be conducted in other, 'foreign' languages (*M.Sot.* 7,1; *M.Meg.* 2,1), and holy scrolls may be written in them (*M.Meg.* 1,8).

[222] Although such an experience is implicit, *a contrario*, in the rabbinic revulsion towards pork and non-Jewish food. See p. 78.

[223] As distinctive Jewish features, Graeco-Roman satirical sources emphasize especially abstention from pork, observance of *shabbat*, and image-less worship: cf Schürer III.1 p. 150–3 (see p. 76, n. 195). In *B.Meg.* 13b (= *Est.R.* 7,12) Haman is said to describe the Jews as a people "who (amongst other things) do not eat our food" (see also *Eliyahu R.* 27, p. 146 (already quoted): a non-Jew exclaimed, "When will I convert and be among Israel who eat nice food?"). M.D. Herr ("Anti-Semitism in the Roman Empire as seen in Rabbinic Literature" (Hebrew), in E.Z. Melamed (ed.), *Sefer Zikaron le-Binyamin De-Fries*, Jerusalem: Univ. of Tel Aviv Press, 1968–9, pp. 149–59) suggests that Haman's speech reflects Tacitus' account of the Jews, and shows the extent to which the Talmud was aware of anti-semitism in non-Jewish writings. Yet this awareness does not appear to have influenced the rabbinic experience of being Jewish, since to the authors of our sources, in this context, dietary laws are only of marginal importance.

embody a covenantal bond between the Almighty and Israel. Thus rather than a 'religious' group, the early rabbinic 'Israel' should be defined, in rabbinic terms, as a *covenantal* group, which perceives itself as belonging to the Almighty's covenant by observing a specific set of bodily, dynamic practices.

APPENDIX TO CHAPTERS I-II

ISRAEL IN SYMBOLIC IMAGERY

The symbolic imagery which is found to represent the notion of Israel may function in itself as a component of the experience of being Jewish. Symbols could be seen, indeed, as a relative embodiment or concretisation of this notion.[1] However, as we shall see, it is difficult to interpret these symbols and especially to assess their experiential significance. My inability to draw significant conclusions from this material has led me to present it in an appendix rather than in the main body of the chapters.

A. *Rabbinic sources*

In rabbinic sources I have encountered the following symbols of Israel:
- Animals: dove,[2] lamb,[3] small cattle,[4] wild animals,[5] bird,[6] worm.[7]
- Trees: vine,[8] vineyard,[9] olive,[10] date,[11] all kinds of beautiful trees.[12]
- Produce: olive oil,[13] wheat,[14] fig,[15] nut.[16]

---

[1] See section I.4, and beginning of chapter II. In this respect this appendix pertains both to chapters I and II.

[2] *B.Ber.* 53b; *B.Shab.* 49a & 130a; *Ex.R.* 21,5; *Song R.* 1,15,2; 1,15,4; 4,1,2; 6,9,5; *Tanh. Beshalah* 23; *Tanh. Tetzave* 5. As opposed to the raven who is a liar: *B.Git.* 45a. On the raven, cf *Y.Taan.* 1,6; *Lev.R.* 18,1.

[3] *Lev.R.* 4,6; *Pes.R.* 9,2.

[4] *Ex.R.* 24,3; 34,3.

[5] *B.Sot.* 11b; *Ex.R.* 1,16; etc.

[6] *Ex.R.* 5,12; *Tanh. Shemot* 29.

[7] *Tanh. Beshalah* 9.

[8] *B.Hul.* 92a; *Ex.R.* 44,1; *Lev.R.* 36,2; *Tanh. Vayehi* 10. Cf *Targum Onkelos ad Gen.* 49:11.

[9] *Ex.R.* 34,3; *Lev.R.* 32,1; *Song R.* 7,13.

[10] *B.Men.* 53b; *Ex.R.* 36,1.

[11] *Gen.R.* 41,1; *Num.R.* 3,1.

[12] *Ex.R.* 36,1; *Est.R.* 9,2.

[13] *B.Men.* 53b; *Ex.R.* 36,1; *Deut.R.* 7,3; *Tanh. Tavo* 3; *Song R.* 1,3,2. Cf *Tanh. Tetzave* 5; *Pes. dRK* 21,4.

[14] *Num.R.* 1,4; *Song R.* 7,3,3; *Midrash Tehillim* 2,12; *Pes.R.* 10,3.

[15] *Gen.R.* 46,1.

[16] *Song R.* 6,11; *Pes.R.* 11,2.

– Miscellaneous: sand,[17] dust,[18] stars,[19] moon,[20] moonlight,[21] fire,[22] lily,[23] incense,[24] bride,[25] female.[26]

Exegesis and general significance
Many of these symbols are found explicitly in the Bible;[27] others are inferred from scripture through exegetical means. In many cases, therefore, their occurrence in rabbinic sources is dictated by no more than exegetical necessity. Since their relevance is restricted to the interpretation of particular scriptural passages, these symbols are unlikely to affect the *general* rabbinic perception of the identity of Israel.

Some symbols, however, appear to transcend the limitations of scriptural exegesis. The dove, vine(yard), olive oil, wheat, and stars, are frequently repeated in our sources, which suggests that they are generally associated with the notion of Israel, without reference to any specific verse or exegesis; sometimes, indeed, the scriptural source of these symbols is unmentioned and apparently taken for granted. In some sources (olive oil in particular, as we shall see), the analogy between the symbol and Israel is elaborately explained. It would appear, therefore, that these symbols participate significantly in the rabbinic perception and experience of Israel.[28]

The dove and olive oil
Appreciation of the symbolic significance of the dove and olive oil would require a thorough, phenomenological study of these items as they are treated in Aggadic and Halakhic sources.

The *Midrash* explains that in the same way as doves are faithful to each other and do not mate with more than one partner,[29] so

---

[17] *Ex.R.* 1,29; *Num.R.* 2,17; *Tanh. Shemot* 9; *Tanh. Ki Tissa* 9.
[18] *Gen.R.* 41,9; *Num.R.* 2,13. When they are unworthy: *Sifre Deut.* 47; *B.Meg.* 16a.
[19] *B.Ber.* 56b (interpretation of dreams); *Sifre Deut.* 306 (end); *Num.R.* 2,17. When they are worthy: *Sifre Deut.* 47; *B.Meg.* 16a.
[20] *Gen.R.* 6,3; cf *PdRE* 51.
[21] *B.Ber. ib.*
[22] *Avot dRN (B)* 43; *Midrash Minian* (ed.Wertheimer) 2,3.
[23] *Lev.R.* 23, 3–6.
[24] *Tanh. Tetzave* 15.
[25] *Tanh. Ki Tissa* 18; *Pes.R.* 38,3; *Pes. dRK* 22,5.
[26] In this world—and male in the world-to-come: *Song R.* 1,5 (s.v. *shehora*), 3.
[27] E.g. lamb: *Jer.* 50:17. Small cattle: *Ez.* 34 *passim*. Sand and stars: *Gen.* 22:17. Dust: *Gen.* 28:14, etc.
[28] The same applies to the pig as a symbol of Rome, see p. 57.
[29] See *B.Eruv.* 100b.

Israel are faithful to the Almighty, and the Almighty to them.[30] This observation, whether true or not, was shared by others in Antiquity: according to Aelian, both ring-doves (*phattai*) and turtle-doves (*trugones*) marry and remain faithful to each other.[31] This explains why our sources would associate the dove with Israel's covenantal relationship with the Almighty, to which we have referred.

Among the numerous meanings attached to the symbolism of olive oil, the *Midrash* mentions that Israel bring light to the world just as olive oil.[32] If we consider that the main uses of olive oil in Antiquity were lighting and anointing,[33] it is likely that this symbol of Israel would have evoked to the authors of our sources the familiar experience of light and, perhaps, bodily cleanliness (though I have found no reference to the latter in our sources). But whilst olive oil was widely produced and distributed throughout the Mediterranean in Late Antiquity, in Babylonia olives could not be grown; consequently, in Babylonia olive oil would have been an unusual, exotic commodity, with very different familiar associations.[34] Thus, a comparison between Babylonian and Palestinian sources on the symbolism of olive oil, if at all possible, may yield some significant conclusions.

---

[30] And similarly, perhaps, that both the dove and Israel are modest: *Song R.* 1,15,2; 1,15,4; 4,1,2; *Midrash Shir* 6,9.

[31] Aelian, *Hist. Anim.*, III.44 (ring-doves) and X.33 (turtle-doves; I am assuming that these species correspond to the dove (*yona*) of rabbinic texts). In VI.45 Aelian describes the hatred between ravens and turtle-doves. Rabbinic sources tend to denigrate the raven (cf *B.Git.* 45a; *Y.Taan.* 1,6; see however *Lev.R.* 18,1) because of its poor performance in the Noah episode, but there is no suggestion that it should be regarded as a symbol of the nations.

[32] *Song R.* 1,3,2.

[33] (I.e., body cleansing). This is implied in *M.Shab.* 8,1; cf *B.Ber.* 35b–36a; *B.Shab.* 40b; *B.Yoma* 76b. See also the *Greek Anthology* 14,37 (transl. W.R. Paton, London: Loeb, 1926, vol. 5, pp. 44–5), where olive oil is referred to as "light for the lamp, cure for men, protection in contests", but not as food to be consumed (courtesy of Lin Foxhall). In rabbinic sources olive oil is only occasionally referred to as food, e.g. spread on bread or mixed with vegetable stock (*B.Ber.* 35b–36a; cf *B.Pes.* 39b; *pace* Hamel (*op.cit.* p.10) who misinterprets *T.Suk.* 2,3 (cf *T.Eduyot* 2,2; *B.Yev.* 15b) which actually refer to whole olives (maybe pickled, cf *M.Ter.* 2,6)). In the Temple cult, however, the bread offering was prepared with oil; furthermore, "the remaining oil is to be eaten by the priests" (*M.Men.* 6,3).

[34] Cf J.N. Postgate & M.A. Powell (eds.), *Bulletin on Sumerian Agriculture*, vol. II, Cambridge U.K.: Faculty of Oriental Studies, 1985, pp. 39–66, 153–8.

Concerning R. Tarfon's ruling that only olive oil may be used for lighting *shabbat* lamps, the *Babylonian Talmud* (*B.Shab.* 26a) asks what should be done in Babylon, Media, Alexandria, and Cappadocia, where olive oil cannot be obtained.

B. *Archaeological sources*

Material culture represents the *milieu* within which Jewish identity is experienced in first instance as a bodily reality. It is fair to assume, moreover, that bodily experience is often better expressed through material culture than it is through the written word. Archaeological evidence may provide us, therefore, with some insights into the rabbinic experience of Jewish identity, which our literary sources do not— and could not—yield.

I will restrict myself to Jewish iconography, because its interpretation, in this context, remains relatively the easiest. A number of motifs referring to Jewish ritual recur in this period in Palestine as well as in the Diaspora: most common is the seven-branched *menora* (candelabrum); other motifs comprise the *lulav* (palm) with the other three species (citron, myrtle, willow), the *shofar* (horn), and the incense shovel (the latter belonging exclusively to the then defunct Temple ritual). In Palestine they are found on coins[35] and in various sites such as Caesarea, the synagogue of Hammat-Tiberias, the catacombs of Beth Shearim, and elsewhere.[36] Their pervasiveness throughout the Jewish world suggests that they were more than purely ornamental. It is generally assumed that they served the Jews as symbolic, pictorial expressions of Jewish identity, hence as universal identity-markers in the Ancient world.[37]

Yet in rabbinic literature, these motifs (especially the *menora*) are never mentioned as symbols of Jewish identity.[38] This lack of corroboration requires perhaps an explanation.[39] It is interesting to note that similar cases of dissonance between literary and pictorial expression

---

[35] In so far as the last Jewish coins were minted during the Bar-Kokhba revolt (132–5CE), they belong to an earlier period than that which we are considering. The *Tosefta* does refer to the contemporary use of Bar-Kokhba coins (*T.Ma'aser Sheni* 1,6; cf *Y.ib.* 1,2; *B.BK* 97b), which may suggest that they were still in circulation in the third century; however this reference may be no more than theoretical.

[36] See E.R. Goodenough, *Jewish symbols in the Graeco-Roman period*, (13 vols.), New York: Bollingen, 1953–68.

[37] V. Klagsbald argues however (p. 438) that in an all-Jewish necropolis such as Beth Shearim, the *menora* must have been more than a symbol of Jewish identity; other possible meanings are thus suggested ("La symbolique dans l'art juif", in *Revue des études juives* 144, 1985, pp. 408–38).

[38] The *lulav* however symbolises the victory of Israel over the nations (*Midrash Tehillim* 17,1; 118,1), and the four species bound together represent the unity of the Jewish people (*Tanh. Emor* 17).

[39] There is no reason to suggest that early rabbinic authorities did not use or approve of these motifs. They are found in areas which the rabbis probably frequented

can be found in Judaism today. Moses' Tablets of the Law are described in Talmudic sources as deep and with square angles,[40] whilst they are traditionally depicted in Jewish (also in Christian) late mediaeval and modern iconography as shallow rectangles, rounded in a semi-circle at the top; I am not aware of any rabbinic explanation of this diverging pictorial representation. Another case is the Star of David (*magen David*), which has been used since the late 18th century as a symbol of Jewish identity in secular (political) contexts as well as in religious settings (e.g. in synagogues), but which is nowhere accounted for in contemporary rabbinic literature.[41]

These cases demonstrate, I think, that pictorial symbols can be effective without being explained or even mentioned in writing. This is why archaeology and rabbinic literature do not necessarily meet. Clearly the experience of Jewish identity went well beyond what is depicted in early rabbinic writings. The case of the *menora*, as an alternative but maybe central, experiential feature of Jewish identity, alerts us to the limitations of our study which has to rely, in its greater part, on literary evidence alone.

---

and may have even sponsored: e.g. the synagogue of Ḥammat-Tiberias and the catacombs of Beth Shearim. Admittedly, a relatively small number of *menorot* was found in Beth Shearim—only 14 in total—of which 9 were found on objects which according to N. Avigad (*Beth She'arim: report on the excavations during 1953–58—vol. III: the catacombs 12–23*, transl. P. Shagiv, New Brunswick: Rutgers Press, 1976, ch. 6) must have been imported from the Diaspora; other Jewish symbols are equally rare. Avigad argues quite convincingly that the Jews of Palestine were not accustomed to using these symbols in burial sites, unlike Diaspora Jews who used them extensively (e.g. in the catacombs of Rome). It does not follow, however, that Palestinian Jews (or indeed their rabbis) did not attach importance to these identity markers, as indeed they are commonly found in Palestine in synagogues, on coins, and on various inscriptions.

[40] *Y.Shek.* 6,1; *Y.Sot.* 8,3; *Y.Taan.* 4,5; *B.Ned.* 38a; *B.BB* 14a: each tablet was 6 handbreaths long, 6 (or 3) wide, and 3 deep, thus neatly fitting into the Ark. See G.B. Sarfatti, "The Table of the Covenant as a Symbol of Judaism", in *Tarbiz* 29(4), July 1960, pp. 370–393 (on Talmudic sources, p. 372).

[41] Although it does appear in mediaeval Kabbalistic works. See Gershom Scholem, "The Star of David: History of a Symbol", in *id.*, *The Messianic Idea in Judaism*, London: Allen and Unwin, 1971, pp. 257–81; and *id.*, in *Encyclopedia Judaica*, s.v. *magen David*.

CHAPTER THREE

THE PEOPLE OF ISRAEL
CENTRE AND PERIPHERY

Judaism was divided into seven sects: . . . (Sadducees, Scribes, Pharisees, Hemerobaptists, Nasaraeans, Ossaeans, Herodians) —Epiphanius, *Panarion* I,14–20.

If one would rightly consider it, one would not admit that the Sadducees, or similar sects of Genistae, Meristae, Galileans, Hellenists, Pharisees, Baptists, are Jews—Justin Martyr, *Dialogue with Trypho*, 80.

1. INTRODUCTION: LINEAL IDENTITY AND THE 'PERIPHERY'

Having discussed in previous chapters the distinctive features of Israel and of Jewish identity, we may now ask who are the people whom our sources call 'Israel', and with whom they identify as belonging to a single collectivity.

Jewish identity, or the Halakhic status of an 'Israel' (singular), is in first instance hereditarily transmitted. According to the *Mishna*, transmission of Jewish identity is exclusively matrilineal;[1] but this view was occasionally challenged by outsiders. We are told, indeed, that Jacob from Navurai, a self-styled rabbi who is called elsewhere a heretic,[2] taught in Tyre that fish requires ritual slaughter, and that the son of a Jew and a non-Jewess is Jewish and should be circumcised even on *shabbat*. He was arguing, in other words, that Jewish identity was patrilineally transmitted.[3] But R. Ḥaggai swiftly refuted him, and flogged him for his erroneous teachings.[4] This much-repeated story

---

[1] *M.Kid.* 3,12; *M.Bikkurim* 1,4; *B.Yev.* 17a; *ib.* 23a; *B.Kid.* 68b; *Y.Yev.* 2,6; minor tractate *Gerim* 3,7; etc. See Shaye J.D. Cohen, "The origins of the matrilineal principle in Rabbinic law", in *AJS Review*, 10 (1985), pp. 19–53. He notes (pp. 36–7) that except for two Midrashic passages (*Sifra Emor* 14,1, which appears to deny matrilineal transmission, and *Avot dRN*, 16,2 which implies patrilineal transmission), rabbinic sources unanimously accept this principle. Cohen argues (see "The Matrilineal Principle in Historical Perspective", in *Judaism* 34, 1985, pp. 5–13) that matrilineality was only introduced by the rabbis after the Bar-Kokhba revolt; but L. Schiffman ("Jewish identity and Jewish descent", *ib.* pp. 78–84) disagrees.
[2] A *min*: *Eccl.R.* 7,26,3; see also *Y.Shab.* 19,5; *Y.Bikkurim* 3,3; *Y.Ber.* 9,1.
[3] See however Shaye Cohen, *op.cit.*, for a possible alternative interpretation.
[4] *Y.Yev.* 2,6; *Y.Kid.* 3,12; *Gen.R.* 7,2; *Num.R.* 19,3; *Eccl.R.* 7,23,3–4; *Tanh. Ḥukkat* 6.

illustrates to what extent, among common Jews, basic notions of Jewish identity and kinship could still remain unclear and open to discussion;[5] it shows simultaneously the determination of the rabbis in our sources to uphold the Halakhic principle of matrilineality without equivocation.[6]

The issue however is not so simple. Firstly, a non-Jew by birth may acquire Jewish identity by converting. Although many conditions are attached to the procedure of conversion, I will argue that the status acquired through a valid conversion is as irreversible as lineal status acquired by birth. Nonetheless, we shall have to inquire whether the identity of convert is equivalent in all respects to that of an 'Israel'.

Secondly, we must consider the implications of apostasy. Indeed, I have defined Jewish identity (in the second chapter in particular) in terms of a set of practices and moral virtues to which Israel adhere. The question arises, therefore, as to the status of a Jew by birth who forsakes these distinctive features: does he remain an 'Israel', and if so, in what respect can he experience the identity of Israel?

We may then extend this question to the bulk of the Jewish-born people, whose general standards of religious observance may not have satisfied the Halakhic demands of 'our' rabbis: was their identity, as Israel, in any way affected?

By concentrating on the 'peripheral' sections of the Jewish people, the ambiguity of the boundaries between Jew and non-Jew will be fully explored. We will have to ask, in the final section of this chapter, how the existence of these 'grey areas' might affect the rabbinic distinction between self and other, and the rabbinic conception of a single homogenous Israel, with which, as we have seen,[7] the authors of rabbinic writings claim to identify as a collectivity.

2. CONVERTS

A. Regular conversion

The procedure of conversion
Any non-Jew may undergo a process of conversion. Although our

---

[5] On similar uncertainty in the first century CE, see M. Goodman, "Identity and Authority in Ancient Judaism", in *Judaism* 39(2), Spring 1990, pp. 192–201.

[6] In this respect Israel are again implicitly contrasted with the 70 nations, whose nationality is transmitted patrilineally (i.e. before the nations were blurred by Sennacherib, presumably—see pp. 13–4): *Y.Yev.* 8,3; *B.Yev.* 78b; *B.Kid.* 67a-b.

[7] Section I.2.B.

sources do not advocate active proselytising,[8] they welcome any non-Jew wishing to convert "for the sake of Heaven" (i.e. not for ulterior motives).[9] The Almighty, likewise, does not reject any prospective convert;[10] He seeks in particular for "righteous non-Jews" to convert.[11]

The Talmudic procedure of conversion has been discussed in detail by Shaye Cohen.[12] It consists basically of verbal acceptance of the *Torah*, followed by circumcision (for males), immersion in a *mikve* (ritual bath),[13] and sacrifice (not applicable after the destruction of the Temple). The reason for this ritual is explained as follows:

> Rabbi says: Just as your fathers did not enter the covenant except by means of circumcision, immersion, and the acceptance of sacrificial blood, so it is the same with the converts.[14]

Thus the convert re-enacts the ritual which Israel is said to have performed at Mount Sinai, so as to enter himself the covenant with the Almighty and thus become an Israel.

The covenant at Mount Sinai demanded above all acceptance of the *Torah*; consequently, the *Talmud* treats it as an essential feature of conversion. The convert is taught only a few laws of the *Torah*, but his commitment to the observance of *all* the commandments is thoroughly investigated.[15] If he was fully committed with the exception of a single command (even, according to some, a minor point from the detailed laws of the Scribes), his conversion cannot be valid.[16]

His *motives* are subject to similar scrutiny. If he wishes to convert out of love (for a person, e.g. in view of marriage), or in order to

---

[8] As convincingly argued by Martin Goodman, "Proselytising in Rabbinic Judaism", in *JJS* 40:2, Autumn 1989, pp. 175–85. See for instance *Num.R.* 10,4, where proselytism is rejected as being a form of intermarriage.

[9] *Mekh. Yitro Amalek* 1; *Lev.R.* 2,9. Shammai, however, was renowned for having been less welcoming then Hillel: *B.Shab.* 31a.

[10] *Ex.R.* 19,4.

[11] Only when Israel are worthy: *Y.Ber.* 2,8.

[12] Shaye J.D. Cohen, "The Rabbinic conversion ceremony", in *JJS* 41:2, Autumn 1990, pp. 177–203. The most comprehensive account of this procedure in early rabbinic sources is found in *B.Yev.* 47a-b (paralleled in minor tractate *Gerim*, on converts). See also L.H. Schiffman, *Who was a Jew?*. I shall not consider what conversion may have consisted of in the pre-Talmudic period, as this is beyond my scope (see introduction).

[13] Whether circumcision or immersion, or indeed both, constitute the decisive factor in conversion is disputed (*Y.Kid.* 3,12; *B.Yev.* 46a; minor tractate *Gerim*, 1,6); see Schiffman, *Who was a Jew?*, pp. 32–6.

[14] *B.Ker.* 9a; *Sifre Num.* 108; *Gerim* 2,5.

[15] Cf *B.Yev.* 47a-b; *Gerim*, 1.

[16] *T.Demai* 2,5; *B.Bekh.* 30b; *Tanh. Vayikra* 2.

eat from the (Jewish) king's table, he is not accepted; the same applies
to those who convert out of fear, such as the *Kutim* who were afraid
of lions,[17] and the Judaizers at the time of Esther's and Mordecai's
victory.[18] Whether they can be regarded *a posteriori* as valid converts
is however a matter of dispute.[19] Tractate *Gerim* concludes: "whoever
does not convert for the sake of Heaven is not a convert".[20]

Converts as 'Israel'
Once this procedure is over, the convert (*ger*, or *ger tzedek*) becomes
a new creature, "similar to a newborn infant"; his previous, non-Jewish
kinship ties are completely severed.[21] He is now included in the category
of 'Israel',[22] and is treated as "an Israel in all respects".[23] As a Jew,
he is now subject to all the commandments, as emphasized by the
Midreshei halakha: "the convert and the Jewish-born are equal regarding
all the commandments in the *Torah*".[24]

The *Midreshei halakha* appear to contradict themselves when they
say elsewhere that wherever scripture addresses itself with a commandment to 'Israel', this does not include converts; therefore another
exegetical inference is "necessary" so as to include them[25] (for instance,
converts are to be inferred from the more inclusive term *adam* (man)[26]).
However, these exegetical exercises do not imply that converts are
not Israel. These *Midrashim* assume all along that converts must be
included in the commandment, which is why it is *"necessary"* for them
to seek for another inference. Their insistence on inferring converts
from a separate source, rather than from the term 'Israel', is simply
to prevent anyone from claiming, against the principle enunciated
above, that converts are not subject to the commandments. If anything,

---

[17] See below.
[18] *Est.* 8:17—*Y.Kid.* 4,1; *Gerim* 1,7.
[19] *Y.Kid.* 4,1; *B.Yev.* 24b. The latter favours the view that they are valid converts.
A classification of converts according to the purity of their original motives is established
in *Eliyahu R.* 27 (p. 146) as follows: "some converts are like our father Abraham;
some are like donkeys; and some, like total non-Jews" (the latter eventually lapse
and return to their old ways). On this comparison with donkeys and its sexual
connotations, see above p. 39.
[20] *Gerim* 1,7.
[21] *B.Yev.* 22a; 48b; 62a; 97b; *B.Bekh.* 47a.
[22] For instance, in the terminology of oaths: *T.Ned.* 2,4.
[23] *B.Yev.* 47b.
[24] *Mekh. Bo* 15; *Sifre Num.* 71; *ib.* 109.
[25] *Tzarikh lehavi et haGerim*: e.g. *Mekh. Bo* 10; *Sifre Num.* 111. For an extensive list
of such passages see *Encyclopedia Talmudit*, vol.6, s.v. *ger*, pp. 254–6.
[26] *Sifre Num.* 39; *Sifra Vayikra* 2,3.

therefore, they are attempting to prove through exegetical means that Jewish-born and converts are equal before the law, and in this respect that converts are actually full members of Israel.[27]

Other sources emphasize at length the identity of converts with Israel.[28] Just as Israel, circumcision distinguishes the converts from the non-Jews.[29] Just as Israel, converts enjoy the exclusive love[30] and protection of the Almighty, hence:

> Whoever perverts judgement and turns the verdict against a convert, it is as though he is turning it against the Almighty.[31]
> Converts are dear, for they are always given the same names as Israel.[32]
> Converts are essential like Israel.[33]
> "Your wife is like a vine" (*Psalms* 128:3)—(this means), a (woman) convert is like an Israel (i.e. a Jewish woman).[34]

The possibility of conversion is explained in a variety of ways. Typically, it is the "righteous non-Jews"—i.e. who display qualities intrinsic to Israel—who make the decision to convert.[35] The *Babylonian Talmud* maintains that the *mazal* (fate, or possibly 'soul') of all future converts was already present at Mount Sinai, together with Israel;[36] they were also included in the covenant in the plains of Moab, prior to Moses' death.[37]

---

[27] See B.J. Bamberger, *Proselytism in the Talmudic period*, New York: Ktav, 1968 (1939). An exception to this principle is found however in *B.Yev.* 101b (and in Rashba's version of *B.Kid.* 14a) according to which a court of converts may not conduct the ceremony of *halitza* because converts are not included in the verse (*Deut.* 25:10) referring to "Israel".

[28] By stating, for instance, that as soon as Ruth decides to convert the Bible treats her as equal to Naomi: *Ruth R.* 3,5.

[29] *Ex.R.* 19,4.

[30] *Mekh. Nezikin* 18; *Num.R.* 8,2; *Gerim* 4,3.

[31] *B.Hag.* 5a. This echoes similar references to Israel, quoted above in pp. 41–3.

[32] *Mekh. Nezikin* 18; *Num.R.* 8,2 ("they are comparable to Israel"); *Gerim* 4,3. The expression *havivim* ('dear') is usually attributed to Israel (see pp. 248–9); in this passage, it is clearly used to draw a parallelism between the converts and Israel. See also *Ruth R.* 3,5.

[33] *Ikar keYisrael*: *Lev.R.* 1,2; *Num.R.* 8,1.

[34] *Num.R.* 8,9. Israel is commonly compared to the vine: see appendix to previous chapter. As to the comparison of converts to 'your wife', we may see this *Midrash* as being addressed to men who had married convert wives; alternatively, the *Midrash* may be implying that in a collective sense, converts are the wife of Israel.

[35] Cf *Y.Ber.* 2,8 (quoted above) and p. 30.

[36] *B.Shab.* 146a.

[37] *B.Shevu.* 39a, on *Deut.* 29:14.

Lineage and ethnic identity

In certain contexts the convert is distinguished from the Jewish-born as having inferior status.[38] In the liturgy, he cannot refer to the Patriarchs as "our forefathers".[39] More importantly, his lineage is inferior to that of most Jewish-born, as according to the Mishnaic scale of lineages (*yoḥasin*—in decreasing order):

> Priest (*cohen*), Levite, 'Israel', impaired priest, convert, freedman, bastard, *natin* (Gibeonite), 'silent' (of unknown fatherhood), foundling.[40]

This scale of lineages, which regulates the laws of marriage, is of extreme importance: a large section of tractate *Kiddushin* is devoted to it. Converts themselves, moreover, are not unaware of their lineal inferiority. According to the *Babylonian Talmud*, one non-Jew asked to convert on the condition that he should be made High Priest.[41] It may be in order to comfort the converts that later *Midrashim* stress the possibility for their grandchildren (from a daughter) to be born as priests;[42] they argue, moreover, that converts who occupy themselves with *Torah* are equivalent to high priests,[43] and they promise that in the future-to-come converts will become priests.[44]

Nevertheless, inferior lineage does not appear to affect the convert's identity as 'Israel'. All the lineages listed by the *Mishna*, up to and including foundlings, are considered to belong to 'Israel'.[45] As the *Mishna* goes on to explain, this lineage scale affects exclusively the right of

---

[38] This may be implicit, for instance, in the usage of the *kal va-ḥomer* (argument *a minori*) from converts to Jewish-born and vice-versa in *Num.R.* 5,9 and in *B.Shab.* 31a (= *Avot dRN* 15,3) respectively.

[39] *M.Bikkurim* 1,4.

[40] *M.Kid.* 4,1. In this context 'Israel' is a technical term referring to a patrilineal sub-group within the ethnic people of 'Israel' (in the common wider sense). On this narrow usage of the term 'Israel', see J. Neusner, *op.cit.* 1989, pp. 56–7.

[41] *B.Shab.* 31a; *Avot dRN* 15,3. Priesthood is not only at the top of the lineage scale, but also a prestigious title which the people of Israel as a whole enjoy (see *Sifre Num.* 119; *B.Zev.* 19a, quoting *Ex.* 19:6, above-quoted in section I.3.B; *Avot dRN ib.*).

[42] *Ex.R.* 27,5; *Num.R.* 8,9. A woman convert herself may not marry a priest (*M.Kid.* 4,1), and it is debated whether her daughter may; all agree, however, that the daughter of a man convert (and of a Jewish-born woman) may marry a priest (*M.Kid.* 4,7; see the conclusion of *B.Kid.* 78a-b). Therefore, since the lineage of priesthood is patrilineally transmitted, only the grandchildren of converts can be born priests. R.Yehoshua saved Aquilas (the convert) from lapsing and returning to his old ways, by assuring him that if a non-Jew converts "for the sake of Heaven", he deserves that his daughters be married into priesthood: *Eccl.R.* 7,8.

[43] *Tanḥ. Vayak'hel* 8.

[44] *Ex.R.* 19,4.

[45] *Freedmen* (formerly non-Jewish slaves) are Israel: see below pp. 96–7. The *Gibeonites*

marriage: it prevents, for instance, a convert from marrying a priest.[46] In the *Babylonian Talmud*, some rabbis go further and recommend all Jewish-born not to marry a woman convert.[47] According to the *Talmud*, moreover, lineage also carries 'spiritual' advantages: the Almighty only rests his Presence among the families of Israel with lineage, whom He originally elected (whereas converts needed first to approach Him); in this respect Israel (i.e. the Jewish-born) are at a higher level (*ma'ala yetera*) than converts.[48] But—I would stress—it is hardly suggested that because of these 'lineal' limitations, the identity of converts as 'Israel' should be, in any other respect, impaired.

Lapses and shortcomings
Converts are occasionally upheld as examples to be emulated;[49] but they also display shortcomings. They are not as versed in the details of the commandments as are the Jewish-born.[50] Though fully converted, the stigma of *avoda zara* can linger on among them for generations.[51] Long after her conversion, Ruth needed (before she met Boaz) to clean herself from the "filth of *avoda zara* upon her".[52] Even after his conversion, Jethro was upset at the downfall of Egypt; to which the *Talmud* remarks that non-Jews should not be spurned in the presence of a convert, even (of descendants of converts) until the 10th generation (*B.Sanh.* 94a).

Above all, converts are subject to the temptation of lapsing and returning to their old ways.[53] This temptation may be due to fear or social pressure.[54] The *Palestinian Talmud* tells us of the difficulties

---

are considered to be valid, albeit mediocre, converts (*gerim gerurim*); although II.*Sam.* 21:2 refers to them as "not among the children of Israel", the *Talmudim* interpret this verse as only meaning that they were excluded, by special decree, from "adhering" to the Jewish-born through marriage: *Y.Kid.* 4,1; *Y.Sanh.* 6,7; *B.Yev.* 79a; *Num.R.* 8,4; *Midrash Tehillim* 1,2 and 17, end. *Foundlings* are "Israel", provided they were found in a Jewish town: *M.Makhshirin* 2,7. On *bastards*, however, see *Targum Jonathan ad Zekh.*9:6 (also in *B.Kid.* 72b) which translates *mamzer* (lit. 'bastard') as "resembling a foreigner", implying at least that the bastard is somewhat akin to the non-Jew.

[46] *M.Kid.* 4,1.
[47] *B.Ber.* 8b.
[48] *B.Kid.* 70b.
[49] *Lev.R.* 2,9; *Num.R.* 5,9.
[50] *B.Yev.* 48b.
[51] *B.Kid.* 75a.
[52] *Ruth R.* 5,12; what this exactly entailed is not explained.
[53] This is apparently the meaning of the frequent expression: *suro ra* (*Mekh. Nezikin* 18; *B.BM* 60a; *Gerim* 4,2; etc.).
[54] Cf *B.Git.* 45b.

experienced by an astrologer who had to abandon, after his conversion, his former trade.[55] Even such a distinguished convert as Aquilas came close, on one occasion, to returning to his old ways.[56] Consequently, it is the converts from Egypt who are blamed for having made the Golden Calf and incited the Jewish-born to worship it.[57] In a later *Midrash*, we are told that converts were once found to be eating on *Yom Kippur*, and consuming leaven on Passover; as soon as they were discovered, they decided to return to their old ways; whereupon the *Midrash* remarks: "do not trust the convert, even after the 22nd generation"[58] (according to another source, for 7 generations a convert cannot be trusted not to have returned to his old ways[59]).

Again, the convert's tendency to lapse does not impair his ethnic identity as Israel. The *Talmudim* rule indeed that a convert who returns to his old ways receives the status of an apostate Israel.[60]

At worst, therefore, his tendency to lapse is considered a liability to Israel, which explains Rabbi Ḥelbo's well-known saying: "converts are as difficult to Israel as leprosy".[61] The *Babylonian Talmud* treats the converts with suspicion: it wonders whether their motives were indeed sincere, and why they waited so long to convert; it also suspects them of acting out of fear rather than out of love.[62] If a convert is suspected of (transgressing) a single commandment, he must be suspected of (transgressing) the whole *Torah*.[63]

On the other hand, the convert's tendency to lapse is met by our sources with sensitivity. This is why, they say, God commanded Israel

---

[55] *Y.Shab.* 6,9.

[56] *Gen.R.* 70,5; *Eccl.R.* 7,8 (other cases are also mentioned).

[57] *Lev.R.* 27,8; *Pes. dRK* 9,7.

[58] *Pes.R.* 22,5.

[59] *PdRE* 28 (ed. Higger).

[60] As we shall see in section III.3.A, a Jew who apostatizes retains forever his identity as Israel. The same applies to the lapsing convert: *B.Yev.* 47b (hence he retains the ability of marrying a Jewish woman); cf *B.Bekh.* 30b. He is called 'your enemy', but one is still obliged to return his lost property: *Mekh. Kaspa* 2. He is automatically classified as a (Jewish) *min* (heretic), the worst form of apostate (see below), except if it is known that he lapsed out of fear; in which case, his inner beliefs have remained unsullied, and he may be trusted to write holy scrolls with the right intention: *Y.Git.* 4,6; *Y.AZ* 2,2; *B.Git.* 45b.

[61] *B.Yev.* 47b; *ib.* 109; *B.Kid.* 70b; *B.Nida* 13b. Converts are also a hindrance to the coming of the Messiah: minor tractate *Kalla R.* 2, end. *B.Yev.* (*ib.*) takes R. Helbo's statement as an attack on those who allow non-Jews to convert; but see E.E. Urbach, 1975, pp. 549–553.

[62] *B.Yev.* 48b: their trials and tribulations constitute a punishment for these shortcomings.

[63] *B.Bekh.* 30b.

to look after the convert[64] and not to afflict him, lest he returns to his evil ways;[65] for the same reason, the rabbis granted the convert some dispensations regarding laws of patrilineal inheritance.[66] And the *Midrash* adds:

> In the same way as he loves you, so you, show your love to him.[67]

Conclusion

The shortcomings of the convert do not appear to affect, in any of our sources, the integrity of his Jewish identity. Rabbinic sources emphasize in many places that a valid convert becomes irreversibly "Israel, in all respects". Although originally outsiders, the converts are thus no longer, in any way, at the 'periphery' of Israel.

Yet in the sub-sections that follow, I shall examine special categories of converts—residents, slaves and Samaritans—which do not conform to the standard model of conversion and are thus considered peripheral to Israel, if not totally excluded.

B. *Residents and slaves*

Ger toshav

According to the *Babylonian Talmud*, the *ger toshav* ('foreign resident') is a non-Jew who formally undertakes (according to R. Meir) not to worship *avoda zara*, or (according to the Sages) to observe the seven Noahide laws,[68] or even (according to others) to observe all the commandments with the exception of dietary prohibitions.[69] Unlike the regular 'convert' (the *ger* or *ger tzedek*), there is no suggestion that he may become thereby an 'Israel'. Both *Talmudim* concur that he

---

[64] *Mekh. Nezikin* 18; *Num.R.* 8,2; *Gerim* 4,2.

[65] *B.BM* 60a; *Gerim* 4,2. There is the story of a barber who had killed scores of Jews before converting; when this was found out, "they prayed and eventually he returned to his old ways" (*Y.AZ* 2,2). He could not have lost, as a result, his Jewish status (for according to the same Talmudic passage, conversion is irreversible), but at least the Jews were rid of his unpleasant company. This is one of the rare passages where an attempt is made to squeeze a convert out of the Jewish fold.

[66] *B.AZ* 64a; *B.Kid.* 17b.

[67] *Eliyahu R.* 27, p. 146.

[68] See section V.1.B.

[69] Specifically, the prohibition of eating carrion: *B.AZ* 64b-65a. According to minor tractate *Gerim*, 3,1, the latter view is R. Yehuda's. Cf *Y.Yev.* 8,1; *Sifra Behar, parasha* 5,1 and *perek* 8,1.

is "in all respects like a non-Jew".[70] Just as a non-Jew, he is considered intrinsically impure.[71]

Nonetheless, his status entitles him to certain benefits which are generally not granted to the non-Jews. Thus, it is permissible to give him a free present[72] and to assist him in his livelihood.[73] As his name conveys, he is entitled to reside within the land of Israel.[74] The *Talmud* stipulates, however, that nowadays the status of foreign resident no longer exists.[75]

Canaanite slaves

The non-Jewish slave, usually referred to as 'Canaanite'[76] and frequently as 'slave' *tout court*, is conceived of in the *Babylonian Talmud* as an incipient convert.[77] Like a convert, the slave must immerse at the time of his acquisition; he also circumcises, although this can be somewhat delayed.[78] Yet he only becomes an 'Israel' when he is finally freed: as a slave,

---

[70] *Y.Yev.* 8,1. Similarly, according to *B.Git.* 44a, all agree that "a foreign resident is like a non-Jew", whereas the status of an apostate or a *Kuti* is subject to dispute (this passage refers however to their status in one specific Halakhic case, rather to their general intrinsic status). According to *B.AZ* 64b, the wine of a foreign resident is forbidden to drink, but it is not forbidden (as with ordinary non-Jewish wine) to derive any other benefit from it; the *Talmud* concludes, however, that "in all other respects he is like a non-Jew".

In p. 36 I have suggested that the term 'like' (*ke-*) generally denotes similarity rather than actual identity; I will argue the same with reference to the Jewish apostate (p. 108, n. 158). However, in these passages on the foreign resident the phrase "like a non-Jew" might well refer to actual identity, since (unlike the apostate Jew) we do not find that he is ever given the title of 'Israel'.

[71] *T.Zavim* 2,1; minor tractate *Gerim* 3,3; cf section II.1.A.

[72] *B.Pes.* 21b. On ordinary non-Jews, see p. 148.

[73] *B.AZ* and *B.Pes.ib.*

[74] *Sifre Deut.* 259; *Gerim* 3,4.

[75] As it only applies when the Jubilee is in application: *B.Arakh.* 29a. On the status of the foreign resident, see further *Encyclopedia Talmudit*, s.v. *ger toshav*.

[76] This is a technical term, derived from *Gen.* 9:25 (Rashi *ad B.Kid.* 22b, s.v. *sede*), which does not necessarily mean that he is an ethnic Canaanite; although in *B.Yoma* 67a it is apparently suggested that all slaves (including the exemplary Tavi) are descended from Canaan.

[77] See Schiffman, *Who was a Jew?*, pp. 36–7, and references quoted; also P.V.M. Flesher, *Oxen, Women or Citizens? Slaves in the System of the Mishnah*, Atlanta: Scholars Press, 1988 (*n.v.*).

[78] This is subject to debate: some hold that he must circumcise forthwith; others, that he may wait up till twelve months; others, finally, that he need not circumcise at all. It is also debated whether he can be circumcised by force: *B.Yev.* 48a–b.

he has departed from the category of the non-Jew but has not entered that of Israel.[79]

The status of the slave is thus interstitial. He is obliged to observe the commandments, but only to the same degree as a (Jewish) woman;[80] it takes twelve months for him to be no longer suspected of *avoda zara*.[81] On the other hand, at the time of his release, he does not need to undergo the ritual of conversion, nor even to make a formal commitment to the observance of the commandments,[82] as he is already involved in their observance.[83]

In many respects non-Jewish slaves are treated in the same way as outright non-Jews.[84] Particularly suggestive, in this context, is their alleged affinity with animals,[85] reminiscent of the rabbinic image of the non-Jews (see section I.4.A). As with non-Jews, this affinity is considered tangible enough to be given *practical*, Halakhic significance. Thus, the *Palestinian Talmud* rules that the death of one's slave should be mourned no more than the loss of one's ox or donkey, "because slaves are like animals".[86] According to the *Babylonian Talmud*, likewise, a woman slave cannot be betrothed before she is freed, for she is an animal;[87] and again, a foetus in her womb is deemed as in an animal's womb.[88] In the *Palestinian Talmud*, the story is told of a man who proposed to a woman slave of Rabbi; the woman, who had acquired some learning from her master, told him that she first had to purify herself from menstrual impurity. He pleaded: "but are you not like an animal?"—to which she retorted: "have you not heard that he

---

[79] *B.Sanh.* 58b.

[80] *B.Hag.* 4a; *B.Nazir* 61a; *B.Ker.* 7b; cf *M.Ber.* 3,3. On the obligations of a woman, see pp. 238–40. See E.E. Urbach, "Halakhot regarding slaves as a source for the social history of the 2nd Temple and the Talmudic period", in *Zion* 25, 1960, pp. 141–189, esp. 162–6 (Hebrew).

[81] *B.AZ* 57a.

[82] *B.Yev.* 47b.

[83] *Ib.* 48a. Cf *ib.* 23a, etc.

[84] It is forbidden to teach them *Torah* (*B.Ket.* 28a), just as it is to the non-Jews (see pp. 212–3). Slaves and non-Jews are often juxtaposed with one another, e.g. *M.Kid.* 3,12.

[85] This affinity is inferred in *Gen.R.* 56,2 from the juxtaposition of "slave" and "animal" in *Ex.* 20:10. See *B.Kid.* 22b: "a minor slave is like an animal". On the other hand, the reference to a slave as an "ox" in *B.Sanh.* 19a is probably not significant, as it is only a Talmudic adage which can be applied in a totally different context, cf *B.BK* 112b.

[86] *Y.Ber.* 2,8; minor tractate *Semahot* 1,10; cf *B.Ber.* 16b.

[87] *B.Kid.* 62b.

[88] *B.Kid.* 69a.

who comits bestiality is stoned to death?".[89] In this instance, the shrewd slave was able to turn her status as animal, tongue in cheek, to her own advantage . . .

Just as non-Jews, slaves are considered to be specifically akin with donkeys (see pp. 37–9), although this affinity is inferred from a different scriptural source: namely, Abraham's command to his servants to remain "with the donkey" (*Gen.* 22:5), and which the *Midrash* interprets as meaning: "you people who resemble the donkey".[90] Again, this statement is sufficiently concrete to be given practical, Halakhic significance. According to the *Babylonian Talmud*, all agree that slaves have no legitimate parenthood, for they are "a people who resemble the donkey";[91] and for the same reason, betrothal is not effective on a woman slave.[92] It is also ruled that if an ox gores a woman slave and causes her to miscarry, its owner's liability is the same as in the case of damage caused to another animal:

> . . . For what reason? He has only damaged a pregnant donkey, for the verse states . . . "a people who resemble the donkey".[93]

This direct, unqualified reference to the slave as a "pregnant donkey" suggests that it is considered, in some way, as an actual reality. On the other hand, however, the *Talmud* does not accept the argument that marital intercourse in the presence of one's slaves may be permitted on the grounds that slaves are "a people who resemble the donkey".[94]

---

[89] *Y.Ber.* 3,4.

[90] *Gen.R.* 56,2; *Lev.R.* 20; *Tanh. Vayyera* 23; *Tanh.B. ib.* 46, *ib. Aharei* 3; *PdRE* 31; *Midrash HaGadol ad Gen.* 22:5. For a historical account of the development of this *Midrash*, see J. Heinemann, *op.cit.* pp. 122–5.

[91] *B.Yev.* 62a (cf *ib.* 23a; *B.BK* 15a); *Midrash HaGadol ad Gen.* 22:5. In this respect slaves are worse off than non-Jews (see p. 37, n. 267), as their lack of parenthood also extends to the commandment of procreation and to the status of first-borns.

[92] *B.Kid.* 68a.

[93] *B.BK* 49a.

[94] *B.Nida* 17a. J. Heinemann takes this passage as evidence that rabbinic sources do not treat the affinity of slaves with the donkey as an actual identity, but rather as a mere metaphor (pp. 125–9); this is to ignore, however, the attitude of the *B.BK* passage which I have just quoted above. On the apparent absurdity of equating people (e.g. slaves) with donkeys, see my remarks in p. 38. Mention should also be made of R. Abbahu's statement that even a woman slave, if she lives in the Land of Israel, has a share in the world-to-come because she is called a "people" in the phrase, "a *people* who resemble the donkey" (*B.Ket.* 111a). Heinemann (pp. 128–9) rightly points out that although the main purpose of this saying is to praise the Land of Israel, R. Abbahu is effectively negating the traditional message of the *Midrash* on *Gen.* 22:5, by emphasizing the 'peopleness' of the woman slave and totally ignoring her equation with the donkey. On other idiosyncratic views attributed to R. Abbahu, see p. 181.

The equation of slaves with donkeys may well be related to the lowly social status which was generally attributed to slaves in Antiquity.[95] It may also be related to their abiding non-Jewish status, in so far as they are only incipient converts.

The *Talmudim* disapprove of the release of slaves,[96] and condemn them, in this sense, to their liminal, semi-non-Jewish status. Just as 'foreign residents', therefore, non-Jewish slaves remain peripheral to the ethnic identity of Israel.

C. *Kutim (Samaritans)*

The Biblical account

The origin of the Samaritans, or '*Kutim*' (or '*Kutiim*')[97] as our sources call them, was in Late Roman Palestine a controversial issue. Samaritans regarded themselves as Israelites, whilst rabbinic sources conceded at best that they were not ordinary non-Jews. The controversy found its roots in the book of Kings,[98] which tells that after the Assyrians deported the ten tribes of Israel from Samaria, they settled in it a number of peoples from Babylon and from Kuta. Whereas the Samaritans claimed that they were remnants of the ten tribes of Israel, rabbinic sources assumed, on the strength of the Biblical account, that contemporary Samaritans were descendants of these immigrants from Kuta. Rabbinic texts asserted this view by insisting in calling them '*Kutim*.[99]

---

[95] This would explain why slaves are in some ways *more* 'animal-like' than the non-Jews, for instance in the context of parenthood. J. Heinemann, pp. 231–2 nn. 27–9, rejects this suggestion on the grounds that in some Halakhic contexts, e.g. life-saving, the slave is treated as equal to a free, Jewish man. But as I have stated in the previous note, this does not prove that slaves are *never* given a sub-human status in rabbinic writings.

[96] *Y.Yev.* 11,6; *Y.Ket.* 3,10; *B.Ber.* 47b; *B.Git.* 38a. By contrast, K. Hopkins argues that in Rome and in mainland Greece the release of slaves was frequent and common practice, and indeed intrinsic to the institution of slavery and to its socio-economic viability (*Conquerors and Slaves*, Cambridge: Cambridge University Press, 1978, pp. 115–32 (Rome) and 169–70 (Delphi)). The historical importance of slavery in Late Antique rabbinic society is yet to be assessed; slaves may have constituted an important source of converts, even though our sources disapprove of their release.

[97] Censorship has frequently substituted the term '*Kuti*' for 'non-Jew', which can be extremely misleading, as in fact early rabbinic *halakha* makes clear distinctions between the *Kutim* and the non-Jews. These occurrences can usually be corrected on the basis of context and of variant readings.

[98] II*Kings* 17:24–41.

[99] The Biblical term *Shomronim* (i.e. Samaritans) is rarely used in our sources; it is discussed in *Gen.R.* 81,3; *ib.* 94,7; *PdRE* 38, end. In *Gen.R.* 94,7 R. Meir concedes that the Samaritans are descended from the tribe of Issachar (although the Samaritans

Now the Bible goes on to tell us that the *Kutim* were plagued with lions soon after they had settled in Samaria; they understood this to be a message from the God of Israel, and they decided accordingly to convert. The Bible emphasizes however that their conversion was not complete, as they continued to worship their native gods alongside the God of Israel. Already according to the Bible, therefore, their status appears ambivalent.[100]

Ambivalence towards the Samaritans' conversion is also found in rabbinic sources, although, for some curious reason, they are rarely discredited for the reasons stated in the book of *Kings*.[101] In this context we may distinguish between the *Mishna* and the *Talmudim*, where the ambiguity of the *Kuti* status is approached in different ways.

The Mishna: an interstitial category

In the *Mishna* the *Kutim* are presented as an interstitial category, neither Jewish nor non-Jewish. As one Tannaitic text puts it:

> The ways (or: practices) of the *Kutim* are sometimes like non-Jews, sometimes like Jews (*Israel*), (though) mainly like Jews.[102]

The origin of this extraordinary Halakhic status is nowhere explained. But far from being problematic to the *Mishna*, the *Kutim* serve the purpose of testing the limits of many Halakhic rulings where the distinction between Jew and non-Jew applies.[103] The *Mishna* is noted elsewhere for its use of similar interstitial categories, often only theoretical, for the sake of defining such Halakhic distinctions.[104]

---

insist that they are descended from Joseph). On rabbinic attitudes towards the Samaritans and their origins, see Alon, *op.cit.*, pp. 354–73. On pre-rabbinic attitudes towards the Samaritan community, see F. Dexinger, "Limits of tolerance in Judaism: the Samaritan example", in E.P. Sanders et al., *op.cit.* pp. 88–114.

[100] II*Kings* 17:40–41. For a critical analysis of this Biblical passage (which would not, however, correspond to the early rabbinic reading of it), see Dexinger (*op. cit.*).

[101] Cf *Num.R.* 8,9.

[102] Beginning of minor tractate *Kutim*. Although this passage is not found in earlier sources, I take it to be Tannaitic in origin; indeed, we shall see that in the Amoraic period, *Kutim* are no longer considered to be "mainly like Jews", but on the contrary virtually identical with non-Jews (see introduction to the *Soncino* translation of this minor tractate, concurring with my interpretation). On the distinctions between *Kutim* and non-Jews in *Mishna* and *Tosefta*, see Porton (1988) pp. 132–40.

[103] Examples to this effect abound (cf *M.Ber.* 7,1; *ib.* 8,8; *M.Demai* 3,4; *ib.* 5,9; etc.), and many of them are collected in minor tractate *Kutim*. This topic is too vast to be treated in this present work; for a sample of such cases (with detailed analysis) see L. Schiffman, "The Samaritans in Tannaitic Halacha", in *JQR* 75:4, 1985, pp. 323–350.

[104] E.g. the land of Syria, neither inside the land of Israel nor outside it; the *tumtum*,

Consequently, the *Kuti* figures in the *Mishna* as an identity of its own which is Halakhically excluded from that of Israel.

The Talmudim: a doubtful conversion

In attempting to explain the *Kuti* of the *Mishna*, the *Talmudim* do not appear to accept the possibility of an interstitial status (neither Jew nor non-Jew), because its origin would be Halakhically inexplicable.[105] Instead, the status of *Kutim* is presented as subject to a Tannaitic dispute: some hold that the *Kutim* are Jewish, others that they are not.[106] This dispute depends on whether they were originally 'converts in truth'—in which case they are Jewish—or 'converts of lions', which is to say that they converted solely out of their fear of the lions—in which case their conversion was *ab initio* invalid.[107]

Thus at first sight, the factor which may have invalidated their conversion was their original *motivation*. We have seen, indeed, that a non-Jew cannot convert for ulterior or insincere motives, and that according to some opinions "whoever does not convert for the sake of Heaven is not a convert".[108] However others hold that converts for ulterior motives, including in fact 'converts of lions', are accepted *a posteriori* as valid converts; and the *Babylonian Talmud* rules decisively in favour of this opinion.[109]

So the invalidation of the conversion of the *Kutim* as 'converts of lions' may be due, instead, to their original lack of *commitment* to keeping all the commandments. Indeed, many Mishnaic rulings on *Kutim* as interstitial are predicated on the assumption that the *Kutim* are not

---

neither male nor female; the *androgynos*, both male and female at once; and the *koy* (or: *kevi*), which the *Mishna* describes as being at once either a domesticated animal, or a wild beast, or neither, or both (*M.Bikkurim* 2,8). Although the practical relevance of the latter cases is limited, they are frequently referred to in the *Mishna* and *Tosefta* purely for the sake of Halakhic reasoning. On the importance of ambiguous and interstitial categories in the *Mishna*, see J. Neusner, *Judaism: the evidence of the Mishna*, Univ. of Chicago Press: Chicago, 1981, pp. 259–61.

[105] In the case of the *koy*, by contrast, the *Babylonian Talmud* is willing to consider that it may constitute a category in its own right (*beriya bifnei atzmah*) as opposed to a doubtful category (i.e. doubtful as to whether it is wild or domesticated): *B.Yoma* 74a-b (cf *Tosafot ad loc.*, 74b). See also *T.Bikkurim*, 2,1–7, on *koy*, *tumtum* and *androginos*.

[106] Already in the *Tosefta* (*T.Terumot* 4,12 and 4,14), R. Shimon b. Gamliel holds that *Kutim* are "like Jews", whilst his son Rabbi holds that they are "like non-Jews" (whether "like" means, in this context, similarity or actual identity is admittedly not clear; see my remarks in p. 96, n. 70 and p. 108, n. 158). See also *Y.Ket.* 3,1; *B.Git.* 44a.

[107] *Y.Git.* 1,4; *B.Kid.* 75b; *B.BK* 38b; *B.Nida 55a*; *Kutim* 2; etc.

[108] *Gerim* 1,7.

[109] *Y.Kid.* 4,1; *B.Yev.* 24b. See Schiffman in *JQR* 1985, pp. 325–6.

fully observant. Although they keep the *shabbat*[110] and separate all tithes,[111] the *Mishna* states that they do not make pilgrimages to Jerusalem,[112] that they have relations with their menstruant wives,[113] and that their fatherhood is doubtful;[114] moreover, it is forbidden to answer *amen* to their blessing without having heard it completely (which would suggest, in line with the Biblical account, that they covertly worship some *avoda zara).*[115] R. Shimon b. Gamliel is quoted as saying that they are *more* meticulous than the Jews in the observance of those commandments that they have adopted, e.g. in the making of *matza* (unleavened bread) for Passover.[116] Nonetheless, the underlying assumption remains that the *Kutim* do not observe all the commandments. This may well explain their doubtful status as converts, since non-acceptance of even a single commandment, at the time of their conversion, would have been sufficient for it to be disqualified.[117]

Their status in Talmudic times

In the post-Mishnaic, Talmudic period, the authors of the Talmudim believe the status of the *Kutim* to have changed. The *Palestinian Talmud* argues that the statement of R. Shimon b. Gamliel (above mentioned) only applies to the period when the *Kutim* were still entrenched in their villages; 'nowadays', the *Kutim* cannot be trusted with any commandment at all.[118] They have recently become corrupted (*nitkalkelu*[119]), as they now worship idols which are concealed under Mount Gerizim

---

[110] *M.Ned.* 3,10—they also keep a Jewish custom of eating garlic; cf *Eccl.R.* 2,16,1. According to *B.Ned.* 31a, they are moreover *commanded* to keep the *shabbat*, implying that they did properly convert and that it is now incumbent upon them to observe the commandments.

[111] According to *B.Ber.* 47b.

[112] *M.Ned. ib.*, in the days of the Temple. Indeed the locus of their worship is Mount Gerizim.

[113] *M.Nida* 4,1.

[114] Similarly to the 'silent' (of unknown fatherhood) and to the foundling: *M.Kid.* 4,3; *T.Kid.* 5,1–2 (L: 5,1); *B.Kid.* 75a.

[115] *M.Ber.* 8,8; *T.Ber.* 5,22 (L: 5,21, see apparatus).

[116] *Contra* R. Eliezer, who holds that they may not be trusted with the preparation of *matza*: *T.Pes.* 1,15 (L: 2,3); *Y.Pes.* 1,1; *B.Git.* 10a; *B.Hul.* 4a; etc.

[117] As we have seen above, on the basis of *T.Demai* 2,5 and *B.Bekh.* 30b.

[118] *Y.Pes.* 1,1.

[119] The notion of corruption (*kilkul*) is found already in the *Tosefta*, albeit with specific reference to tithing, which the *Kutim* are said to have begun neglecting in the early-mid 2nd century CE (*T.Demai* 5,24). The same term is also applied to the *Kutim* in *M.RH* 2,2, but this only refers to their conflict with rabbinic authority, and does not necessarily connote a deterioration of their religious observance or—certainly not—of their Jewish status (*pace* Schiffman).

(where the Samaritan cult is indeed located).[120] Hence, a *Kuti* may not circumcise a Jew, as he will direct his intention towards Mount Gerizim.[121]

Similarly, in the *Babylonian Talmud* we hear that by the Amoraic period, the *Kutim* did not keep the *Torah* at all. Once it was discovered that they worshipped the image of a dove at the top of Mount Gerizim; thereupon, the rabbis "refused to budge until they made the *Kutim absolute non-Jews*".[122] Because of this decree, the *Kutim* may no longer, for instance, slaughter animals for Jews.[123]

It remains unclear whether the rabbis decreed, in this passage, that the *Kutim* were *really* non-Jewish, or that they should be treated, in Halakhic terms, only *as though* they were non-Jews. The plain reading to the text would suggest that the rabbis declared the *Kutim* to be really and 'absolutely' non-Jewish.[124] Although we have seen that the status of convert is irreversible, the discovery of the dove may have indicated to the rabbis that the *Kutim* had never abandoned *avoda zara*, and hence that their conversion had never been valid to start with.[125] Consequently most of the Mishnaic material on *Kutim* would have to be declared null and void, since their status as converts was now fully and formally invalidated.[126]

On the other hand, the same Talmudic text apparently equates

---

[120] Therefore their wine can no longer be trusted: *Y.A.Z* 5,4. The *Palestinian Talmud* considers this change to have taken place at a specific point in time, within the Tannaitic or early Amoraic period, and in specific circumstances which vary according to the different accounts (brought down in *Y.A.Z ib.*). It is generally agreed that it took place sometime in the Tannaitic or early Amoraic period. Some Mishnaic passages already assume that the *Kutim* are covert *avoda zara* worshippers, e.g. with the prohibition of answering *amen* to their blessing without hearing it completely. According to *Tanh. Vayyeshev* 2, end, Ezra already ruled that eating their bread is like eating pork (see *M.Sheviit* 8,10), because they had hindered the re-building of the Jerusalem Temple.

[121] I.e. to its *avoda zara* (according to R. Yehuda): *T.A.Z* 3,13; *Y.Shab.* 19,2; *Y.Yev.* 8,1; *B.A.Z* 27a; *Kutim*, 1.

[122] *B.Hul.* 6a (*goyim gemurim*).

[123] *Ib.*—as they will slaughter for the sake of *avoda zara*.

[124] The Vilna and Warsaw editions read *AKUM*, which *could* mean no more than '*avoda zara* worshippers'; but since this term is only a censorial substitution (see *Dik.Sof. ad loc.*: the correct reading, in manuscripts and more reliable editions of this passage, is *goyim* (non-Jews); on the term *AKUM* in general as a censorial substitution, see p. 9), it is totally insignificant.

[125] It should be noted that in the *Babylonian Talmud*, there is no explicit reference to the notion of sudden 'corruption' and change, as found in the *Palestinian Talmud*. It would be consistent with the Biblical account for the *Babylonian Talmud* to consider that the *Kutim* had *always* worshipped *avoda zara*.

[126] As Maimonides argues in his commentary on *M.Ber.* 8,8.

the *Kutim* with apostates,[127] suggesting perhaps that as apostates, the *Kutim* are to be treated only *as though* they were non-Jews.[128] Indeed, if it was assumed (as in the *Palestinian Talmud*) that the *Kutim* had only recently turned to *avoda zara*, their conversion, albeit doubtful, could not have been invalidated; at most they would have been declared 'lapsed converts', which is to say apostates;[129] as apostates they would have remained, to some extent, Jews.[130]

Conclusion: a failed conversion
Kutim are frequently referred to in rabbinic writings, and their ethnic status is subject to intense controversy. The validity of their original conversion is doubtful, both in terms of motivation and of commitment. In the *Mishna*, their slack observance of the commandments turns them into a separate, interstitial category, which renders them Halakhically different from Israel. This becomes all the more pronounced once they are declared in the *Talmud* "non-Jews in all respects", which either means apostates, or literally non-Jews. Considering that in Late Roman Palestine, the Samaritans were a social reality of considerable importance, we may wonder why our sources remain so ambiguous about their ethnic status.

In some ways, the *Kutim* take on the features of a separate religious sect: according to the *Talmudim*, they restrict their observance to that

---

[127] At least, the same ruling (pertaining to *eruvin*) is applied to *Kutim* and apostates without distinction: *B.Hul. ib.*

[128] We shall see in the next section that apostates remain Jews but are treated, in most Halakhic cases, as though they were non-Jews. The expression 'absolute non-Jews', in this passage, may be applied to the *Kutim* as a derogatory substitution for 'apostates'.

[129] See above p. 94.

[130] In favour of this latter possibility I would quote a similar passage in *B.Yev.* 17a, where the phrase, "they refused to budge until they made them absolute non-Jews" is applied to the ten lost tribes of Israel. There the *Talmud* is trying to establish not only that these tribes apostatised (or rather: assimilated), but also that their ability to marry (which apostates normally retain—*B.Yev.* 47b, see p. 108) has become invalid. Since it is may be assumed that the rabbis do not have the power to abolish their lineal belonging to Israel, mediaeval commentators understand this passage to mean that the rabbis decreed, with *specific* reference to marriage, that the ten tribes should be treated *as though* they were non-Jewish (i.e., that their marriages should be invalid—Ritva and Meiri *ad loc.*); but not that they actually became non-Jews. By analogy, this phrase may mean the same when applied in our passage to the *Kutim*.

The present-day status of the Kuti—whether apostate or non-Jew—remains unresolved in later rabbinic literature: cf R. Joseph Karo, *Shulḥan Arukh, Even HaEzer*, 44,10 and ancillary commentaries.

which is explicitly written in the Bible,[131] they have their own books, and interpret Scripture in their own way.[132] Thus the identity of the *Kutim* is not necessarily 'peripheral' to Israel: it may be regarded by our sources as an independent identity in its own right.

The *Kutim* cannot be accepted as Jews unless they undergo once more conversion. Thus tractate *Kutim* concludes:

> they can only be accepted (i.e. as converts?) if they renounce Mount Gerizim, and recognize Jerusalem and the resurrection of the dead.[133]

Other late traditions confirm that *Kutim* would require conversion, but add that they are not allowed to convert.[134] *Kutim* are thereby irrevocably excluded from entering the fold of Israel.

3. APOSTATES

Let us now approach the question of marginality from the opposite angle: the Jew who departs and 'converts' *away* from the community of Israel. On the one hand, the apostate remains permanently and irreversibly 'Israel', whether he was originally Jewish-born or just a convert (as we have seen in the previous section). On the other hand, as we shall now see, rabbinic sources ignore by and large the Jewish identity of the apostate, and emphasize as much as possible his affinity with the non-Jews.

---

[131] *B.Hul.* 4a; *B.Nida* 57a; *B.Ber.* 47b.

[132] For instance, as to the location of *Elonei More*: *B.Sot.* 33b (R. El'azar b.R. Yose proves them wrong). Their minimalist interpretation of Scripture is illustrated in *Y.Pes.* 1,1.

[133] Minor tractate *Kutim*, end. This passage does not indicate whether the *Kutim* are considered non-Jews or apostates, and it may thus refer not to their "acceptance" as converts, but rather to their "acceptance" as repentant apostates. But it seems to me that since the whole issue remains doubtful in Tannaitic and Talmudic sources, this passage may well be implying that in any case the *Kutim* require some form of conversion so as to remove them from their doubtful status.

(Immediately preceding this conclusion, tractate *Kutim* states that "(*Kutim*) were originally proper converts". However this statement is separate from the conclusion, and only represents the view of the Tanna whom the tractate is still quoting. It should be noted that the conclusion here quoted, unlike the main body of the tractate, is not a quotation from earlier Talmudic or Tannaitic sources but (presumably) an original statement by its redactor(s)).

[134] *Tanh. Vayyeshev* 2, end; *PdRE* 38. According to *Eliyahu Z.* 1 (p. 169), this is because some of the ten lost tribes are mingled among them, and one should wait for the arrival of Elijah to come and identify them.

A. *Apostasy: limited and comprehensive*

Definition

The apostate is called *mumar* (lit. 'converted') or *meshumad* (lit. 'destroyed'); both terms are interchangeable in the various recensions. Curiously, *mumar* and *meshumad* are nowhere mentioned in the *Mishna*. But the *mumar* enjoys a relatively well-defined Halakhic status in subsequent sources. According to the *Tosefta*, the apostate is

> he who eats carrion and non-kosher meat, abominations and 'creepies', and pork, who drinks forbidden wine,[135] or who desecrates the *shabbat* and who is decircumcised.[136] R. Yose b. Yehuda says, even he who wears a garment of wool and linen;[137] R. Shimon b.El'azar adds, even he who commits a transgression for which there is no natural desire.[138]

The *Babylonian Talmud* understands this passage to mean that apostasy can be *limited* to the rejection of only one or a few commandments. 'Limited apostates' mentioned in the *Talmud* include apostates from circumcision, apostates from dietary laws, apostates from the *shabbat* (which they desecrate either privately or publicly), apostates who make libations to *avoda zara*, and apostates who worship *avoda zara*. Only the latter, and certainly the "apostates from the whole *Torah*", may be regarded as *comprehensive* apostates.[139] The terms *mumar* (*tout court*) and *meshumad* refer in general to comprehensive apostates.[140] Limited apostates, on the other hand, can be far removed from outright apostasy, in so far as they are fully observant in all other respects.[141]

The *Babylonian Talmud* distinguishes moreover between the apostate out of convenience (*mumar le-te'avon*, lit. apostate out of appetite), and the apostate out of conviction (*mumar le-hakh'is*, lit. apostate out of spite).[142] Again, it is the latter who is generally referred to as *mumar*

---

[135] On account of having been used for a libation to *avoda zara* (*yein nesekh*).

[136] So ms. Erfurt. But ms. Vienna reads instead of the last item: 'who makes libations (to *avoda zara*)'. *B.Hor.* 11a omits this item altogether.

[137] Cf *Lev*.19:19; *Deut*.22:9–11.

[138] *T.Hor.* 1,5. *B.Hor.* 11a reads also: he who eats forbidden fats (*helev*).

[139] *B.Hul.* 4b–5a; *B.Eruv.* 69a-b. This notion is subject however to some debate in these passages; it is not found in any other early rabbinic source.

[140] Or to apostates who worship *avoda zara*: *B.Hul.* 41a.

[141] As argued by J. Petuchowski, "The Mumar. A study of Rabbinic psychology", in *HUCA* 30, 1959, pp. 179–90. He quotes (p. 189) *B.Hul.* 4a according to which even an 'apostate from dietary laws' can be trusted to perform a valid slaughtering, provided his knife is in a proper condition: indeed, given the choice, this person would prefer to eat kosher meat.

[142] *B.AZ* 26b; *B.Hor. ib.*; *B.Hul. ib.*

(*tout court*).[143] In some cases, however, the apostate out of conviction is deemed more trustworthy than the apostate out of convenience.[144] The 'apostate out of conviction' corresponds perhaps to the 'overt apostate' (*mumar be-gilluy panim*) mentioned elsewhere in the *Talmudim*.[145]

Talmudic sources condemn the apostates in no uncertain terms: unlike mere sinners, apostates are locked into Gehenna where they are punished forever.[146] "Your enemy", according to the *Mekhilta*, is a reference to the apostate;[147] therefore, according to *Avot dRN*, the apostate must be hated.[148]

Jewish identity and affinity with non-Jews

The apostate remains irreversibly Jewish in the following respects:

1. His name, *Israel mumar*. Jacob Katz points out that in this expression, *Israel* is the substantive whereas *mumar* is only the epithet.[149] That the apostate belongs to the category of 'Israel' is implied, as Schiffman has shown,[150] in the following exegetical passage in *B.Hul.* 5a (= *B.Eruv.* 69b):

> "Of you" (*Lev.* 1:2)—i.e. not all of you; which excludes the apostate. "Of you"—i.e. *among you* have I made a distinction (excluding apostates) but not among the nations (i.e., the nations are not excluded).

Hence the apostates are "among you", among the people of Israel.

2. His abiding obligation to observe the commandments. This concept is only implicit in our sources. We are told in the *Midrash Tanhuma* that Israel cannot divest themselves from their oath of allegiance to the Almighty.[151] According to the *Talmud*, indeed, every Jew is bound by oath to observe all His commandments.[152] This would imply that the apostate is expected to repent (as he is Israel, moreover,

---

[143] Passages which I shall quote in this section *may* thus refer exclusively to the comprehensive apostate out of conviction.

[144] According to Rava in *B.Sanh.* 27a, since the latter is motivated by greed he is unfit for testimony (as he is liable to be bribed, perhaps)—whereas the former is not.

[145] *Y.Eruv.* 6,2 and *B.Eruv.* 69a–b.

[146] *T.Sanh.* 13,4–5; *B.RH* 17a.

[147] *Mekh. Kaspa* 2.

[148] *Avot dRN* 16.

[149] J. Katz, "*Af al pi she-hata, Yisrael hu*", reprinted in *Halakha veKabbala*, Jerusalem: Magnes Press, 1984, p. 262.

[150] Schiffman, *Who was a Jew?*, pp. 46–9.

[151] *Tanh. Nitzavim* 3 (*Tanh.B. ib.*7), quoting *Ezekiel* 20:33.

[152] *B.Shevu.* 21b; 22b; 23b; *B.Yoma* 73b.

he does not need to convert). When R. Meir wished that bandits in his neighbourhood should die, his wife Beruria suggested instead that he should pray for their repentance.[153] There are cases of illustrious 'heretics' who repented.[154] According to the *Palestinian Talmud*, it would seem that a repenting apostate takes precedence over a converting non-Jew.[155]

3. The apostate man retains the ability of marrying a Jewish woman (and presumably vice-versa, a Jewish man of marrying an apostate woman), just as any other 'Israel'. In a Halakhic context, the distinction between apostate and non-Jew is narrowed down *exclusively* to this.[156]

Otherwise, in practical terms, the apostate is always treated as a non-Jew:[157] "the overt apostate is like a non-Jew in all respects".[158] In *Ex.* 12:43, which excludes a *ben nekhar* ('foreigner') from eating the Passover sacrifice, Onkelos translates this term as "an Israel apostate". According to the *Mekhilta* on the same verse, *ben nekhar* includes both a non-Jew and an Israel apostate, for it is written: "every *ben nekhar* is uncircumcised in the heart" (*Ez.* 44:9).[159]

---

[153] Which he did, and eventually they repented: *B.Ber.* 10a. It is not clear, admittedly, that they belonged to the category of 'apostates' (rather than 'sinners').

[154] *B.A.Z* 17a; I argue below that heretics are even worse than apostates.

[155] *Y.Hor.* 3,5. The *Talmud* does not specify in what respect he takes precedence. My interpretation follows traditional commentators, but the text simply reads: "a convert and an apostate—the apostate comes first". Commentators take "convert" as meaning 'prospective convert' rather than 'actual convert', for as we have seen, the actual convert is treated as 'Israel' in all respects and should thus take priority over the apostate. Commentators also assume, by analogy, that "apostate" refers to a repenting apostate. Note however that *Otiyot dR.Akiva* 7–8 (1st recension, ed. Wertheimer) places converting (righteous) non-Jews and repenting (wicked) Jews on a par.

[156] *B.Yev.* 47b. In *T.Hul.* 1,1, however, it is ruled that slaughtering by a *meshumad* (as opposed to by a non-Jew) is valid; see *B.Hul.* 4a–5b. See also *B.Git.* 44a whereby apostates may be treated as Jews in one other case.

[157] In *M.A.Z* 4,4 the non-Jews are distinguished from Jews worshipping *avoda zara*; however it is not clear that the latter are *mumarim*—this passage may only be referring to occasional offenders (see however *Turei Zahav* on *Shulhan Arukh Y.D.* 139,1).

[158] *Y.Eruv.* 6,2. As stated above in p. 36, 'like' (*ke-*) generally means *similarity* rather than actual identity. Although we have seen (p. 96, n. 70) that in the case of the 'foreign resident' the phrase *"like a non-Jew"* probably meant actual identity (on the *Kutim*, see p. 101, n. 106), this interpretation is unlikely to apply to the apostate, as there is no evidence that the inherent Jewish identity of the *'Israel' mumar* is at any stage abolished.

[159] *Mekh. Bo* 15. In *B.Shab.* 87a, it is stated that apostates are excluded from receiving the *Torah*, which is why Moses broke the tablets in the episode of the golden calf; this is reminiscent of the non-Jews' exclusion from the *Torah* (see section V.1.C). The similarity between the nations and the "wicked of Israel" (probably meaning apostates and heretics) is also conveyed in a *Midrash* on *Isaiah* 56:11, which suggests that dogs are symbolic of both (*Midrash Tehillim* 4,11).

In some cases, the apostate is even worse than the non-Jew. Whereas sacrifices from the non-Jews may be accepted,[160] sacrifices from apostates may not, as they have rejected the covenant with the Almighty.[161] Moreover, the *Tosefta* issues the following ruling:

> Non-Jews, and small cattle shepherds and rearers are neither brought up nor brought down; heretics, apostates and informers are brought down and not brought up.[162]

This text is admittedly obscure, but it intimates at least that heretics and apostates are treated worse (they are "brought down") than the non-Jews (who are not). The *Babylonian Talmud* understands this passage in most drastic terms: non-Jews are not to be saved from death by being 'brought up' from a pit in which they have fallen,[163] but they may not be cast into it ('brought down') in the first place; whereas apostates and heretics should be cast into pits ('brought down'), and thus indirectly put to death.[164]

In a sense, the apostate is the mirror image of the convert: just as the latter is "Israel in all respects", so the apostate is "as a non-Jew in all respects". However, the apostate differs from the convert in that the latter divests himself entirely from his original non-Jewish identity, whereas the apostate retains his basic identity as Israel, even though it is seldom referred to.

B. *Minim and heresy*

The *minim*—literally 'types', but best translated as 'heretics'—are frequently identified by modern scholars with the Christians;[165] but

---

[160] *M.Shek.* 1,5; *T.Shek.* 1,7; *Sifra Emor, parasha* 7,2; *B.Naz.* 62a; cf *B.Hul.* 13b.

[161] Sacrifices from sinners are however accepted: *Sifra Vayyikra* 2,3; cf *B.Hul.* 5a (= *B.Eruv.* 69b).

[162] *T.BM* 2, end; *B.AZ* 26a-b.

[163] According to *M.Yoma* 8,7, if it is doubtful whether the person is Jewish or not, one may transgress *Yom Kippur* (and by extension, presumably, *shabbat* and other festivals) so as to save him. This implies that if he were definitely non-Jewish, he should not be saved, at least where desecration of *Yom Kippur* would be involved.

[164] *B.Sanh.* 57a; *B.AZ* 13b. For a radically different interpretation of this passage in *Tosefta*, see J. Neusner, *A History of the Mishnaic Law of Damages—part 2, Baba Mesia: translation and explanation*, Leiden: Brill, 1983, p. 40. Neusner suggests that the passage, far more benign, is concerned with one's obligation to return lost property to its (Jewish) owners. However I do not think the Talmudic interpretation is any more 'far-fetched' than his.

[165] As demonstrable in a few cases: for instance, *B.Shab.* 116a-b, where the Gospel is mentioned and quoted from; *T.Hul.* 2,24, where we hear that "words of *minut*" were circulating in the name of *Yeshua b.Pantira* (identified by many scholars with

this identification is often misleading and probably unwarranted.[166] On the one hand, with very few exceptions the term *minim* refers to *Jewish* heretics alone: as according to the *Babylonian Talmud*, indeed, "there are no *minim* among the nations".[167] On the other hand, in many Mishnaic and Talmudic passages the *minim* are attributed *non-Christian* heretical practices and beliefs, such as the worship of *avoda zara*,[168] and the denial of the world-to-come[169] and of the resurrection of the dead.[170] Thus the category of *minim* undoubtedly includes Jewish Christians, but equally all other 'types' of Jewish heresy.[171]

Jesus). See Schiffman, *Who Was a Jew?*, with a compendium of early rabbinic references to the *minim*.

[166] As argued by R. Kimelman, "*Birkat haMinim* and the lack of evidence for an anti-Christian Jewish prayer", in E.P. Sanders et al., *Jewish and Christian self-definition*, vol. II (1981), pp. 226–44, esp. pp. 228–32; cf Ch. Milikowsky, "Gehenna and the "Sinners of Israel" in the light of *Seder Olam*", in *Tarbiz* 55, 1985–6, p. 332, with extensive bibliography in n. 92 (Hebrew).

[167] *B.Hul.* 13b: hence, a non-Jew who adheres to practices of Jewish *minut* remains a non-Jew and is distinguished from a *min* (in the same passage a reference is made to "non-Jewish *minim*", but this is swiftly interpreted by the Talmud as meaning in fact non-Jewish worshippers of *avoda zara*). Consequently a sacrifice from a non-Jewish Christian (for instance) would be acceptable (since he is only a non-Jew), whereas it would not be from a Jewish Christian, because he is a *min* (on the distinction between a *min* and a non-Jew who holds the same beliefs, see also *B.Git.* 45b).

M.Sot. end (= *B.Sanh.* 97a) predicts that in Messianic times, the whole (Roman) Empire will have converted to *minut*; in this context, the term refers without doubt to Christianity, Jewish and non-Jewish alike; but this usage is most exceptional. Interestingly the Talmud (in *B.AZ* 65a) also says that a prospective convert who fails to circumcise (and thus remains equivalent to a *ger toshav*—cf section III.2.B) is considered after twelve months to be "like a *min* among the nations", i.e. a special, heretical 'type' of non-Jew (or is this a suggestion that he resembles, in his Judaizing practices, the Christians?).

It should also be noted that according to Kimelman, in the *Babylonian Talmud* (but not in Palestinian sources) the term *min* refers occasionally to imperial officials, as a substitute for their Graeco-Roman titles (e.g. *hegemon*, as found in the parallel Palestinian sources: e.g. *B.Pes.* 87b, cf *Eliyahu R.* p. 54; *B.AZ* 6b, cf *Y.AZ* 1,1).

[168] According to *T.Hul.* 1,1, the *min* slaughters animals for *avoda zara*. Even if we argue that Christianity was considered to be *avoda zara* (see section I.3.A), the practice of ritual slaughter was generally not Christian; hence the term *min*, in this passage, cannot refer specifically to Christians. It is debated in the *Babylonian Talmud* whether the term *min* refers primarily to a Jew who worships *avoda zara*, or to the 'apostate out of spite': *B.AZ* 26b, cf *B.Hor.* 11a. In *B.Hul.* 13a it is assumed, however, that the *min* worships *avoda zara*. In *B.AZ* 17a, a sexually promiscuous person is also called a *min*.

[169] *M.Ber.* 9,5.

[170] *B.Sanh.* 90b. The *minim*, informers, *meshumadim* and *apikorsim* are listed together with those who reject the *Torah* and the resurrection of the dead, who sin and cause the public to sin: *B.RH* 17a (see *Dik.Sof.*). These passages may be referring to the heresy of the Sadducees (see below). Cf also *M.Meg.* 4,8, on the heretic way (*darkei minut*) of laying *tefillin*. I have not found evidence of any historical change in the semantic meaning of *minim* (such as originally as 'heretics' and then as 'Christians').

[171] See Sokoloff, *op.cit.* p. 306, s.v. *minii*.

In some respects, the *minim* are no more than a variety of apostates. Just as apostates, they must be hated.[172] Heretics must be cast into a pit and not brought up from it;[173] after death, they are permanently condemned to Gehenna.[174] But since heretics deviate from the *Torah* by giving it a new interpretation[175] and/or by actively embracing *avoda zara*, they are treated as non-Jews to an even greater extent than are ordinary apostates. The *Tosefta* rules that the bread of *minim* is like non-Jewish bread, their wine is a 'wine of libations',[176] their produce is untithed, their books are books of magic, and their children are bastards.[177] As with non-Jews, commercial transactions are forbidden with heretics, and it is forbidden to be healed by them.[178] According to the *Babylonian Talmud*, imitating their customs is equivalent to following the customs of the nations.[179]

As with apostates (see section III.3.A), furthermore, heretics are presented as worse than the non-Jews, even if the latter worship *avoda zara*. Indeed, according to the *Tosefta*, non-Jews are unaware of the Almighty, whereas heretics know Him but have rejected Him; therefore it is preferable to enter a non-Jewish *avoda zara* temple for refuge than to enter the heretic houses (of worship).[180] An animal slaughtered by a heretic is assumed to have been dedicated to *avoda zara*, whereas slaughtering by non-Jews is simply invalid.[181] A *Torah* scroll written by a heretic must be destroyed; whereas if written by a non-Jew, it is only put away and concealed.[182]

The fact that the *minim* are distinguished in this way from the non-

---

[172] *Avot dRN* 16 (quoted above, p. 107).

[173] See above, quoting *T.BM* 2, end; *B.AZ* 26a–b.

[174] *T.Sanh.* 13,4–5; *B.RH* 17a. On the evils of heresy, see also *B.AZ* 16b-17a; it is compared to leprosy in *B.Sanh.* 97a.

[175] As do the Christians, or as is evident from references to a heretical way of laying *tefillin* (above mentioned).

[176] I.e. to *avoda zara*; see above p. 27.

[177] *T.Hul.* 2,20.

[178] *T.Hul.* 2,21–24, with the story of individuals who died rather than be healed by a *min* (also *Y.AZ* 2,2; *B.AZ* 27b). On forbidden transactions with non-Jews, see section IV.1.A-B.

[179] *B.Hul.* 41b; see further section IV.2.D.

[180] *T.Shab.* 13,5; *B.Shab.* 116a.

[181] *T.Hul.* 1,1 (above quoted, note 168); cf *ib.* 2,20. This entails that no benefit whatsoever may be derived from an animal slaughtered by a *min*. According to *M.Hul.* 2,9, heretics are accustomed to slaughter over a pit into which the animal's blood drips; their covert aim, it would seem, is to offer the blood to some chthonic deity (see also *B.Hul. ad.loc.*). Cf *B.Tamid* 31b: heretics bind together the limbs of a lamb before slaughtering it as a daily sacrifice.

[182] *B.Git.* 45b.

Jews[183] is itself significant, as it indicates that they retain, just as do ordinary apostates, a distinctive identity as 'Israel'. The same is implied in the Talmudic statement that through their heretical writings, they cast hatred, strife and dissension between Israel and their Father in heaven.[184]

However, that the *minim* are part of Israel is only, at best, implicit. To some extent they have forsaken this identity: they forsake it completely at the entrance of Gehenna, where, according to a late *Midrash*, they are decircumcised by an angel.[185] Thus, as with ordinary apostates, our sources play down the Jewish identity of heretics and emphasize instead their distinct affinity with the non-Jews.

C. *The Sadducees*

The Sadducees (*tzedukim*) are the heretic sect most commonly referred to by name. Although the Sadducees appear to have faded away after the destruction of the Temple in 70CE, the *Mishna* speaks of them not only as a sect of the past,[186] but occasionally also as a contemporary reality.[187]

According to the *Mishna*, the Sadducees disagree with the Pharisees (*Perushim*), who represent the later 'rabbinic' view, on a number of Halakhic issues. They do not necessarily argue for more lenient positions, nor do they always rely on alternative Biblical exegesis;[188] but their opinions consistently challenge the authority of the rabbis and the logic of their reasoning.[189] The *Babylonian Talmud* implies that

---

[183] See also references in note 167 above.

[184] Therefore, their books should be remorselessly burnt, even if they contain names of the Almighty: *Y.Shab.* 16,1; *B.Shab.* 116a.

[185] Hence they do not escape Gehenna: *Ex.R.* 19,4 (applying a Talmudic saying from *B.Eruv.* 19a to the heretics and the "wicked of Israel").

[186] Contemporary with the Pharisees (*Perushim*): *M.Yadayim* 4,6–8. In *M.Eruv.* 6,2, R. Gamliel (presumably the Elder, prior to 70CE) talks of a Sadducee who shared a courtyard in Jerusalem with him and his father's family. In *M.Yadayim* 4,6, R. Yohanan b. Zakkai's argument with the Sadducees may also be attributed to a date prior to the destruction of the Temple.

[187] See Shaye D. Cohen, "The significance of Yavneh: Pharisees, rabbis, and the end of Jewish sectarianism", in *HUCA* 55, 1984, pp. 27–53. One must beware that the term *tzeduki* is often used as a censorial substitution for *min*, for instance in *B.Hor.* 11a (see *Dik.Sof.*).

[188] They do in *M.Mak.* 1,6. Cf also *Y.BB* 8,1 (= *B.BB* 115b).

[189] *M.Yadayim* 4,6–8. *M.Hag.* 2,4 mentions those who claim that *Shavuot* always falls on a Sunday, without explicit reference to Sadducees; in *M.Men.* 10,3, the same opinion (concerning however the harvesting of the *omer*, which takes place on the same day of the week as *Shavuot*, seven weeks earlier) is attributed to the Boethusians

the Sadducees only accept what is explicitly found in the Bible,[190] and this view is also expressed in the *Mishna*.[191] According to later sources, the Sadducees deny the existence of reward in after-life, and indeed the existence of a world-to-come and of the future resurrection of the dead;[192] in the *Babylonian Talmud* it is even suggested, perhaps hyperbolically, that they do not believe in God.[193]

Talmudic sources debate whether, in some contexts, the Sadducee is to be treated in the same way as a non-Jew.[194] In the context of menstrual impurity, the *Mishna* rules that Sadducee women are like *Kuti* women, unless they have abandoned the ways of their fathers, in which case they become like Jewish women[195]—which implies again that Sadducees remain basically 'Israel', for whom it is still possible, and perhaps expected, to repent. And yet, the *scholium* to *Megillat Taanit* treats Sadducees and "Israel" as distinct people;[196] and we find an early *Midrash* exclaiming that whoever denies the existence of a world-to-come is not among the descendants of Abraham.[197] These passages suggest reluctance, as with other heretics, to consider the Sadducees as 'Israel'.

(*Beitusim*), a sect related to the Sadducees (according to *Avot dRN* 5,2). On Sadducee polemics and the Boethusians, see Y. Sussman, "The History of Halakha and the Dead Sea Scrolls", in *Tarbiz* 59, 1989–90, pp. 11–76 (Hebrew).

[190] *B.Sanh.* 33b; *B.Horayot* 4a. The passage reads: "(the laws) that the Sadducees accept, anyone can go and *read* at the rabbis' house" (i.e. those laws are accessible for anyone to learn). The word 'read' suggests that the reference is to laws which are written explicitly in the Scriptures.

[191] *M.Mak.* 1,6; *M.Para* 3,7.

[192] *Avot dRN* 5,2, which also explains the origins of this sect. Doctrinal heresies of the same kind are listed, without specific reference to Sadducees, in *M.Sanh.* 10,1: he who denies the resurrection of the dead, or that the *Torah* is from Heaven, and the *apikoros* (see also *B.RH* 17a, mentioned above in note 170). Schiffman points out the similarity between these doctrines and those of Josephus' Sadducees (*Who was a Jew?*, pp. 41–46; on Sadducees in pre-rabbinic and in rabbinic sources, see also Schürer vol. II, pp. 404–14.). Incidentally, the exclusion of these characters from the world-to-come in *M.Sanh.* 10,1 suggests implicitly their exclusion from Israel, who, as stated in the same *mishna*, are all righteous and all have a share in the world-to-come (see p. 30).

[193] *B.Yev.* 63b.

[194] *B.Eruv.* 68b–69a (*tzeduki ke-nokhri*), in connection with the laws of *eruv*.

[195] *M.Nida* 4,2. *B.Nida* 33b (cf *T.Nida* 5,3) describes how they are fearful of the Pharisees. The similarity between the Sadducees and the *Kutim* may be explained in so far as both reject the authority of the rabbis and observe only what is explicit in Scriptures.

[196] Hans Lichtenstein, "Die Fastenrolle", in *HUCA* 8–9, 1931–2, pp. 257–51, on the 28th of *Tevet* (pp. 342–3).

[197] *Gen.R.* 53,12. This may be aimed at Sadducees, or at other *minim* contemporary of the rabbis in the Late Roman period.

4. THE COMMON PEOPLE

The common Jewish people, or *amei haAretz* as they are referred to in our sources, correspond in first instance to all Jews (Jewish born and Jewish converts) who would identify themselves as Jewish. According to rabbinic sources, common Jews in Palestine and in the Diaspora were generally faithful to the *Torah* and its commandments, e.g. the prohibition of *avoda zara*, circumcision, prayer, *shabbat*, festivals, charity, dietary laws, and others.[198] This would suggest that unlike the apostates, those who identified as Jews maintained what we have defined in chapter II, in rabbinic terms, as the *constitutive* features of the identity of Israel. Consequently, the identity of the common people as 'Israel' should be, at first sight, the least problematic to our sources.

However, rabbinic sources not unfrequently complain about the failure of the common people to conform to rabbinic teachings—which amounts, in rabbinic terms, to slackness of observance.[199] The category of 'common people' or *amei haAretz* is always referred to in our sources in *contradistinction* with that of the rabbis and their disciples, or in the *Mishna*, in contradistinction with the meticulously observant *ḥaver*. The question arises, therefore, whether this relative slackness of observance meant, in rabbinic terms, that the common people failed to achieve, effectively, the distinctive features of the rabbinic 'Israel'; and hence, whether the distinction of the rabbis from the common people may have extended as far as excluding the latter, in some way, from the distinctive category of 'Israel'.[200]

A. *Amei haAretz*

The category of *am haAretz*, or 'common people',[201] represents the largest single group of Jews referred to in rabbinic sources. As I have stated, *amei haAretz* are always distinguished from the rabbis and contrasted

---

[198] Classical and epigraphic sources would also confirm this. See Schürer vol. III.1, esp. pp. 138–149; E.P. Sanders, *Judaism: Practice and Belief. 63BCE–66CE*, London: SCM Press & Philadelphia: Trinity Press Int., 1992.

[199] See L.I. Levine, *The Rabbinic Class of Roman Palestine in Late Antiquity*, New York & Jerusalem: Jewish Theological Seminary, 1989, pp. 117–127.

[200] The restriction of the identity of 'Israel' to a limited, rabbinic circle might find some parallels, for instance, with the Qumran sect: see Schürer vol. II pp. 575–80 and 590.

[201] The term *am haAretz* literally means: 'the people of the land'. Although it is used differently in different periods, it usually refers to the common (Jewish) people. In rabbinic writings the term *am haAretz* is employed as a singular, i.e. 'common

with them. It is generally assumed in our sources that the *amei haAretz* nominally affiliate to the rabbis and their teachings;[202] nevertheless, rabbinic sources suspect them of slack observance, and despise them for their lack of knowledge and lack of respect for the rabbinic class.

Slack observance

A whole Mishnaic tractate, *Demai*, is based on the assumption that the *amei haAretz* do not fully tithe their produce, and that their word may not be trusted in this respect.[203] They are also careless about laws of purity,[204] but Talmudic sources suggest that this stems from ignorance rather than from deliberate neglect.[205]

In the *Babylonian Talmud*, the *amei haAretz* are defined, according to various Tannaim, as those who neglect the daily recitations of the *shema*, or who do not wear fringes or *tefillin*, or who do not observe the commandment of *mezuza*, or who fail to teach *Torah* to their children and to attend the *Torah* scholars.[206] Ignorance and lack of *Torah* learning is ascribed elsewhere to the *amei haAretz*.[207] In their ignorance, *amei haAretz* call synagogues 'the houses of the people'.[208] In a later source

---

person', with *amei haAretz* as its plural. For a concise description of the *amei haAretz* and rabbinic attitudes towards them, see L.I. Levine, *op.cit.*, pp. 112–117. For a general study, see Aharon Oppenheimer, *The 'Am Ha-Aretz*, Leiden: Brill, 1977.

[202] For a well-balanced assessment, see Levine *op.cit.* pp. 98–106, 127–33, and especially 192–5.

[203] *M.Demai, passim*. See also *B.Sot.* 48a.

[204] *M.Demai* 2,3. In *T.AZ* 3,10 (= *B.Ber.* 47b etc.) it is debated whether the *am haAretz* is Halakhically defined as a person negligent in tithing (the Sages' view) or rather in the laws of purity (R.Meir's view). In practice, however, Tannaitic sources show plainly that the *amei haAretz* were negligent in both.

[205] He is trusted if he says: a) that his produce has not become liable to impurity (through being wet); but he is not if he claims: b) that it is liable to impurity but has not become impure: *Y.Demai* 2,3; *B.Hag.* 22b. Oppenheimer (*op.cit.*, p. 92) rightly argues that he cannot be suspected of *lying* in the latter statement (b): indeed, if he really wanted to lie and be believed, he could have made instead the former statement (a) (as the *Mishna* explicitly argues in a similar case in *M.Demai* 6,11). It must be that he is actually concerned not to mislead his customers in matters of purity, but is simply *not sufficiently knowledgeable* in the complex laws of purity for his latter statement (b), albeit sincere, to be reliable (whereas laws of liability to impurity are considerably simpler and hence are known to the *am haAretz*). In *M.Tohorot* 10,1, the *am haAretz* is said not to be 'knowledgeable' in the laws relating to moving things impure (*heyset*). Significantly, the *am haAretz* who wishes to become a *haver* (i.e., reliable in matters of purity) must first be *taught* the laws of purity: *T.Demai* 2,10; *B.Bekh.* 30b.

[206] *B.Ber.* 47b; *B.Sot.* 22a.

[207] *B.Ket.* 111b.

[208] *B.Shab.* 32a; they also call the Holy Ark *arana* ('Ark'), *tout court*. Cf Levine *op.cit.* p. 114 n. 77.

the *amei haAretz* are accused of speaking maliciously ("evil tongue") of *Torah* scholars;[209] but the same *Midrash* concedes that

> they have good manners (*derekh eretz*) and keep away from (sexual) transgression, theft, and all evil things.[210]

Affinity with non-Jews

Impurity itself points to an affinity between *amei haAretz* and the non-Jews. Rabbis are depicted in the *Mishna* as refraining from commercial exchanges and social contacts with the *amei haAretz*,[211] as well as from attending their synagogues.[212] In this respect, *amei haAretz* are treated in a similar manner to non-Jews.[213] In the *Babylonian Talmud*, we find that rabbis do not dine with them[214] or even sit with them[215] and enjoy their company.[216] They warn against living in the neighbour-hood of *amei haAretz*, even of pious ones.[217] Even in a period of famine, R. Yehuda the Patriarch strove not to distribute his corn to the *amei haAretz*; he had to be forced, eventually, to allow them into his granaries.[218]

Significantly, the rabbi/ *am haAretz* divide is explicitly compared, in a passage in *B.Pes.*, with that of Israel and the nations: the *amei haAretz* (and particularly their wives) are said to hate *Torah* scholars more than the non-Jews hate Israel.[219] The similarity between *amei haAretz* and non-Jews is reiterated, in the same Talmudic passage, in many other ways. The *am haAretz* is lustful, as we have seen with the non-Jews.[220] R. Akiva recalls that as an *am haAretz*, he used to want to bite *Torah* scholars "like a donkey".[221] Consequently, *amei haAretz* are

---

[209] *Eliyahu R.* 13 (beginning and end).

[210] *Ib.* 15, p. 69.

[211] Mainly because they are perpetually impure, as *M.Demai* 2,2–3, and *M.Tohorot* 7,2–5 and 8,1 plainly convey. But even when, in the later period, the rabbis became less particular about purity (see my remarks in pp. 54–5), untithed produce would have remained a problem of considerable importance.

[212] *M.Avot* 3,10.

[213] See sections IV.1.A-B.

[214] *B.Ber.* 34b; cf *B.AZ* 27b; *B.Shab.* 147b; *Eliyahu R.* 12, pp. 59–61. A *haver* does not attend, as a guest, the house of an *am haAretz*: *M.Demai* 2,3.

[215] *Derekh Eretz Z.* 6,1.

[216] *B.Ned.* 20a.

[217] *B.Shab.* 63a.

[218] *B.BB* 8a; minor tractate *Kalla R.* 2.

[219] *B.Pes.* 49b.

[220] Section I.3.A.

[221] His pupils ask: "why not like a dog?". On the affinity between non-Jews and donkeys (and dogs), see pp. 35–8. In *B.BB* 8a an '*am haAretz*' asked Rabbi, during the famine above mentioned, to feed him "as he would a dog or a raven"; however,

to be treated in much the same way as a non-Jew. It is forbidden to marry their daughters, for they are 'abominations', their wives are 'creepies', and marrying their daughters amounts to bestiality.[222] Learning *Torah* before an *am haAretz* is like having intercourse with one's bride in front of him.[223] Just as non-Jews, the *amei haAretz* are suspected, according to R. El'azar, of murder: "if they did not need us for their business, they would be killing us all"; therefore one is forbidden to travel together with an *am haAretz*, for "in the same way as he does not care for his own life, so he does not care for yours".[224] R.El'azar adds that it is permissible to stab an *am haAretz*—even on a *Yom Kippur* that coincides with *shabbat*; his pupils suggest that the *am haAretz* should be ritually slaughtered (as an animal), but R. El'azar answers maliciously that stabbing is better, as this would not require a blessing. R. Yohanan makes a similar statement; but neither, I think, should necessarily be taken *au pied de la lettre*.[225]

The amei haAretz as Israel

This virulent, vitriolic passage is unique in its kind in our sources. Elsewhere the *Babylonian Talmud* can be quite sympathetic towards the *am haAretz*. Contrary to what is taught in the passage just quoted, other passages praise those who endeavour to teach *Torah* to the *amei haAretz*.[226] Indeed, our sources describe how the common people would commonly attend the rabbis' public preachings.[227] R. Shimon b. Gamliel holds that it is better for an *am haAretz* to commit a serious offense than for a Sage to commit a minor one, but his son R. Yehuda the Patriarch argues the reverse, that it is better for the Sage to commit

---

this comparison was not an *am haAretz*'s self-ascription, but actually a rabbinic statement, as this '*am haAretz*' turned out to be a rabbi in disguise . . .

[222] On intermarriage with non-Jews, see section IV.1.D. Animals are commonly associated with the non-Jews (see section I.4.A), especially abominations and 'creepies' (see p. 58); consequently, it is marriage with non-Jews which is usually considered as bestiality (see p. 165).

[223] The *Torah* is indeed the bride of Israel (see p. 74). Similarly one may not reveal "secrets" to an *am haAretz*: (*ib.*). In this respect, again, the *am haAretz* is similar to a non-Jew, to whom it is forbidden to teach *Torah* (*B.Hag.* 13a) or to reveal one's "secrets" (*B.Ket.* 111a—see p. 221, n. 142).

[224] Cf minor tractate *Kalla R.* 2. As we have seen, there are restrictions on travelling with non-Jews for exactly the same reasons (p. 23; also p. 147).

[225] All passages in this paragraph are quoted from *B.Pes.* 49b.

[226] *B.BM* 85a; and *Lev.R.* 34,13.

[227] See Levine *op.cit.* pp. 102–5; M. Hirshman, "The Preacher and his Public in Third Century Palestine", in *JJS* 42(1), Spring 1991, pp. 108–114.

a minor offense than for the *am haAretz* to commit a serious one.[228] Whereas inadvertent offenses committed by Sages are judged (by the Almighty) as though they were deliberate, deliberate offenses committed by *amei haAretz* are judged as though they were inadvertent.[229] Concerning the fate of the *amei haAretz* in the world-to-come, the rabbis are divided. R. Yoḥanan is 'upset' at the suggestion that they might not have a share in it, for, he argues, the *amei haAretz* are not *avoda zara* worshippers.[230] According to *Avot dRN*, one should not love *Torah* scholars and hate *amei haAretz*; rather, one should love them all.[231]

Unlike the passage in *B.Pes.*, a number of sources would stress the identity of the *amei haAretz* as Israel.[232] According to the *Tosefta*, the *am haAretz* is not suspected of lying as to whether his produce has been tithed, provided he has nothing to gain from it: "Israel are not suspected of this".[233] In the *Babylonian Talmud*, Israel is compared to a vine of which the clusters are the *Torah* scholars and the leaves are the *amei haAretz*; hence, the following instruction was once sent to Babylon from the land of Israel: "let the clusters pray for the leaves, for without the leaves, the clusters would not last".[234] The *Midrash* explains that the *amei haAretz* 'cover' (i.e. protect) the rabbis in the same way as the leaves cover the clusters.[235] Similarly, elsewhere, Israel is compared to a nut: in the same way as the shell of a nut protects its fruit, so the *amei haAretz* protect (or: support) *Torah* learning.[236] Israel is also compared to a date-tree: just as the date-tree yields dates of various qualities and also thorns, so Israel comprises *Torah* scholars, *amei haAretz* as well as boors.[237] These similes confirm, in one sense, the distinction between the rabbis and the *amei haAretz*; nevertheless, both are depicted as forming part, in organic solidarity, of the same

---

[228] *Y.Maaserot* 2,1; *B.Eruv.* 32a. See also the dispute in *B.Men.* 99b as to whether one should disclose to the *am haAretz* that reciting the *shema* twice a day constitutes a fulfilment, albeit minimal, of one's duty of daily *Torah* learning.

[229] *B.BM* 33b.

[230] *B.Ket.* 111b.

[231] *Avot dRN* 16.

[232] See *B.BM* 33b.

[233] Whereas a non-Jew in any case cannot be trusted, as he is liable to mislead his customers for no reason: *T.Demai* 5,2.

[234] *B.Hul.* 92a.

[235] *Lev.R.* 36,2.

[236] *Song R.* 6,11 (s.v. *maḥzikin be-divrei Torah*); cf *Pes.R.* 11,2. According to *Song R.* 7,3,3, Israel are compared to wheat which is measured together with its waste: similarly, among Israel are included "wood-cutters and water drawers" (*Deut.* 29:10).

[237] *Num.R.* 3,1; cf *Tanh. Bamidbar* 15 (*Tanh.B.* 17), *Midrash Tehillim* (ed. Buber) 92,11.

symbolic entity: the *amei haAretz* are an intrinsic, as well as an indispensable part of the people of Israel.

Ambiguity and contradiction

The image of the *am haAretz* is undoubtedly mixed, and even, at times, contradictory. In some sources, *amei haAretz* are emphatically portrayed as indispensable members of the people of Israel; whilst in other sources, their affinity with non-Jews is given much the same emphasis—albeit not to the same extent as with apostates and heretics (the *amei haAretz* are never treated as "non-Jews in all respects").

This apparent contradiction has been explained by some in terms of a historical change. Levine claims, for instance, that outright hostility towards the *amei haAretz* in the Tannaitic period was gradually superseded, in the Amoraic period, by a more balanced, two-sided point of view (and that by the early Middle Ages the *am haAretz* faded away completely from rabbinic literature).[238] But as I have argued in my introduction, individual sayings cannot be tied down to a fixed point in historical time, as they were transmitted, initially orally, over many centuries. The mere fact that the early mediaeval editors of the *Babylonian Talmud* recorded and learnt Tannaitic sayings on the *amei haAretz* suggests that they had remained relevant, to some extent at least, to their lived experience.[239]

The ambiguity of Talmudic sources vis-a-vis the *amei haAretz* is better accepted for what it is and at face value, rather than 'explained away'. According to our sources, indeed, it is the same R. Yehuda who barred the *amei haAretz* from his granaries, but who disagreed with his father in their favour (see above). It is the same R. Yoḥanan who urges that an *am haAretz* be "torn like a fish",[240] but who is upset at the suggestion that *amei haAretz* have no share in the world-to-come.[241] Clearly, the *Talmud* considers that it was possible for the rabbis to

---

[238] See also Oppenheimer, *op.cit.*, ch. 5 (pp. 170–99).

[239] Levine admits this objection to his argument *in extremis*, on p. 117 n. 93. It is clear that rabbinic conflicts with *amei haAretz* or 'common people' have endured until today, even though it is not explicitly accounted for in each rabbinic generation. Levine also claims that little material is found on the *am haAretz* in sources of Palestinian origin, in contrast for instance with *B.Pes.* 49b, which suggests that the issue of the *am haAretz* only endured in Babylonia (in post-Tannaitic centuries: p. 117 and n. 93); but this suggestion does not account for the outstanding ambiguities in the *Babylonian Talmud* itself, as it is presently redacted.

[240] *B.Pes.* 49b.

[241] See Levine (*op.cit.*) pp. 115–6. Resh Lakish and other rabbis also display 'inconsistent' views on the *am haAretz*.

entertain both notions simultaneously. Their ambivalent attitude towards *amei haAretz*, and its implications regarding the definition of 'Israel', will be discussed in the conclusion to this chapter.

B. *"Sinners of Israel"*

Problems of definition

Unlike most groups which we have so far considered (converts, apostates, *amei haAretz*, etc.), the "sinners of Israel" do not constitute a Halakhic category in its own right; indeed, the term seldom appears in Halakhic sources. This suggests that it is unlikely to have a standard meaning in rabbinic writings.[242] But although the terms "sinners of Israel", "wicked of Israel", apostates and heretics tend to overlap with each other in Aggadic sources,[243] I have found in the *vast majority* of cases that the term "sinners of Israel" refers to a distinguishable group: our sources treat them in a more conciliatory manner, reminiscent in some respects of the *amei haAretz*.[244]

Indeed, one Talmudic passage draws an explicit, Halakhic distinction between the sinners on the one hand, and the apostates, those who make wine libations to *avoda zara*, and the desecrators of *shabbat* in public on the other—whose offenses are much more severe.[245] Elsewhere we hear that unlike apostates, sinners are confined to Gehenna for only a limited period of twelve months,[246] or even that the fire of Gehenna does not take hold of them at all, for the merit of circumcision redeems them.[247]

---

[242] A. Marmorstein, in *Studies in Jewish Theology*, London: OUP, 1950, pp. 179–224, considers the *posh'ei Yisrael* (lit. 'sinners of Israel') to be a "peculiar sect of Jews" (p. 185) identifiable as a Jewish Christian sect. In my opinion, however, this term is too vague and its usages too diverse to represent a specific, well-defined group.

[243] Thus in *Tanh. Lekh* 20, the 'sinners of Israel' are described as "those who denied the Almighty and followed the customs of the nations", which would place them firmly, against normal usage, in the category of apostates. I would accept that as an Aggadic term, its usage need not be free of inconsistencies.

[244] The term *rish'ei Yisrael* (the wicked of Israel) may be confused at times with *posh'ei Yisrael*, particularly as their spelling is similar; but they are clearly distinguished in *T.Sanh.* 13, 1–4, and I have generally found that the 'wicked of Israel' are considered worse than the 'sinners' and closer to the category of apostates and heretics (e.g. in *Ex.R.* 19,4).

[245] *B.Hul.* 5a (= *B.Eruv.* 69b).

[246] Whereas apostates are confined forever: *T.Sanh.* 13,4–5; *B.RH* 17a.

[247] *B.Eruv.* 19a; *B.Hag.* end; more on this below. In later *Midrashim* we are told that the sinners of Israel answer *amen* from the depths of Gehenna to the praises offered by the righteous to the Almighty in the Garden of Eden, whereupon the Almighty redeems them: *Eliyahu Z.* 20; *Otiyot deR.Akiva* 7 (1st recension, ed.Wertheimer).

What does the distinction between "sinners" and "apostates" consist of? It would seem that sinners are not committed to a formal and permanent rejection of the commandments, as the apostates are: their offenses are no more than casual and intermittent.[248] This *informal* character would explain why "sinners" are not treated as an established Halakhic category: indeed, unlike apostates or *amei haAretz*, it would be impossible for anyone to define or describe them in a definitive, universal manner.

Affinity with non-Jews

The sinners may be treated to some extent as non-Jews, inasmuch as it is forbidden to hate a Jew, but if one sees in him something improper (*devar erva*) one is commanded to hate him.[249] Interestingly, in the same Talmudic passage which distinguishes apostates from sinners, the latter are referred to as "people who are like animals",[250] which reminds us of the rabbinic image of the non-Jews.[251] However, few passages suggest direct affinity between the sinners and non-Jews. In one specific context, the *Talmud* explains that the term *nokhri* (usually meaning 'non-Jew') may refer to a sinful Jew, though only as a euphemism (*lishna ma'alya*).[252]

The sinners as Israel

By and large, the *Babylonian Talmud* adopts a remarkably positive attitude towards the sinners of Israel. It boldly states that the sinners of Israel are "full of commandments as a pomegranate (is with seeds)", which is why the fire of Gehenna does not take hold of them after their death.[253] This is because unlike non-Jewish sinners, the sinners of Israel eventually repent.[254] Sinners of Israel are preferable even to divinely

---

[248] Sinners of Israel are characterized in one place as being those who do not wear *tefillin* (whilst the 'sinners of the nations' are guilty of sexual offenses—*B.RH* 17a), similarly to *amei haAretz*, as we have seen elsewhere (*B.Ber.* 47b; *B.Sot.* 22a); see pp. 70–1.

[249] *B.Pes.* 113b.

[250] *B.Hul.* 5a (= *B.Eruv.* 69b).

[251] Section I.4.A. This phrase also emphasizes that although distinct from apostates, sinners should not be fully exonerated.

[252] *B.Sanh.* 54a.

[253] *B.Eruv.* 19a; *B.Hag.* end; cf *Midrash Tehillim* 92 (according to the *textus receptus*).

[254] *B.Eruv. ib.* In this respect sinners are also distinguished from the apostates, in that only sinners are allowed to bring sacrifices to the Temple for repentance, whereas apostates are presumed beyond repentance: *B.Hul.* 5a (= *B.Eruv.* 69b).

inspired non-Jews.[255] A later *Midrash* maintains that even the bad among Israel perform good deeds.[256]

This idealistic view of the sinners of Israel is backed up in the *Babylonian Talmud* with an emphasis on their identity as Israel. For instance: "although he has sinned, he is an Israel"[257]—implying not only that his Jewish status is retained, but also that this should mitigate the gravity of his offenses. In another passage which I have already quoted, Abraham redeems the sinners of Israel at the entrance of Gehenna through the merit of their circumcision;[258] circumcision appears to represent their enduring Jewish identity, which distinguishes them from the heretics whom an angel decircumcises,[259] and *a fortiori* from the non-Jews.

Likewise, the priviledged relationship between the Almighty and Israel, which we have frequently encountered in connection with Jewish identity,[260] applies in the same measure to the sinners of Israel. R. Meir emphatically maintains that

> although Israel are full of blemishes, they are called "(My) sons" ... when they do not perform (commandments), they are called "My people".[261]

---

[255] As Onkelos found out after conjuring the spirits of Balaam and Titus from after-life: *B.Git.* 56b–57a.

[256] *Num.R.* 3,1. "Bad" is an uncertain translation of *surim*. The parallel source in *Midrash Tehillim* (ed. Buber) 92,11 reads *amei haAretz* instead of "bad".

[257] *B.Sanh.* 44a. Such emphasis and explicitness are not paralleled in the case of the *Yisrael mumar*. According to Rashi (*ad loc.*), this statement refers to the people of Israel collectively. However, the fact that the word "Israel" is treated here as a singular suggests that it refers to an individual, who in this context would be Achan (see *Joshua* 7), described in the same passage as transgressing (*avar*) the *Torah* and decircumcising (he is not described as worshipping *avoda zara* or as *rejecting* the *Torah*, which might explain why the Talmud refers to him as a sinner, but not as anything worse, e.g. an apostate). On this see J. Katz, *op.cit.* (1961) pp. 67–74, especially 71–2, and *op.cit.* (1984) pp. 255–69, who shows that although this saying, in its original context, was Aggadic and not applicable to apostates, Rashi applied it in his responsa (171; 173; 175), for Halakhic purposes, to the apostate. I would add that the same occurs in the 11th century *Midrash Aggada*, ed. S. Buber p. 162 (*parashat matot*). In practical terms, nevertheless, Rashi's view of the Halakhic status of the apostate seems not to have differed significantly from that of early rabbinic writings.

[258] *B.Eruv.* 19a; *B.Hag.* end.

[259] See p. 112.

[260] See conclusion to chapter II.

[261] *Sifre Deut.* 308, beginning, *contra* R. Yehuda. Cf *Sifre Num.* 1 (= *Num.R.* 7,8): "although they are impure, the Divine Presence is among them". According to *Num.R.* 7,9, however, the Divine Presence departs from them if they are guilty of murder or of forbidden relations. Cf also *Ex.R.* 24,3.

and again, whether worthy or not "in any case, you are called 'My sons'".[262] Israel are dear to the Almighty (as much as Elijah[263]), even if they sin.[264] The mercy of God is upon all Israel, wicked and righteous alike.[265]

As the *amei haAretz*, the sinners are treated as indispensable components of Israel. According to an early *Midrash*, which interprets the four species which are taken on *Sukkot* as representing different sections of the people of Israel, the willows, which have no taste nor smell, correspond to those who have neither *Torah* nor good actions; since, in the words of the *Midrash*, "it is impossible to reject them", they must be *physically bound together* with the other three species.[266] In the *Babylonian Talmud*'s comparison of Israel with the vine, the rods are taken to represent the "empty ones", i.e. the worthless.[267] Although inferior even to the *amei haAretz*, whom we have seen are represented by the (less worthless) leaves, they remain, as rods, an intrinsic component of the vine.[268] Finally, according to the *Babylonian Talmud*, a public fast which does not include the sinners of Israel (i.e. where they do not participate, or alternatively, where they are not included in the public prayers) is not considered a fast; this is inferred from the fact that although galbanum has a bad smell, it is, in the Temple, an *indispensable* ingredient of the incense.[269]

Thus even if the sinners of Israel are less righteous than the *amei haAretz*, our sources show the same determination, in contrast with the apostates, to mitigate their sins so as to have them included amongst the people of Israel.

---

[262] *Sifre Deut.* 96; *B.Kid.* 36a; *contra* R. Yehuda. In *Y.Kid.* 1,7, however, only the latter's view is quoted.

[263] *Song R.* 7,6.

[264] *Num.R.* 2,15.

[265] *Eliyahu R.* 14, p. 62 (text as amended by Friedmann on the basis of the *Yalkut Shimoni*).

[266] *Lev.R.* 30,12; *Tanh. Emor* 17 (with slight variations).

[267] *B.Hul.* 92a, quoted above in p. 118. The term "empty ones" (*rekanim*) is equated with the sinners of Israel in *B.Eruv.* 19a.

[268] The same idea is expressed with reference to the "bad among Israel" in a comparison of Israel with the date-tree in *Num.R.* 3,1, above mentioned (see footnote 237). With similar reference to the *am haAretz* and the date-tree, see above p. 118.

[269] *B.Ker.* 6b, quoting *Amos* 9:6 which is taken literally as meaning: "He (God) has founded on earth His bondage (*agudato*)". This interpretation is found again in *B.Men.* 27a where the 'bondage' of the people of Israel is paralleled to the physical bondage of the four species of *Sukkot*, which include fruit-bearing as well as fruitless species.

5. The Rabbis and the People: A Centripetal Experience

A. *The problem of the 'grey areas'*

A dichotomous model

As I have tried to suggest, the 'peripheral' groups which we have studied might fall into two distinctive categories. Converts, *amei haAretz* and sinners are often described emphatically as full members of Israel; whilst *Kutim*, apostates, and heretics are virtually excluded from Israel, and treated in *halakha* as though they were completely non-Jewish. This clear dichotomy is founded, I will suggest, on two possible considerations: the first is subjective and self-definitional; the second is objective and related to the constitutive features of Jewish identity. However, I shall argue that this model fails to account for a number of outstanding ambiguities, which are so pervasive to the social context of rabbinic literature that they cannot be lightly dismissed.

Self-definition

The exclusion of apostates from the category of Israel was primarily self-inflicted: by definition, they did not identify themselves as being 'Israel'. This was not the case with some *minim* who may have regarded themselves as 'Israel', for instance, as we know, the Christians and the Samaritans/*Kutim*. However their notion of 'Israel' was *incompatible* with that of the rabbis; which rendered impossible any form of ethnic solidarity between the authors of our sources, and the apostates, the heretics and the *Kutim*.

Converts, on the other hand, strove, by definition again, to be identified as legitimate members of Israel; and so, in all likelihood, did the common Jewish-born people and even a substantial proportion of what rabbinic sources would refer to as 'sinners'. It is probable, moreover, that the common people were sufficiently affiliated to the rabbis and their teachings[270] so as to identify themselves with an 'Israel' which was, unlike the heretics', at least compatible with rabbinic teachings. *Amei haAretz* and sinners could be severely criticised for their shortcomings, but evidently this did not prevent rabbinic sources from appreciating their genuine desire to be recognized as Israel, and from giving full sanction to this subjective, self-ascribed identity.

Thus the dichotomy between apostates, heretics and *Kutim* on the

---

[270] See above p. 115.

one hand, and converts, *amei haAretz* and sinners on the other may be explained in terms of their own, subjective self-definition.

Objective features

According to our sources, the shortcomings of converts, common people and even sinners are, we have seen, relatively benign. The convert is no more than *prone* to returning to his non-Jewish ways. The *am haAretz* is slack for the most part in matters of tithing and of purities. The 'sinners of Israel' are clearly distinguished from apostates and from those who desecrate the *shabbat* in public and make libations to *avoda zara*; it is assumed, moreover, that sinners adhere to Jewish practices such as circumcision, which in a passage above quoted symbolizes their adherence to Jewish identity and hence redeems them from Gehenna. In 'objective' terms, therefore, it appears that the common people are unquestionably 'Israel' as they display the essential features which are constitutive of Jewish identity.

This cannot be said of the *Kutim*, apostates and heretics, as nearly all reject the *Torah* (or at least, the Oral *Torah*) and are accused of *avoda zara*, which constitutes a palpable departure from the fold of Israel. Interestingly, they are not accused of murder, forbidden relations or theft:[271] I think this is because the latter, although major transgressions, do not constitute in themselves a violation of the distinctive characteristics of Israel. Furthermore, we have found that even 'limited apostates' are guilty of transgressions which significantly affect their Jewish identity: they eat carrion and non-kosher meat, pork, abominations and 'creepies'; they desecrate the *shabbat*[272] and are decircumcised.[273] As *Avot dRN* states, apostates and *minim* may not be loved because they do not "act like your people".[274] By renouncing the objective features of Israel, their Jewish identity is necessarily forlorn.

---

[271] See Petuchowski, who notes (1959, p. 182) concerning the apostate "a total absence of references to sexual transgressions, for instance, or to infringements of civil law". It seems that whoever commits these crimes would probably be regarded as a 'sinner of Israel', albeit the worst of its kind.

[272] See p. 106. Desecration of *shabbat* leads to apostasy: we are told that once people were found catching fish on *shabbat*, a ban was placed on them, whereupon they apostatized (*ishtemud*—*B.Kid.* 72a).

[273] Quoted above in p. 106. On non-kosher meat, pork, abominations and 'creepies': section II.1.B. On circumcision: section II.2.A.

[274] *Avot dRN* 16, in explicit contrast with the *amei haAretz*.

'Grey areas'

The dichotomous model I have presented is unfortunately not so clear-cut. First of all, it is not absolutely symmetrical: whereas the convert becomes fully Jewish, the apostate and heretic cannot divest themselves entirely of their identity as Israel. This irreversibility remains to be explained; all I have suggested is that it may be due to the fact that all Jews are bound by oath to adhere to the commandments of the Almighty. Nevertheless, it raises the paradoxical possibility of being 'Israel', albeit in a limited sense, without however displaying or experiencing any of its constitutive features.

Secondly, the position of the *am haAretz* in this dichotomous model remains ambiguous, as in some passages he is compared unequivocally to the non-Jew in his worst, animal-like features. As I have shown, this ambiguity cannot be accounted for as representing divergent rabbinic opinions, since we find conflicting views attributed in the *Babylonian Talmud* to the same rabbinic figures. It should also be noted that although *shabbat*-observant and circumcised, the *am haAretz* is described as neglectful of *tefillin*, fringes, and above all *Torah* learning, all of which are treated by our sources as powerful constituents of Jewish identity.[275] Thus in our model, the *am haAretz* appears to occupy a 'grey area', emphatically Israel but simultaneously akin to the non-Jews, in view of his failure to adhere to 'Israel' in *all* its constituent features. Thus far from obtaining a clear dichotomy between Israel and (virtual) non-Jews, we now find a wide spectrum ranging from Israel to *amei haAretz*, sinners of Israel, partial apostates, full apostates, heretics and *Kutim*, and finally outright non-Jews.

Dual identity

However, rather than occupying a theoretical middle-ground, the *am haAretz* is presented in our sources as being *either* Israel *or* akin to the non-Jews, or even both at once. In this respect, to define the *am haAretz* as a static, stable 'grey area' within our dichotomous model would not do justice to the paradox, indeed the contradiction which his ever-shifting, 'dual' identity continues to present.

Yet it must be recognized that dual identity is neither problematic nor impossible, but actually quite plausible and realistic. Our perception of people and things is not static but dynamic and changing, according

---

[275] See section II.2–3.

to time, context and conditions. In a case involving self-identity, the perceiving self can draw on a panoply of alternative identities, some inclusive of the outside world and others more exclusive, so as to adjust and orient himself in the ever-changing environment in which he is engaged. It is reasonable to assume, therefore, that in some contexts a rabbi may have been inclined to include the *am haAretz* within Israel, whereas in others he would have excluded him. The ambiguous status of the *am haAretz* is thus not problematic, even when expressed by the same rabbinic figure, but reflects if anything the realities of human perception and experience.[276]

But although it might be fair to assume, in this way, that the rabbinic perception of the *am haAretz* was largely context-bound, this assumption finds no substantiation in our sources. We might have expected, for instance, that it was in passages dealing with the nations that the *amei haAretz* would be distinguished from them and treated emphatically as 'Israel'; but I have not found this to be the case. It is difficult, however, to draw any conclusions from this observation. We must not lose sight of the fact that in the complex process of oral transmission and redaction of our sources, rabbinic sayings became considerably decontextualised; the context of a saying relating to *amei haAretz* may thus have been considered irrelevant, or self-evident and ignored.

B. *"Israel" and centripetal experience*

Who are 'Israel'?

Let us approach the same problem from the other end: to whom do rabbinic sources refer with the term 'Israel'? In the first chapter, we found that 'Israel' was experienced as an idealized, homogenous and collective entity, righteous and quasi-angelic, which was

---

[276] At least from the perspective of rabbinic sources. What identity the *am haAretz himself* experienced, and more to the point, what identity rabbinic sources *thought* he experienced, is a matter which is never raised. Indeed, since he fails to display essential features of Jewish identity, one wonders what, in rabbinic terms, his experience of being Jewish could consist of . . .

The same question could be asked with reference to women: the most important features of Jewish identity which we have described, *Torah* learning and circumcision, are not to be performed by or on women, even though their belonging to the people of Israel is absolutely unquestionable. However, women are substantially different from all the social groups we have analyzed, in so far as they are not kept aloof by the rabbis but part of the rabbis' restricted social circle; moreover, women are *exempt* from these commandments, as opposed to the common people who *fail* to perform them. Therefore the problem of women's Jewish identity calls upon a radically different set of considerations; I shall tentatively address it in section V.2.D.

distinguished and diametrically opposed to the entity of the non-Jews. We saw in the second chapter that this experience depended essentially on Israel's adherence to the Almighty through the observance of His commandments. Yet in this chapter, we find that the so-called people of Israel are neither homogenous nor matching this idyllic description. Jewish heretics, albeit 'Israel', are by no means "faithful sons of faithful" as Israel are elsewhere described.[277] Apostates, though 'Israel', have rejected the covenantal yoke of the Almighty without which Israel would not be a nation. The common people do not learn *Torah*. If so, in phrases such as "Israel are not suspected", "Israel are holy", "Israel are dear because they have been given the *Torah*"—whom are these sources referring to? How inclusive is the term 'Israel'?

This question is not merely one of textual interpretation; it concerns the rabbinic ontological experience of belonging to a collectivity called 'Israel'. If the idyllic, rabbinic image of Israel did not obtain in actual reality, we may wonder why and how the authors of our sources could sustain it, in practice, as the basis of their experience of being 'Israel'.

As I have argued above concerning the identity of the *am haAretz*, we may suggest a model of multiple and ever-changing identities; i.e. that according to context, the term 'Israel' (collective plural) may have a variety of meanings, some inclusive, others exclusive, which in our sources are never explicitly distinguished.[278] This would entail, however, that various usages of the term 'Israel' would often be incompatible and contradictory. Without denying entirely the validity of this approach, I would like to suggest two other interpretations—Utopia and centripetalism—which would entail a more consistent meaning to the term 'Israel'.

Utopia and reality

Jacob Neusner has often maintained that much of the *Mishna*, as well

---

[277] *B.Shab.* 97a.

[278] Besides the Halakhic usages of 'Israel' as a singular, discussed in section I.2.A, to which I am not referring here. I have found no evidence to suggest that the various meanings of Israel correspond to a divergence of opinions among the rabbis of our writings. We have seen that 'conflicting' statements about the *am haAretz* can be issued by the same rabbi (pp. 119–20). The sayings I have quoted in chapters I–II are attributed, by and large, to the same authorities as those quoted in this chapter, and they are found in the same rabbinic sources. We must assume, therefore, that this paradoxical perception of Israel, including at once an idyll and a set of 'grey areas', could be sustained *in toto* by the same individual rabbi.

as subsequent writings, legislate for a Utopian world rather than for the realities of Late Antique Palestinian society. Most of the order of *Kodashim* ('Holy things') and substantial section of the other orders (e.g. tractates *Bikkurim*, *Yoma*, *Sota*) deal with Temple ritual, which by the time of the redaction of the *Mishna* had long been extinct. It is questionable whether rabbinical courts had the power, in this period, to exercise the civil and criminal jurisdiction described in the order of Damages. In this respect, rabbinic writings account for the life of Israel only as it should be in an ideal world.[279] Nonetheless, this Utopia is not depicted for purely 'academic', theoretical reasons: it represents to the authors of our sources a potential reality, which is to be actualised with the imminent redemption of the Jewish people.[280]

The rabbinic, idyllic image of Israel as fully righteous and observant is another aspect of this Utopia and ideal. In phrases such as "Israel are holy", 'Israel' does not refer to the multifarious Jewish people of Late Antiquity, including heretics, apostates, and *amei haAretz*, but rather to an *ideal* people, who all adhere to the commandments as expounded by the rabbis and collectively display the same, distinctive features of rabbinic Jewish identity.[281]

However, our sources do not refer to 'Israel' as some Utopia pertaining, as the Temple and its cult, to some imminent Messianic future. 'Israel' are presented as a concrete, present-day reality. The image of Israel as 'righteous' is so 'real' to the authors of our sources that it forms the basis of a number of practical, Halakhic rulings:

---

[279] Neusner may have over-emphasized the theoretical nature of Mishnaic writings. Some passages of the *Mishna* are actually quite 'realistic': for instance tractate *Demai*, which is entirely devoted to the unfortunate reality of the *amei haAretz* and the doubts surrounding the tithing of their produce.

[280] Neusner may not have taken sufficient account of this point. The *Mishna* talks of the imminent re-building of the Temple (*M.Tamid* 7,3, also *M.Taan.* 4,8; *Avot* 5,10; *B.BM* 28b) and the return of Elijah (*M.BM* 1,8, 2,8, 3,4–5; cf *M.Eduyot* 8,7); it even refers to the possibility of making sacrifices today (*M.Eduyot* 8,6). According to the *Babylonian Talmud* many rulings from after the destruction of the Temple are based on the assumption that it will be imminently re-built: thus priests must remain sober *at all times*, in case they are suddenly called to the new Temple (*B.Sanh.* 22b; *B.Taan.* 17b); the supply of animals suitable for sacrifice must be maintained (*B.Bekh.* 53b; cf also *B.RH* 30b, *B.Suk.* 41a, *B.Betza* 5b, *B.Men.* 68b). The *Babylonian Talmud* also reports that the Amoraim of Galilee were producing some food in a state of purity, to be offered in the Temple when it would be restored (*B.Hag.* 25a, *B.Nida* 6b, quoted in pp. 54–5, note 25).

[281] It may be of some significance that in Halakhic passages, the term "Israel" (singular) refers to the *theoretical* Jew rather than to an observable reality (see p. 11).

for instance, the laws of *yiḥud* (private meetings), which assume that Israel, unlike the non-Jews, cannot be tempted into sexual transgressions (see p. 26). Remarkably, however, our sources state elsewhere that the *amei haAretz*—who may well represent the majority of the Jewish people—are just as lustful as non-Jews.[282] Thus although the idyllic image of 'Israel' is treated as a practical, Halakhically significant reality, rabbinic sources could themselves concede that in empirical terms, and in the majority of cases, this image simply did not obtain.

It is difficult to understand how the authors of our sources could have conceived of 'Israel' and identified with it as an *actual*, ontological experience, when in empirical reality, of their own admission, it did not exist. Similar difficulties have been encountered by ethnographer Michael Jackson in his attempt to make sense of the Kuranko belief in shape-shifting (e.g. that some men can change into elephants)—which is empirically impossible—especially as it is not merely a mythical account, but a faculty which some individuals experience as part of their actual ontological identity. The question is, under which the conditions could such a belief (shape-shifting, or idyllic 'Israel') "be entertained as reasonable and made intelligible and, most important, *realized as a sensible truth*".[283]

Jackson argues that beliefs of this kind should not be justified or made sense of on the basis of their theoretical truth or 'rationality', but rather on the basis of their *pragmatic use* and *experiential veracity*. This approach has also been advocated by philosopher William James;[284] to paraphrase him, I would say that Utopian 'Israel' can become a reality to the authors of rabbinic sources firstly if it has "practical cash-value", and secondly "if it can help them to get into satisfactory relation with other parts of their experience"; it would hence be "true for just so much, true in so far forth, true *instrumentally*".[285]

The 'cash-value' of treating Utopian Israel as real might consist

---

[282] *B.Pes.* 49b, see p. 116. See also *T.Demai* 5,2, quoted below.

[283] Jackson (*op.cit.* ch. 7, esp. pp. 105–6, his emphasis).

[284] Whose 'pragmatist viewpoint' (as opposed to the 'intellectualistic' viewpoint) is applied to ethnography by Jackson, cf pp. 63–4. This is related to Jackson's notion of 'radical empiricism', i.e. a method designed "to encourage us to recover a lost sense of the immediate, active, ambiguous "plenum of existence" in which all ideas and intellectual constructions are grounded" (p. 3) (see above, pp. xx–xxii).

[285] W. James, *Pragmatism*, Indianapolis: Hackett Publishing Company, 1981 (1907), pp. 28–30 (his emphasis). He also writes: "all our theories are *instrumental*, are mental modes of adaptation to reality . . ." (p. 87).

of the escapist comfort which 'wishful thinking' generally provides.[286] Because of its cash-value, wishful thinking has the power to turn dreams into reality, which is to say, into a subjective perception of reality which constitutes nonetheless a real experience in its own right. Rabbinic sources *want* 'Israel' to be real—and so, through the sheer power of their subjective will, it becomes true in so far forth, instrumentally.

But in order to ascertain how this Utopia can be 'realized' as a '*sensible*' truth, we need also to establish whether it can help the authors of rabbinic sources, in pragmatic terms, to "get into satisfactory relation with other parts of their experience".[287] At first sight, Utopian Israel is in blatant contradiction with all the Talmudic derogatory statements about the *amei haAretz* and the common people. How then could rabbinic sources sustain as a reality the belief in Utopian Israel?

The belief in 'Israel' as real may proceed from the notion that in spite of their well-established shortcomings, the people of the grey areas conform '*deep down*' to the ideality of Israel. We have seen, indeed, that in some cases our sources disregard their shortcomings and emphasize instead their intrinsic characteristics as 'Israel'. Thus they refuse to suspect the *am haAretz* of lying, on the grounds that "Israel are not suspected of this".[288] Similarly, the *Babylonian Talmud* assumes that given the choice, the (limited) apostate would still prefer kosher to non-kosher meat.[289] Although one may not trade with a non-Jew on his way to an idolatrous pilgrimage, one may do so with a Jew, as it is assumed that he may still change his mind and not attend it.[290] Most distinctive is the passage claiming that the sinners of Israel will eventually repent; and that although in some sense 'empty', they are "full of commandments as a pomegranate (is with seeds)".[291] 'Deep down', indeed, all Jews share the distinctive features of Israel. In this sense, 'Israel' is no longer a Utopia, but an actual reality. Again, an outsider may consider this 'deep Israel' to be no more than a wishful delusion; but in so far as it satisfies the general, experiential worldview

---

[286] As we have found concerning Israel's alleged immunity among the nations: section I.5.A.

[287] Jackson's explication of the belief in shape-shifting refers essentially to its articulation within the broader cultural *context* of Kuranko thinking.

[288] Provided he has nothing to gain from it: *T.Demai* 5,2, quoted in p. 118.

[289] *B.Hul.* 4a, quoted in p. 106, n. 141.

[290] *B.AZ* 32b–33a (this would not apply, however, if the Jew was established to be an apostate).

[291] *B.Eruv.* 19a; *B.Hag.* end.

of rabbinic writings, in pragmatic terms it can be sensibly treated by the latter as real.

Yet only the few passages I have quoted suggest the notion that the grey areas share, 'deep down', the idyllic nature of Israel. In most cases our sources emphasize the shortcomings of *amei haAretz* and sinners, which distinguish them from the rabbinic ideal of 'Israel'. Even when Israel are compared to a single vine, the *amei haAretz* are the 'leaves' and the sinners the 'rods', in contradistinction with the rabbis who are the 'clusters'.[292] The extent to which 'wishful thinking' transforms the 'grey areas' into an idyllic 'Israel' is therefore limited; it does not fully account for the rabbinic belief in 'Israel' as an actual reality.

The rabbis and centripetal experience

I would like to suggest, instead, that rabbinic sources can treat idyllic 'Israel' as an actual reality by ignoring the Jewish 'grey areas' as though they were non-existent, and by focussing attention, exclusively, on the rabbis and the so-called 'rabbinic class'.[293] Indeed, as we have seen, it is the study of the Oral *Torah*—the distinctive profession of the rabbinic class—which is considered one of the most essential features of Israel.[294] In this respect, only the rabbis and their disciples could correspond to 'Israel' in *all* respects, and hence, unlike the common people, be unequivocally 'Israel'. Therefore, since the rabbis alone represent the true identity of Israel, we may infer that it is essentially to *themselves* that phrases such as "Israel are holy", in early rabbinic writings, refer. At this restricted, 'rabbinic' level, the experience of "Israel" would not constitute a Utopia or wishful thinking, but quite on the contrary a most tangible and concrete reality, which the authors of rabbinic writings could experience in their immediate surroundings as an intrinsic part of their daily lives.

This interpretation requires however qualification, as it would be simplistic and wrong to conclude that our sources adopt a policy of sectarian exclusiveness, as may have been found in Qumran,[295] restricting the title 'Israel' to the adherents of their own group alone. This is clearly not the case: as we have seen, throughout rabbinic writings the title 'Israel' is granted indiscriminately to all Jews, even

---

[292] See pp. 118 and 123.
[293] Term used by Levine, 1989 (for a definition of it, see pp. 13–4).
[294] See pp. 74–5.
[295] See p. 114, n. 200.

to apostates and heretics of the worst kind. When our sources wish to refer exclusively to the rabbis, it is the term '*Torah* scholars', not 'Israel', which they use.[296] All I would suggest, therefore, is that although the category of 'Israel' includes the totality of the Jewish people, rabbinic sources define its distinctive features, such as 'holiness' and observance of the commandments, with *exclusive reference* to the rabbis and their restricted 'class'. This is because, as a collectivity, the people of 'Israel' is deemed to consist *essentially* of the rabbinic class; whilst the *amei haAretz* and sinners, albeit numerous, are ignored by our sources as being merely 'peripheral' to the description of the identity of Israel, hence only of marginal importance.

This attitude is evident in a number of *Midrashim*. We have seen, in the simile of the vine, how the *Babylonian Talmud* insists that *amei haAretz* and sinners are included, as 'leaves' and 'rods' respectively, within the category of 'Israel'. Similarly, *Leviticus Rabba* refers to *amei haAretz* as the vine's leaves, and *Torah* scholars as its clusters.[297] Yet alongside this reference, *Leviticus Rabba* goes on to present a rather different account of the same simile, as follows:

> in the same way as a vine has grapes and raisins, so Israel have masters of Scripture, masters of *Mishna*, masters of *Talmud*, and masters of *Aggada*.[298]

As if to counterbalance the previous, inclusive account, this passage presents Israel as though it consisted exclusively of different types of *Torah* scholars.

In *Genesis Rabba*, we find that in the same way as a date tree has no waste (its dates are good for eating, its sprouts (*lulavim*) for (reciting) *hallel*, its branches for roofing, its fibres for ropes, etc.),

---

[296] *Talmidei ḥakhamim*, literally 'the students of the wise', often translated as 'the Sages'. Our sources are replete with references to them as a distinct and unique social group: see Levine, *op.cit.* pp. 47–53.

[297] See pp. 118–23, quoting *B.Hul.* 92a and *Lev.R.* 36,2 respectively.

[298] *Lev.R.* 36,2. Most mss. list also wine; some also list vinegar. The term "masters" is found in most mss. (mss.Oxford 147 and 2335; ms.Vatican; ms.Jerusalem 245) and in first editions. It is omitted, however, in ms.London, in *Yalkut Makhiri* 80,23, and in *Midrash Shemuel* 16, which read: "Israel . . . have Scripture, *Mishna*, *Talmud*, and *Aggada*" (see *Lev.R.* ed. M.Margaliot). According to this version, the *Midrash* would be referring to the *Torah* of Israel rather than to its *people*, and hence would be irrelevant to my argument.

so Israel *have no waste*, but some are masters of Scripture, some are
masters of *Mishna*, some are masters of *Talmud*, and some are masters
of *Aggada*.[299]

The omission of *amei haAretz* and sinners, and the assertion that all
Israel are learned and "have no waste", is a remarkable case of
apparently deliberate obliviousness.

The ability of our sources to ignore the common people and describe
'Israel' with exclusive reference to the rabbis may account for sayings
such as "Israel are holy", but remains, nevertheless, surprising. In
demographic terms, indeed, it must have been obvious to our sources
that the *amei haAretz* constituted the vast majority of the Jewish people,
which could hardly be treated as merely 'peripheral' or of negligible
importance. It is likely that the authors of our sources had regular
social and commercial transactions with *amei haAretz*, as indeed the
latter have with 'rabbis' in numerous passages in our sources. We
may ask, therefore, how our sources could *sensibly* ignore, in certain
contexts, the existence of the non-learned majority of the Jewish people,
and describe 'Israel' only with reference to the rabbinic class.

Let us return to Jackson's contention that cognitive notions cannot
be defined simply as true or false, as real or as illusory, but must
be pragmatically articulated into the wider context of one's lived
experience. William James has similarly suggested that in certain
contexts certain 'truths' can be successfully and sensibly ignored:

> The practical value of true ideas is thus primarily derived from the
> practical importance of their objects to us. Their objects are, indeed,
> not important at all times . . . Yet since almost any object may some
> day become temporarily important, the advantage of having a general
> stock of *extra* truths, of ideas that shall be true of merely possible situations,
> is obvious. We store such extra truths away in our memories . . . Whenever
> such an extra truth becomes practically relevant to one of our emergencies,
> it passes from cold storage to do work in the world and *our belief in
> it grows active*.[300]

The authors of our sources were not unaware of the *amei haAretz*,
particularly when they had to engage in commercial transactions with

---

[299] *Gen.R.* 41,1. This passage is quoted in *Num.R.* 3,1, but with, in addition: "masters
(i.e. performers) of commandments, masters of charity, etc. (*sic*)". This addition may
constitute an inclusion of the common people; indeed, *Num.R.* 3,1 is explicitly 'inclusive'
further on in the same passage, with reference to the "bad" among Israel (quoted
above in p. 122).
[300] James, *op.cit.* p. 93, my emphasis.

them. But it appears, as James would suggest, that whereas in certain contexts their awareness of the 'grey areas' could be "actively embraced" and "realized", in others it could be left aside "in cold storage" as a subsidiary, irrelevant aspect of their lived experience.[301] Thus it is not unreasonable to suggest that in the context of Jewish identity and the notion of 'Israel', the rabbinic class—which to our sources may have been perceived as most immediate and momentous—became to them the object of *"focal awareness"*, whereas the common people could be 'put in brackets', treated as irrelevant, and relegated to the realm of *"subsidiary awareness"*.[302] I would stress, however, that rabbinic sources could only effectively and 'sensibly' marginalize the common people if they *focused* awareness on themselves and on their narrow ideal-like environment. In other words, in order to be credible, the conception of 'Israel' as holy, learned and observant must have been to them an essentially self-centred, implosive, and *centripetal* experience.

C. *Jewish identity and 'boundaries'*

My conclusions to this chapter have theoretical implications concerning the nature of ethnicity and identity which I shall now explore. In 1969 anthropologist Fredrik Barth edited a volume entitled *Ethnic groups and boundaries*, which for the first time set out to study the concept of ethnicity in a systematic way. As a seminal work it has had a profound influence on subsequent research in this area; it has become in some ways a text-book of anthropological orthodoxy.[303]

With a structuralist outlook, Barth lays down as a premise that ethnic identity proceeds from the boundaries which demarcate the ethnic group from others and distinguish between 'us' and 'them'. A study of ethnicity must focus therefore on these boundaries:

> we shift the focus of investigation from internal constitution and history of separate groups to ethnic boundaries and boundary maintenance (p. 10).

The 'internal' cultural contents of identity, on the other hand, are only incidental to its establishment and its maintenance:

---

[301] M. Jackson *op.cit.*, p. 111 and generally ch. 7.

[302] Terms borrowed from Polanyi; cf Jackson pp. 106 & 111.

[303] Fredrik Barth (ed.), *Ethnic Groups and Boundaries*, Bergen/Oslo/London, 1969. Barthian anthropological and sociological studies abound, and I shall not refer to them here. G. Porton is also heavily indebted to Barth's theory (*op.cit.*, esp. in ch. 12 and p. 201f.).

the nature of continuity of ethnic units is clear: it depends on the maintenance of a boundary. The cultural features that signal the boundary may change, and the cultural characteristics of the members may likewise be transformed, indeed, even the organizational form of the group may change—yet the fact of continuing dichotomization between members and outsiders allows us to specify the nature of continuity, and investigate the changing cultural form and content (p. 14).

Therefore,

the critical focus of investigation from this point of view becomes the ethnic *boundary* that defines the group, not the cultural stuff that it encloses (p. 15, his emphasis).

"Cultural stuff" is thus distinguishable from ethnicity, which consists of no more than a structural boundary.[304]

On empirical grounds I cannot accept this distinction, nor the reification of the structure of ethnicity into a separable object of inquiry. Barth's focus on 'boundaries' as divorced from their 'cultural', social and bodily substance does not correspond in any sense to the pragmatic reality of lived experience (as I have argued in chapter II); it is therefore irrelevant, in my opinion, to ethnographic or historical inquiry. I shall return to this point at the end of the next chapter; in the context of this chapter, however, I would like to criticize his theory on two other important points.

Firstly, Barth seems to assume that ethnic groups are objectively distinguished from each other in a dichotomous manner (hence "ethnic dichotomies" and "dichotomization between members and outsiders"—pp. 14–5). However, in the case of Israel we have found (see p. 126) a range of 'grey areas', e.g. *am haAretz*, sinners and apostates, which in various contexts can be included or excluded from the category of Israel. Far from unusual or exceptional, these grey areas may constitute in objective, demographic terms the majority of the ethnic group. As I have argued, they entail a flexible and fluid definition of the boundaries of Israel: according to context, the category of 'Israel', as opposed to 'non-Israel', will vary subjectively in inclusiveness.

---

[304] He also writes: "when one traces the history of an ethnic group through time, one is *not* simultaneously, in the same sense, tracing the history of a 'culture': the elements of the present culture of that ethnic group have not sprung from the particular set that constituted the group's culture at a previous time, whereas the group has a continual organizational existence with boundaries (criteria of membership) that despite modifications have marked off a continuing unit" (p. 38).

The ambiguous, multi-levelled and ever changing identity of Israel, which I suspect may be just as common among other ethnic groups, weakens Barth's case for clear, "continuing" and changeless boundaries between 'us' and 'them' which he uses as the starting-point of his investigation.

Secondly, the rabbinic perception of Israel (as discussed in section 5.B) indicates that Barth's model is inadequate in fundamental, experiential terms. In Barth's approach, the experience of ethnic identity appears to be focused on its *external* boundaries, on the dichotomy between self and other. Similarly, at the beginning of this study I posited that the notion of 'Israel' implied the existence of a contrastive 'non-Israel', namely the nations, and that the opposition between them was an important element in the rabbinic experience of self-identity. But although this must remain to some extent a logical truism, I would question whether this contrastive dichotomy constitutes indeed the main, *formative* feature of the rabbinic experience of Israel.

In this chapter we have seen that the attention of our sources is focused away from the realities of the 'grey areas', the 'periphery' and the external boundaries of Israel. Their experience of themselves as Israel is self-referential, hence self-centred and centripetal. It should also be noted that the 'nations' in rabbinic writings do not represent an observable reality 'out there', but rather a logical opposite to the identity of Israel, thus defined in rabbinic writings in purely self-referential terms. In fact, in many passages on the holiness or righteousness of Israel, the contrasting nations are not even mentioned.[305] I have explained that the rabbinic orientation *must* remain ontologically 'inward' if its experience of idyllic Israel is to be sensibly

---

[305] Unfortunately, the frequency with which our sources refer to 'Israel' with or without reference to the nations would be difficult to assess, especially as many rabbinic sayings were decontextualised in the process of their redaction and transmission, as I have earlier argued. For instance, the saying that Israel are merciful, modest, and kind (see p. 31), is quoted on its own in *Deut.R.* 3,4 in the name of R. Ḥiyya (a late Tanna), for purely exegetical purposes; in the *Talmudim* (*Y.Kid.* 4,1; *Y.Sanh.* 6,7; *B.Yev.* 79a; also *Num.R.* 8,4) this exegesis is incorporated in the account (attributed to Palestinian *Amoraim*, Resh Lakish especially) of King David and the Gibeonite converts, as a justification for the Halakhic exclusion of the latter from the right of marriage; the saying is quoted again on its own in *Kalla R.* 10 in the name of Rava (a later Babylonian *Amora*), by analogy with another saying just quoted. If there ever was an original context to this saying, it is now impossible to ascertain.

sustained. The rabbinic definition of 'Israel' is essentially based on an *introspective* analysis of the rabbis' own features, rather than on an external outlook, as Barth contends, towards ambiguous boundaries which our sources prefer deliberately—and with good reason—to 'put in brackets' and ignore.[306]

---

[306] I have suggested in p. 100 that in the *Mishna* and *Tosefta*, the interstitial category of the *Kuti* (neither Jew nor non-Jew) serves the purpose of testing the theoretical limits of Halakhic rulings where the distinction between Jew and non-Jew applies. Frequent reference to the *Kutim* in these sources could thus be seen as a general attempt to define the identity of Israel through its *external* boundaries. I would argue, however, that this way of experiencing Israel is no more than *implicit* in Tannaitic sources; whilst *explicit* descriptions of Israel, in early rabbinic writings, are made (as we have seen) with exclusive reference to its rabbinic 'centre' and *not* to its interstitial periphery.

I would also point out that according to the *Talmudim*, who regard the *Kutim* as virtually non-Jewish, the Tannaitic category of the *Kuti* is interpreted as a purely theoretical notion, not as a lived reality. In this context, therefore, the historical reality of the Samaritans as a potential interstitial boundary between Israel and the nations is completely ignored in Talmudic sources. In the next chapter I will assess the extent to which Barth's notion of boundaries may be applied, in other contexts, to the rabbinic experience of Jewish identity. We shall find again that rabbinic boundaries do not correspond to external, historical reality, but rather to Halakhic *theory*. I will show, in my conclusion to the next chapter, how this distinction undermines further the validity of Barth's model.

CHAPTER FOUR

THE PROTECTION OF JEWISH IDENTITY
DISSOCIATION AND DISSIMILATION

They did not change their name, they did not change their language, they did not change their clothing—modern, popular *Midrash*, based on *Mekhilta Bo*, 5.[1]

Ethnic identities are naturally exposed to assimilation and erosion; in order to survive, external threats must be continually resisted. Resistance to assimilation is a theme which may have acquired inordinate importance in the modern Jewish world since the emancipation; it may be somewhat anachronistic to search for it in other cultures, even in rabbinic writings of Late Antiquity. Many historians assume, nevertheless, that the latter were faced, initially, with threats of Hellenic influence,[2] and later with the theological challenge of triumphant Christianity,[3] against which their identity as Jews required to be protected. There is little *explicit* evidence in our sources that 'Hellenism' and Christianity were ever perceived as a challenge or threat to Jewish identity; it may be rash, therefore, to see in rabbinic teachings a reaction to specific historical conditions. Nonetheless, as I will argue in this chapter, we find that *regardless* of any historical context the rabbis are constantly engaged in the erection of 'boundaries' between themselves and the non-Jews, and thus in the protection of their distinctive identity as 'Israel'.[4]

I will argue on the one hand that our sources try to exert a form of 'social control', and encourage the Jews to dissociate from the non-Jews. This would serve to minimize non-Jewish influence and to maintain the distinctiveness of the Jews as an independent social group. On the other hand, they exert 'cultural control', by banning elements of non-Jewish culture. This would have the obvious function of maintaining the integrity of their Jewish cultural identity.

---

[1] This modern version of *Mekh. Bo*, commonly found in 20th century rabbinic works, is of doubtful origin; but see *Midrash Lekaḥ Tov ad Ex.* 6:6 (quoted in p. 192, n. 325).

[2] This view is further discussed in section IV.2.A.

[3] E.g. Neusner *op.cit.* (1989) pp. 97ff.

[4] This view is already expressed by Porton, *op.cit.* esp. p. 201f.

This chapter explores a new dimension in the experience of Jewish identity. The need to protect it against assimilation and erosion may force rabbinic sources to adopt a more reflexive attitude towards it, and to begin to treat identity as an end in its own right. It remains unclear, however, to what extent their policies of social and cultural control were conscious and deliberate attempts to foster their identity and to protect it. This unclarity, I will finally argue, may prove in itself to be significant. We will have to assess, in conclusion, the extent to which the rabbinic apparent 'erection of boundaries' could be seen to lend support to Barth's model, which I have already criticised in this study.

1. Social Control: 'Boundaries' and Dissociation

It is well established in rabbinic writings that Israel are, or should be, separate from the nations.[5] This notion constitutes an important component of the weekly liturgy of the *havdala*.[6] It is also emphasized in a number of later *Midrashim*: for instance, we are warned that if Israel were to mix with the nations, they would be learning from their practices.[7] Israel are compared to oil, for in the same way as oil cannot mix with water, so Israel cannot mix with the nations.[8] Israel prefer to be martyred rather than to mix with the nations;[9] they are secluded in this world, and there is no foreigner among them.[10]

It remains questionable, however, to what extent the rabbis promoted the dissociation of Israel from the non-Jews by actively erecting Halakhic

---

[5] *Mekh. Baḥodesh* 2; *Sifra Kedoshim* 11,22. This is also a Biblical theme: see *Lev.* 20:24–26. In *Est.R.* 7,11 it is suggested that this separateness was created on the second day of Creation.

[6] *B.Pes.* 103b. Interestingly, *PdRE* 20 (cf Higger's edition and the version in *Tur, Oraḥ Ḥayim*, 296) states that whoever performs the *havdala* (or participates in it), "the Almighty elects him as his treasure as it is written: "and I have separated you from all the nations" (*Lev.* 20:26) "and you will be my treasure of all the nations" (*Ex.* 19:5)".

Cf also *Eliyahu Z̧.* 2 (p. 173): "He separates Israel as a heave-offering from all the nations"; *Song R.* 6,16,5: "as one who separates the good from the bad". Cf also *Y.Taan.* 2,6.

[7] Which justifies mutual hatred between them: *Midrash Temura HaShalem* (ed. Wertheimer) 5,26, (ed. Eisenstein) 3,26, quoting *Psalms* 106:35.

[8] *Deut.R.* 7,3; *Tanh. Tavo*, 3. Cf *Ex.R.* 36,1. *Song R.* 1,3,2 relates this saying to the prohibition of intermarriage.

[9] *Ex.R.* 15,7. Cf *ib.* 19,6; *Num.R.* 13,2.

[10] *Eliyahu R.* 25, p. 137. This is why Israel do not actively proselytize: *Num.R.* 10,4.

boundaries between them. Porton has argued that commercial transactions with the non-Jews were not particularly restricted. In the
following sub-section, I will disagree with Porton and maintain that
relations with non-Jews in the market-place were substantially restricted.
I will then show that dissociation from non-Jews was similarly promoted
in other areas of social life.[11]

I will then inquire whether these 'boundaries' were specifically designed to protect the identity of Israel, rather than simply to ensure
the proper observance of the *Torah* and the commandments. Although
in most cases there is little explicit evidence to this effect, I will argue
that the prohibition of intermarriage reveals, on the part of our sources,
a firm commitment towards the preservation of Jewish identity.[12]

A. *Commercial transactions*

The first chapter of *Mishna AZ* is almost entirely devoted to restrictions
on commercial transactions between Jews and non-Jews.[13] The chapter
begins with the prohibition of dealing with non-Jews during their festive
(*avoda zara*) seasons,[14] and within the areas of the *avoda zara* cult.[15]
There follows a list of items which may never be sold to non-Jews:
fir-cones, white figs, frankincense, white cocks, or anything else which
may be used for *avoda zara* purposes.[16] Large (and in some places,
also small) cattle, calves or foals may not be sold to non-Jews,[17] as
well as other animals, such as bears and lions, which may be used
for harmful purposes.[18] Finally real estate, including unharvested crops,
may not be sold or even hired to non-Jews in the land of Israel;
dwelling-houses may not be hired to them in any place, because they

---

[11] Sections IV.1.A–B.

[12] Sections IV.1.C–D.

[13] See David Rosenthal, *Mishna Aboda Zara—a critical edition with introduction* (PHD
thesis), Jerusalem: Hebrew University, 1980 (2 vols.).

[14] *M.AZ* 1,1–3. "Dealing" includes borrowing, lending, settling debts, and according to *T.AZ* 1,1 and *B.AZ* 6b, purchase and sale. These are all prohibited as being
a shade (lit.: 'dust') of *avoda zara*: *T.AZ* 1,13.

[15] *M.AZ* 1,4. Cf *M.AZ* 2,3.

[16] *M.AZ* 1,5. R. Meir prohibits also various types of dates.

[17] *M.AZ* 1,6. According to *B.AZ* 14b, this is related to the prohibition of working
Jewish-owned animals on the *shabbat*. Some scholars have suggested that these animals
are also likely to be used in *avoda zara* sacrifice: G. Porton, "Forbidden Transactions:
Prohibited Commerce with Gentiles in Earliest Rabbinism", in J. Neusner & E. Frerichs
(eds.), *"To see ourselves as others see us"*, Atlanta: Scholars Press, 1985, pp. 317–335,
on p. 323, n. 26.

[18] *Ib.* 7.

might bring in idols; and the same restriction applies to bath-houses.[19]

Additional restrictions on trade are found in *Tosefta AZ*. If it is known that the non-Jew will use his purchase for *avoda zara* purposes, it is forbidden to sell him even water or salt.[20] Large animals are forbidden just as large cattle; besides bears and lions, harmful items such as implements of war, swords and their accessories, stocks, neck-chains, ropes, or iron chains may not be sold to a non-Jew.[21] It is forbidden to sell him a slave; if this occurs, the slave must immediately be freed.[22] Finally, it is forbidden to conduct business in a non-Jewish fair, if the latter constitutes a celebration of *avoda zara*.[23] Any benefit derived from such a fair must be destroyed: if one purchased an animal, it must be put down; cloth and clothes must be left to rot; metallic goods and money must be cast into the Dead Sea; produce must be burnt or buried.[24]

Other tractates of *Tosefta* mention additional items which may not be sold to non-Jews: eggs of forbidden birds,[25] linen dyed with blacking,[26] as well as village dogs, porcupines, cats, and apes.[27] Furthermore, a wide range of foods could not be purchased from non-Jews because they were intrinsically forbidden: it was assumed, for instance, that meat sold by a non-Jew was not kosher,[28] and similarly non-Jewish wine[29] because it had been used in a libation.

On the basis of this extensive evidence, we may conclude that the

---

[19] *Ib*. 8–9. The problem with hiring bath-houses is that they will be known to belong to the Jew (*ib.*) whilst being used by the non-Jewish tenants on the *shabbat* (*T.AZ* 2, end).

[20] *T.AZ* 1,21.

[21] *Ib*. 2,2–4; *B.AZ* 15b. According to *B.AZ* 16a, it is permissible 'nowadays' to sell weapons to the Persians, since they will use them for the military protection of Israel (rather than for harassing them; see *Tosafot ad loc.*).

[22] *T.AZ* 3,16–19.

[23] *T.AZ* 1,7. See Z. Safrai, "Fairs in the land of Israel in the Mishna and Talmud period", in *Zion* 49, 1984, pp. 139–58, esp. 147–50 (Hebrew), who shows how the prohibition from attending fairs was gradually relaxed in Palestine between the 2nd and the 4th centuries CE. His suggestion that this development was due to economic factors is however unsubstantiated.

[24] *T.AZ* 3,19; *B.AZ* 13a.

[25] Unless they are cracked into a dish, so that one need not fear that another Jew may mistakenly buy them: *T.Hul*. 3,24.

[26] Lest another Jew buys it thinking it is wool: *T.Kilayim* 5,24.

[27] *T.Sheviit* 5,9. Also *T.AZ* 2,3, where the text probably requires amending: cf *T.BK* 8,17, and S. Lieberman, *Tosefta Kifshuta—Zera'im vol. II*, New York: Jewish Theological Seminary, 1955, pp. 552–3.

[28] *Y.Shek*. 7,4; cf *B.Hul*. 95a.

[29] *M.AZ* 2,3. Non-Jewish food will be discussed further in the next section.

rabbis erected firm boundaries between Israel and the nations, sub-stantially restricting their commercial relations in the market-place. Porton however has taken quite the opposite view, concluding that

> regular interaction took place between the gentile and the Israelite in the market-place and the rabbis put few restrictions in the way of this activity.[30]

His view deserves our full consideration.

Porton notes that Tannaitic sources actually allow Jews to purchase a wide range of items from non-Jews, including most essential staples:[31] grain,[32] vats of olives,[33] grapes,[34] raisins,[35] pulse, dried figs, garlic, onions, summachtree and cedar wood,[36] eggs in their shell,[37] animals,[38] sheep, cows, asses,[39] the embryo of an ass[40] and of a cow,[41] slaves,[42] and metal filings.[43] It is even permissible to purchase ritual items from non-Jews, such as scrolls, *tefillin*, and *mezuzot*, provided they are properly prepared,[44] as well as animals for sacrifices.[45] To this I could add that the sale of the following items to non-Jews is permitted: pigs, wine,[46] frankincense in large quantities,[47] harvested crops,[48] jars,[49]

---

[30] Porton *op.cit.* (1985), p. 335.

[31] p. 332, n. 62.

[32] *T.Peah* 4,1 (cf *ib.* 2,9). Porton erroneously infers from this passage that wine may also be purchased from a non-Jew, which would surprisingly contradict the strict and well-established prohibition of non-Jewish wine in tractate *AZ* (e.g. *M.AZ* 4,8–12 and 5,3–6).

[33] *T.Tohorot* 10,5.

[34] *Ib.* 11,8. Cf *T.Peah* 3,12.

[35] *T.Tohorot* 11,9.

[36] *T.AZ* 4,11.

[37] *T.Hul.* 3,24.

[38] *Ib.* 9,3 (to be slaughtered); *T.Bekh.* 2,11 and 2,14.

[39] *M.Bekh.* 2,11.

[40] *Ib.* 1,10.

[41] *Ib.* 2,1.

[42] *T.AZ* 2,1.

[43] *Ib.* 5,3.

[44] *Ib.* 3,6–7.

[45] *Ib.* 2,1.

[46] One need not be concerned that the non-Jew will make an *avoda zara* sacrifice of the pigs, or a libation of the wine: *T.AZ* 1,21.

[47] In such quantities that the non-Jew is unlikely to use it for *avoda zara* purposes. *T.AZ* 1,21; cf *B.AZ* 14a.

[48] *M.AZ* 1,8; *T.AZ* 2,4; cf *T.Peah* 2,9 and 3,12.

[49] *M.Sheviit* 5,7.

animals to be slaughtered,[50] and according to Ben Betyra, horses.[51] In quantitive terms, it appears that a greater number of commercial transactions between Jews and non-Jews would have been allowed rather than forbidden. Porton concludes that the rabbis did not attempt to draw sharp borders "between the two segments of Palestinian society" (p. 333); indeed, restrictions on trade were "few and relatively innocuous" (p. 335, n. 67).[52]

This conclusion, however, is not the impression conveyed by the authors of our sources. Porton's permitted items are only *implicit* in rabbinic writings, and inferred by him from sporadic and unrelated Halakhic cases. That one may purchase essential staples from non-Jews such as grain, olives, grapes, raisins, animals, and slaves, is merely implicit in our sources.[53] Similarly, from the end of *M.AZ* Porton might infer that it is permitted to buy utensils from non-Jews; however, the main point of this passage is clearly that these vessels may not be

---

[50] The non-Jew must slaughter it in his presence: *T.AZ* 2,1. As to village dogs, weasels, porcupines, cats, and apes, it is unclear whether or not the *Tosefta* allows them to be sold to non-Jews, or whether again it is a matter of dispute. *T.Sheviit* 5,9 appears to forbid it, but the prohibition may be to purchase these pets with the *intention* of selling them to non-Jews. In *T.AZ* 2,3, R. Shimon b. El'azar allows the sale of these pets, but the text is somewhat doubtful. See Porton, p. 329, n. 54.

[51] *M.AZ* 1,6.

[52] He also writes: "It is significant that the earliest rabbis did not attempt to draw sharper borders between the two segments of Palestinian society. Either the economic factors were so important that they superseded any concern for contact, or the rabbis simply ignored or did not consider as significant any threat to the coherence of the Israelite community which might result from the economic interaction of Israelite and gentile" (p. 333). The *significance* of the absence of borders is a further point in his argument which will be discussed in section IV.1.C.

[53] Grain can be inferred from the following passage:
"If a poor person said: 'I bought this grain from a non-Jew (and therefore it is exempt from tithes)', he is not to be believed" (*T.Peah* 4,1; cf Porton's other references, listed above). I do not dispute the validity of such an inference; I am stressing, however, that it is no more than an inference, whereas forbidden transactions are listed *explicitly* in our sources.
Nonetheless I must concede that in some cases our sources do explicitly allow certain transactions with non-Jews, for instance:
"it is permitted to purchase from non-Jews fields, houses, animals, and slaves" during *hol haMoed* (when business is normally forbidden) (*T.Moed* 2,1 (L: 1,12)) or in a non-Jewish market (*T.AZ* 1,8; *B.AZ* 13a; cf *Y.AZ* 1,1; *ib.* 1,4), "because it is like redeeming these items from them". This passage might be labelled as 'permissive', although the latter clause indicates that it is not sympathy for the non-Jew which motivates the rabbis in this case ... Other explicitly 'permissive' passages are occasionally found in tractate *AZ*: *T.AZ* 2,1 (animals to be sacrificed), *T.AZ* 4,11 (pulses etc.), *M.AZ* 4,8 (trodden grapes; *contra B.AZ* 56b, *T.AZ* 7,1). These passages are however in a distinct minority.

used unless they are immersed and thoroughly cleansed;[54] this passage, as indeed the whole of the tractate, is thus not permissive but essentially restrictive. It is forbidden transactions, indeed, which are given most emphasis in rabbinic sources, as they are expressly listed in *M.AZ* and *T.AZ* in a consistent, systematic manner;[55] clearly, this is what our sources consider most significant.

The subjective perspective of the authors of our sources, emphasizing forbidden relations rather than permitted ones, is more relevant to our assessment of rabbinic social boundaries than Porton's quantitative observations. Indeed, 'boundaries' should not be taken as objective and measurable features of the social landscape, as the topographical metaphor may misleadingly convey, but rather as a subjective, socio-cultural interpretation of external reality. Restrictions may have been "few" in number, as Porton remarks, but few does not necessarily mean "innocuous". From the perspective of our sources, it was these restrictions which essentially characterized their interaction with non-Jews.

It should be noted, moreover, that every commercial transaction with a non-Jew could be affected, potentially, by one of these prohibitions; it may have been taking place, for instance, on some inconspicuous *avoda zara* festive day. In so far as every transaction had to be subject to continual scrutiny, interaction with non-Jews was continually hindered, conditioned and restricted.[56]

Yet in only partially restricting relationships with non-Jews, our sources implicitly recognize that this relationship, to some extent at least, should be allowed to exist. Thus instead of outright 'isolationism',

---

[54] *M.AZ* 5, end.

[55] They are listed together without taking account of the *different* Halakhic principles upon which they are predicated (such as the 'suspicion' that non-Jews are murderers, and avoidance of *avoda zara*). This confirms the *Mishna*'s intention to stress what these prohibitions have in common, namely the restriction of relations between Jews and non-Jews.

[56] Porton *op.cit.* 1988 (pp. 257–8) raises this point but then concludes: "the concern with avoiding idolatry did not *predominate* in determining how the two groups should interrelate". He argues, indeed, that it is possible for the Jew to distinguish between the gentile as an idolater and the gentile *qua* gentile: "unless it is clear that the gentile is engaging in religious activity, the Israelites need not be concerned with interacting with non-Israelites". However, I doubt that in practice such an abstract distinction could be made, or that the Jew could always be sure whether the non-Jew was engaging in *avoda zara* or not. Indeed, even if the non-Jew had only touched Jewish wine, he could be suspected of having made a quick libation (see above p. 27). In so far as the non-Jew was considered a worshipper of *avoda zara*, his actions and intentions had to be scrutinized at all times.

they adopt a policy of measured *dissociation* from the outside world.[57] The possibility of appearing in non-Jewish markets with conspicuous restraint constituted in itself a way of conveying a message to the non-Jews, albeit one of boundaries and of rejection.[58] As Merleau-Ponty has written: "refusal to communicate is again a form of communication".[59]

B. *Social relations*

The same conclusions may be drawn in non-commercial domains. It is quite possible that in quantitative terms, social relations with non-Jews were usually permitted; but, as our sources emphasize, they were qualified and conditioned by numerous restrictions. Dissociation extended, therefore, to the widest range of social experience.

Courtesy

The *Mishna* and *Talmud* make some concessions to the policy of dissociation, but this is not without considerable reluctance. The *Mishna* allows one to greet a non-Jew, but only "for the sake of peaceful relations";[60] hence, one should greet him "in a mumbling tone and with downcast head".[61] One may not give him a double greeting.[62]

It is forbidden, according to both *Talmudim*, to praise non-Jewish ladies for their beauty.[63] R. Gamliel saw a beautiful non-Jewish woman and made a blessing to the Almighty for His creation; however, the *Palestinian Talmud* specifies, he refrained from giving *her* his good wishes.[64] If a non-Jew blesses a Jew, he should answer *amen*; but R. Yishmael

---

[57] The notion of isolationism will be re-considered, however, in the final chapter of this work.

[58] Although there is no evidence that the rabbis explicitly informed non-Jews of their commercial restrictions, their public restraint in the market-place must have been available for all non-Jewish traders to observe. See Porton 1988, pp. 201–3.

[59] Merleau-Ponty *op.cit.* p. 360.

[60] *Mi-penei darkei shalom*: *M.Sheviit* 4,3; ib. 5,9; *M.Git.* 5,9. See Porton 1988 (pp. 231–2): this expression implies that greeting a non-Jew is not ideal, but forced upon the Jew by circumstantial necessity.

[61] *B.Git.* 62a; cf *T.AZ* 1,2–3. According to these passages, however, the Mishnaic ruling refers specifically to non-Jewish festive days; on other days, any single greetings are permitted. Greeting with a "mumbling tone" is a sign of mourning: cf *T.Taan.* 4,12 (L: 3,12); *Y.Taan.* 1,8 (on the fast-day of the 9th of *Av*).

[62] This applies on any day: *B.Git. ib.*

[63] As inferred from *Deut.* 7:2: "do not grant them grace"—*Y.Ber.* 9,1; *Y.AZ* 1,9; *B.AZ* 20a. I have not found that Babylonian and Palestinian sources differ significantly on the principle of dissociation from the non-Jews.

[64] *Ib.* Quoted in p. 39, n. 274.

would dismiss his blessing, by telling him that it was unnecessary and to no avail.[65] It is forbidden to be light-headed with non-Jews on *avoda zara* festive days.[66]

Nevertheless, a favourite saying of Abaye was that a person should always strive to be on peaceful terms with his brothers, his relatives, and everyone else *including* "the non-Jew in the market-place", so as to be beloved to Heaven and to his fellow people.[67] They said, the *Talmud* goes on, of R. Yohanan b. Zakkai that no one ever gave him a greeting first, "even a non-Jew in the market-place".[68] R. Yohanan (Nap'ha) used to rise in the presence of elderly non-Jews, in respect for the tribulations they had suffered.[69]

Coexistence and private meetings

The *Tosefta* rules that a husband may force his wife to move from a non-Jewish city to a Jewish one, but he may not do so in the opposite direction.[70] Because the non-Jews are suspected of murder,[71] the *Babylonian Talmud* considers it unusual for a Jew to live on his own in a non-Jewish courtyard.[72]

Moreover, because they are suspected of murder, rape, and pederasty, the *Mishna* and *Tosefta* rule that a Jewish man, woman or child may not have a private meeting (*yihud*) with one or many non-Jews,[73] whether in the bath-house, in the lavatory, or on a journey.[74] But Jews and non-Jews are allowed to work together.[75] In a case cited in the *Babylonian Talmud*, Jew and non-Jew shared the same cooking-stove in Tyre.[76]

---

[65] *Y.Ber.* 8,8.

[66] *T.AZ* 1,2.

[67] *B.Ber.* 17a; quoted, without attribution to Abaye, in *Eliyahu Z.* 1 and 15.

[68] *B.Ber. ib.*

[69] *B.Kid.* 33a; text and translation unclear.

[70] *T.Ket.* 13,2 (L: 12,5). It is preferable, however, to live in a non-Jewish city in the Land of Israel than in a Jewish city outside it: *T.AZ* 4,3; *B.Ket.* 110b; according to *Y.Ket.* 12,3, this is because the Land of Israel is like one mother's bosom, whereas outside it is like a stranger's.

[71] See section I.3.A (pp. 22–3).

[72] *B.Eruv.* 62a.

[73] *M.AZ* 2,1 (man and woman); *T.AZ* 3,2 (child); cf *T.Kid.* 5,9 (L: 5,10) (with special emphasis).

[74] *T.AZ* 3,4; *Y.AZ* 2,1; *B.AZ* 25b; quoted in detail in pp. 23 and 26. Cf *Gen.R.* 78,15: Rabbi never accepted non-Jewish escorts, emulating Jacob's mistrust in Esau (*Gen.* 33:12–15).

[75] *M.AZ* 4,9: treading grapes, but not cutting them. The reverse is taught in *T.AZ* 8,1; *B.AZ* 55b–56a.

[76] *B.AZ* 11b–12a.

Services

The *Mishna* and *Tosefta* rule that a Jewish child may not be entrusted
to a non-Jewish teacher for his education or apprenticeship, as the
latter is suspected of pederasty.[77] One may not use a non-Jewish doctor
or barber, as they are suspected of murder.[78] A Jewish barber may
cut a non-Jew's hair, but without approaching his *belurit* (hair-lock),
as it is dedicated to *avoda zara*.[79] According to a popular saying quoted
by the *Babylonian Talmud*, if you are singeing the hair of an Aramean
and he is pleased with it, set fire to his beard and "you shall hear
no laughter from him"[80]—in other words, non-Jews should not enjoy
your services. A Jewess may not assist a non-Jewish woman in childbirth,
nor may she nurse a non-Jewish infant, as she is assisting in the growth
of a future *avoda zara* worshipper.[81] A non-Jewish nurse may be used,
but provided she stays in a Jewish house.[82] A non-Jewish midwife
may also be used,[83] but only, according to some, if she is continually
watched.[84] A Jew may not work for a non-Jew on *avoda zara* festive
days.[85]

For the sake of peaceful relations,[86] one is permitted to raise charity
from non-Jews[87] and to distribute it among them; one may also deliver
funeral eulogies on their behalf, bury them, and comfort their
bereaved.[88] On the other hand, one may not give them a free gift,
for it is written: 'do not grant them grace'.[89]

The *Babylonian Talmud* forbids a Jew to turn to non-Jewish law-
courts, even if their laws are identical to the laws of Israel[90]—and
even, the *Midrash Tanhuma* adds, if one's opponent is not Jewish.[91]

---

[77] *T.AZ* 3,2.
[78] *M.AZ* 2,2; *T.AZ* 3,4–5. However, a non-Jewish barber may be used in a public
place (*M.AZ*) or if the Jew can see himself in a mirror (*T.AZ*).
[79] *T.AZ* 3,6; cf *Deut.R.* 2,18.
[80] *B.Sanh.* 96a.
[81] *M.AZ* 2,1; *T.AZ* 3,3.
[82] *M.AZ* 2,1.
[83] *M.AZ* 2,1.
[84] *T.AZ* 3,3.
[85] *T.AZ* 1.3.
[86] See note 60.
[87] See further p. 201, n. 13.
[88] *T.Git.* 5,4–5 (L: 3,13–4). *B.Git.* 61a adds: visiting their sick, and allowing their
poor to gather gleanings, forgotten sheaves, and the corner of the field. In this respect,
non-Jews are to be treated equally as Jews.
[89] *T.AZ* 3,15; *Y.AZ* 1,9; *B.AZ* 20a (quoting again *Deut.* 7:2).
[90] *B.Git.* 88b; this is a scriptural prohibition, inferred from *Ex.*21:1.
[91] *Tanh. Shoftim* 1; again a scriptural prohibition, inferred from *Psalms* 147:20.

The same *Midrash* suggests that if one has the choice between a Jewish and a non-Jewish shop, it is sinful to enter the latter.[92]

Partnership

Many Halakhic cases in our sources deal with partnership with non-Jews, thus implying that it is permissible. Jews and non-Jews make joint purchases;[93] they own together fields, vineyards, and cattle;[94] they are partners in dwellings,[95] and joint tenants of gardens, orchards and fields.[96]

Yet on the other hand, Shemuel's father is said in the *Babylonian Talmud* to forbid one to enter a partnership (*shuttafut*) with a non-Jew, lest a dispute between the partners should lead the non-Jew to take an oath and swear by his *avoda zara*.[97] Furthermore, according to a later *Midrash*, partnership with a non-Jew is like a covenant with him, and like worship of *avoda zara*.[98] This prohibition may have been widely transgressed, however, as one *Amora* boasted of never having made a partnership with a non-Jew—implying that this was rather exceptional;[99] his brother boasted of never having even looked at a non-Jew.[100]

The imperial service

Halakhic sources do not prevent Jews from joining the imperial service, and many appear to have done so;[101] but the *Midrashim* condemn

---

[92] *Tanh. Vayikra* 6; *Tanh.B. ib.*10. In the parallel (earlier?) versions in *Lev.R.* 4,3 and *Eccl.R.* end, however, the choice is between shops selling kosher or non-kosher meat.

[93] *T.AZ* 3,17. In all these passages the term *shuttafut* (partnership) is explicitly used.

[94] *T.Peah* 2,9; 3,12; and especially *B.Hul.* 133a–b and 135a–136a (and parallel sources). They are also joint owners of a stew (*Y.AZ* 2,9), and even of an object of *avoda zara* (*B.AZ* 53a)!

[95] *B.Hul. ib.*

[96] *B.AZ* 22a.

[97] *B.Sanh.* 63b. This ruling is in contradiction with the Halakhic cases just listed, where partnership with non-Jews is mentioned without any indication that they may be forbidden (as noted by the *Tosafot ad B.Bekh.* 2b s.v. *asur*; cf *Hagahot Maimoniyot* on Maimonides, *Mishne Torah, Shuttafim,* 5,10).

[98] *Eliyahu R.* 8, end, at length.

[99] As noted by the *Tosafot ad B.Bekh.* 2b, and R. Asher (the *Rosh*) *ad Sanh.* 63b.

[100] *B.Meg.* 28a.

[101] See A. Linder, *The Jews in Roman Imperial Legislation*, Detroit: Wayne State Univ. Press and Jerusalem: Israel Academy of Sciences and Humanities, 1987, pp. 76–7, 222–4 and 280–3. In 418CE the Jews were barred by imperial edict from the imperial service, and instructions were issued for the dismissal of Jewish State agents, (*agentes in rebus*), financial officials (*palatini*), and soldiers (*Codex Theodosianus* 16:8:24).

this practice in no uncertain terms. The story is told of an ignoramus in Babylon who behaved with excessive pride; "in the course of that year and the second and the third" (*sic*), he went up to the Land of Israel and was appointed commander of Caesar's army and of all the castles in the Land of Israel; he built a city to dwell in and was given the hereditary title of *coloni*;[102] and the *Midrash* concludes: "whoever displays pride in His presence suffers disgrace".[103] With much irony, this *Midrash* considers high military office and hereditary titles to be fit for an ignoramus, and a form of disgrace.[104]

Moreover, Israel are praised in early and later *Midrashim* for rejecting imperial offices:

> The nations say to Israel: "For how much longer will you die and be martyred for the sake of your God? . . . Come to us and we will appoint you *ducsin*, *eparkhin*, and *istratlin* (i.e. generals and governors)!". Israel answer: ". . . we will not worship *avoda zara*".[105]

In this passage, the imperial service is implicitly portrayed as a betrayal of God and as *avoda zara*.[106]

Similar edicts were issued in the course of the 5th and 6th centuries, indicating that the law may not have been thoroughly enforced.

[102] What this title corresponds to, in historical terms, is totally unclear.

[103] *Num.R.* 4,20; also *Eliyahu R.* 13.

[104] The *Midrash* may even imply that his imperial appointment was a form of *punishment* for his empty pride, by analogy with a similar incident which is told in the same *Midrash* (*ib.*). In that incident, an ignoramus was punished "in the course of that year and the second and the third" (*sic*) by death, for himself and all his family. The hereditary title granted to our ignoramus and all his family may represent, by analogy, some form of *ethnic death*, as he had excluded himself from the fold of Israel.

[105] *Song R.* 7,1,2. Also *Num.R.* 2,4 (& *Tanh. ib.*), which reads: 'Adhere to us and we will appoint you etc.'. In *Pes.R.* 21,15 and *Pes.dRK* 19,4, Israel ignore the nations' offer by entering synagogues and houses of learning.

[106] On the other hand, in the 390's CE imperial legislation (recorded in the *Codex Theodosianus*) refers to the Jewish Patriarch with the honorific, senatorial titles of *spectabilis*, *clarissimus* and *illustris* (see Linder, pp. 70 and 221f.); furthermore, in the early 5th century the Patriarch was given the supreme honour of an (honorary) prefecture, which was then removed by imperial legislation in 415CE (*Codex Theod.* 16:8:22; cf Linder, pp. 267–272). We may have to distinguish between imperial *service*, which entailed active involvement in the administration of the Roman Empire, and imperial *honours*, which in practice meant little or no commitment to it at all, and may thus have been acceptable to the Patriarchs. Furthermore, the fact that the Patriarch's honorific titles are nowhere mentioned in rabbinic writings may indicate that the Patriarchs never endorsed the titles which the emperors had willy-nilly bestowed on them (even though the prefecture entailed the official reception of *codicilli*, documents, as implied in *Codex Theod. ib.*).

On the avoidance of *civic* service as *bouleutai* on local councils (which, unlike avoidance

Weddings, dinners, and food

Non-Jewish weddings are listed in the *Mishna* as one of the festivals of *avoda zara*.[107] According to the *Tosefta*, Diaspora Jews are commonly invited by non-Jews to their wedding banquets; even though they eat their own food, drink their own wine, and are served by their own waiters, they are unknowingly committing *avoda zara* and eating, as it were, *avoda zara* sacrifices.[108] The *Palestinian Talmud* rules that it is forbidden to act as *shushbin* (bride's or bridegroom's friend) at a non-Jewish wedding, because this resembles intermarriage.[109]

According to the *Babylonian Talmud*, state-sponsored dinners are also forbidden: whoever attends them ends up in exile.[110] The reason why the Jews at the time of Ahasuerus were threatened with extermination (by Divine decree) was because they had enjoyed the banquet of the wicked king.[111] It is forbidden to invite a non-Jew for a meal at one's home; this is also punished by exile.[112] Later *Midrashim* forbid one in general to eat with a non-Jew at the same table: it amounts to eating 'abominable meat',[113] or to eating with a dog,[114] or again, to committing *avoda zara* and eating *avoda zara* sacrifices.[115] Thus the mere fact that it is eaten together with non-Jews renders this food, albeit initially kosher, 'abominable' and even an '*avoda zara* sacrifice'.

Similarly, a number of foods become forbidden if they are merely produced or manufactured by non-Jews. The *Mishna* (*M.A.Z.* 2) lists

---

of the imperial service, was widespread in the Late Roman Empire), see S. Safrai, "The Avoidance of Public Office in Papyrus Oxy.1477 and in Talmudic Sources", in *JJS* 14, 1963, pp. 67–70, and Linder, *op.cit.*

[107] *M.A.Z.* 1,3.

[108] *T.A.Z.* 4,6; *B.A.Z.* 8a; *Avot dRN* 26,4.

[109] *Y.A.Z.* 1,9. On intermarriage, see below section IV.1.D.

[110] *B.Pes.* 49a.

[111] As told in *Est.* 1: *B.Meg.* 12a (but according to *Song R.* 7,8, it was because "they ate non-Jewish cooked food"). In *Num.R.* 21,20 (= *Tanh. Pinhas*, 13) R. Dostai says that he once attended a public, non-Jewish dinner; however, it was sponsored by a private individual.

[112] *B.Sanh.* 104a. The connection between dinners and exile is to me unclear.

[113] *PdRE* (ed.Higger) 28.

[114] *Ib.* in text of first editions, quoted by Friedlander, *op.cit.*, p. 208, n. 5, and above in p. 35 and p. 60, note 65.

[115] *Eliyahu R.* 9 *passim*; cf *ib.* 13 where the same is said of an *am haAretz*.

them as follows: wine and all its by-products,[116] fish-brine,[117] cheese,[118] milk, bread, oil, minced fish, salt,[119] locusts from a basket,[120] as well as all cooked foods.[121] It would appear that these foods are forbidden because the non-Jew cannot be trusted to have prepared them in a kosher way;[122] this explanation is stated, for instance, with reference to cheese[123] and to salt.[124] However, according to the *Babylonian Talmud*, non-Jewish bread, oil, alcohol and even wine were banned "on account of (i.e. lest they led to) intermarriage".[125] The prohibition of non-Jewish foods is thus interpreted by the *Babylonian Talmud*, quite explicitly, as a means of separating and dissociating the Jews from the non-Jewish world.[126]

Public baths; theatres, circuses and stadia
The *Mishna* rules that Jews may build public baths together with non-

---

[116] E.g. vinegar, wine skin-bottles and jars, grape-stones and grape-skins: *M.AZ* 2,3–4; vegetables pickled in wine or vinegar: *ib.*, 6. Grape juice is not distinguished from wine: since the non-Jew is suspected of having made a libation of them, they are forbidden as *avoda zara*.

[117] *Ib.* 4 & 6.

[118] *Ib.* 4–5.

[119] *Ib.* 6.

[120] *Ib.* 7.

[121] According to *Y.AZ* 2,6; *B.AZ* 37b–38b; cf *Est.R.* 7,8 (quoted above). It is debatable whether the prohibition of cooked foods can be traced back to the *Mishna*. Danby translates *M.AZ* 2,6 as forbidding "stewed or pickled vegetables into which it is their custom to put wine or vinegar". Both *Talmudim* (*Y.AZ ib.* & *B.AZ* 37b–38b), however, treat "stewed vegetables" as an independent item, which unlike pickled vegetables are forbidden regardless of whether it is the custom to prepare them with wine or vinegar. The *Talmudim* infer from there the general prohibition of 'non-Jewish cooked foods'. (Besides ignoring the Talmudic tradition, Danby ignores that in *M.AZ* 2,7 "pickled vegetables" are mentioned on their own and without reference to "stewed vegetables", and that in the text of *M.AZ* 2,6 according to *Y.AZ* "stewed vegetables" are positioned independently, earlier on in the *mishna*. Nonetheless, R. L'azar, at the beginning of *Y.AZ* 2,7, may have understood the *mishna* like Danby.)

[122] This would not apply, however, to honey, honeycombs, raw vegetables, whole fish, certain brines, and olive cakes, which are all permitted: *M.AZ* 2,7.

[123] *M.AZ* 2,5.

[124] It is told that once an old non-Jew smeared salt with pork fat: *Y.AZ* 2, end; *B.AZ* 36b.

[125] *Mi-shum hatnut.* Bread: *B.AZ* 35b and 36b. Alcohol: *ib.* 31b. Oil and wine (perhaps, if it is known *not* to have been made a libation to *avoda zara*): *ib.* 36b.

[126] As already intimated in *Lev.* 20:24–26, where the separation of animals permitted for eating from those forbidden is emphatically related to the separation of Israel from the nations. The rabbinic prohibition of non-Jewish foods is also related, no doubt, to the repulsiveness which is generally attributed to the non-Jews and to their food (see sections II.1.B and II.3.C).

Jews, except for the vault where an object of *avoda zara* is to be placed.[127]

There are some restrictions on frequenting public baths together with non-Jews, since private meetings with them are forbidden;[128] according to a late *Midrash*, Jews should not bathe together with the uncircumcised, as it is like bathing with carrion.[129] The *Mishna*, however, allows one to attend baths which are run and attended by non-Jews.[130] R. Gamliel attended the baths of Aphrodite in Acco, and had a conversation, albeit abortive, with Proclus the son of a *philosophos*.[131] He argued that bathing in the presence of a statue of Aphrodite did not constitute *avoda zara*: indeed, the baths had not been built as an ornament to Aphrodite, but quite on the contrary, the statue had been erected as a mere ornament to the baths; moreover, it was not the object of religious worship.[132]

Theatres, circuses and stadia, on the other hand, are forbidden by the *Sifra* (i.e. to attend, or possibly to build[133]) as being 'customs of the nations'.[134] According to the *Tosefta* and *Talmudim*, attending theatres and circuses is tantamount to *avoda zara* (perhaps because pagan sacrifices were commonly performed on those premises); others condemn them as a 'seat of the scornful'[135] and places where *Torah* learning is neglected; as to attending stadia, this is tantamount to murder, as it is the place where convicts are put death.[136]

---

[127] *M.AZ* 1,7.

[128] *T.AZ* 3,4; *B.AZ* 25b (see above).

[129] *PdRE* (ed.Higger) 28.

[130] *M.Makhshirin* 2,5.

[131] *M.AZ* 3,4. On the identity of these characters see A. Wasserstein, "Rabban Gamliel and Proclus the Philosopher", in *Zion* 45, 1980, pp. 257–67 (Hebrew).

[132] *M.AZ ib.* See also *Y.Sheviit* 8, end. But according to *Midrash Ḥesed Le'ummim* (ed. Wertheimer), the non-Jews build public baths where to worship *avoda zara* and conceal their prostitutes.

[133] Elsewhere we are told that stadia may not be built: *M.AZ* 1,7.

[134] *Sifra Aharei, perek* 13,9. The notion of 'customs of the nations' will be explained and discussed in section IV.2.D with reference to cultural resistance to assimilation; I am quoting this passage in this section, as it is also relevant to social interaction with non-Jews.

[135] Quoting *Psalms* 1:1; cf *Avot dRN* 22,1.

[136] *T.AZ* 2,5–7; cf *Y.AZ* 1,7; and at greater length, *B.AZ* 18b where *karkom* (perhaps a military camp, as the same term refers to an invading military contingent in *M.Ket.* 2,9) and *kynegion* (a hunting show?) are also mentioned as forbidden to attend, and much attention is given to the evils of being among the 'scornful'. Some argue, however, that stadia may be attended in order to save the convicts through acclamation, or alternatively to be able to certify that they were actually put to death and thus to enable their widows to re-marry (*T.AZ ib.*, etc.); see also *B.Shab.* 150a (= *Tanh. Bereshit* 2): one may attend theatres, circuses and 'basilicas' even on the *shabbat* in order to keep an eye on public affairs.

The contrast between theatres (etc.) and synagogues is frequent in rabbinic sources. According to the *Palestinian Talmud*, a *Torah* scholar leaving his 'house of learning' (*beit midrash*) should recite:

> I thank You .. that You have allotted me to the houses of learning and synagogues and not ... to theatres and circuses.[137]

The *Babylonian Talmud* states that in the future the theatres and circuses of Rome will be transformed into synagogues and houses of learning where "the princes of Judah will publicly expound the *Torah*".[138]

The *Midrashim* depict theatres and circuses as places where the non-Jews laugh[139] and jeer at the customs of the Jews[140] and arouse the Almighty's anger.[141] They desert their homes on "theatre days".[142] The Jews, by contrast, shun theatres and circuses[143] and attend instead synagogues and houses of learning.[144] Naomi told Ruth that daughters of Israel are not accustomed to go to the theatres and circuses of the nations.[145] Likewise, a scholar has no benefit in entering these places.[146] The Assembly of Israel prides itself as follows:

> Never in my life have I entered the theatres or circuses of the nations in order to jeer and rejoice together with them ... instead, I am sitting alone. . . .[147]

The avoidance of theatres and circuses is not only a social gesture of dissociation from the non-Jews and from their civic institutions.

---

[137] *Y.Ber.* 4,2.

[138] *B.Meg.* 6a.

[139] *Eccl. R.* 2,2,1; *Pes. dRK* 26,2; *Tanh. Aharei* 1.

[140] Such as the *shabbat* and the Sabbatical year: *Lam.R. pet.* 17; 3,5.

[141] *Pes. dRK* 28,1. Still, the Jews must be grateful for theatres and circuses, for they distract the non-Jews and keep them out of mischief: *Gen.R.* 80,1 (cf various readings). Theatres and circuses also entertain imperial rulers: *Est.R. pet.* 5.

[142] *Gen.R.* 87,7.

[143] Theatre and circus attendants are so prestigious among the nations that they are put in charge of the imperial icons (*Lev. R.* 34,3); by contrast, the Jews consider this profession to be insulting (*Y.Taan.* 1,4). In Egypt, however, the Israelites are said to have thronged theatres and circuses: *Tanh.B. Shemot* 6. On the apostasy of the Israelites in Egypt, see p. 67.

[144] E.g. *Pes. dRK* 28,1; *Eccl.R.* 1,7,5. The latter adds that if the Almighty had given wisdom to the fools (the non-Jews), they would be sitting and discussing it in lavatories, in theatres and in baths; so He gave it to the wise (Israel), and they discuss it in synagogues and in houses of learning.

[145] *Ruth R.* 2,22. This statement is presented by the *Midrash* as part of the formal procedure of conversion.

[146] *Eccl.R.* 2,2,1.

[147] *Lam.R., pet.* 3; *Pes. dRK* 15,2.

It is also significant in terms of material culture: inasmuch as Jews and non-Jews identify with different public buildings, the boundaries between them may be written into the physical planning of the city. Dissociation from the non-Jews is thus not only 'social', but also material and in a sense, 'embodied'.

C. Dissociation and Jewish identity

Although I have established that rabbinic sources erected substantial boundaries between themselves and the non-Jews, it would be wrong to assume, *prima facie*, that these were designed to protect or enhance the integrity of Jewish identity, or at least were seen to fulfil this purpose.[148] If we take our sources at face value, indeed, the reasons for these boundaries would appear extraneous and unrelated to Jewish identity. These reasons could be classified as follows:

1. *Personal safety*. Social restrictions can be means of protecting Jews against the physical danger which the non-Jews, in their intrinsic wickedness, represent: for instance, the prohibition of selling them weapons, of using their doctors and barbers, and of having private meetings with them.

2. *Avoidance of scriptural prohibitions*. Many restrictions we have listed are designed to safeguard the avoidance of scriptural prohibitions: for instance, the Mishnaic prohibition of non-Jewish cheese, salt, and other non-Jewish foods, is to ensure that dietary laws are not infringed. Restrictions on the sale of land to non-Jews,[149] on praising non-Jews

---

[148] Although Porton (1985) dismisses the existence of substantial dissociation, he takes it for granted that the purpose of dissociation, were it to exist, would be to protect the integrity of Jewish identity. He writes: "the rabbis simply ignored . . . any threat to the *coherence of the Israelite community* which might result from the economic interaction of Israelite and gentile" (p. 333—my emphasis). But as I will now argue, the "coherence of the Israelite community" need not be the only reason for the rabbis to restrict relations with non-Jews.

[149] This is the scriptural prohibition of "granting (the non-Jews) residence in the Land": *Y.A.Z* 1,9; *B.A.Z* 20a. This applies specifically to the Land of Israel, and would have the effect of reducing non-Jewish land ownership and hence the size of the non-Jewish population in the Land of Israel. We may speculate, therefore, that this prohibition was also seen as a means of reducing social interaction between the Jews and non-Jewish land-owning neighbours. It has even been argued that Israel's exclusive possession of their land would enhance the integrity of their national identity: see R. Jankelewitz, "The Gentiles' struggle for land ownership in Eretz-Israel", in A. Kasher, A. Oppenheimer, U. Rappaport (eds.), *Man and Law in Eretz-Israel in Antiquity*, Jerusalem: Yad Ben-Zvi, 1986, pp. 117–127 (Hebrew). I have found, however, that the Land of Israel is hardly ever associated in our sources with Jewish identity or with the people of Israel (with the exception perhaps of *Y.Ket.* 12,3, quoted above:

for their beauty, on giving them free gifts, and on resorting to non-Jewish courts, are explained by the *Talmud* as constituting scriptural prohibitions in their own right.

3. *Avoidance of avoda zara*. Most common is the concern to avoid scriptural prohibitions related to *avoda zara*. Thus, one may not provide non-Jews with sacrificial animals for *avoda zara*. Non-Jewish wine is forbidden because it is presumably a libation to *avoda zara*. Partnerships with non-Jews are forbidden as they may be induced to swear by their *avoda zara*. Attendance at non-Jewish weddings, dinners and public shows, as well as the imperial service, are anathematized as a form of participation in *avoda zara*. Porton argues, against Saul Lieberman and E.E. Urbach, that the practice of *avoda zara* was seen by the *Mishna* and *Tosefta* as a potential attraction to the Jews, even in their own period, and that prohibitions such as these are designed to avert this threat.[150] I have argued elsewhere, however, that the *Mishna* and *Talmud* consistently assume that in their own time, *avoda zara* was no longer attractive to the Jews.[151] The concern with *avoda zara*, in these prohibitions, does not necessarily proceed from a fear that Jews may come to worship *avoda zara* themselves:[152] in most cases, it is either

---

to a Jew, the Land of Israel is "like his mother's bosom").

See also Y. Cohen, "The attitude to the Gentile in the Halakhah and in Reality in the Tannaitic Period", in *Immanuel* 9, 1979, pp. 32–41, who argues that commercial restrictions were designed to weaken the 'Gentile economy' in the Land of Israel (p. 39); but this is unlikely, as the 'Jewish economy' would have suffered just as much from these same restrictions.

[150] Porton *op.cit.* 1988 (pp. 241–3). See also M. Hadas-Lebel, "Le paganisme à travers les sources rabbiniques des IIe et IIIe siècles. Contribution à l'étude du syncrétisme dans l'empire romain", in *Aufstieg und Niedergang der Römischen Welt*, vol. II.19.2, Berlin and New York: Walter de Gruyter, 1979, pp. 397–485, esp. 398–9. On the persistence of paganism in the Late Roman Near East, see above p. 28, n. 186.

[151] See "The Death of Idolatry?", in *Le'ela*, April 1993, pp. 26–8, where I argue that the Mishnaic tractate *Avoda Zara*, where one would expect to find reference to Jewish worship of *avoda zara*, is significantly reticent in this respect; inasmuch as it is entirely devoted, instead, to relations with the non-Jews, this tractate conveys that *avoda zara* is intrinsically a *non-Jewish* problem. Likewise the *Babylonian Talmud*, in *B.Sanh.* 102b, expresses genuine difficulty at understanding Menasheh's attraction to *avoda zara*. See also above, p. 28, referring to the Talmudic accounts of the *eradication* from the Jewish people, in the days of Ezra, of the attraction to *avoda zara*; which may explain why Jews are not suspected, according to Halakhic sources, of *avoda zara*. The sole proof-text quoted by Porton (1988, p. 241, n. 2) is *T.Ber.* 6,2, which only shows awareness that *some* Jews still worship *avoda zara*—a reference, perhaps, to the *minim*; it does not prove that in *general* terms, *avoda zara* presented a temptation to the common Jewish people.

[152] Except in the case of intermarriage, which we shall examine in the next section. It must be noted, however, that in the case of intermarriage, relationship with the

a matter of refraining from assisting a non-Jew in his worship (e.g. by selling him sacrificial animals), or of avoiding any benefit derived from the (non-Jewish) practice of *avoda zara* (e.g. from non-Jewish wine), which are treated as scriptural prohibitions in their own right.[153]

It may be argued that the protection of Jewish identity constitutes the 'real' purpose of these prohibitions, for which personal safety and avoidance of *avoda zara* are no more than Halakhic 'excuses'. However, the scope of these prohibitions suggests that this is not the case. We find, indeed, that a non-Jewish barber *may* be used in public places, where he is not susceptible to murder.[154] Likewise, it is permissible to trade with non-Jews *outside* a city where there is *avoda zara*.[155] Whereas theatres, circuses and stadia, where *avoda zara* and murder are committed, are strictly forbidden to attend, R. Gamliel rules that public baths may be attended since their statues of *avoda zara* are no more than insignificant. Thus, relations with non-Jews are not *per se* curtailed; it is personal safety, scriptural prohibitions and avoidance of *avoda zara*, and not some general concern for Jewish identity, which determine the scope of these prohibitions.[156]

Yet in a certain sense, these prohibitions do reflect an implicit desire to protect the identity of Israel. Firstly, as we have seen in the first chapter, *avoda zara* constitutes a distinctive feature of the nations, and is thus antithetic to the identity of Israel. Avoiding any benefit derived from (non-Jewish) *avoda zara*, although perhaps a scriptural prohibition in its own right, would thus serve to protect the integrity of Jewish identity. Secondly, by taking pragmatic precautions against the non-Jewish threat of rape and murder, as well as against the non-Jews' attachment to *avoda zara*, the authors of our sources would conceptually enhance this negative image of the nations, against which their own image as Israel could be contrasted. Finally, restrictions on social relations, albeit limited in scope, could not fail to exercise some social

---

non-Jews is far more intimate than in the socio-economic relations which we have so far discussed. Accordingly, as we shall see, intermarriage is associated not only with *avoda zara* but also with apostasy and loss of Jewish identity. In the context of apostasy, it is hardly surprising or inconsistent that *avoda zara* should be treated in our sources as a potential lure.

[153] Assisting the non-Jew in his *avoda zara* pertains, among others, to the prohibition of "placing a stumbling-block before the blind" (*Lev.* 19:14), according to *BAZ* 6a–b, 14a, etc. The prohibition to derive any benefit from *avoda zara* is inferred from *Deut.* 13:18 in *MAZ* 3:4, etc.

[154] *MAZ* 2,2.

[155] *MAZ* 1,4.

[156] This is also argued by Porton (1988), p. 243.

control on Jews and non-Jews and to enhance, at least as a 'side effect', the social distinctiveness of Israel.

There is some evidence that the authors of our sources are aware of this 'side effect', and accordingly experience these prohibitions as means of protecting their identity. In one passage we quoted, the Talmud explains the prohibition of non-Jewish foods as being "on account of intermarriage", thus implying that restrictions of this kind promote the dissociation of Jews from the non-Jews. In a *Midrash*, Jewish identity is invoked as an explanation to the Mishnaic ruling that for the ritual of *havdala* the light of a non-Jew may not be used.[157] According to the *Babylonian Talmud*, such a light is unfit because "it has not rested over *shabbat*";[158] but the *Midrash Tanḥuma* adds:

> also, if you make *havdala*[159] on the light of a non-Jew, you are treating him as though he were respectable, whereas in fact it is written: "all the nations are nothing before Him".[160]

Thus a prohibition grounded on the Halakhic principle of Sabbatical rest is experienced simultaneously, in a more informal Midrashic context, as means of enhancing the identity of Israel. This indicates that the Halakhic considerations which bring about and define restrictions on relations with non-Jews do not constitute the only way in which they are experienced.

This Midrashic interpretation is admittedly unparalleled in the rest of rabbinic literature. Since the liturgy of the *havdala* refers to the distinction between Israel and the nations, awareness of Jewish identity is bound to be more distinctive in this context. I would argue, nonetheless, that a similar identity-related experience lurks behind *all* restrictions on relations with non-Jews, even though they are formally and primarily based on other Halakhic reasons. This multiplicity of purposes, involving at once avoidance of *avoda zara* (or other Halakhic

---

[157] *M.Ber.* 8,6.

[158] *Lo shavat: B.Ber.* 52b–53a. This light has been used by the non-Jew for the purpose of work forbidden to Jews on *shabbat* (Rashi *ad loc.*).

[159] Literally: "if you separate". In chapter I we have seen that the ritual of *havdala* asserts the separation between Israel and the nations as much as that between *shabbat* and weekdays.

[160] *Tanh. Vayyeshev* 3, quoting *Isaiah* 40:17. It can be argued that this *Midrash*, being of later composition, does not represent the opinion of the Talmud; nonetheless my analysis remains valid as to the *Midrash* itself. Porton (*op.cit.* 1988 pp. 44–5) argues, however, that the *Mishna* appears to forbid lamp and spices for no other reason than that they are not Jewish.

motives) and the protection of Jewish identity, is most visible in the prohibition of intermarriage, to which I shall now turn.

D. *The prohibition of intermarriage*

Intermarriage and avoda zara

The prohibition of exogamy, or of 'intermarriage' between Jews and non-Jews, finds its origin in the Bible:

> Neither shall you make marriages with them: your daughter you shall not give unto his son, nor his daughter shall you take for your son (*Deut.* 7:3).

The prohibition is justified as follows in the next verse:

> For he will turn away your son from Me, and they will serve other gods; so will the Lord be kindled against you, and He will destroy you quickly (*ib.*4).

This occurred indeed at Shittim, where the Israelites had sexual relations with the daughters of Moab: the latter enticed them to worship and make sacrifices to their gods.[161]

As any other Biblical commandment, the rabbis could adhere to it without inquiring into its significance. But since the scriptures invest it with a specific purpose—the avoidance of *avoda zara*—this *rationale* is given prime importance in rabbinic writings. It is invoked by the *Babylonian Talmud* as evidence that the prohibition of intermarriage is not restricted to the 'seven nations' (of the land of Canaan), but applies to all nations liable to lure the Jews into *avoda zara*;[162] whereas it is permitted, by the same logic, for one to marry converts.[163] Moreover, according to Rav, the rabbinic decree against non-Jewish "daughters" was passed as a precaution against the lure of *avoda zara*.[164]

---

[161] *Num.* 25:1–2. The connection between intermarriage and *avoda zara* is also expressed in *Ex.* 34:15–6 and I*Kings* 11:4–8. *Ezra* 9–10, which deals extensively with the issue of intermarriage which confronted him, refers to the abominations (*to'avot*) of the non-Jews they married, which may be identified as their *avoda zara* (*Ezra* 9:11; 9:14; cf Nehemiah 13:23–27). Cf G. Vermes, "Leviticus 18:21 in Ancient Jewish Bible Exegesis", in *Studies in Aggadah, Targum and Jewish Liturgy in Memory of Joseph Heinemann*, Jerusalem: Magnes Press, 1981, pp. 108–124.

[162] *B.Yev.* 23b; *B.Kid.* 68b.

[163] *B.Yev.* 63b.

[164] *B.AZ* 36b. The same applies to the rabbinic decree against non-Jewish bread, oil, and wine. The *Talmud* concludes that the rabbinic decree against non-Jewish "daughters" cannot be a reference to intermarriage, since intermarriage is anyway prohibited by Biblical law, but rather a reference to having *yihud* (private meetings)

Intermarriage leads, indeed, to *avoda zara*. It is the next step after apostasy,[165] a "marriage with *avoda zara*".[166] Its offspring follows the same path: *Deut.* 7:4 (quoted above) refers to the Jewish son of a non-Jewish father[167] who goes and worships *avoda zara* in his father's footsteps;[168] or according to the *Palestinian Talmud*, to the non-Jewish son of a Jewish father, who will eventually become, as all non-Jews, an enemy of the Almighty.[169]

(This may explain the Talmudic reference to the 400 children of King David's army born from non-Jewish captives, who grew a *kome* hair-style and a *belurit*, which are distinctly non-Jewish.[170] Although these captive women *may* have converted beforehand,[171] their offspring persisted in adopting, if not *avoda zara*, at least forbidden non-Jewish hair-styles.[172])

Avoda zara and intermarriage are, in this sense, virtually interchangeable. A verse in *Lev.* 18:21, which reads: "and you shall not give your offspring (lit.: seed) to be passed on to *Molekh*", is translated by *Targum Ps-Jonathan* as follows:

> and you shall not have intercourse with a non-Jewish woman and give her your seed, and make her pregnant for the benefit of some other worship.[173]

---

with non-Jewish women, which was prohibited by the Houses of Hillel and Shammai. On the extent to which *avoda zara* is considered an attraction to the Jews in early rabbinic sources, see p. 156, note 151.

[165] As implied from the story of Miriam b.Bilga in *T.Suk.* 4,28; *B.Suk.* 56b.

[166] *B.Sanh.* 82a.

[167] Jewish identity is transmitted matrilineally: see p. 87.

[168] *B.Yev.* 63b.

[169] *Y.Sanh.* 9,7.

[170] *B.Kid.* 76b. On *kome* and *belurit*, see pp. 68–9. On their prohibition, see pp. 187–8. The "400 children" may be a reference to I.Sam.30:10.

[171] See *Deut.* 21:10–14. Indeed, women captives must first abandon *avoda zara* (*Sifre Deut.* 213; *B.Yev.* 48b) and become Jewish (*B.Yev.* 47b; *B.Kid.* 68b). According to R. Yohanan, intercourse with them is forbidden until this procedure is completed (*Y.Mak.* 2,6).

[172] Although converts are normally considered Jewish, as I have shown in section III.2.A, the case of the captive woman may be frowned upon by our sources because her conversion is not based on genuine religious motivations (see *B.Kid.* 21b).

S.R. Shimoff ("Hellenisation among the rabbis, some evidence from early Aggadot concerning David and Solomon", in *JSJ* 18.2, 1987, pp. 168–87) interprets *B.Kid.* 76b as laudatory rather than derogatory, and sees the praise of non-Jewish hair-style as "evidence of rabbinic hellenization" (pp. 176–8; see below pp. 171–3). However, if laudatory, this passage would be inconsistent with all other Talmudic passages prohibiting non-Jewish hair-style.

[173] I.e. *avoda zara*, which her non-Jewish children are liable to worship. It must be pointed out that *M.Meg.* 4,9 rejects this translation ("with rebuke"), as the verse

Preserving Jewish identity

Are we to conclude that the prohibition of intermarriage is primarily designed to avert the cult of *avoda zara*, whilst the protection of Jewish identity would be no more than its implicit 'side effect' or 'by-product'? I would like to argue that rabbinic sources see this particular prohibition, together with its rabbinic appendages,[174] as a 'social boundary' which is *directly and explicitly* aimed at the protection of the identity of Israel.

The prohibition epitomizes, indeed, the dissociation of Israel from the nations, as an early *Midrash* puts it:

> (Israel) do not mix with the nations, as it is written: "Neither shall you make marriages with them".[175]

Intermarriage appears, in one Talmudic account, as a form of surrender to the enemies of Israel: for it is when King Solomon married the daughter of Pharaoh that Gabriel came down and laid the foundations of the city of Rome.[176] But most significant is the fact that according to some sources, avoidance of intermarriage preserves the identity of Israel *even if they worship avoda zara*, as we shall now see.

According to a well-known *Midrash*, the Israelites in Egypt were "soaked in *avoda zara*" and ignored Moses' instructions to forsake it. Nevertheless, although *avoda zara* is equivalent to the transgression of the whole *Torah*, the Israelites were redeemed from Egypt through the merit of having kept four '*mitzvot*',[177] as follows: 1. they did not indulge in forbidden relations; 2. they did not inform against each other; 3. they did not change their names; 4. they did not change their language.[178] It is clear from the context of some versions of the *Midrash* that item 1 refers specifically to avoidance of intermarriage,

---

plainly refers to the cult of *Molekh*. Nonetheless, *B.Meg.* 25a brings down that the verse is talking of "an Israel who had intercourse with a non-Jewish woman and begot a child for *avoda zara*" (also *Y.Meg.* 4,9, which reads: "and begot enemies to the Almighty"). Cf Vermes *op.cit.*

[174] E.g. casual, extra-marital sexual relations, as well as private meetings, which were gradually forbidden by successive rabbinic courts: *B.AZ* 36b (just quoted).

[175] *Song R.* 1,3,2. Haman is said to have told Ahasuerus that the Jews were 'different' in so far as they would not intermarry: *B.Meg.* 13b.

[176] *B.Shab.* 56b; *B.Sanh.* 21b; *Y.AZ* 1,2 (Michael).

[177] Meaning in this context 'good deeds', since the last two items do not correspond to any scriptural commandment or rabbinic ruling—see pp. 192–4. The term *mitzvot* is not used in all the versions of this *Midrash*.

[178] This well-known *Midrash* is found in *Pes.dRK* 11,6; *Lev. R.* 32,5; *Song R.* 4,13; *Num.R.* 20,22; *Mekh. Bo* 5; *Tanh. Balak* 16; *Midrash Tehillim* 114. Its text varies considerably from version to version, although its contents, namely the 'four things', remain almost invariably the same.

rather than simply to incest or adultery. Indeed, the examples of Sarah
and Joseph are quoted as illustrations to item 1, both having avoided
intercourse with Egyptians (Pharaoh and Potiphar's wife, respectively);
conversely the example of Shelomit, the only Israelite woman to have
had intercourse with an Egyptian man, is quoted by the same *Midrash*
as an exceptional case.[179] Thus, in spite of their practice of *avoda zara*,
the Israelites' avoidance of intermarriage is implied to have maintained their integrity as a distinctive social group, without which they
could not have been redeemed.[180] Moreover, in this *Midrash* dissociation
from the non-Jews and the integrity of Israel's identity are presented
as a goal to be achieved in its own right.[181]

Intermarriage and loss of identity

In what respect does intermarriage constitute a *particular* threat to the
identity of Israel? Two propositions are suggested in our sources: firstly,
intermarriage disrupts the purity of Jewish lineage; secondly, sexual
intercourse with a non-Jew affects one's bodily identity as a Jew. Both
these propositions, which I will examine in turn, confirm that avoidance
of intermarriage is considered essential to the preservation of Jewish
identity.

　1) Intermarriage is a threat to the hereditary transmission of Jewish
identity, since the latter is only matrilineally transmitted.[182] Consequently, the *Talmudim* rule that "your son from a non-Jewish woman
is not called your son".[183] This does not affect a Jewish woman who
intermarries, as her offspring remains Jewish; nonetheless, some hold

---

[179] *Lev.R.* 32,5; *Song R.* 4,13. Joseph is omitted in *Pes. dRK* 11,6, but in the same
text (immediately preceding this passage) it is explicitly stated that the Egyptians
did not master the Israelites' wives. *Num.R.* 20,22 (= *Tanh. Balak* 16) brings this *Midrash*
in order to contrast Israel's behaviour in Egypt with their sin at Shittim, where
they had intercourse with the daughters of Moab (*Num.* 25:1). This confirms that
the *Midrash* understands item 1 as referring specifically to sexual intercourse with
non-Jews.

[180] We may assume that without a distinctive identity, the Israelites would have
totally merged with the Egyptian population—there would have been no Israel, and
hence their redemption could no longer have taken place.

[181] The significance of items 2, 3, and 4, in the context of the protection of Jewish
identity, will be examined in pp. 192–4 and 222.

[182] See pp. 87–8.

[183] *Y.Yev.* 2,6; *B.Yev.* 17a, 23a; *B.Kid.* 68b etc. This phrase implies not only that
is he non-Jewish, but also that he is not considered his father's son; indeed, his
non-Jewish mother would be suspected of adultery just as any non-Jew (see section
I.3.A). Similarly, intermarriage itself is not considered a valid marriage: *T.Ket.* 1,3.

that her offspring from a non-Jewish man would have the inferior lineage of a 'bastard'.[184]

By disrupting the purity of Jewish lineage, intermarriage can also be seen as a threat to the holiness of Israel. We are told in an early *Midrash* that in the days of Ezra, the Almighty guarded the families of Israel from intermarriage "so that the *holy seed* should not mix with the nations".[185] Ruth's redeemer refused to marry her because he did not know that her conversion had been valid, and he would not "mix his seed" and "mix a worthless offspring with his own sons".[186] A late *Midrash* goes as far as saying that the sons of Jacob (the ancestors of Israel) would only marry their own sisters, so as not to marry with the nations; they earned thereby the title of 'a truthful seed'.[187] A list of the 14 (!) negative prohibitions which are transgressed through intercourse with a non-Jewish woman includes the (agricultural) prohibitions of mixing seeds (*kilayim*).[188]

2) Talmudic sources consider that sexual intercourse with a non-Jewish partner leads to the surrender of one's Jewish identity; in this respect, it is the spouse, not the offspring, that is under threat. This may be implied in the account that Potiphar's wife threatened Joseph with "making him an Aramean".[189] But the *Babylonian Talmud* is more explicit: it claims that whilst the sinners of Israel are redeemed by Abraham at the entrance of Gehenna through the merit of their circumcision, those who had a sexual relationship with a non-Jewish woman are not redeemed, for they have become decircumcised and Abraham can no longer recognise them.[190] In other sources too, sexual relations

---

[184] Just as the offspring of any forbidden relation: *T.Kid.* 4,16. On lineage, see pp. 92–3.

[185] *Lev.R.* 16,1 on *Ezra* 9:2 (my emphasis).

[186] *Ruth R.* 7,7. In these passages 'seed' *may* be taken literally as semen: in *Tanh. Naso* 7 the description of Israel as a 'seed of truth' and a 'seed of holiness' is associated with the holiness of their act of conception. However the term 'seed' is generally used metaphorically of the people as a whole, e.g. in the expression 'seed of Abraham' (*M.Ned.* 3,11; *B.Betza* 32b; *B.BB* 60b; *B.Sanh.* 104b; *Kalla R.* 10; *Eliyahu R.* 2, p. 10); in the following passages, its usage is clearly metaphorical.

[187] *Pirkei HaYeridot* 1 (appended to *Eliyahu Z.*).

[188] *Derekh Eretz R.* 1, as in the recension of *Yalkut Shimoni*, 931. On the importance of purity of lineage (without specific reference to intermarriage), see *Num.R.* 9,7 and 12,4.

[189] *Avot dRN* 16,2. On "Aramean" as meaning non-Jew, see p. 17 n. 110. It is unclear whether becoming a non-Jew would have been the *consequence* of their sexual relationship, or simply a pre-condition which would have encouraged Joseph to yield.

[190] *B.Eruv.* 19a. The translation of *mivashkar* as 'recognized' is based on Rashi.

with non-Jewish women are set in parallel with the neglect of circumcision.[191] Decircumcision, or the neglect of circumcision, symbolizes
no doubt the loss of Jewish identity which intermarriage entails.

But decircumcision is more than simply symbolic in this context;
it may also correspond, in some way, to a concrete, bodily experience.[192]
Circumcision and sexuality are indeed related. These passages seem
to consider that it is from the core of the sexual act with a non-
Jewish woman that loss of identity spreads to the whole person. By
penetrating into the vaginal tract of a non-Jewish woman, the penis
becomes infected, so to speak, with her non-Jewishness, and is in this
sense decircumcised. Sexual intimacy with a non-Jewish woman entails
therefore, according to these sources, a *bodily* experience of ontological
demise.[193]

(Again, decircumcision would not affect a woman; I have found
no clear indication that she may lose her bodily identity through having
intercourse with a non-Jew.[194])

The repulsiveness of intermarriage
Sexual intercourse with an non-Jewish man is considered, for a woman,
to be bodily repulsive. This is related first and foremost to his prepuce,
which as we have seen is particularly repulsive.[195] Already in the Bible
Dinah's brothers tell Shechem:

> We cannot do such a thing, to give our sister to a man who has a
> prepuce, for this is a reproach to us (*Gen.* 34:14).

This may explain, incidentally, why Rebecca is praised in *Genesis Rabba*

Parallel versions of later compilation, such as in *Tanh. Lekh* 20, refer instead to 'apostates'
who are decircumcised and not redeemed.
    [191] Through the equation of Phinehas with Elijah: cf *PdRE* (ed.Higger) 28, end.
    [192] See my remarks in chapter II (pp. 51–2, 63–7).
    [193] Sexual intercourse and loss of personal identity may be understood in terms
of the commonplace association between love and death, Eros and Thanatos, which
is studied in detail by George Bataille, *L'Eroticisme*, Paris: Editions de Minuit, 1957.
He argues in his introduction that love entails the bodily, emotional and spiritual
fusion of one individual with another, hence his destruction, deconstruction and virtual
death (death of the individual gives rise, however, to a new sense of the continuity
of being).
    [194] We are told that Orpah had intercourse with 100 *prepuces* of non-Jews (*Ruth
R.* 2,20—my emphasis). Although this orgy was *subsequent* to Orpah's departure from
the fold of Israel rather than a cause of it, the *Midrash* may be implying that intercourse
with uncircumcised men sealed, in a bodily manner, her rejection and loss of Jewish
identity.
    [195] See pp. 59–60.

as the first woman to have had intercourse with a man circumcised when eight days old.[196] Non-Jewish semen is equally repulsive: the *Babylonian Talmud* describes Sisra's intercourse with Yael as "evil" to her, because he "polluted" her with his seed; this is associated, moreover, with the snake's intercourse with Eve.[197]

To a man, intercourse with a non-Jewish woman is similarly repulsive. In many passages this is related to the rabbinic perception of non-Jewish women as animals,[198] which leads to the remarkable suggestion that intercourse with them may be equivalent to bestiality. In the Talmudic story of R. Sheila, which we have quoted in the first chapter[199] and to which we will presently return, a man who had had intercourse with a non-Jewish woman was pronounced guilty of bestiality with a donkey.[200] According to the later Midrashic rephrasing of another Talmudic passage, a non-Jewish woman with whom a man has intercourse clings to him "like a dog", wrapping him up and leading him down to Gehenna;[201] the notions of "clinging" and "wrapping" imply, incidentally, that the physical intimacy of such intercourse is particularly repulsive.

This repulsiveness is associated specifically with a revulsion towards non-Jewish food. We have already encountered the story of R. Akiva, who would not be seduced by non-Jewish women because he had been put off by their stench of carrion and abominable foods.[202] Similarly, we are told in the *Babylonian Talmud* the story of a *matronita* who tried to seduce R. Tzadok; as he warded her off with the excuse that he was very hungry, she offered him some forbidden food; whereupon he remarked:

---

[196] *Gen.R.* 60,5.

[197] *B.Yev.* 103a-b. It should be noted however that *M.Mikvaot* 8,4 deals with a Jewish woman who excreted the semen of a non-Jew, without expressing indignation at the fact that she must previously have had sexual intercourse with him.

[198] See section I.4.A. *Y.Ber.* 9,1 refers to the beauty of non-Jewish women, but emphasizing that camels, donkeys and horses can also be considered beautiful: see p. 39, n. 274 and p. 146.

[199] Section I.4.A.

[200] *B.Ber.* 58a.

[201] *Tanh. Vayyeshev* 8. The Talmudic passage which the *Tanhuma* paraphrases is *B.Sot.* 3b, which only says that a "transgression"—not the non-Jewish woman—"wraps up" the person and "clings to him like a dog"; the transgression in question, however, is clearly intercourse with non-Jewish women as the *Talmud* quotes as evidence a verse from the episode of Joseph and Potiphar's wife. The *Tanhuma* re-phrases this passage as referring not to the transgression but to the actual woman.

[202] *Avot dRN* 16,2; quoted in p. 58.

this indicates that whoever *does* this (i.e. intercourse with a non-Jewish woman) *eats* this (i.e. forbidden food).[203]

The relationship between non-Jewish sex and non-Jewish food—both equally repulsive—may be explained in terms of the analogy between food and sex which is generally found in early rabbinic writings.[204] In this context, however, it is effectively employed for the purpose of enhancing the bodily repulsiveness of intercourse with the non-Jews.

Interestingly, in a Halakhic context, we also find that the prohibition of non-Jewish food is explicitly related to that of intermarriage: non-Jewish bread and alcoholic drinks are forbidden by rabbinic decree, according to the *Babylonian Talmud*, "on account of intermarriage" (i.e. the danger that their consumption may lead to intermarriage).[205] According to another passage, their bread and oil were forbidden "on account of their wine", but their wine, in turn, was forbidden "on account of their daughters".[206]

Repulsiveness is graphically conveyed, finally, in the Midrashic rendering of Phinehas' deed at Shittim, where the Israelites had sexual intercourse with the daughters of Moab. I will quote the more extensive version of the *Midrash*, as found in *Num.R.*:[207]

> "And Phinehas... took a spear in his hand. And he went after the man of Israel into the chamber, and he pierced them both through, the man of Israel and the woman through her belly..." (*Num.* 25:7–8).
>
> He pierced them both, one on top of the other, through both their genitals [lit: 'their impurity']. lest Israel should say there had been no intercourse [lit: 'impurity']. He avenged the name of the Almighty, who wrought 12 miracles for him:
>
> 1. The couple did not separate from each other, but an angel made them cleave.
>
> 2. The angel shut their mouths so that they should not shout.
>
> 3. He directed the spear into her genitals in such a way that his genitals should be visible inside hers...

---

[203] *B.Kid.* 40a (my emphasis).

[204] See *B.Yoma* 74b–75a, following the simile in *Prov.* 30:20; *B.Pes.* 49b; *B.Ber.* 20a; *Targum Ps-Jonathan ad Gen.* 39:6; *Gen.R.* 86,6; *Tanh. Shemot* 11.

[205] *B.AZ* 31b and 35b. Mediaeval Talmudic commentators interpret likewise the rabbinic prohibition on non-Jewish cooked foods.

[206] *B.AZ* 36b (see above note 164); their daughters, in turn, were forbidden 'on account of something else', which is interpreted by Rashi—probably on the basis of Rav's statement, which I have quoted in p. 159—as referring to *avoda zara*. The association between their bread, oil, wine, and daughters, is confirmed in that they were all forbidden as a *single* decree, according to *B.Shab.* 17b.

[207] *Num.R.* 20,25 (= *Tanh. Balak* 21). Cf *Sifre Num.* 131; *B.Sanh.* 82b.

4. He lengthened the spear-head so that it should pierce them both.

5. He gave strength to [Phinehas'] arm to lift them up.

6. He gave strength to the spear-shaft, that it should bear both their weight.

7. They did not slip down the spear-shaft, but remained at the top of the spear.

8. The angel turned them round in such a way that their turpitude should be visible to all.

9. They did not drip any blood which might have defiled Phinehas.[208]

10. The Almighty kept them alive, so that they should not defile him [as corpses].

11. The angel lifted up the lintel, to enable Phinehas to walk out of the room with both hanging between his shoulders, in the eyes of everyone.

12. ... [the angel protected Phinehas from blood-feud].

The length of this account is most remarkable, especially as it has no exegetical foundation. It is sheer passion, it seems, which drives the *Midrash* to describe, with much gory detail and emphasis on sexual body-parts, Phinehas' public exposure of a most revolting "turpitude".

No doubt, it is because the non-Jews are generally repulsive that sexual intercourse with them is presented in this way.[209] The prohibition of intermarriage is thus experienced by the authors of our sources as an vigorous rejection of non-Jewishness, and hence as a protective enhancement of Israel's distinct identity.

"Zealots may descend on him"

Phinehas' deed is echoed in an extraordinary Mishnaic ruling which deserves our full attention. This is the passage in full:

> If one stole a service-vessel, or cursed with *Kosem, or had sexual intercourse with a non-Jewish [lit: Aramean] woman—zealots may descend on him.*
>
> If a priest served in impurity, his brothers the priests do not bring him to Court, but the young men of the priesthood take him outside the Temple court and split his skull open with logs.
>
> If a non-priest [lit: 'foreigner'] ministered in the Temple, R. Akiva says [he must be put to death] by strangling, but the Sages say, at the hands of Heaven.[210]

---

[208] As a priest, it would have been sinful for Phinehas to become impure.

[209] See section II.1. It may be noted that intermarriage is associated with non-Jewish impurity in *Ezra* 9:11–12.

[210] *M.Sanh.* 9,6. On this *Mishna*, see M. Hengel, *The Zealots* (trans. D. Smith), Edinburgh: T & T Clark, 1989, esp. p. 67 (on *kisva*—a sacrificial service-vessel), and p. 186 (*kosem*, meaning magic). *Aramit* (Aramean) refers in all probability to a non-Jewish woman (see p. 17, n. 110; a similar usage is found in *B.Ber.* 8b). "May

The composition of this *mishna* is somewhat peculiar, as it lists intercourse with a non-Jewish woman together with offenses related, in general terms, to the desecration of the Temple. This suggests that intercourse with a non-Jewish woman is a form of sacrilege: more than simply 'repulsive', it is a defilement of the *sanctity* intrinsic to the Jewish people.[211]

But it is the harshness of this *mishna*, advocating effectively the 'law of lynch', which I would like to emphasize. The ruling on intercourse with a non-Jewish woman is based on the scriptural precedent of Phinehas, as explicitly noted in the *Talmud* and alluded to by the *Mishna* with its usage of the term *kanna'in* ('zealots'), which is applied in the Bible to Phinehas.[212] Like Phinehas, 'zealots' are allowed to by-pass the authority of the courts and to kill instantaneously whoever is caught having intercourse with a non-Jewish woman.[213]

Capital punishment is not unknown to the *Mishna*; it is applicable, indeed, to a number of major transgression such as murder, incest, and *avoda zara*. However, in the same tractate the *Mishna* describes in detail how capital punishment may be exercised only by a legitimate law-court with reliable witnesses, and after a laborious, circumspect procedure to ensure that no error is committed.[214] The *Mishna* is so cautious as to conclude elsewhere:

> a Sanhedrin that kills (*sic*) once in seven years is considered destructive; R. El'azar b. Azaria says, once in seventy years; R. Akiva and R. Tarfon say, had we been in a Sanhedrin, nobody would have ever been put to death.[215]

---

descend on him" translates *pog'in bo*, which means literally 'may hit upon him' or 'may harm him', but is traditionally understood as meaning: 'may kill him', i.e. lynch him; Hengel appears to accept this interpretation.

[211] Cf G. Alon, *op.cit.*, pp. 118–9, suggesting a similar notion in *Jubilees* 30: 14–5. Cf also Hengel, pp. 186–90. On the holiness of Israel, see pp. 31–2.

[212] *Num.* 25:11. The source of the other rulings in the *mishna* is actually unclear.

[213] As the *Talmudim* interpret this *mishna*. This would imply that the prohibition on *extra-marital* intercourse with a non-Jewish woman is not rabbinic but scriptural (indeed, that it is punishable by death), which would contradict the Tannaitic material quoted in *B.AZ* 36b (cf note 164). The *Talmud* resolves the contradiction by stating that only extra-marital intercourse *in public*, such as Zimri's (at Shittim), was forbidden by the Scriptures, and that the rabbis decreed against intercourse in private. In *B.Sanh.* 82a the *Talmud* infers from the Scriptures that if this offense goes unpunished by man, the offender is liable to *karet* ('extermination'—one of the worst divine punishments); see also *Derekh Eretz R.* 1, as in the recension of *Yalkut Shimoni*, 931.

[214] *M.Sanh.* 1,3–6; 4,1–6,1.

[215] *M.Mak.* 1, end. R. Shimon b. Gamliel objects, however, that without this deterrent R. Akiva and R. Tarfon "would have increased murder among Israel" (*ib.*). Pharisees

In this context, a *mishna* advocating the law of lynch appears to be remarkably incongruous.[216] In spite of its scriptural precedent, it is difficult to understand how the redactors of the *Mishna* could reconcile this passage with their otherwise over-cautious ethos in matters of capital punishment. Not surprisingly, perhaps, the *Palestinian Talmud* rules that this *mishna* does not correspond to the 'will of the Sages'.[217] But even if at a later date this *mishna* was in some sense rejected, its preservation in the main body of the *Mishna*, in the *Talmudim* and even in mediaeval legal codes,[218] cannot be dismissed as insignificant. It suggests that unlike any other transgression, intercourse with a non-Jewish woman was so repulsive and so ontologically threatening to the identity of the Jew, as to justify its passionate and spontaneous elimination.[219]

We do not know whether this Mishnaic ruling was ever put into practice; but Babylonian *Amoraim* are said to have applied exceptionally harsh punishments against this transgression. Whether the following accounts actually took place, in historical reality, is irrelevant to us. The main point is that our sources *believed* that such events had happened, and that the behaviour of these *Amoraim* had been legitimate.

We are told that R. Sheila lashed a man who had had intercourse with a non-Jewish woman. When questioned by the Persian authorities, he exonerated himself by claiming that the man was actually guilty

---

showed a similar reluctance towards capital punishment in the first century CE: cf Hengel, pp. 168–9, nn. 124–5, quoting Josephus *Ant.*13,294 (cf *Ant.*14,167; *Bell.Jud.*1,209).

[216] It is incongruous, indeed, in many other respects. Its terminology is unparalleled in the rest of the *Mishna*: for instance, *kisva* is a *hapax* in the *Mishna*, and so is *kosem* (at least in the context of curses); I do not know why a non-Jewish woman should be called *Aramit* (Aramean), and not, as elsewhere, *nokhrit* (foreigner; *Aramit* cannot be a reference to the Biblical episode of Phinehas, as Zimri's concubine was a Midianite). The precise meaning of 'may descend on him' (*pog'in bo*) remains unclear, in spite of the *exemplum* of Phinehas' murder which it appears to refer to.

[217] *Y.Sanh.* 9,6; indeed, it is argued, Moses' Sanhedrin would have excommunicated Phinehas were it not for his Divine, *post facto* dispensation. Hengel argues, but with little substantiation, that this *mishna* is an early text, which accounts for its incongruities; it is dated to the period between 7 and 66CE, when the Sanhedrin had lost its penal powers and entrusted them to private individuals—none other, in fact, than the 'Zealots' mentioned in Josephus (pp. 66–8; 168; 186–90; 394–6); this ancient tradition was then rejected by the rabbis, already in the Tannaitic period (pp. 158–60 & 168–70).

[218] Moses Maimonides, *Code of Law: the Book of Judges* (A.M. Hershman (trans.), New Haven: Yale University Press, 1949), Laws of Sanhedrin 18,6.

[219] Conversely, we are told that rabbis were willing to give up their lives, even to surrender to demons, rather than being enticed by the proposals of *matronitae* (non-Jewish ladies of influence): *B.Kid.* 39b–40a.

of bestiality with an ass. When the man threatened to appeal again
to the Persian authorities, R. Sheila reckoned that his own life was
at risk; in self-defense he killed the man, so that he should not inform
against him.[220] In another incident, Rava personally lashed a man
whom his court had found guilty of intercourse with a non-Jewish
woman, and inadvertently killed him.[221] R. Sheila's final blow and
Rava's 'accidental' excess may have been justified, implicitly, by this
Mishnaic ruling.[222]

E. *Preliminary conclusion*

I have argued that separateness or dissociation constitutes a form of
social control, designed to protect the integrity of Israel as a distinctive
social group. This may explain the numerous restrictions on social
and commercial relations with non-Jews, even though they are primarily
designed to secure the safety of the Jews, their observance of various
scriptural laws, and their avoidance, above all, of *avoda zara*. Intermarriage, in particular, may be perceived as related to *avoda zara*,
but it is equally considered a threat to Jewish identity; as we have
seen, its prohibition implies a passionate commitment to preserving
the integrity of Israel.

In the following section, similar conclusions are to be reached:
maintenance of identity and the avoidance of *avoda zara* appear to
be closely intertwined. The significance of this apparent interdependence will be fully discussed at the end of this chapter.

2. CULTURAL CONTROL: RESISTANCE TO ASSIMILATION

A. *Introduction: assimilation and dissimilation*

"Learning from their practices"
We now turn to 'boundaries' of a completely different order: those
which constitute cultural difference.[223] Cultural difference is highly

---

[220] *B.Ber.* 58a, quoted in more detail in p. 39.

[221] *B.Taan.* 24b.

[222] Strictly speaking, however, and according to the interpretation of the *Talmud*,
the ruling of the *Mishna* did not apply in these cases, since R. Sheila and Rava
were not acting on the spur of the moment but only after juridical deliberation in
their courts.

[223] The term 'boundary' may appear less suitable in a cultural context, where
it refers to *difference* rather than to a dividing line secluding the Jews from the non-

valued in our sources. The *Targum* praises Israel for not following the "customs of the nations".[224] Halakhic *Midrashim* strive to protect this cultural distinctiveness by forbidding Jews to learn from the non-Jews, "resemble them, or follow their practices",[225] even when Israel are in exile.[226] Some rabbinic decrees are explained by the *Babylonian Talmud* as measures preventing Jews from "learning from their practices": the prohibition of usury with non-Jews,[227] and restrictions on living in a non-Jewish courtyard.[228] These passages suggest, as I will argue in this section, that the authors of rabbinic sources attempted to protect their identity against the threat of non-Jewish assimilation.

The debate on 'Hellenisation'
The extent to which the rabbis of Late Antiquity welcomed the influence of non-Jewish, especially Graeco-Roman culture, has been and still is the subject of intense, scholarly debate. Jewish scholars have taken different views on the matter, often reflecting their own religious convictions. Daube contended that rabbinic methods of interpretation and reasoning were directly borrowed from Greek rhetoric.[229] Similarly, in an early work, Lieberman argued that the rabbis had good knowledge of Greek language, literature and culture, and that they were tolerant towards Hellenism and its adoption.[230] Alon strongly opposed this thesis,

---

Jews. It remains nonetheless a useful term in that it suggests that cultural difference is not merely an abstract concept but in most cases a *concrete* reality.

[224] *Nimusei*, from the Greek *nomoi* (customs): *Targum Ps-Jonathan ad Num.* 23:9 (*Targum Yerushalmi ib.* praises Israel for not "mingling" with the customs of the nations).

[225] *Sifre Deut.* 81. "Whoever learns a single thing from the *Magi* is punishable by death": *B.Shab.* 75a.

[226] *Sifra Behukkotai, perek* 8,4. Although Menasseh and Ephraim were brought up in Egypt, they succeeded in not "learning from their practices": *Pes.R.*, end. According to a late *Midrash*, mutual hatred prevents the Jews from learning from the nations' practices: *Midrash Temura HaShalem* (ed. Wertheimer) 5,26.

[227] However a scholar is exempt from this prohibition, as he may be trusted not to learn from their practices: *B.BM* 70b–71a. These 'practices' must be understood as non-Jewish practices in general; the *Talmud* probably means that if usury was allowed with non-Jews, Jews would conduct most of their business with the latter rather than among themselves, and thus would come under the pernicious influence of non-Jewish culture. These 'practices' cannot be interpreted as a specific reference to the (non-Jewish) practice of usury itself, for then the *Talmud* would have explicitly stated: "lest he learns to conduct usury even among his fellow-Jews".

[228] *B.Eruv.* 62a.

[229] D. Daube, "Rabbinic Methods of Interpretation and Hellenistic Rhetoric", in *HUCA* 22, 1949, pp. 239–62.

[230] Saul Lieberman, *Greek in Jewish Palestine*, New York: Jewish Theological Seminary, 1942 (2nd ed. 1965). Cf also *id.*, *Hellenism in Jewish Palestine*, New York: Jewish Theological Seminary, 1950 (2nd ed. 1962), pp. 105–114. Rabbinic literature is

refuting quite convincingly Lieberman's evidence and suggesting that Hellenism had only a marginal impact on the rabbis and their writings.[231] Twenty years later Lieberman retracted his earlier claims, finding no evidence that rabbinic Judaism was influenced by Greek philosophy, religion and law in any significant manner.[232] Still, many scholars have continued to argue that the rabbis willingly embraced Hellenistic culture.[233] Sandmel favours this view but maintains that Hellenisation did not necessarily constitute a threat to Jewish identity:

> ... hellenization could be both extensive and intensive, but still it was a tenacious Judaism ... being hellenized, this without any loss of identity or loss of essential characteristics.[234]

The method which all these scholars have adopted consists in searching for 'Greek' elements in early rabbinic writings, and on this basis assessing the extent to which the rabbis effectively resisted Hellenisation or, on the contrary, embraced it. This is to assume however an objective definition of what is 'Greek', hence what is 'Hellenisation', and conversely, what are the Jewish "essential characteristics". Yet it is plain that these concepts are highly subjective, and depend entirely upon one's own ethnic or religious standpoint. Even if a consensus could be reached among contemporary scholars—which I strongly doubt—their modern definition of 'Greek' and 'Jewish' would not correspond, necessarily, to that of the rabbis of Late Antiquity.

For instance, modern historians tend to regard public baths in Late Antique Palestine as 'Greek' institutions, on the grounds that they were probably introduced by Hellenistic rulers; some conclude, therefore, that public baths "reflect the influence of Hellenism".[235] Late

---

certainly aware of some Graeco-Roman myths; for instance, the story of Romulus and Remus is mentioned in *Est.R.* 3,5.

[231] G. Alon, review article on S. Lieberman (1942), in *Kirjath Sepher* 20, 1943–4, pp. 76–95 (Hebrew).

[232] S. Lieberman, "How much Greek in Jewish Palestine?", in A. Altmann (ed.), *Biblical and Other Studies*, Cambridge Mass.: Harvard Univ. Press, 1963, pp. 123–41. For a similar argument see, more recently, L.H. Feldman, "How much Hellenism in Jewish Palestine?", in *HUCA* 57, 1986, pp. 83–111; *id., Jew and Gentile in the Ancient World*, Princeton, NJ: Princeton Univ. Press, 1993, ch. 1 (pp. 3–44).

[233] E.g. Martin Hengel, *Judaism and Hellenism* (trans. J. Bowden), 2 vols., Philadelphia: Fortress Press, 1974; see S.R. Shimoff, *op.cit.*, listing other recent scholars who have argued this.

[234] S. Sandmel, *Judaism and Christian Beginnings*, New York: Oxford University Press, 1978, p. 258, quoted by Shimoff.

[235] Schürer, *op.cit.*, vol. II, p. 55. On the introduction of public baths in Jewish Palestine, see R. Reich, "The Hot Bath-House (*balneum*), the *Miqweh* and the Jewish

Midrashic sources, however, describe them as ancient Hebrew institutions. King Solomon is said to have built public baths;[236] so did Yoav, thus providing "livelihood" to the people of Israel.[237] It is quite possible, indeed, that by the late Roman period an institution established for centuries in Jewish Palestine would no longer be regarded by its inhabitants as 'Greek'. By this period, bath attendance was a widespread practice which was completely taken for granted.[238] R. Gamliel, at the baths of Aphrodite in Acco, was challenged with the suggestion that the statue could expose him to *avoda zara*; but it was not suggested that his public bathing may have been considered a 'custom of the nations'.[239] It would be absurd to suggest, therefore, that in attending public baths the rabbis 'embraced Hellenisation', since in their terms, public baths were not intrinsically non-Jewish.[240]

The modern debate on early rabbinic 'Hellenisation' has not sufficiently distinguished between Hellenisation in *our* own terms and Hellenisation in *the rabbis'* terms. The degree to which the rabbis desired to embrace Hellenisation or to resist it and ensconce their Jewish cultural identity can only be assessed on the basis of what *they* considered to be 'Jewish', 'Greek', or 'non-Jewish'. It would be safer, therefore, to adopt a minimalist approach and restrict our analysis to practices which rabbinic sources themselves refer to *explicitly* as 'non-Jewish'.

Community in the Second Temple Period", in *JJS* 39(1), Spring 1988, pp. 102–7; *id.*, "The Warm Bath and the Jewish Community in the Early Roman Period (2nd Jewish Commonwealth)", in A. Kasher, V. Rappaport, G. Fuks (eds.), *Greece and Rome in Eretz Israel* (Hebrew), Jerusalem: Yad Ben-Zvi and IES, 1989, pp. 207–11.

[236] *Eccl.R.* 2,8,1.

[237] *Midrash Shemuel* 25. I see no reason to assume that these passages should not be taken in their literal sense.

[238] Bath attendance is mentioned as a matter of course in *Sifra Behar, perek* 7,2; *B.Kid.* 22b. Many rabbis are depicted as attending public baths: R. Meir (*B.Shab.* 40b), R. Yehuda and R. Zeira (*B.Shab.* 41a), R. Yohanan (*B.Eruv.* 27b; = *B.Sanh.* 62b, *B.BM* 41a) and R. Yehoshua b. Levi (*Y.Sheviit* 8,end). Hillel the Elder is reported as saying that it is a *mitzva* ('commandment'?) to attend public baths: *Lev.R.* 34,3; *Avot dRN (B)* 30. On public bathing in Babylonia see M. Beer, "Notes on three edicts", in S. Shaked (ed.), *Irano-Judaica* vol.1, Jerusalem: Yad Ben-Zvi, 1982, Hebrew section p. 31.

[239] *M.AZ* 3,4; see p. 153.

[240] According to *Eccl.R.* 1,7,5, however, the non-Jews are distinguished from the Jews in that the former sit and talk in toilets, in theatres and in baths, whereas the latter, in synagogues and houses of learning; a similar opposition is drawn in *B.Taan.* 20a. Public baths are one of the Empire's main sources of income, together with customs, theatres, and *annonae*: *Avot dRN* 28,4; but they are also a form of munificence, as Esau builds them for the benefit of poor travellers (*Tanh. Mishpatim* 14), and they are open to rich and poor alike (*Midrash Hesed Le'ummim*, ed. Wertheimer).

They belong, by and large, to three Halakhic headings which I will examine in turn: *hokhmat yevanit* (Greek wisdom), *darkei haEmori* (ways of the Amorite), and *hukkot haGoy* (customs of the nations). All three are prohibited.

The heading of *avoda zara* ('foreign worship') may arguably be added to this list. It should be noted, however, that practices such as *avoda zara* are not necessarily prohibited because they are non-Jewish:[241] as I shall argue in conclusion to this chapter, *avoda zara*, or the cult of 'foreign' deities, *may* only *happen* to be non-Jewish, i.e., in so far as the non-Jews perform it. A similar interpretation may also apply to the prohibition of the 'ways of the Amorite', and also, though to a lesser extent, to the 'customs of the nations'. The extent to which these prohibitions were aimed at protecting Jewish identity against assimilation is thus somewhat debatable. This is a problem, in fact, which we have already encountered with reference to social dissociation.

Strategies of resistance
Before assessing the evidence, in early rabbinic sources, of resistance to cultural assimilation, it is worth noting that against this threat a variety of strategies could have been employed. Some of these strategies are conveyed in a remarkable Talmudic passage (*B.Sanh.* 52b) which I shall now outline. In the *Mishna*, the Sages rule that decapitation should be performed with the sword, "as is done by the Kingdom" (i.e. the imperial authorities). R. Yehuda objects that this method is a "hideous disfigurement"; he advocates, instead, the use of the axe. The Sages reply: surely, "no death is more disfiguring than this!".[242] A sequel to this intriguing debate is found in the *Tosefta*. R. Yehuda agrees with the Sages that the axe is more disfiguring, but reveals the *true* reason for his objection to the sword: "what can I do?", he says—the *Torah* forbids it as a 'custom of the nations'.[243] As to the Sages, the *Babylonian Talmud* explains that they allowed the sword because it is explicitly mentioned in the Bible, which proves that "we

---

[241] Lieberman interprets a number of rabbinic prohibitions as *covert* attempts to resist Hellenisation: for instance, the ban by Yohanan the High Priest against stunning calves before their sacrificial slaughtering, "as it is done for *avoda zara*" (*T.Sot.* 13,10; cf Lieberman, 1950, pp. 140–2). There is no reason to assume, however, that this ban was aimed at anything else but *avoda zara*; besides, the reason *explicitly* stated in that text is that wounding the animal before its slaughtering would render it unfit for food or for sacrifice.

[242] *M.Sanh.* 7,3.

[243] *T.Sanh.* 9, end; cf *Y.Sanh.* 7,3.

have not learnt it from them (the non-Jews)". The same argument is repeated to justify the practice of royal funeral pyres.[244]

The strategy of R. Yehuda deserves attention. It does not simply consist in resisting assimilation through the prohibition of a non-Jewish practice, decapitation by the sword. Indeed it is debated, in the *Talmud*, whether the sword should be at all identified as 'non-Jewish'. R. Yehuda's strategy is therefore at once prescriptive and descriptive: the prohibition of the sword as a 'custom of the nations' entails, simultaneously, its unequivocal definition as non-Jewish. This re-definition of the boundaries between Jewish and non-Jewish culture constitutes *in itself* a strategy of resistance to assimilation. It could be said, in fact, that the prohibition of *any* non-Jewish practice brings about, simultaneously, a positive enhancement to the perception of these distinctive boundaries. R. Yehuda employs therefore a strategy of *'dissimilation'* (my term), which, contrary to the process of assimilation, consists not only in stemming the influx of assimilation but also in actively *increasing* Israel's dissimilarity from the non-Jews.

Although the Sages permit the sword, they are also engaged, in a certain sense, in a process of resistance to assimilation; but their strategy is somewhat more subtle. No doubt, they share with R. Yehuda a concern to resist assimilation; but they deny his claim that the sword is intrinsically non-Jewish, and argue, with scriptural support, that in fact it has always been 'Jewish'. Thus by appropriating the sword and making it 'theirs', the Sages prevent it from becoming a threat to their experience of Jewish identity. I have found however that this strategy of *'cultural appropriation'* occurs but rarely, at least in an observable form, in early rabbinic writings.[245]

---

[244] *B.Sanh.* 52b (royal funeral pyres are mentioned in *Jer.* 34). See further p. 188.

[245] By contrast, cultural appropriation has become a powerful anti-assimilatory weapon among contemporary Orthodox Jewry. Solomon Poll argues that instead of opposing the introduction of modern technology (as did the Amish of Pennsylvania), the Hasidim of Williamsburg have been able to welcome it by investing it with a semi-religious character. For instance, refrigerators are equipped with automatic timers (*Shabbath Zeigers*, allowing one to open them on *shabbat* without causing their motor to start), and are re-named *Frig-o-matic Shabbath Zeiger*; consequently, selling them becomes a semi-religious act (S. Poll, *The Hasidic Community of Williamsburg*, New York: Schocken, 1969 (1962), pp. 101 & 222ff.). In some cases, modernity is not re-named as 'Jewish', but simply treated as ethnically 'neutral', hence not a threat to Jewish identity; in this process, assimilation is 'neutralised'. For instance, S.R. Hirsh considered so-called 'factual' elements of science to be acceptable: "it is possible to accept the *factual* knowledge which science provides without being perturbed by unproven hypotheses which seemingly contradict the tenets of the *Torah*" (I. Grunfeld, introduction

B. *Greek wisdom*

> Do not deal with anything else but them (*Torah* and commandments),
> do not mix other things into them, saying, "I have learnt the wisdom
> of Israel, I shall now learn the wisdom of the nations".[246]

Aside from this *Midrash*, it is usually *Greek* wisdom, rather than wisdom
of the nations in general, which our sources anathematise. This tradition
may find its origin in the Maccabean revolt against Hellenistic rule
(mid 2nd century BCE), where the Jews had objected to the introduction
of an idolatrous cult into the Temple as well as to certain elements
of Greek culture.[247] For some reason, however, rabbinic sources do
not associate the Maccabean revolt, nor the festival of *Hanuka* which
commemorates it, with resistance to Hellenistic culture.[248] The decrees
against Greek wisdom are ascribed, instead, to historical events which
postdate the Maccabean period.

The decree and its origins

In the *Babylonian Talmud* there are two accounts as to their origin.
The first is a well-known episode which is said to have taken place
during the Hasmonean dynastic wars in the 60's BCE:

> Aristobulus was inside the city (Jerusalem), and Hyrcanus was (besieging
> him) outside it. Everyday they would send money down the city-walls
> in a container, and haul up in exchange (courtesy of their foes) the
> animals for daily sacrifice. An elder who knew Greek wisdom informed[249]
> on them in Greek wisdom and said (to the besiegers): 'as long as they
> observe the worship, you will not defeat them'. The next day, after
> the monies had been sent down, they were given in exchange a swine.[250]
> When the swine was half way up the wall, he dug his nails into it

---

to the English edition of S.R. Hirsch, *The Pentateuch*, Gateshead: Judaica Press, 1982
(1963), p. xxix, author's emphasis). The assimilatory influx is thus *controlled* (rather
than kept in check, as in the strategy of dissimilation) by willingly but selectively
appropriating some of its elements. Strategies such as re-naming or 'neutralization'
do not appear to have been much used in early rabbinic writings.

[246] *Sifra Aharei, perek* 13,11; *Sifre Deut.* 34.

[247] At least according to II*Macc.* 4:7–15 and 6:9; cf also I*Macc.* 1:14–15 (on gymnasia).
On pre-rabbinic attitudes to Greek culture, see J.A. Goldstein, "Jewish acceptance
and rejection of Hellenism", in E.P. Sanders et al. (eds.), *op.cit.*, pp. 64–87.

[248] According to early rabbinic sources (which we are considering), the festival
of *Hanuka* celebrates only the military victory of the Maccabeans and their subsequent
purification of the Temple; but no mention is made of "Greek wisdom" or Hellenistic
culture: *B.Shab.* 21b ff.; *Pes.R.* 2 *passim*.

[249] *La'az*. In the substantive form (*la'az*), this term also means 'foreign language';
thus we have here a *double entendre*.

[250] Which meant the end of sacrificial worship.

and the land of Israel trembled over a distance of 400 parasangs. This is when they said: "Cursed is he who rears swine; cursed is he who teaches his son Greek wisdom".[251]

The second episode is briefly related in the *Mishna*; this time, the context is that of the Jewish wars against the Romans:

> During the war of Vespasian, they decreed against the crowns of the bridegrooms and against the *erus*;[252] during the war of Titus[253] they decreed against the crowns of brides, and that one should not teach one's son Greek wisdom;[254] during the last war, they decreed that the bride should not go out in a litter across the city, but our rabbis allowed it.[255]

Since both stories are quoted together in the *Babylonian Talmud*,[256] it would appear that they are not duplicative, hence inconsistent with each other, but rather complementary. According to mediaeval commentators, in the first stage the teaching of Greek wisdom was only cursed; whereas in the second stage, it was formally banned.[257]

Greek wisdom in the Hasmonean episode

Two questions need to be investigated: firstly, what our sources mean by 'Greek wisdom'; secondly, whether this decree is designed to resist the threat of Hellenic or non-Jewish cultural assimilation. As to 'Greek wisdom', we are at first sight on familiar terrain: to us, Greek wisdom evokes the founding figures of Western philosophy, Socrates, Plato and Aristotle. However these philosophers are nowhere mentioned in rabbinic writings;[258] it is clear that the rabbis' awareness of Greek

---

[251] *B.Sot.* 49b; *B.BK* 82b-83a; *B.Men.* 64b. References to Greek wisdom are entirely omitted in the version of the *Palestinian Talmud*: *Y.Ber.* 4,1; *Y.Taan.* 4,5. On the historical background, see Schürer vol. I, pp. 235–6.

[252] This *hapax legomenon* is derived from the term *erusin* ('betrothal'); it is traditionally interpreted as a drum used in weddings.

[253] According to some manuscripts, *Quietus*, which would be a reference to the revolt of 115–7CE: S. Lieberman, 1950, p. 101 (and generally on Greek wisdom, pp. 100–105). According to this reading the "last war" (below) could be the Bar-Kokhba revolt of 132–5CE rather than some final campaign of the First Revolt (against Vespasian and Titus, circa 66–74CE).

[254] According to ms. Munich and as quoted by *Tosafot* in *B.Men.* 64b; this is probably the original version of the *Babylonian Talmud*. The printed text reads: "Greek" (*tout court*), which may well represent the original version of the *Palestinian Talmud*, as we shall later see (note 273).

[255] *M.Sot.* 9,14.

[256] In *B.Sot.ib.*

[257] *Tosafot* in *B.BK ib.* and in *B.Men.ib.*

[258] On references to Oenomaus of Gadara in early rabbinic writings, see most recently Menahem Luz, "Oenomaus and Talmudic Anecdote", in *JSJ* 23, 1992,

philosophy must have differed considerably from ours. Moreover, it is unlikely that 'Greek wisdom' refers in the Hasmonean episode to philosophy, for the phrase "he informed on them in Greek wisdom" would then be nonsensical.[259] Nor could it mean that the elder spoke in Greek language, for then the term *lashon* (language) would have been used instead of *hokhma* (wisdom).

Mediaeval commentaries on the Hasmonean episode interpret 'Greek wisdom' as being a special method of dropping hints, verbally or through other means, which the elder successfully employed to betray his people.[260] This interpretation is clearly tailor-made to this specific passage; nonetheless, it appears to correspond to the understanding of the Talmudic redactor, who goes on to describe, in the same passage, how Mordecai could unravel enigmas—suggesting that in his understanding, 'Greek wisdom' consists of a similar technique.[261] The term 'wisdom' is found elsewhere with the same restricted sense: *leshon hokhma* (language of wisdom), referring to the rabbis' technique of dropping verbal hints.[262]

It may be argued that the expression 'Greek wisdom', thus defined, has no more 'ethnic' significance than the English expressions 'Dutch courage' or 'French horn'; if so, its prohibition could not be seen as a form of resistance to assimilation. This however is not the case, because 'Greek wisdom' is implied by our sources as being *intrinsically* non-Jewish. Indeed, in the Hasmonean passage, 'Greek wisdom' leads to the gift of a swine—which embodies, in some sense, the identity of the non-Jews.[263] The teaching of Greek wisdom is cursed together

---

pp. 42–80, with bibliography.

[259] It should be noted however that some manuscripts omit this clause. *Dik.Sof.* believes this clause to be authentic and erroneously omitted in those sources; but one could argue, on the contrary, that it is an interpolated gloss which fails to clarify the issue and rather confuses it.

[260] Rashi in *B.Men. ib.*; Meiri in *B.Sot. ib.*; *Shita Mekubbetzet* in *B.BK ib.*

[261] *B.Men. ib.*: Mordecai could decipher the gestural language of mutes, as well as other verbal statements. The juxtaposition of the Hasmonean episode with the Mordecai passage is ostensibly required for the Talmud's interpretation of *M.Men.* 10:2, and irrelevant, *prima facie*, to the definition of 'Greek wisdom'. Nonetheless, I would suggest that the similarity between the elder's hints and Mordecai's riddles is more than simply coincidental.

[262] *B.Eruv.* 53b.

[263] See pp. 56–7. The land of Israel, which is entirely shaken at the approach of the swine, may be seen as a personification of the people of Israel (or of their "mother's bosom", in the words of *Y.Ket.* 12,3—quoted above in pp. 155–6, note 149). However, the overt purpose of the Talmud is to account for the destruction of the land of Israel and particularly of the outskirts of Jerusalem during the later Second Temple period.

with swine-herding: this suggests that they are similar activities, perhaps because teaching one's son Greek wisdom means rearing him into non-Jewishhood and turning him, so to speak, into a swine. Thus, the ban on 'Greek wisdom' may be perceived as designed to ward off the threat of non-Jewish assimilation.

The Roman episode

The context of the second passage does little to enlighten us on the meaning of 'Greek wisdom'. The decree against it is listed incongruously amidst decrees relating to weddings.[264] Nonetheless, in so far as it is explicitly related to the military struggle against the Romans, it could be interpreted as a form of parallel 'cultural warfare', designed to counter a perceived threat of Graeco-Roman cultural assimilation.

'Greek wisdom' in a wider sense

Another passage appears to forbid the learning of 'Greek wisdom' (according to some versions: of a 'Greek book', or even of 'Greek') in a much wider sense than in the Hasmonean episode. The Talmudim rule that since one is obliged to learn Torah by day and by night, there is no time—"which is neither day or night"—for one to learn Greek wisdom.[265] Lieberman has argued that in this ruling "the study of Greek wisdom is not forbidden per se, but only because it leads to the neglect of Torah study".[266] However, this does not account for the fact that this ruling refers specifically to 'Greek wisdom', rather than to general extraneous studies. This may suggest that the cultural integrity of Israel is again, somehow, at stake.

The Palestinian Talmud reaches the conclusion, in the same passage, that Greek (again, it seems, in its widest sense) may not be taught to one's son 'because of informers'.[267] This apparently means that Greek studies may lead one to befriend non-Jews or even non-Jewish rulers, and hence to inform against one's fellow people.[268] Strangely,

---

[264] T.Sot. 15,8–9, lists in addition a decree on home decorations.

[265] B.Men. 99b, in the name of R. Yishmael. Idem in the name of R. Yehoshua, with reference to teaching one's son: T.AZ 1,20 ("a Greek book"); Y.Peah 1,1 and Y.Sot. 9,15 ("Greek"—see below note 273).

[266] S. Lieberman, 1950, p. 100. He also discusses the distinction between learning oneself and teaching one's son (pp. 100–2), but I do not think it is in any way significant to our topic.

[267] Y.Peah 1,1; Y.Sot. 9,15.

[268] Cf Penei Moshe, ad Y.Sot. ib., and Lieberman, 1950, p. 101. Here, the decree appears to be a measure of social rather than of cultural control.

this passage reminds us of the Hasmonean episode, according to the *Babylonian Talmud*, where knowledge of 'Greek wisdom' was used by an elder to inform. The reverse is argued in the exceptional case of R. Gamliel (the patriarch) who was allowed, together with half his school (500 students!), to learn Greek wisdom for the sake of improving relations with the Roman authorities.[269] This dispensation, never (it seems) to be repeated, must have depended on the fact that the Patriarch would presumably not inform.

Greek song, Greek language, and 'Greek'

Elisha b. Abuya is said in the *Babylonian Talmud* to have apostatized because "Greek song did not cease from his mouth".[270]

However, not everything 'Greek' is forbidden. All early sources concur that holy books may be translated, written and even read out publicly in Greek;[271] Greek language is generally commended in the *Talmud*,[272] where it is explicitly distinguished from 'Greek wisdom'.[273]

In the *Palestinian Talmud* we find in the name of R. Akiva:

---

[269] *T.Sot.* 15,8; *T.Shab.* 6,1; *T.AZ* 2,2; *B.Sot. ib.; B.BK ib.*

[270] Or 'Greek music', or again, 'Greek poetry' (*zemer yevani*): *B.Hag.* 15b.

[271] *M.Meg.* 1,8; *T.Meg.* & *B.Meg. ad loc.; Deut.R.* 1,1. However, minor tractate *Soferim* 1,6–7 forbids the use of Greek; this may reflect a change of attitude in some later period (see Maimonides' *Code, Laws of Tefillin*, 1,19).

[272] *B.Sot.ib.* and *B.BK ib.*: it is preferable to Syrian Aramaic. Cf also *T.Sot.* 7,2; *T.Meg.* 1,8. On non-Jewish languages, see further pp. 193–4.

[273] *B.Sot.ib.* and *B.BK ib.* It has been suggested, however, that according to the *Palestinian Talmud* the ban on Greek wisdom applies also to Greek language: cf Lieberman, 1950, pp. 100–5; E.E. Hallewy, "Concerning the Ban on Greek Wisdom", in *Tarbiz* 41, 1971–2, pp. 269–74 (who also notes that on the other hand, the *Palestinian Talmud* forbids only the teaching of 'Greek', but not its learning). Indeed, the Babylonian distinction between wisdom and language is not found in the *Palestinian Talmud*; moreover, the *Palestinian Talmud* refers generally to 'Greek' tout court rather than to 'Greek wisdom' (for instance, R. Gamliel was given dispensation to teach 'Greek'; because *Torah* must be learnt day and night, the study of 'Greek' is forbidden (see references above); 'Greek wisdom' is not mentioned in the Palestinian version of the Hasmonean episode). The only *explicit* evidence that Greek language would be forbidden, however, comes from secondary mediaeval sources which quote the *Palestinian Talmud* as saying that R. Gamliel was allowed to teach "Greek language", implying that it is generally forbidden (see *Encyclopedia Talmudit* s.v. *hokhmot hitzoniot*, n. 51).

These various recensions alert us however to the difficulty of relying, in this area, on accurate mediaeval transmission. Uncertain transmission can be documented in the case of *T.AZ* 1,20, which reads in our texts "Greek book", but is quoted by R. Hananel (*ad B.AZ* 22a) as reading "Greek wisdom" (cf also R. Shimshon of Sens *ad M.Peah* 1,1). One wonders, in fact, whether the term 'Greek wisdom' was not deliberately left ambiguous, so as to allow each generation to redefine it, and even re-word it, according to its current conditions. It is questionable, therefore, whether Lieberman and Hallewy's evidence can be considered reliable and sufficient.

the books of Homer (?) and all books subsequently written (?) (are permitted to read, for) reading them is like reading a letter . . . they are meant for pleasure, not for toil.[274]

R. Abbahu of Caesarea permitted, in the name of R. Yoḥanan, the teaching of Greek to one's daughter: but this was vehemently disputed by Shimon, claiming that R. Yoḥanan had never made such a statement.[275]

To conclude, although the prohibition of 'Greek wisdom' is clearly related to the protection of Jewish cultural identity, the criteria which make certain 'Greek' elements forbidden (e.g. Greek 'wisdom', Greek song) and others permitted (e.g. Greek language and literature) remain somewhat unclear.

C. *The ways of the Amorite*

The 'Amorite chapters'

The 'ways of the Amorite', which are but mentioned in the *Mishna*,[276] are fully listed in two chapters of the *Tosefta*.[277] This list is well known in rabbinic writings, which refer to it elsewhere as the *Amorite chapters*.[278] As it is rather lengthy, I shall only quote the beginning of it:

These are the ways of the Amorite:
he who cuts his hair in *kome* style and grows a *belurit*, . . .[279]
she who drags her child among graves,

---

[274] *Y.Sanh.* 10,1. The meaning of 'books subsequently written' is unclear. *Homer* is a conjectural emendation which I would accept. It should be noted, however, that in *M.Yadayim* 4,6 it is stressed that the books of Homer, unlike holy books, do not defile the hands because they are "not dear"; the contrast between holy books and Homer is then compared to that between the bones of R. Yoḥanan the High Priest and the bones of donkeys . . .

[275] *Y.Peah* 1,1; *Y.Sot.*9,15. According another version in *Y.Shab.* 6,1, it was R. Abbahu who vehemently defended his position. R. Abbahu maintained close contacts with the imperial authorities in Caesarea (*B.Yoma* 73a; *B.Sanh.* 14a) and interceded to them on behalf of the Jewish community (*B.Hag.* 14a): cf L. Levine, *Caesarea under Roman rule*, Leiden:Brill, 1975; also *op.cit.* (1989) pp. 85–6. The *Talmud* may be implying that R. Abbahu was emulating somehow R. Gamliel and his school, who, in a similar situation, had enjoyed even broader dispensations. On the significance of this passage regarding women, see pp. 242–3. On the unusual stance attributed to R. Abbahu regarding (women) slaves, see p. 98, n. 94.

[276] *M.Shab.* 6 end; *M.Hul.* 4 end.

[277] *T.Shab.* 6–7. Cf also minor tractate *Semahot* 8.

[278] *B.Shab.* 67a–b, where another, shorter version of the list is given. The list is also referred to in *Sifra Aharei perek* 13,9: "the ways of the Amorite which the Sages listed". See also *Y.Shab.* 6,9.

[279] See pp. 68–9. There follows a clause of which the meaning is doubtful.

he who ties a pad unto his thigh and a red thread on his finger,
he who counts and throws pebbles into the sea or river,
he who claps and strikes and dances before a flame . . .
If a piece of bread dropped from him and he said: "give it back to
me, lest I lose my blessing",
"put a light on the ground, so that the dead be pained",
"do not put a light on the ground, so that the dead be not pained",
if sparks fell from it and he said: "we shall have guests today". . .
if he started a job and said: "let so-and-so come whose hands are skilful
and let him begin it",
"let so-and-so come whose feet are swift and let him walk in front of
us". . .
regarding a jar or a dough, "let so-and-so come whose hands are blessed
and let him begin it". . .
he who stops up a window with thorns,
he who ties a piece of iron to the leg of the bed of a woman in childbirth,
he who lays a table in front of her -
however, it is permissible to stop the window with blankets or with
sheaves, and to place a cup of water in front of her, and to tie a hen
to keep her company, for this is not the ways of the Amorite . . . .[280]

To this fairly representative sample of the 'ways of the Amorite', I
should add a number of obscure incantations which are listed in the
next chapter of *Tosefta*, and of which the reading and meaning are
unclear: e.g. *yam'mya u-botziya, dani dani*, etc.

I will argue that whereas the *term* 'ways of the Amorite' suggests
resistance to non-Jewish culture, the *contents* of the *Amorite chapters* suggest
that the prohibition is actually aimed against—for want of better
terms—magic, divination and undesirable 'superstitious' practices.[281]

Who are the 'Amorites'?
These practices are not attributed to the non-Jews in general, but
only to the nation of the Amorites.[282] The identity of these Amorites
is remarkably unclear. Late Antique historical sources do not mention
the existence of such a nation; nor do they corroborate the existence

---

[280] *T.Shab.* 6,1–4. For further quotations see M. Hadas-Lebel, 1979, pp. 454–477; and generally, Y. Avishor "*Darkhe haEmori*" (Hebrew), in H. Rabin *et al.* (eds.), *Studies in the Bible and the Hebrew Language offered to Meir Wallenstein*, Jerusalem: Kiryat Sepher, 1979, pp. 17–47.

[281] As suggested by Hadas-Lebel, *ib.*

[282] There is no indication in rabbinic literature that the term "Amorite" should be taken as referring to the non-Jews as a whole, unlike the Romans, Edomites, Egyptians, Canaanites, and others (see p. 9).

of the ways of the Amorite, as described in detail in our sources, among non-Jewish peoples of the Late Antique Near East.

It appears, therefore, that the 'Amorites' of rabbinic writings can be none other than the Canaanite nation whom Moses and Joshua conquered, and who become extinct, it seems, by the period of the Kings.[283] Thus they are seldom mentioned in rabbinic sources, and only with reference to the distant Biblical past.[284] The *Amorite chapters* conclude themselves with a description of the Amorite people which is clearly cast in the Biblical past tense.[285] This suggests that the 'ways of the Amorite' had been practised by an ancient Canaanite people who are now extinct; it may imply, furthermore, that by the rabbinic period these particular practices had fallen into complete disuse.[286]

It is not unknown for Tannaitic sources to deal with such antiquated and outdated topics;[287] but we may wonder, nevertheless, why our sources take care to preserve the *Amorite chapters* with such length and detail. No doubt, these chapters convey Halakhic principles which retain full relevance in the rabbinic period: namely, that non-Jewish practices *of this kind* must be forbidden. In this sense, the 'ways of the Amorite' may *symbolize* certain aspects of non-Jewish culture which

---

[283] Their last appearance as an existing nation is in I*Sam.* 7:14; by the time of I*Kings* 9:20 (= II*Chron.* 8:7–8), they are already extinct (in *Ezra* 9:1 the reference to them is merely metaphorical).

[284] See *T.BM* 2,12 (= *Y.BM* 2,4; *B.BM* 25b); *B.Ber.* 54a; *B.Ket.* 112a. R. Isaac Nap'ha says that the children whom Elisha cursed and thus caused to die (in II*Kings* 2:23–4) were growing a *belurit* "like the Amorites" (*B.Sot.* 46b). It should be pointed out, however, that already by the time of Elisha the Amorites are no longer mentioned in the Bible as a contemporary nation; R. Isaac's statement may be no more than a reference to the fact that the *belurit* is listed as one of the 'ways of the Amorite'.

[285] *T.Shab.* 7 end.

[286] For a comparison with ancient Canaanite and Babylonian practices, see Y. Avishor, *op.cit.* R. Eliezer of Metz (12th cent.) writes that the Talmud did not define the 'ways of the Amorite' on the basis of *sevara* (reasoning, through observation and empirical means), but only on the basis of earlier traditions (*Sefer Yere'im*, 313 (88)). We may wonder whether this list was monolithically composed at a given time and with reference to one particular non-Jewish group (the 'Amorites'), and henceforth transmitted orally, in a rigid and changeless form, until it was eventually put into writing; or whether it was redacted over a lengthy period of time, eclectically and in a cumulative manner (as were indeed most rabbinic writings), with reference to a variety of peoples and cultures referred to metaphorically as 'Amorites'.

[287] The Mishnaic order of *Kodashim* (holy things) deals almost entirely with Temple ritual, although redacted well after its destruction; but then again, rabbinic writings see the Temple as imminently to be restored (see p. 129, n. 280). Nevertheless, some passages in the *Mishna* deal with specific historical periods which had no prospects of ever being returned: e.g. *M.Meg.* 1,10–11, which deals with the period prior to the building of the First Temple, when sacrifices were conducted on altars and at the Tabernacle of Shiloh.

the authors of our sources, in their own period, were determined to avert. To our sources, however, the Amorite tradition enjoys in addition the authority and venerability of Biblical antiquity.

'Ways of the Amorite' and 'customs of the nations'

At first sight, the term 'ways of the Amorite' suggests that they are, *by definition*, non-Jewish practices, and that it is as such that our sources forbid them. Indeed, the *Babylonian Talmud* implies that the 'ways of the Amorite' come under the scriptural prohibition of 'customs of the nations'.[288] According to R. Meir, in the *Sifra*, this scriptural prohibition consists *exclusively* of the "ways of the Amorite which the Sages listed".[289] As customs of the nations, therefore, the ways of the Amorite would constitute a cultural threat to the integrity of Israel's identity. I would like to argue, however, that in many respects this interpretation does not obtain.

Magic and divination

Although, as Halakhic categories, 'ways of the Amorite' and 'customs of the nations' tend to overlap, they remain distinguished in name and, to a large extent, in content. The 'ways of the Amorite' are distinctively related, as we have noted, to magic, divination, and superstitious practices. Indeed, a short, parenthetical section in the *Amorite chapters* is devoted to the scriptural prohibitions of magic and divination (*me'onen* and *menahesh*); the similarity between the latter and the ways of the Amorite is quite striking.[290] According to the *Babylonian*

---

[288] *B.AZ* 11a (referring to royal funeral pyres); cf also *B.Sanh.* 52b. *Belurit* and *kome* hair-style are forbidden as 'ways of the Amorite' at the beginning of the *Amorite chapters* (see above), but as 'customs of the nations' according to R. Yehuda b. Beteira in *Sifra Aharei perek* 13,9.

[289] *Sifra Aharei perek* 13,9.

[290] *Me'onen* and *menahesh* are forbidden in *Deut.* 18:10. I am referring to *T.Shab.* 7,13–14, which reads:

> What is a *menahesh*? He who says: "my stick fell out of my hand; my piece of bread fell out of my mouth; so-and-so called me from behind; a raven called at me; a dog barked at me; a snake passed me on the right, and a fox on the left; a stag crossed the road in front of me; don't start with me, for it is morning; for it is the new moon; for it is the end of *shabbat*".
> What is *me'onen*? R. Yishmael says: he who passes over his eye. R. Akiva says: those who reckon the seasons and say: "today is good to go out; today is good to buy; today the sun is covered, tomorrow it will rain"; . . . the Sages say: hypnotisers.

Talmud, the incantations listed in the *Amorite chapters* (e.g. *dani dani*) are addressed to divinities of *avoda zara*.[291]

This raises the possibility that the ways of the Amorite may be forbidden not as non-Jewish customs, but primarily because of their affinity with these scriptural prohibitions. Indeed, it could be argued that the term 'Amorite' does not connote non-Jewishness as such, but rather *avoda zara* and other abominable practices which are forbidden by Scriptures in their own right and only incidentally associated with the pagans of the days of old.[292] This may explain why practices which appear non-Jewish but are effective remedies (as opposed to mere superstitions) are not considered to be 'ways of the Amorite'.[293] It would not be inconceivable, indeed, to suggest that the 'ways of the Amorite' were practised in rabbinic times by none other than the Jews themselves; the *Tosefta* would thus be aiming at undesirable elements of popular Jewish folklore.[294] If so, the relevance of the *Amorite chapters* to the protection of Jewish identity would be considerably reduced.

D. *Customs of the nations*

Unlike the ways of the Amorite, of which the origin remains obscure, the 'customs of the nations' (*hukkot haGoy(im)*) are mentioned in the Bible and prohibited in no ambiguous manner:

> ... and their (i.e. of Egypt and Canaan) customs do not follow.[295]
> Do not follow the customs of the nation which I am expelling before you.[296]

---

[291] *B.Shab.* 67b.

[292] Already in the Bible the 'Amorites' are mentioned as paradigmatic of *avoda zara* worshippers: *Gen.* 15:16; *Jud.* 6:10; *Jos.* 24:15; *IKings* 21:26; *IIKings* 21,11 (as previously mentioned, the latter two passages belong to a period where the Amorites, as a people, were apparently already extinct). On references to Amorites in the Apocrypha, see Porton *op.cit.* (1989) p. 33 n. 68. Similarly *Gen.R.* 97,6 calls Esau an 'Amorite', on the grounds that "he did Amorite deeds" (*ma'ase Emori*'—a paraphrase of the verses, rather than a reference to the rabbinic 'ways of the Amorite', *darkei haEmori*). It should be noted, however, that the 'ways of the Amorite', though similar to magic and divination, are explicitly distinguished as a Halakhic category from *avoda zara* in *Y.Shab.* 6,9. The expression *darkei haEmori* is not found in any Biblical passage—its origin remains therefore unclear.

[293] *Y.Shab.* 6,9; *B.Shab.* 67a; cf *B.Hul.* 77a. Similarly, the practice of spouting wine and oil through pipes before brides and grooms, which has no other purpose but to increase their merriment: *T.Shab.* 7,16.

[294] As suggested by M. Hadas-Lebel (1979, p. 455).

[295] *Lev.* 18:3.

[296] *Lev.* 20:23. In keeping with rabbinic interpretation, I am translating *hukkot* as

Yet in spite of its scriptural foundation, the prohibition of 'customs of the nations' is rarely mentioned in rabbinic sources. It is defined in passages of the *Sifra*, and occasionally referred to in the *Tosefta* and the *Talmud*. I will argue that although this prohibition appears to ban non-Jewish customs indiscriminately, its application is rather unpredictable and sporadic; it is also closely related to the prohibition of *avoda zara*.

The prohibition defined

The *Sifra* on the foregoing verses expresses difficulty at defining 'customs of the nations' as a distinct, Halakhic prohibition. It begins with the following question:

> Does this mean that one should not have buildings or plantations like theirs? . . . (the verse) is only speaking of customs to which they, their fathers and their grandfathers have been accustomed.[297]

Thus not everything non-Jewish is forbidden, but only well-established, hereditary traditions. As an example, the *Sifra* goes on to suggest the practices of male and female homosexuality, marriage to a mother and her daughter, polyandry, which the nations allegedly practised in the Biblical period.[298] This would suggest that the 'customs of the nations' correspond to sexual abominations which are anyway forbidden. This prompts the *Sifra*, further down, to raise the following objection:

> Is there anything that Scripture has not already mentioned? Has it not already forbidden the rites of *Molekh*, *hover haver*, etc. etc.? What does the verse "do not follow their customs" teach us?.[299]

In answer to this the *Sifra* appears to return, at first, to its original definition of the prohibition, but this time it is followed with examples which successfully establish the 'customs of the nations' as a distinct Halakhic category:

'customs', although this term normally refers to 'laws'.

[297] *Sifra Aharei parasha* 9,8: *hukkim haHakukim lahem* etc.

[298] *Ib.* The *Midrash* infers this from the fact that the Biblical text goes on to list the forbidden sexual relations (*Lev.*18:6–30), and especially from verse 24 which accuses the nations of indulging in them. Similarly, *Lev.*20:23 (above quoted) comes at the end of a list of forbidden relations.

[299] *Sifra Aharei perek* 13,9.

That you should not follow their laws (*nimusot*, from the Greek *nomoi*),
things which are established (*haHakukim*, from the term *hukkot*, customs)
among them,
such as theatres, circuses and stadia.
R. Meir says: those are the 'ways of the Amorite' which the Sages listed.
R. Yehuda b. Beteira says: that you should not beautify yourself (?),[300]
grow hair-locks (*tzitzit*), or cut your hair in *kome* style.[301]

We have already dealt with the contents of the first two opinions.[302]
I shall now examine the last.

Hair-style

We have seen, in the second chapter, that Israel are described as
distinguished from the nations in their hair-style, particularly as the
nations have a *kome* hair-style and a *belurit* (hair-lock).[303] Both these,
in the passage just quoted, are forbidden as being 'customs of the
nations'. At first sight, therefore, the prohibition of 'customs of the
nations', according to R. Yehuda b. Beteira, would appear to be aimed
at the maintenance of the Jews' distinct external appearance, and hence
at the protection of their cultural identity. Indeed, we are told, in
the *Babylonian Talmud*, that similarly to R. Gamliel's dispensation to
study Greek wisdom, an exceptional dispensation was given to an
Avtolos b. Reuven to cut his hair in *kome* style for the sake of his
relations with the Roman authorities;[304] which suggests that the
prohibition of non-Jewish hair-style is not unrelated to that of Greek
wisdom.

However, *Deut.R.* ascribes the prohibition of *kome* style to the scriptural
prohibition of shaving the corners of one's hair,[305] and the prohibition of *belurit* to *avoda zara*:

---

[300] Text and translation are both doubtful.

[301] *Ib.* It is unclear whether this dispute is Halakhic, and refers to the actual extent
of the prohibition, or whether it is merely exegetical, and only refers to the meaning
of the verse.

R. Yehuda b. Beteira appears to be making a distinction between *kome* and the
"ways of the Amorite which the Sages listed", even though *kome* is listed among
them in the Amorite chapters (see p. 181). It should be noted that restrictions on
hair style (*kome* and *belurit*) do not readily fit into the category of the the 'ways of
the Amorite' which otherwise refer, as we have seen, to magic, divination and
'superstitious' practices.

[302] Theatres etc.: pp. 153–5 (this is the only passage where theatres are explicitly
forbidden as 'customs of the nations'). 'Ways of the Amorite': pp. 181–5.

[303] See pp. 68–9.

[304] *B.Sot.* 49b; *B.BK* 83a; see p. 180.

[305] *Lev.* 19:27.

the *belurit* is only grown for the sake of *avoda zara*, and no punishment is graver than that of *avoda zara*.[306]

This may suggest, as I will argue, that non-Jewish customs are not forbidden merely because they are non-Jewish (and hence a potential threat to Jewish identity), but rather because they are intrinsically connected to *avoda zara*.

Capital punishment

On the other hand, in the *Tosefta* and the *Talmudim* the prohibition of 'customs of the nations' is applied to a context which concerns neither physical appearance nor *avoda zara*: methods of capital punishment. As we have seen in the introduction to this section, R. Yehuda (distinct from R. Yehuda b. Beteira) forbids decapitation by the sword (*sayif*) "as is done by the Kingdom" (i.e. the Imperial authorities) on the grounds that it is a 'custom of the nations'; he advocates instead the use of the axe.[307] The Sages, according to the *Babylonian Talmud*, argue against him that the sword is not intrinsically non-Jewish. From a historical standpoint, it is actually unclear why R. Yehuda should have considered decapitation by the sword to be more 'non-Jewish' (e.g. Roman) than by the axe.[308]

---

[306] *Deut.R.* 2,18. This is already implicit in the *Mishna*: *M.AZ* 1,3; cf *B.AZ* 29a. It is not unreasonable, therefore, to assume that the *Sifra* itself may also have had this view in mind. The dedication of hair-locks to pagan deities is well attested in Greek and Roman sources, but hardly with reference to the Levant (except for Lucian, *De Dea Syria*, 60, referring to the cult of Hierapolis in Northern Syria: M. Hadas-Lebel (1979), pp. 438–9). Hadas-Lebel uses rabbinic sources as evidence that this practice must have spread in a syncretic manner to the rest of the Levant, and argues the same throughout her article (e.g. concerning the *kalendae*). This is to assume, however, that our sources refer exclusively to local, Syro-Palestinian cults, whilst we know that they commonly refer to outdated, even Biblical cults and deities of *avoda zara* (see above p. 20, n. 125; Hadas-Lebel, *ib.* p. 477), and nothing would have prevented them, likewise, from referring to Graeco-Roman cults from outside the Levant. It should be noted, however, that *T.AZ* 3,6 (quoted in p. 148) seems to treat the *belurit* as a contemporary and *local* non-Jewish practice.

[307] *T.Sanh.* 9, end; *Y.Sanh.* 7,3; *B.Sanh.* 52b.

[308] Ulpian (early 3rd century Roman jurist) does record an undated imperial ruling whereby capital executions should only be performed with the sword, and not with axes, javelins, or any other weapons, and whereby the free choice of death may not be granted to the sentenced man. There is no evidence, however, that this ruling was generally obeyed. According to the same source, the Divine Brothers (Marcus Aurelius and Lucius Verus—contemporary, as it happens, with R. Yehuda) allowed the free choice of death to be granted to the sentenced man (*Digest* 48.19.8.1); this suggests, perhaps, that widespread circumvention of the earlier ruling had to be condoned. It should also be noted that the form of capital execution discussed in this passage of the *Digest* would only apply to high-status convicts (*honestiores*: e.g.

Avoda zara ritual

The Talmudic passage on the sword implies that any practice identified as 'non-Jewish' could be forbidden as a 'custom of the nations'. However, another Talmudic passage implies that the prohibition applies exclusively to practices related to the ritual of *avoda zara*: thus only if funeral pyres constituted among non-Jews a form of *avoda zara*, would they be forbidden as a 'custom of the nations'.[309]

A *mishna* prohibits slaughtering animals straight over a pit; it also prohibits one to slaughter next to a pit and let the blood drip into it, so as not to "imitate the *minim*".[310] The context of this *mishna* indicates quite clearly that these methods of slaughtering are prohibited as resembling overt and covert forms of *avoda zara*, involving perhaps

---

Roman senators and prominent provincial civic councillors), who in practice were more often deported or sent into exile than decapitated; ordinary, low-status convicts (*humiliores*) would be crucified, burnt alive, or delivered to the beasts. See, with reference to the Early Empire, P. Garnsey, *Social Status and Legal Privilege in the Roman Empire*, Oxford Univ. Press, 1970, ch. 4. The same applied, in theory, to the Later Empire (see A.H.M. Jones, *op.cit.* p. 519), but R. MacMullen ("Judicial Savagery in the Roman Empire", in *Chiron*, 16, 1986, pp. 147–66) has shown that in practice, the cruelty of the methods of capital execution increased in this period and was extended to the upper classes, even to the highest ranks of the imperial hierarchy. Thus rabbinic sources could hardly have considered decapitation by the sword to have been the imperial 'norm' (R. Shimon b. Gamliel and R. Yishmael are said to have been martyred by the sword (*Avot dRN* 38,3), but R. Ḥanina b. Teradyon by live cremation (*B.AZ* 17b–18a; minor tractate *Semahot* 8)).

Alternatively, it may be suggested that R. Yehuda associates the sword itself, as an object, with the non-Jews and especially with Rome. Indeed, the *Midrash* says that "the nations live by the *ḥerev*" (sword) (*Num.R.* 20,13), quoting *Gen.* 27:40 which refers to Esau (cf *Gen.R.* 75,1). However, in this context the term *ḥerev* is probably a metonymy for 'war' (as in *M.Taan.* 3,5; *Avot* 5,8) or the 'sword in battle' (cf *M.Sot.* 8,1 and 8,5). *Ḥerev*, moreover, may be distinguishable from the term *sayif* (also translated as 'sword') which occurs in our passage on decapitation. Indeed, *sayif* is nowhere associated with battle, but found instead in a list of weapons and domestic utensils (*M.Kelim* 13,1; 14,5; 16,8); it is a weapon which a Jew would ordinarily carry (*M.Shab.* 6,4—though the Sages frown upon this practice), which suggests that it is not intrinsically 'non-Jewish'.

Finally it may be suggested that execution by the sword is considered a 'custom of the nations' because of the ruling, in *T.Sanh.* 9,10, that a non-Jewish court (in an ideal society ruled by Jewish Halakhic norms), is only entitled to give capital punishment "by the sword" (likewise, in an ideal society a non-Jew can only be put to death by the sword: *B.Sanh.* 56a). However, the expression "as is done by the Kingdom" (in our passage) would appear to refer to actual imperial practice, rather than to a mere Halakhic ideal.

[309] *B.AZ* 11a. From this passage the Ran (R. Nissim), late mediaeval commentator, infers that only those non-Jewish customs which comprise a touch of *avoda zara* are forbidden as 'customs of the nations' (*ad* Rif, *AZ* 2b); whereas the *Tosafot* (*B.Sanh.* ib.), on the basis of *B.Sanh.*, hold that any custom of the non-Jews is forbidden under that heading.

[310] *M.Hul.* 2,9; see pp. 109–10.

the worship of tellurian deities. But although, in the second ruling, the *minim* must be taken as heretical Jews rather than as non-Jews,[311] the *Babylonian Talmud* treats this method of slaughtering as a 'custom of the nations', by virtue, it would seem, of the affinity of the latter with *avoda zara*.[312]

"As the nations do"

In other sources other non-Jewish practices are occasionally forbidden, but without explicit reference to the prohibition of 'customs of the nations': thus it is forbidden to reckon days "as the others do" (i.e. the non-Jews);[313] it is forbidden to pray standing in a valley, "as the nations do".[314]

Conclusion

In spite of the *Sifra*'s attempts to define this prohibition, the scope of the 'customs of the nations' remain somewhat unclear. It is undoubtedly related to Jewish identity: accordingly, those who follow the 'customs of the nations' are referred to in Midrashic sources as apostates[315] and even as 'non-Jews'.[316] But although hair-style is naturally associated with personal identity, methods of decapitation are evidently not. It is difficult to see in this prohibition a *consistent* attempt to protect Jewish identity and to resist non-Jewish assimilation.

Again, we find that with the exception of the sword, this prohibition is generally related to that of *avoda zara*[317]—even in the case of typical 'identity-markers' such as hair-style. This dual purpose—protection of Israel's distinctiveness, and avoidance of *avoda zara*—is already implied in the Biblical sources: the prohibition of 'their customs' (*Lev.*

---

[311] *Pace* S. Lieberman, 1950, p. 135 n.69. In support of my interpretation, I would stress the *cryptic* manner of the *min*, who does not slaughter *directly* over the pit but only indirectly, so as not to draw attention to his practice of *avoda zara;*, and the *Talmud's* ruling that a *Jew* who slaughters in this way must be investigated, as he is suspected of having become himself a *min*.

[312] *B.Hul.* 41b. Alternatively, this may be due to a terminological confusion between *minim* and 'non-Jews'. See further pp. 109–12.

[313] But one should only count days (of the week) with reference to the *shabbat*: *Mekh. Bahodesh* 7.

[314] *Eliyahu R.* 9, beginning.

[315] *Tanh. Lekh* 20, which refers to the "apostates who have denied the Almighty and followed the customs of the nations".

[316] I.e. *goyim*: *Sifre Deut.* 175.

[317] They are juxtaposed in the *Targum* to *Hos.* 9:1; also in *Midrash Tehillim* 1,15: "'my son, do not go with them'—these are the nations, for it is said: 'do not follow the customs of the nations'; 'keep away'—from worshipping *avoda zara*".

20:23) is followed with an emphatic assertion of the separateness of Israel from the nations (*ib.* 24–6), and then with the prohibition of *ov* and *yid'oni*, apparently related to *avoda zara* (*ib.* 27).

E. *Clothes, names, and language*

Restrictions on important identity-markers such as clothing, name, and language are discussed in a number of *Midrashim*, but only in an *edifying* manner. I will argue that the absence of formal and binding Halakhic rulings reduces considerably the practical significance of these passages. Again, however, we will note a close connection between non-Jewish customs and *avoda zara*.

Clothing

We have seen that Jews and non-Jews are not clearly distinguished, according to our sources, by their clothing.[318] Concomitantly, there are no formal prohibitions on non-Jewish clothing. Thus, there is no prohibition on wearing black shoes, although they could be used to conceal one's Jewish identity.[319] Eliezer the younger wore black shoes in mourning for Jerusalem; he was blamed for his arrogance, but not for transgressing the prohibition of 'customs of the nations'.[320]

Nonetheless, the following invective is found in the *Sifra*:

> Do not resemble them (the non-Jews) or follow their practices;
> "Lest you seek after their gods" (*Deut.* 12:30)—lest you say: "since they go out wearing an *avtiga*,[321] so will I go out wearing an *avtiga*; since they go out wearing purple, so will I go out wearing purple; since they go out wearing *tulsim*,[322] so will I too".[323]

This passage would appear to condemn non-Jewish clothing; it may be argued, however, that it censures the *desire to imitate* the non-Jews

---

[318] Pp. 69–71.

[319] See *B.Taan.* 22a quoted in p. 70.

[320] *B.BK* 59b.

[321] Text and translation unsure. Some have suggested *toga*, others *epitogium* (L. Finkelstein (ed.), *Siphre ad Deut.*, New York: Jewish Theological Seminary, 1969, p. 147), and others again *atrebatica* (S. Krauss, *Griechische und Lateinische Lehnwörter im Talmud, Midrash und Targum*, vol. 2, Berlin: Calvary & co., 1899, p. 5); but these are artificial attempts to reconcile the text with our external knowledge of Graeco-Roman clothing.

[322] Text and translation unsure.

[323] *Sifre Deut.* 81.

(to say: "since they go out . . . so will I too") rather than non-Jewish clothing *per se*.[324]

Interestingly, the relationship between *avoda zara* and non-Jewish customs is again apparent in this passage, in that the verse "lest you seek after their gods" is curiously interpreted as referring to non-Jewish clothing. Conversely, a verse in *Zephaniah* (1:8) which reads: "And it shall come to pass . . . that I will punish the princes and the kings' children, and all those *who wear foreign clothing*", is rendered by *Targum Jonathan* as: "and all those *who rush to worship idols*"—thus taking 'foreign clothing', in the verse, as a metaphor for *avoda zara*.

Name and language

I have earlier quoted the *Midrash* whereby the Israelites were redeemed from Egypt through the merit of having kept four *mitzvot*, as follows: 1. they did not indulge in forbidden relations; 2. they did not inform against each other; 3. they did not change their names; 4. they did not change their language.[325]

Item 3. In a number of versions, the *Midrash* is expanded as follows:

> They went down (to Egypt) as Reuven and Shimon, and they came up as Reuven and Shimon. They did not change their name from Judah to Leon, from Reuven to Rufus, from Joseph to Lestes, from Benjamin to Alexander!.[326]

---

[324] As pointed out by the Maharik (R. Joseph Colon, c.1420–1480), *responsum* 88.
Another passage is commonly taken to imply that non-Jewish clothing was forbidden: this is the statement in *B.Sanh.* 74a-b that in public, or alternatively in times of anti-Jewish persecution, one should be martyred rather than transgress the "lightest commandment", up to and including "changing the strap of one's shoe". Why the latter should be forbidden is not explained in the Talmud, but mediaeval commentators ascribe it to the prohibition of 'customs of the nations', on the assumption that the Talmud is referring to a 'non-Jewish' strap (see *Tosafot ad loc.*). Even so, both Rashi and later the Maharik (*ib.*) hold that 'customs of the nations' would not be a sufficient reason, alone, to forbid non-Jewish straps; they conclude that the latter must also have been particularly indecent. Rashi and the Maharik appear to concur with the opinion of the Ran (see above note 87) that 'customs of the nations' are only forbidden when in conjunction with some other prohibition (i.e. *avoda zara*, or indecency).

[325] Quoted above in p. 161: *Mekh. Bo* 5; *Pes.dRK* 11,6; *Lev.R.* 32,5; *Song R.* 4,13; *Num.R.* 20,22; *Tanh. Balak* 16; *Midrash Tehillim* 114. Cf also *Eliyahu R.* 17, p. 85: in the desert, they did not change their name and language. Curiously, according to *Pes. dRK* 12,24 the Israelites in Egypt did learn the Egyptian language, thus forgetting Hebrew. Another item, that they did not change their clothing, is a later Mediaeval addition which is first found in the late 11th century *Midrash Lekah Tov* compiled and written by R. Tovia b. Eliezer: "they did not change their language or their clothing, etc." (*ad Ex.* 6:6).

[326] *Lev.R. ib.*

It has been suggested that this *Midrash* is specifically directed against contemporary *Egyptian* Jews who had adopted, by and large, Greek names and language.[327]

Aside from this touching homiletic address—a vignette, one might say, of Late Antique rabbinic preaching—non-Jewish names are not clearly forbidden in our sources. Their widespread use among converts and in Diaspora communities is mentioned in the *Talmudim* without criticism.[328] We know through rabbinic as well as through external evidence that the use of Greek and Latin names among the Jews of Palestine, including the rabbis themselves, was actually no less frequent.[329] Thus again, we may have to say that in this edifying *Midrash* it is an attitude, rather than a practice, that is being condemned.

Item 4. Rabbinic attitudes towards non-Jewish language are similarly ambivalent. Again, non-Jewish language is nowhere formally forbidden.[330] Greek, Aramaic (Syrian), and Latin are praised in the *Babylonian Talmud* for their distinctive qualities.[331] Members of the Sanhedrin must be able to understand the 70 languages of the nations without the help of interpreters[332]—which implies that their study is permitted. A number of Biblical personalities are said to have known the 70 languages.[333] In historical terms, there is no doubt that the

---

[327] Yitzhak Heinemann, *Darkhey Ha-Aggadah*, Jerusalem: Magnes Press, 1954, p. 18.

[328] In *T.Git.* 8,4 (L: 6,4); *Y.Git.* 1,1; *B.Git.* 11b. In *B.Git.* 11a and 14b, however, the Talmud criticises Jews who bear Iranian names: cf Neusner (*op.cit.* 1976) pp. 143–5. Nonetheless, the Talmud recognizes that not all names are clearly Jewish or non-Jewish (*B.Git.* 11a).

[329] See E. Schürer, vol. II, pp. 73–4. Although in Palestine the majority of Jews (men and women) had Hebrew names, Greek and Aramaic names were also quite common: T. Ilan, "Notes on the distribution of Jewish women's names in Palestine in the Second Temple and Mishnaic periods", in *JJS* 40(2), Autumn 1989, pp. 186–200. Greek names were more widespread in the Diaspora, though often as translations of Biblical names and hence distinctively 'Jewish' (it has been argued, however, that the choice of Biblical names was often influenced by similar-sounding non-Jewish names which happened to be fashionable at a given place and period: N.G. Cohen, "Jewish Names as Cultural Indicators in Antiquity", in *JSJ* 7, 1976, pp. 97–128).

[330] With the possible exception of *Y.Shab.* 1,4, which lists among the "18 decrees" a decree against "their language" (not found in the parallel version of *B.Shab.*), which some commentators (see S. Lieberman, *HaYerushalmi Ki-feshuto, ad loc.*; *Korban haEda ad loc.*) interpret as meaning the Jewish use of non-Jewish languages. Other commentators (*Penei Moshe ad loc.*) argue that the passage "against their language, and against their testimony" must be understood as a single decree, the former meaning that one must not rely on the language (i.e., the words) which *they* (the non-Jews) employ as witnesses in court.

[331] *Y.Sot.* 7,2; *Y.Meg.* 1,8. *Sifre Deut.* 343 also lists Arabic. On Greek, see further p. 180.

[332] *B.Sanh.* 17a; *B.Men.* 65a.

[333] Joseph and Pharaoh: *B.Sot.* 36b, *Gen.R.* 89. Mordecai: *B.Meg.* 13b. Adam, Moses:

Jews of Palestine and Babylonia spoke foreign (i.e. non-Hebrew) languages, namely Aramaic and possibly some Greek,[334] and this was never criticized by the rabbis even in the mildest edifying terms.[335]

Interestingly, according to a late *Midrash* the Israelites refrained from speaking the Egyptian language because of its affinity with '*avoda zara* ways'.[336] Thus again, avoidance of *avoda zara* underpins the prohibition of non-Jewish customs.

3. CONCLUSION

A. *The problem of scope*

In this chapter I have argued that the experience of Jewish identity is maintained and even enhanced through various strategies of preservation. These consist essentially of the erection of social and cultural boundaries between the Jews and the non-Jews. I have found, however, that the scope of these social and cultural boundaries is far from comprehensive: many commercial transactions with non-Jews remain permitted, whilst non-Jewish names, languages and clothing are not formally forbidden. In the case of socio-economic transactions, I have argued that a sufficient number of restrictions was imposed so as to condition and impede relations between Jews and non-Jews. In the case of cultural identity, however, the prohibition of non-Jewish customs is so sporadic, unpredictable and ill-defined that one wonders whether the same argument could be successfully applied.

We may wonder, therefore, whether the prohibition of 'customs of the nations' could have been experienced by the authors of our sources as an effective method of resisting the threat of assimilation. Mediaeval commentators have assumed that the scope of this prohibition is actually much wider, and that the items listed in the *Sifra* are no more than *select examples* of the non-Jewish customs which are all to be forbidden.[337] Alternatively, it may be argued that the prohibition of 'customs of the nations', albeit restricted in scope, could function

---

Tanh. Devarim 2. See p. 211.

[334] Cf E. Schürer vol. II, pp. 20–8 (Aramaic); pp. 74–80 (Greek); also vol. III, pp. 142–4 (on the liturgy).

[335] On language as having little or no function regarding Jewish identity, see pp. 79–80.

[336] *Eliyahu R.* 21, p. 123 and 22, p. 125.

[337] *Tosafot* and R. Nissim, quoted in p. 188, n. 309; see also Meiri *ad B.Sanh.* 52b.

as a symbolic or *tokenistic* rejection of non-Jewish culture. This tokenistic prohibition would be effective in that 'focal awareness' would be directed entirely towards it, whereas permitted items of non-Jewish culture, such as clothing and names, would be *ignored* and assigned to the realm of 'subsidiary awareness'.[338] Although non-Jewish clothes and names would be accepted through some tacit process of 'cultural appropriation',[339] the dominant perception would remain that non-Jewish culture—conceived of as the 'customs of the nations'—had been vigorously repelled.

A broader outlook on our sources would suggest, however, that in spite of their evident concern not to "learn from their practices",[340] rabbinic sources do not seek to engage in a systematic rejection, whether general or even tokenistic, of non-Jewish culture. Indeed, they show little interest in what non-Jewish culture consists of.[341] 'Greek wisdom' and 'customs of the nations' are sporadic notions which are not clearly, if at all, defined. Their limited scope is not likely to be due to a *different* understanding of what 'Greekness' or 'non-Jewishness' consists of, but rather to a general *lack of interest* in the non-Jewish world.

B. *Non-Jewishness and avoda zara*

Rabbinic sources do show interest, however, in one particular aspect of non-Jewish culture and in the threat which it may present: *avoda zara*. Avoda zara (a scriptural prohibition in its own right) is invoked in our sources as a Halakhic justification for many, if not the majority, of their rulings on dissociation and dissimilation from the non-Jewish world. Commercial transactions, partnerships, theatre shows, weddings, and even intermarriage, are all prohibited for the alleged reason of avoiding *avoda zara*; the same is implied concerning the imperial service, the 'ways of the Amorite', *belurit*, and other aspects of cultural dissimilation. The limited scope of the prohibition of 'customs of the nations' becomes readily understandable if we consider, as our sources

---

[338] On these terms, see pp. 134–5.

[339] See p. 175.

[340] See pp. 170–1.

[341] The features ascribed to the nations (see chapters I and II) relate in general to their ethical and ontological nature (e.g. wickedness, repulsiveness), and do not relate to their culture and customs.

appear to convey, that its primary purpose is restricted to the avoidance of *avoda zara*.[342]

It is quite possible that in the context of these rulings, *avoda zara* constitutes a Halakhic metaphor for the notion of 'non-Jewishness' and the threat to Jewish identity which it may represent. We have seen, indeed, that all non-Jews are assumed to worship *avoda zara*, as opposed to Israel,[343] which may suggest that *avoda zara* and 'non-Jewishness' are to some extent coterminous.

Admittedly *avoda zara* and non-Jewishness do not coincide in all respects. Not all non-Jewish ritual is considered *avoda zara*;[344] conversely, objects of *avoda zara* can be, at least in Mishnaic theory, the exclusive worship of (sinful) Jews.[345] Moreover, 'foreign worship' ("*avoda zara*") does not mean, in first instance, 'foreign to Israel' (and hence 'non-Jewish'), but rather 'foreign to the Almighty'.[346] This might suggest that dissociation and dissimilation proceed from a purely 'religious' concern, namely the desire to avoid contact with the illegitimate worship of other gods, rather than from a concern to enhance the distinctiveness of Israel from the nations.

Nevertheless I have argued in this chapter that we cannot ignore, in the context of these prohibitions, a rabbinic concern for the integrity of Jewish identity and for Jewish distinctiveness from the nations. This concern is often no more than implicit in these rulings,[347] but it finds *explicit* expression in the prohibition of intermarriage and in categories such as "customs of the nations". The significant point, however, is that even in cases where non-Jewishness is almost explicitly referred to, our sources deal with non-Jewishness purely *in terms of avoda zara*. *Avoda zara* is in this sense a defining *metaphor* of non-Jewishness, or even its embodiment. This is why in the context of intermarriage

---

[342] In this sense these prohibitions cannot be interpreted as partial or 'tokenistic', in so far as they resist the threat of *avoda zara*, according to Halakhic standards, in a *fully* comprehensive manner. Other scriptural prohibitions are also invoked as justifications to some rulings (e.g. *kome* hair-style, because of the prohibition of shaving the corners of one's hair); but for the sake of simplicity I shall be referring in general to *avoda zara*.

[343] See pp. 27–9 and 156–8.

[344] For instance non-Jewish funeral rites (with the exclusion of pyres, which are regarded as *avoda zara*): *M.AZ* 1,3.

[345] *M.AZ* 4,4; *Y.Ber.* 8,6; cf *T.Ber.* 6,2; *B.Ber.* 57b; *Sifre Deut.* 318.

[346] Note that according to *Ruth R., pet.* 3, the nations are called "foreign" *because* they worship *avoda zara*—and not *vice-versa*.

[347] As I have tried to argue in pp. 158–9.

the avoidance of *avoda zara* and of non-Jewishness are virtually undistinguished.[348]

C. *Boundaries and internalization*

I have argued, throughout this chapter, that rabbinic sources erect social and cultural boundaries between themselves and the non-Jews with the purpose of protecting their identity against erosion and annihilation. This might appear to support the theory of Barth, which I have discussed and criticised at the end of the previous chapter, that boundaries are the constitutive foundation of ethnic identity. However, in view of the foregoing conclusions, the nature of these boundaries must be re-assessed.

It appears, indeed, that these boundaries do not separate Israel from the nations as much as from *avoda zara*. Even if we consider that *avoda zara* refers to non-Jewishness and constitutes a metaphor of it, the distinction between Jewish and non-Jewish identity does not correspond to an empirical, objective dividing line between Jewish and non-Jewish society and culture, but rather to a rabbinic conceptual notion—the prohibition of *avoda zara*. This does not mean that tangible, concrete boundaries between Jews and non-Jews no longer exist: we may refer, for instance, to the substantial restrictions on their socio-economic transactions. However, these boundaries arise from subjective, 'internal' Halakhic imperatives, rather than from objective encounters with the non-Jew outside.[349]

This constitutes a challenge to Barth's contention that the persistence of ethnic identity depends on its external boundaries rather than on its 'contents'.[350] My study suggests that ethnic boundaries are often themselves a cultural construct, or in Barth's words, a product of the

---

[348] This ties in with our conclusions in the second chapter that Jewish identity consists essentially of a covenantal relationship with the Almighty; by contrast, non-Jewish identity or 'non-Jewishness' would consist of a betrayal of the Almighty and of the worship of alien gods.

Consequently, the prohibition of *avoda zara* could be interpreted systematically as an implicit means of protecting Jewish identity (as suggested by Levine *op.cit.* (1989), pp. 85–86 and 110). However, *avoda zara* is such a wide topic that it would deserve a separate study in its own right; I have preferred to limit my study to *explicit* attempts, on the part of our sources, to resist non-Jewishness *per se*.

[349] So notes Porton (1988) in his conclusion to ch. 9. This explains why many historians consider the rabbis to have been oblivious of the 'real', objective threat of Hellenistic assimilation, which leads them mistakenly to conclude that the rabbis willingly 'embraced' it (see pp. 171–3).

[350] See section III.5.C.

'contents' of ethnicity. It is at this 'internal' level, not from without, that self-identity is primarily experienced and conceived.[351]

The displacement of ethnicity and ethnic boundaries to the internal Halakhic realm of *avoda zara* may be seen, furthermore, as a protective strategy in its own right. If boundaries between Israel and the nations were 'objective' and shared by either side, they would belong, as it were, to the non-Jews as much as to the Jews. Such an exposure to the non-Jewish world would render these boundaries particularly vulnerable to non-Jewish interference, e.g. to the threat of cultural influence and allurement. Now that, as we have seen, the boundaries of Israel are withdrawn and internalized into the rabbis' *exclusive* Halakhic frame of reference, they become, to the nations, incomprehensible and totally 'out of reach'. The laws of *avoda zara* are so alien to the non-Jewish subjective perspective that they are certain to remain unchallenged. Thus, the *internalization* of boundaries renders them all the more secure, and all the more protective of the identity of Israel.[352]

---

[351] Consequently, Barth's structuralist distinction between 'boundaries' and 'contents' becomes somewhat confused. This conclusion also confirms our conclusion in the previous chapter that identity is a self-referential, inward-looking experience, rather than outward-looking as Barth's model would imply.

[352] Internalization as a protective device is a familiar notion in psychotherapy; cf H. Guntrip, *Schizoid Phenomena, Object-Relations and the Self,* London: Hogarth Press, 1968, especially pp. 22–3; see further section V.1.D. The process of internalization and exclusiveness will be examined in detail in the following and final chapter of this work.

CHAPTER FIVE

BEING ISRAEL
SOLIPSISM, INTROVERSION AND TRANSCENDENCE

In the course of our study we have encountered two recurrent themes. The first is that Jewish identity, in early rabbinic writings, consists essentially of being in *a special relationship with the Almighty*. This transpires in the notion that Israel are intrinsically holy and angelic,[1] and that they are distinguished from the nations through their observance of Divine commandments, especially those expressing a covenantal bond between the Almighty and Israel.[2] Appropriately, we find that a non-Jew can become Jewish by entering the covenant and observing the commandments,[3] whilst apostates and heretics are virtually excluded from the peoplehood of Israel.[4] We have suggested in the last chapter that *avoda zara*, the antithesis of Israel's covenant with the Almighty, constitutes the main threat of 'non-Jewishness' which our sources strive to avert.

The second theme is somewhat more subtle. I have suggested that although the experience of Jewish identity is embodied in a physical *praxis* and articulated in a wider social environment, it is *self-referential* and oblivious, in some respects, of the 'real' world outside. It is true that rabbinic literature speaks at length of the distinction and boundaries between Israel and the nations: indeed, the dialectical opposition between self and other is indispensable to the experience of self-identity.[5] But as we have seen in the first chapter, that the "nations" in rabbinic writings do not represent an observable reality 'out there', but rather a logical opposite to the identity of Israel, defined by our sources in purely self-referential terms. Similarly, in the fourth chapter, we have found that resistance to the non-Jewish threat is not conceived in terms of an objective socio-cultural reality, but rather 'internalized' and cast in terms of the Halakhic prohibition of *avoda zara*. The rabbinic conception of the people of Israel has also led us, in the third chapter,

---

[1] Sections I.3–4.
[2] E.g. circumcision and *Torah* learning: sections II.2–3.
[3] Section III.2.
[4] Section III.3.
[5] See chapter I.

to conclude that in some contexts the peripheral sections of the Jewish people, and even at times the common people, are ignored in the description of 'Israel'; and hence, that the rabbinic experience of Jewish identity is predicated on the ability to turn away from the reality of the periphery and of its boundaries, and to focus *inwardly* on the rabbis' own, internal world.[6]

In this final chapter I would like to conduct, in further detail, a phenomenological study of both themes. I will argue that the experience of 'transcendence' and 'introversion', which they respectively entail, characterize the rabbinic ontological experience of 'being Israel'. I will begin with the theme of introversion, which is related, I would suggest, to an isolationist world-view which verges on solipsism.

1. SOLIPSISM: THE NATIONS EXCLUDED

"All the nations are like nothing . . ."—*Isaiah* 40:17.

An experience of solipsism, where the other is considered by the self to be non-existent, is fostered in our sources with the suggestion that in some respects, the nations are excluded from the experience of Israel and totally insignificant to it. I shall begin this chapter with a detailed account of how the nations are deemed unable to learn the *Torah* and perform the commandments. The nations are thus excluded from adopting the distinctive *praxis* of the Jews and hence from participating in the experience of 'being Israel'.[7]

A. *The Torah and the commandments*

The nations as exempt, unable, invalid
The *Torah* was not given to the non-Jews; they are generally *exempt*, therefore, from all the commandments.[8] They *may* however observe them, and not without reward. Dama b. Netina, a non-Jew who lived

---

[6] Section III.5.

[7] This exclusion may also be seen as a means of enhancing the distinctiveness of Israel and of its *praxis*, and of protecting Israel's identity against assimilation with the non-Jews. Exclusion of the nations could thus have been discussed in the second chapter or in the fourth; I am dealing with it in this chapter in order to stress the *ontological* significance of the world-view which the exclusion of the nations entails, as I will explain in sub-section D below.

[8] As emphasized in *Ex.R.* 15,23. The exemption of the non-Jews is already implicit throughout the *Mishna*, e.g. *M.Peah* 4,6 (their crops are exempt from the laws of gleanings and of the corner of the field).

in Ashkelon, is praised by the *Talmudim* for the exemplary respect which he gave on a number of occasions to his father, in accordance with the fifth of the Ten Commandments.[9] Similarly, according to R. Jeremiah as quoted in the *Sifra*, a non-Jew who "does the *Torah*" (i.e. observes its commandments) is equivalent to a high priest.[10] However, the *Babylonian Talmud* concludes with the opinion that he would only be rewarded as a person who "performs without being commanded", which is inferior to the reward of a person who "is commanded and performs".[11] A later *Midrash* maintains that even if a non-Jew performs all the commandments in the *Torah*, the Almighty does not show him mercy.[12]

Most of our sources would suggest, however, that non-Jews are intrinsically *unable* to perform the commandments. They cannot give charity and perform good deeds without it being sinful to them: this is because their sole intention is to gain prestige.[13] In Messianic times the non-Jews will abandon *avoda zara*[14] and attempt to convert;[15] but as they will not be able to keep the commandments, they will soon reject them and apostatize.[16] According to a *Midrash*, many non-Jews will claim at this time, in their defense, that they refrained from pork just like the Jews; but the Almighty will reply that even if they did take care not to eat forbidden meat in their own homes, they did not refrain from eating it at their friends.[17] Other *Midrashim* suggest

---

[9] *Y.Peah* 1,1; *B.Kid.* 31a; *B.AZ* 23b.

[10] *Sifra Aharei* 13,13. The parallel version in the *Babylonian Talmud*, in the name of R. Meir, refers instead to a non-Jew who "occupies himself with *Torah*" (i.e. learns it): *B.Sanh.* 59a; *B.BK* 38a; *B.AZ* 3a; see below pp. 212-3.

[11] *B.BK* 38a; *B.AZ* 3a.

[12] *Deut.R.* 1,21.

[13] This view is disputed in *B.BB* 10b, but considered normative in *Pes.dRK* 2,5. It may partly explain the *Tosefta*'s reluctance to accept charity from non-Jews. *T.Git.* 5,4 (L: 3,13) allows charity to be collected from and by non-Jews (and even to be distributed to non-Jews), but this is only for the sake of peaceful relations (cf *Y.Git.* 5,9; *Y.AZ* 1,3; *B.Git.* 61a). *T.Sot.* 14, end (*B.Sot.* 47b) states that "now that many Jews have been accepting charity from the non-Jews, it appears that the latter have increased and the former decreased, and Israel have no peace in the world". See also *B.Sanh.* 26b and *Tosafot ad loc.*

[14] *Mekh. Shira* 8.

[15] *B.Ber.* 57b.

[16] *B.AZ* 3b (also *B.AZ* 3a, with reference to the commandment of *sukka* which they will find themselves unable to keep); cf *Y.AZ* 2,1; *Pirkei Hekhalot R.* 37,1 (ed. Wertheimer); *Tanh. Shoftim* 9. These sources suggest in fact that they will not be *allowed* to convert (cf also *B.AZ* 10b; *B.Pes.* 68a; *Mekh. Nezikin* 10); consequently, one *Midrash* adds, they will be enslaved to Israel (*Eccl.R.* 2,8,1).

[17] *Eccl.R.* 1,9,1.

that it is because of their sinful proclivity that the *Torah* was not given to the nations—such a gift would have been to them a source of embarrassment.[18] It was because Esau knew that he could not refrain from murder, because Ammon and Moab knew that they could not refrain from adultery, and because Ishmael knew that he could not refrain from theft, that they all refused the Almighty's offer of the *Torah*.[19]

Furthermore, the *Mishna* and *Tosefta* are replete with rulings which imply that even if non-Jews do succeed in performing commandments, this performance is considered *invalid*. For instance, if a non-Jew separates a sheave-offering from the produce of a Jew, even with permission of the latter, his action is considered null and void.[20] If he slaughters an animal (even in accordance with *halakha*) it is considered as carrion.[21] If he adjudicates even in accordance with Jewish laws, his verdict is ineffective and not binding.[22] Examples to this effect are numerous, and I shall not list them here.[23] This Halakhic principle constitutes a further, decisive step in the exclusion of non-Jews from the Jewish way of life.

Public worship: an exception

For some reason, in early rabbinic sources the non-Jews are not excluded from public worship. We are told in the *Mishna* that non-Jews may offer voluntary sacrifices to the Temple, just like the Jews[24]—although they are barred from compulsory sacrifices, which if performed by

---

[18] *Num.R.* 2,16. The *Midrash* concedes that Israel are also sinful, but Israel alone benefit from Divine forgiveness, which is why the *Torah* could be given to them without excessive embarrassment. On this 'preferential treatment' of Israel, see below p. 251.

[19] *Mekh. Bahodesh* 5; *Sifre Deut.* 343; *Midrash Tannaim*, ed. D.Z. Hoffmann, p. 210; *Targum Yerushalmi ad Deut.* 33:2; *Pes.R.* 21,3; *PdRE* 41; *Num.R.* 14,10; *Tanh. Berakha* 4; *Tanh.B. Berakha* 3. Cf *Mekh. Bahodesh* 1. This *Midrash* is further discussed in p. 211.

[20] *M.Terumot* 1,1; cf *B.BM* 22a and 71b.

[21] *M.Hul.* 1,1.

[22] *Mekh. Nezikin* 1.

[23] See Porton (1988), *passim*, for a comprehensive list of relevant cases in the *Mishna* and *Tosefta*. We find a similar notion in a non-Halakhic context: "Even if a non-Jew speaks the Holy Language (Hebrew), his language is obscene" (*Num.R.* 20,14; *Tanh. Balak* 9).

[24] *M.Shek.* 1,5; *T.Shek.* 1,7 (they may also sell sacrificial animals to the Temple for the purpose of the public cult); *Sifra Emor parasha* 7,2; *B.Naz.* 62a; cf *B.Hul.* 13b. The *Mishna* and *Tosefta* discuss in a number of places the laws of non-Jewish sacrifices: *M.Zev.* 4,5; also *T.Shek.* 3,12 (L: 3,11) (priests and ordinary Jews may eat their sacrificial meat).

them are invalid.[25] They have full ability to 'consecrate', i.e. to dedicate an animal or object to the exclusive use of the Temple (*hekdesh*). This is treated by Talmudic sources with appropriate concern. A non-Jew may *offer* a chandelier or a lamp to a synagogue;[26] but if he *consecrates* a beam to the synagogue, his intention might have been in fact to consecrate it to *God*, which would make it forbidden to use outside the Temple; therefore it must be hidden away so as to prevent sacrilege.[27] The same applies if a non-Jew separated a sheave-offering from his own produce: although it does not have the specific status of a sheave-offering, it might have been 'consecrated' by the non-Jew, and must therefore be hidden away.[28]

The notion that non-Jews are able to participate in the Temple cult may be related, in historical terms, to the apparently active presence of non-Jewish 'God-fearers' in Jewish synagogues of the Late Roman period.[29] We are taught in the *Tosefta* that if a non-Jew makes a *berakha* (blessing) one should answer *amen* to it,[30] which may suggest—although the evidence is admittedly slim—that non-Jewish participation in synagogal liturgy was not unacceptable to the rabbis of this period.

Significantly, perhaps, it is only in later *Midrashim* that the effectiveness of non-Jewish prayers begins to be questioned, with the claim that their prayers do not reach the Almighty,[31] or the request that the Almighty should not answer them, for the non-Jews act out of opportunism and really remain faithful to *avoda zara*.[32] Moreover, some later *Midrashim* rule that non-Jewish sacrifices, even voluntary, are not acceptable to the Temple—thus contradicting the earlier, Mishnaic ruling.[33] This may indicate a change of attitude on the part of rabbinic writers, although it is difficult to speculate on this.[34]

---

[25] As emphasized in *Pes.R.* 14. Moreover, the voluntary sacrifice of a non-Jew is more liable to invalidation than a Jew's: see *B.Zev.* 45a–b. It is also stated, in *B.Zev.* 45b, that "(sacrifices of) non-Jews are not fit for acceptance".

[26] *B.Arakh.* 6b: thus, an Arab named Sha'azrak donated a candle to the synagogue of R. Yehuda.

[27] *T.Meg.* 3,5 (L: 2,16).

[28] *B.Arakh.* 6a.

[29] See J. Reynolds & R. Tannenbaum, *Jews and Godfearers at Aphrodisias*, Proc. of the Cambridge Philological Society, Suppl. 12, 1987; I would stress, however, that there is little evidence to suggest that the Diaspora community of Aphrodisias ran in accordance with rabbinic norms.

[30] *T.Ber.* 5,22 (L: 5,21); *Y.Ber.* 8,8; *B.Ber.* 51a.

[31] *PdRE* 28 (ed. Higger), for "the dead will not praise God" (*Psalms* 115:17).

[32] *Deut.R.* 2,10.

[33] *Pes.R.* (ed.Friedman) 48,1; *Tanh. Tzav* 1; *Tanh. Behukkotai* 6; *PdRE* 10.

[34] For an alternative interpretation, see Israel Knohl, "The acceptance of sacrifices

I would emphasize that public worship is the only practice which our sources are willing to share, to some extent at least, with the non-Jewish world; otherwise, the non-Jews remain excluded from the vast majority of the commandments.[35] This prevents them from experiencing the distinctive *praxis* of the Jews, and hence from experiencing 'what it is like' to be Israel.

B. *The Noahide laws*

According to rabbinic tradition, seven commandments were given to the sons of Noah and to the nations which they begot. They are listed in *Tosefta* as follows:

> laws (i.e., to establish civic jurisdiction), (and the prohibitions of) *avoda zara*, blasphemy, forbidden relations, murder, theft, and a limb from a live animal (i.e. tearing it off and eating it).[36]

These commandments are given precise Halakhic definitions,[37] and non-Jews are punishable for transgressing them.[38] The *Babylonian Talmud* states that they are binding on non-Jews "just as they are on Israel".[39]

At first sight these commandments provide the non-Jews with a *niche* within the *Torah* framework: indeed, the non-Jews are assigned a *praxis* which is not unlike that of Israel, though considerably reduced in the number of its commandments. However, I would argue that the setting of different standards of observance for the non-Jews constitutes in itself a process of exclusion.[40] As a *Midrash* puts it, it

---

from Gentiles", in *Tarbiz* 48, 1978–9, pp. 341–5.

[35] See Porton (1988).

[36] *T.AZ* end; some add at least one of the following prohibitions: blood from a live animal, castration, magic and related practices, cross-breeding and cross-grafting trees. Thus the number 'seven' is apparently not accepted by all. *B.Hul.* 92a refers to "30 commandments which the Noahides received"; but according to *Y.AZ* 2,1 the Noahides are only to receive these 30 commandments in the future (presumably in Messianic times). *Y.Sanh.* 3,5 rejects the suggestion that the non-Jews are commanded to sanctify God's Name (cf *Y.Shevi.* 4,2), but *B.Sanh.* 74b–75a debates the issue.

[37] *T.AZ* end (definition of what constitutes a 'limb from a live animal', etc.); see also *B.Eruv.* 62a and *B.Yev.* 47b.

[38] However a non-Jew can only be put to death by the sword (*B.Sanh.* 56a; *Sifra Emor* 19,4—as opposed to the four methods applicable to Jews: *M.Sanh.* 7,1).

[39] *B.Hag.* 11b. A more extensive account of the Noahide laws is found in *B.Sanh.* 56a–59b; cf also *Tanh. Shoftim* 1. On this whole topic, see D. Novak, *The image of the non-Jew in Judaism*, Toronto Studies in Theology 14, 1983.

[40] The following saying should be noted as treating the Noahide commandments with condescension and scorn: "God gave the nations shapeless (or: 'unfinished'—*golmiot*) commandments, (only) to keep them busy; he did not distinguish, in them, between impure and pure": *Ex.R.* 30,9.

is like a king who offers a cup of wine to each of his guests, but to his son he offers his whole cellars; so God only gave out individual commandments to the non-Jews and to the Patriarchs, but to Israel he gave them all.[41] The Noahide commandments reflect the nations' inability to observe the whole *Torah*: God would have given the whole *Torah* to Adam, but then He reflected,

> if Adam is unable to keep even six commandments, how can I give him 613, of which 248 are positive commandments and 365 are negative?.[42]

The latter passage suggests, furthermore, that the non-Jews are unable to observe *even their own* commandments.[43] Indeed, it is generally assumed that the Noahide laws are widely transgressed.[44] We have seen how the non-Jews are suspected of *avoda zara*, murder, sexual promiscuity, and theft, all of which are forbidden among the Noahide commandments.[45] As the *Mekhilta* and *Sifre* point out, the laws which Esau, Moab and Ammon, and Ishmael were unable to accept, and which led them to reject the *Torah*,[46] coincided with Noahide commandments, i.e. murder, adultery, and theft, respectively; the non-Jews rejected the Noahide laws from the outset, because they were unable to withstand them.[47]

The final exclusory step, in the context of the Noahide laws, comes with the remarkable Tannaitic saying that because the nations did

---

[41] *Song R.* 1,2(a),5; cf *Ex.R.* 30,9; *Pes.dRK* 12,1.

[42] *Gen.R.* 24,5. Adam is commonly presented as having been given the first six 'Noahide' commandments; the seventh—not to tear a limb off a live animal—was subsequently given to the sons of Noah.

[43] Similarly, in a discussion on the obligations of non-Jewish women in *B.Sanh.* 57b, it is implied that they are *obligated* to give charity to the needy (see R. Nissim—the *Ran*—on *B.Sanh.* 56b, quoting *Ezekiel* 16:49). And yet, we have seen above that the *Babylonian Talmud* considers the non-Jews *unable* to perform charity without ulterior, sinful motives.

[44] Converts are punished for not having kept the Noahide commandments when they were still non-Jewish: *B.Yev.* 48b. Nonetheless, *Midrash Tehillim* (4,11) attributes the prosperity of the nations in this world to their observance of the Noahide commandments (whereas Israel reap the benefits of their observance in the world-to-come).

[45] Section I.3.A.

[46] See above p. 202.

[47] All the more so, the *Mekhilta* concludes, did they reject all the commandments of the *Torah*: *Mekh. Bahodesh* 5; cf *Sifre Deut.* 343. According to a rather sarcastic passage in *B.Hul.* 92a–b, the non-Jews fail to observe their 30 commandments with the exception however of three: they do not seal their homosexual relations with marriage contracts, they do not sell human flesh in meat markets, and—believe it or not!—they show respect for the *Torah*.

not observe these laws, God "stood up and *exempted them*".[48] According to the *Babylonian Talmud*, this means that henceforth, the nations are not rewarded for the Noahide commandments even if they do perform them;[49] nonetheless they remain, even to the non-Jews, moral imperatives in their own right.[50] Our sources retain, thereby, the right to castigate the nations for their immoral conduct, but simultaneously exclude them from the privilege of observing Divine commandments, and hence from sharing even a limited experience of the *praxis* of Israel.

C. *The praxis of Jewish identity*

The exclusion of the non-Jews is most articulately expressed in those commandments which are specifically related to Jewish identity— circumcision, *shabbat*, and *Torah* learning.[51] In this context exclusion is taken yet to further extremes: the non-Jews are not only *unable*, but also *forbidden* by our sources to engage in the covenantal practices of Israel.

Circumcision

Although the non-Jews are referred to as "the uncircumcised",[52] rabbinic sources are well aware that circumcision is practised in some non-Jewish cultures. An informer once pointed out to emperor Hadrian that the Arabs (Ishmaelites) are no less circumcised than the Jews;[53] the *Babylonian Talmud* itself speaks of circumcised Arabs (*Aravim*) and Gibeonites;[54] so much so that a slave belonging to non-Jews is assumed by the *Tosefta* to be non-Jewish even if he is circumcised.[55] However, non-Jewish circumcision is considered *invalid* by the *Babylonian Talmud*:

---

[48] *Sifre Deut.* 322; *ib.* 343; *B.BK* 38a; *B.AZ* 2b–3a; *Midrash Alpha Beitot* (ed. Wertheimer) p. 449. This would explain why, according to *Ex.R.* 15,23, the prohibition of *avoda zara* is no longer binding on the nations. According to *Lev.R.* 13,2, God removed these commandments from the non-Jews and passed them on to Israel.

[49] At most they are rewarded as a person who "performs without being commanded", which, as I have mentioned above, is inferior to the reward of a person who "is commanded and performs": *B.BK* 38a; *B.AZ* 3a.

[50] Thus by undertaking to observe the Noahide commandments, a non-Jew acquires the status of *ger toshav* ('resident convert', see section III.2.B): *B.AZ* 64b–65a.

[51] As described in chapter II.2–3.

[52] See p. 60, n. 68.

[53] *Eccl.R.* 2,16,1.

[54] Or: 'Gabnonites': *B.Yev.* 71a; *B.AZ* 27a; *Mekh. Bo ad Ex.*12:45.

[55] *T.AZ* 3,11.

Even if they are circumcised, it is as though they are not circumcised.[56]

Therefore, according to the House of Shammai, circumcised non-Jews require a fresh circumcision (i.e. blood dripping) if they wish to convert.[57] Their circumcision is thus illusory, and bears no resemblance or relationship with the true circumcision of Israel.[58]

The *Babylonian Talmud* goes further and appears to suggest that it may be *forbidden* to circumcise a non-Jew for any other purpose than conversion.[59] The non-Jews are thus radically excluded from attempting to experience, as non-Jews, this central aspect of the identity of Israel.

Shabbat

We are told in a later *Midrash* that the commandment to "observe" the *shabbat* (*Deut.* 5:12) was given to Israel, whereas the commandment to "remember" it (*Ex.* 20:8) was given to the nations;[60] but this obscure passage must be dismissed as rather exceptional. The *Babylonian Talmud*, as well as a *Midrash*, rule authoritatively that it is *forbidden* for a non-Jew to observe the *shabbat*; if he does so, he is punishable by *death*.[61]

The severity of this Talmudic ruling is explained in the *Midrash* as follows. It is comparable to a king and his *matronita* in conversation with each other: if someone passed between them, he would be

---

[56] *B.AZ ib.*; cf *B.Yev.ib.* This notion is Mishnaic in origin and affects the interpretation of oaths: *M.Ned.* 3,11 rules that if one takes an oath not to derive benefit from the "uncircumcised", this term includes circumcised non-Jews.

[57] *T.Shab.* 15,9; *B.Shab.* 135a.

[58] Similarly, a non-Jew cannot circumcise a Jewish child. Although this restriction is primarily due to the suspicion that he might murder him (*T.AZ* 3,12; *B.AZ* 26b), R. Yehuda (i.e., as the *Talmud* concludes, the Patriarch) and Rav are attributed the view that circumcision performed by a non-Jew is *intrinsically* invalid (*B.AZ* 26b–27a; cf *Y.Shab.* 19,2; *Gen.R.* 46,9).

[59] E.g. for medical purposes: *B.AZ* 26b (but see Rashi and *Tosafot ad loc.*, with a different interpretation). According to *T.Ned.* 2,4, the Divine sentence against the non-Jews is sealed not because of their practice of murder, incest or idolatry—all Noahide laws—but because of their abiding prepuce. It seems unlikely, however, that the non-Jews should be punished for a practice which they have never been commanded to observe (unlike the Noahide commandments; the *Talmud* stresses that the commandment of circumcision does not apply to the sons of Ishmael and of Esau: *B.Sanh.* 59b); this passage *may* mean that the non-Jews are punished for failing to *convert*, inasmuch as circumcision may be a metaphor for conversion.

[60] *Pes.R.* 23,1 (R.Yudan). We also hear, from the ghost of Turnus Rufus' father, that in after-life the nations are forced to observe *shabbat* against their will: *Tanh. Ki Tissa* 33.

[61] *B.Sanh.* 58b (Resh Lakish); unless he has undertaken to circumcise and convert: *Deut.R.* 1,21 (R. Yehoshua b. Hanina; also R. Levi, and R. Hiyya b. Aba in the name of R. Yohanan).

immediately sentenced to death. Similarly, the *shabbat* is "between the Almighty and Israel":[62] if a non-Jew passes between them, he is immediately sentenced to death.[63] A non-Jew who observes the *shabbat* is thus intruding on the privacy of Israel and disturbing their intimate 'conversation' with the Almighty, which is to say, their exclusive relationship with Him.

Appropriately, the *Babylonian Talmud* presents the experience of *shabbat* as a mystery to the non-Jews. All other commandments were given to Israel in the open (in front of all the nations), but *shabbat* was given to them in private,[64] as it is written: "(*shabbat* is) between Me and the children of Israel" (*Ex.* 31:17).[65] Consequently, the non-Jews know the Sabbatical prohibitions, but do not know the rewards of their observance; alternatively, they know the rewards of their observance, but not the 'supplementary soul' which accrues to every Jew on that day.[66] According to *Genesis Rabba*, when Emperor Antoninus marvelled at the fragrance of Rabbi's *shabbat* meal, Rabbi told him that one special spice rendered it inimitable. The emperor exclaimed that there was no spice that the imperial foodstores did not possess; to which Rabbi replied: "this spice is *shabbat*—do you have it?".[67] In the *Babylonian Talmud*'s version, it is R. Yehoshua b. Hanania who told Caesar about the *shabbat* spice; when asked whether he could get a sample of it, R. Yehoshua replied that it was only effective for those who keep the *shabbat*.[68] The non-Jews are thus aware of the spiritual value of *shabbat* and (secretly) desire it, but it is impossible for them to gain access to it or even to comprehend it.

Again, not unlike the passage on circumcision (note 59), we are told in *B.Betza* 16a that the nations are punished "on account of the *shabbat*", which would appear to mean, on account of their *not* keeping it. The Maharsha *ad loc.* suggests that the passage refers in fact to non-Jews who *would be* observing it, thus contravening the ruling of Resh Lakish. Both R. Yohanan and Resh Lakish are mentioned in this passage, but this particular statement is not directly attributed to them; it is just possible therefore that this passage represents a different opinion from that of Resh Lakish, similar to that of the *Midrash* (*Pes.R.* 23,1) just quoted.

[62] Cf *Ex.* 31:17.

[63] *Deut.R. ib.* As commonly found in the *Midrash* the comparison is not entirely rigorous, for the non-Jew must introduce himself somehow between *three* terms—the Almighty, the *shabbat*, and Israel.

[64] *Be-tzin'a*, lit. 'in concealment'. More on this in section V.2.

[65] *B.Betza* 16a.

[66] *B.Betza ib.*

[67] *Gen.R.* 11,4.

[68] *B.Shab.* 119a.

Non-Jewish wisdom

The non-Jews are similarly excluded from *Torah* learning. It should be noted, however, that this does not extend to other types of learning. As the *Midrash* states:

"There is wisdom among the nations"—believe it.
"There is *Torah* among the nations"—do not believe it.[69]

Before turning to *Torah* learning, non-Jewish wisdom deserves some consideration.

Genesis Rabba states that the Almighty gave wisdom, understanding and might to every single nation;[70] according to the *Babylonian Talmud*, a non-Jew who says something wise is entitled to the title of 'wise'.[71] In Palestinian sources, it is the *Arabs*, in particular, who master forms of knowledge which the rabbis do not possess.[72] R. Ḥiyya Rabba was taught by an Arab merchant Aramaic words from the *Targum* which he had forgotten.[73] The language of the Arabs is also used, occasionally, for exegetical purposes.[74] The Arabs are reliable diviners:[75] an Arab heard the ox of a Jew lowing, which he correctly interpreted as meaning that the Temple had just been destroyed, and that the Messiah, whose name was Menaḥem, had been born immediately thereafter[76] (although Rabbi Bun exclaims in this passage, not without irritation, that there was no need to rely on this Arab since these events can be inferred in full from scripture,[77] the Arab's interpretation is nevertheless vindicated). The *Babylonian Talmud* refers in a similar context to *tayi'i* (nomads) rather than to 'Arabs'. A *tayi'a* unwittingly gave Rabba bar bar Ḥanna the meaning of an obscure Biblical verse.[78] The *tayi'i* are master topographers and experts on their desert: they can find their way by picking up sand and smelling it;[79] indeed, a *tayi'a* showed the same Rabba bar bar Ḥanna the site where, in the days of Moses,

---

[69] *Lam.R.* 2,13.
[70] *Gen.R.* 89,6.
[71] *B.Meg.* 16a.
[72] Even though they are said, in a later *Midrash*, to have inherited nine out of ten measures of the world's stupidity: *Est.R.* 1,17.
[73] *Gen.R.* 79,7.
[74] E.g. *Lev.R.* 5,1.
[75] Cf *Lam.R.*, *pet.*23 (with the method of *extispicium*).
[76] *Y.Ber.* 2,4; *Lam.R.* 1,51.
[77] *Y.Ber. ib.*
[78] *B.RH* 26b.
[79] *B.BB* 73b.

Koraḥ was swallowed up by the earth and where those who died in the desert were buried.[80]

Both *Talmudim* depict the rabbis as willing to acknowledge the wisdom of the non-Jews. They consult them for medical advice,[81] and occasionally debate with the "wise of the nations" on issues relating to the physical nature of the world—often conceding victory to the latter.[82] Yet even in this domain, the non-Jews are at times excluded: Shemuel refused to reveal to Ablat, a Persian sage, that the heat of the sun is beneficial on the summer solstice.[83]

Torah learning

Torah learning, on the other hand, is absolutely exclusive to Israel. As we have already seen, the *Babylonian Talmud* stresses that "the *Torah* is our inheritance, not theirs";[84] similarly, the *Sifre* emphasizes that the *Torah* was only given to Israel, and not to the nations,[85] because the nations were unworthy of it.[86] Various *Midrashim* present the *Torah* as something which the nations desire but do not possess,[87] and claim

---

[80] The full version is found in *B.BB* 73b–74a; with reference to Koraḥ only, in *B.Sanh.* 110a; *Num.R.* 18,20; *Tanh. Korah* 11. The latter two sources are probably derived from the *Babylonian Talmud*, as *tayi'i* are not mentioned otherwise in Palestinian writings.

[81] R. Yoḥanan and the daughter of Domitianus(?): *Y.Shab.* 14,4; *Y.AZ* 2,2. R. Yoḥanan and a *matronita*: *B.Yoma* 84a; *B.AZ* 28a. Abaye and a *tayi'a*: *B.AZ ib.*

[82] *B.Pes.* 94b (cf *Y.BB* 8,1). On the other hand, in *B.Bekh.* 8b–9a R. Yehoshua b. Ḥanania is depicted as defeating the "elders of the house of Athens" with his superior wisdom. See also *B.Sanh.* 91b (Rabbi and Antoninus).

[83] *B.Shab.* 129a (variant reading: the winter solstice). However this did not prevent Shemuel from having frequent, amicable exchanges with Ablat: *B.Shab.* 156a; *B.AZ* 30a.

[84] *B.Sanh.* 59a. '*Torah*', in the context of this passage, means '*Torah* learning', and not the commandments as a whole (see p. 74, n. 174).

[85] *Sifre Deut.* 345; *Tanh. Shoftim* 1; cf *Mekh. Bahodesh* 9, ad *Ex.* 20:22.

[86] *Sifre Deut.* 311. These passages have been quoted in p. 74. See J. Heinemann, *op.cit.*, pp. 117–9, interpreting these passages as being anti-Christian polemics.

[87] "Three presents were given to Israel which the nations desire: *Torah*, the land of Israel, and the world-to-come": *Mekh. Bahodesh* 10. This may be the meaning of the saying that the nations "respect the *Torah*": *B.Hul.* 92b (already quoted). According to the *Babylonian Talmud*, many Persian emperors admired the wisdom of the Jews (actually, of the rabbis), e.g. Shapur (*B.BM* 119a; but *Tosafot ad loc.* infer that Shapur was knowledgeable himself in *halakha*). On this account, some rabbis are said to have close contacts with Persian emperors: Shemuel and Shapur I: *B.Ber.* 56a; *B.Suk.* 53a; *B.MK* 26a; *B.Sanh.* 98a. Rav and Shapur I: *B.Ned.* 49b; *B.BM,* 70b. Rava and Ifra Hormizd (mother of Shapur II): *B.Nida* 20b; *B.Taan.* 24b; *B.BB* 10b; *B.Zev.* 116b. Rav Yosef and the same: *B.BB* 8a. Rava and Shapur II: *B.Hag.* 8b; *B.Shevu.* 6b;

that a scholar among the nations is a fool, for he does not know *Torah* words.[88]

The exclusion of the nations from *Torah* learning is accounted for in a well-known *Midrash*, which claims that the Almighty originally approached the nations, especially Esau, Ishmael, and (in some versions) Ammon and Moab, and offered them the *Torah*; however, in contrast with Israel, these nations immediately rejected it.[89] One version of this *Midrash* takes this refusal of the *Torah* as *exonerating* the nations from punishment for any subsequent transgression;[90] but according to another version, also found in the *Babylonian Talmud*, this refusal constitutes an *indictment* against the nations:[91] once the nations rejected the *Torah*, the Almighty "released them and threw them into Gehenna".[92]

Similarly, we are told in the *Babylonian Talmud* and various *Midrashim* that the words of God, at Mount Sinai, were translated into the 70 languages of the nations so that each nation may comprehend them,[93] and that again, before dying, Moses expounded the *Torah* in 70 languages.[94] According to the *Mishna* and *Tosefta*, when the *Torah* was written on stone at the crossing of the Jordan and at Mount Eval (*Deut.* 27:1-8), it was translated again into 70 languages,[95] and every nation sent secretaries (*notarii*) to make copies of these translations.[96]

---

cf *B.AZ* 76b. Yazdgard I: *B.Ket.* 61a–b; *B.Zev.* 19a.

[88] *Midrash Tehillim* 92,6. But R. Akiva is reported to have told Turnus Rufus— sarcastically, perhaps?—that he was an "expert in the *Torah* (or: the teachings) of the Hebrews": *Pes.R.* 23,8.

[89] This *Midrash* is based on *Deut.* 33:2, and found in various forms in *Mekh. Bahodesh* 5; *Sifre Deut.* 343; *Midrash Tannaim*, ed. D.Z. Hoffmann, p. 210; *B.AZ* 2b; *Targum Ps-Jonathan* and *Yerushalmi ad Deut.* 33:2; *PdRE* 41; *Ex.R.* 27,9; *Num.R.* 14,10; *Lam.R.* 3,1; *Pes.R.* 21,3; *Tanh. Berakha* 4; *Tanh.B. Berakha* 3. One of its main versions has been mentioned above in p. 202. For a likely (but somewhat speculative) account of the historical development of this *Midrash*, see J. Heinemann, pp. 156–62. Heinemann (*ib.* and pp. 117–9) sees the notion that the *Torah* was offered to the nations as an apologetic response to non-Jewish, Hellenistic charges against Jewish exclusivism. See also *Mekh. Bahodesh* 5, end (*Num.R.* 1,7): "the *Torah* was given to all inhabitants of the world". These passages do not imply, however, that the *Torah* should be made available *nowadays* to the non-Jews: as an apology, it is sufficient for our sources to claim that the *Torah* was *once* offered to the nations, and that they should blame themselves for not having accepted it.

[90] *Ex.R.* 27,9, as pointed out by J. Heinemann, *op.cit.*, p. 161.

[91] *B.AZ* 2b.

[92] *Tanh. Berakha* 4; *Tanh.B. Berakha* 3; *Midrash Alpha Beitot* (ed. Wertheimer), p. 449. See J. Heinemann, pp. 157 and 160.

[93] *B.Shab.* 88b; *Ex.R.* 5,9. Cf *B.Betza* 16a: the *Torah* was given to Israel in full public view of the nations (unlike the *shabbat* which was given to Israel 'in private').

[94] *Tanh. Devarim* 2.

[95] *M.Sot.* 7,5.

[96] *T.Sot.* 8,6; *Y.Sot.* 7,5; *B.Sot.* 35b.

The Babylonian Talmud concludes that the nations were then doomed irreversibly for the 'pit of destruction', for they should have learnt the (written) *Torah* but failed to do so.[97]

The oral *Torah*, on the other hand, appears in a later *Midrash* never to have been offered to the non-Jews. Indeed, Moses asked that the *Mishna* be given in writing, but the Almighty foresaw that the nations—a probable to the Christians—would take the scriptures from the Jews, translate them into Greek and claim themselves to be 'Israel'; therefore the *Mishna*, the *Talmud* and the *Aggada* were given orally, so as to remain untarnished and out of the nations' reach.[98] The *Mishna* remained henceforth a exclusive *secret* of the Almighty, which was only revealed, *ab initio*, to the righteous (i.e. Israel).[99]

This exclusion of the nations from the oral *Torah* is obviously most significant, as it is the oral *Torah* which is considered most central to Jewish identity[100] and which is most central, at the same time, to the activity of *Torah* learning. A passage in the *Babylonian Talmud* suggests that the nations are incapable of contributing towards it. Cleopatra "the Greek queen of Alexandria" is said to have made a discovery concerning the formation of the human foetus, which could serve as proof for a Halakhic ruling in *M.Nida* 3,7. R. Yishmael, however, rejects this proof and exclaims: "I am bringing you a proof from the *Torah*, and you bring me a proof from the fools?".[101]

Elsewhere, the *Babylonian Talmud* stipulates that *Torah* learning is guarded from the nations, just as the *shabbat*, with prohibitions of the severest magnitude. It is *forbidden* to hand over *Torah* words to a non-Jew,[102] even to teach *Torah* to one's slave.[103] R. Meir is reported as

---

[97] *B.Sot. ib.*

[98] *Ex.R.* 47,1; *Num.R.* 14,10; *Tanh. Vayyera* 5; *Tanh. Ki Tissa* 34; *Pes.R.* 5,1; quoted in pp. 74–5.

[99] *Tanh. Vayyera ib.*; *Tanh. Ki Tissa ib.*; *Pes.R. ib.* Although such an emphasis on the Oral *Torah* is not *explicit* in earlier sources, it should be noted that this *Midrash* is based on *Y.Peah* 2,4 and *Y.Hag.* 1,8 (see pp. 74–5).

[100] See pp. 74–5.

[101] *B.Nida* 30b.

[102] *B.Hag.* 13a; cf *Tanh. Mishpatim* 3. This ruling was apparently infringed by the 70 elders who are said to have translated the Pentateuch into Greek for King Ptolemy (*B.Meg.* 9a), but they were probably acting under royal duress. Nonetheless, our sources add that they all made a number of emendations to the text, ostensibly to prevent the non-Jewish king from misunderstanding it; these are listed in *Mekh. Bo* 14 and more extensively *B.Meg.* 9a–b (some are found in our extant version of the Septuagint). A detailed study of these emendations would indicate which aspects of *Torah*, according to these sources, are *least* fit to be transmitted to non-Jewish readers.

[103] *B.Ket.* 28a. On the status of the (non-Jewish) slave, see section III.2.B.

saying that a non-Jew who occupies himself with *Torah* learning is equivalent to a high priest;[104] however, according to one passage in the *Talmud*, this refers specifically to the study of the seven Noahide laws; for otherwise, the *Talmud* concludes, a non-Jew who occupies himself with *Torah* learning is punishable by *death*.[105] His offense is comparable to theft and adultery[106]—indeed, it is an inroad on Israel's possessions as well as on their bride.[107] This marital *simile*, reminiscent of the 'king and *matronita*' *simile* which we saw with reference to *shabbat*, implies that the non-Jew learning *Torah* would be intruding on the most *intimate* constituents of the identity of Israel.

Midrashic sources, on the other hand, consider the *Torah* to be *dangerous* to the non-Jews, more than merely forbidden. Its study by non-Jews is compared again to adultery but associated, in *Exodus Rabba* with the following verses:

---

[104] Also in *B.BK* 38a and *B.AZ* 3a. See above, p. 201.

[105] *B.Sanh.* 59a. This may appear to contradict the frequent references in all our sources to dialogues between rabbis and eminent non-Jewish personalities (e.g. philosophers, *matronita*'s, Roman emperors and their relatives, Roman governors) on Halakhic and 'theological' issues. On dialogues with philosophers, see for instance Luz, *op.cit.* Tannaitic dialogues with non-Jewish dignitaries are listed and studied in detail by M.D. Herr, "The historical significance of the Dialogues between Jewish Sages and Roman Dignitaries", in *Scripta Hierosolymitana* 22, Jerusalem: Magnes Press, 1971, pp. 123–50 (such dialogues are rare, however, in Babylonia: see Neusner, 1976, pp. 140–1). Herr argues in favour of their historicity, on the grounds that the topics discussed in each dialogue appear to be suited to the historical background in which they are set. I would not rule out, however, that a sizable proportion of this material is in fact a literary *topos*, which does not record actual events or even claim to do so, but rather enables our sources to introduce provocative questions and thereupon to answer them (see Z.H. Chajes, *The Student's Guide through the Talmud*, J. Shachter transl., London: East and West Library, 1952, ch. 29). Moreover, even if these dialogues did actually happen, they do not imply that the rabbis *willingly* engaged in *Torah* learning with non-Jews: in these passages, it is always the non-Jewish dignitary who initiates the discussion with an aggressive and taunting question; being often in a position of power, he virtually compels the rabbi to respond. Finally, in many cases the rabbis remain successfully reticent: thus according to both Talmudim, the answer which R. Gamliel gave to Proclus outside the baths of Acco (*M.AZ* 3,4, quoted in p. 153) was deliberately fallacious so as to divert him (*Y.AZ* 3,4; *B.AZ* 44a). King Shapur asked R. Hama from what passage in the *Torah* the law of burial was derived; "he remained silent and said not a word". R. Aha b. Yaakov called him a fool for not having answered, but R. Hama replied that the King would not have understood his exegetical deduction . . . (*B.Sanh.* 46b).

[106] *B.Sanh. ib.*

[107] The *Torah* is Israel's bride: *B.Sanh. ib.*; cf also *B.RH* 4a; *B.Pes.* 49b; above, p. 74.

Can a man take fire in his bosom and his clothes not be burned? If
a man walks on hot coals, will his feet not burn?—so it is with he
who commits adultery with his fellow's wife (*Proverbs* 6:27–9).[108]

According to *Leviticus Rabba*, the *Torah* is honey to Israel, but a sting
to the nations; a potion of life to Israel, but a lethal poison to the
non-Jews.[109] At Mount Sinai, the words of God gave life to Israel
but instantaneously killed the non-Jews who heard them.[110]

Finally our sources claim, as with circumcision, that to the non-
Jews *Torah* learning is *of no avail*. When Aquilas informed Emperor
Hadrian of his intention to convert, the latter, horrified, suggested
instead that he learn *Torah* without circumcising; but Aquilas replied
that "even the wisest man in your empire cannot learn *Torah* if he
is not circumcised".[111] In another incident, a Roman emperor sent
two officers to Palestine to study the *Torah* of the Jews and find out
what were its virtues. They studied it in depth,[112] and concluded on
their departure that it was true in all respects, with the exception
of one or a few Halakhic rulings where non-Jews are given, for no
apparent reason, a treatment inferior to the Jews; but out of affection
for the rabbis, they promised not to mention these critical remarks
to the emperor.[113] However the story does not end there. According
to one source, as soon as they reached the 'ladder' (promontory) of
Tyre, all their *Torah* was forgotten[114]—as non-Jews, their knowledge
of *Torah* could not possibly have been retained. According to another
source, the officers were instructed by the emperor to convert before
commencing their studies[115]—the emperor may have realised that *Torah*
learning, to an uncircumcised non-Jew, would have been impossible.[116]

---

[108] *Ex.R.* 33,7.

[109] *Lev.R.* 1,11; cf *Deut.R.* 1,6.

[110] *Lev.R. ib.*; *Ex.R.* 5,9.

[111] *Ex.R.* 30,12. In the more expanded version of *Tanh. Mishpatim* 5 (= *Tanh.B.
ib.*3), this dialogue took place after Aquilas' conversion.

[112] As *Tosafot* in *B.BK ad loc.* points out, the rabbis (like the 70 elders) were probably
given no option but to comply.

[113] *Sifre Deut.* 344; *Y.BK* 4,3; *B.BK* 38a.

[114] *Y.BK ib.*

[115] *Sifre ib.* Some manuscripts read, however, that they were only instructed to
"make themselves Jews", which probably means to *pretend* to be Jewish, rather than
to convert.

[116] This might explain why a prospective convert is taught relatively little *Torah*
before his conversion: "One informs him (*modi'in oto*) of a *few* light commandments
and of a *few* severe ones . . . of the punishment . . . and reward of the commandments . . .
one does not elaborate or go into fine details" (*B.Yev.* 47a–b). The sole purpose of this summary
instruction, according to the *Talmud*, is to give him the opportunity to change his

D. *Solipsism: an interpretation*

Exclusion: distinction and dissimilation

Throughout this section we have seen the non-Jews excluded from the practice of the commandments, and hence from the ability to share the distinct experience of being Israel. This exclusion unfolds in a series of successive stages: from being merely *exempt* from the commandments, even from their own Noahide laws, the non-Jews are then presented as *unable* to perform them; their performance is moreover *invalid*, and in certain cases—where Jewish identity is most at stake—it is dangerous to them or sternly *forbidden*.

This process of exclusion can be interpreted in a variety of ways. The *inability* of the non-Jews to perform the commandments confirms, for a start, that the latter are distinctive features of the Jewish people. Moreover—as an additional precaution, one might say—the non-Jews must be *prevented* from engaging in them, lest this leads to the erosion of the distinctiveness of Israel. The prohibitions for a non-Jew to circumcise, observe *shabbat* or learn *Torah* may thus be seen as protective measures, even as a process of dissimilation *in reverse*: in the same way as the Jews are forbidden to adopt the 'customs of the nations',[117] so the nations must be forbidden to adopt the practices of the Jews.

Exclusion and solipsism

Without denying the validity of such an analysis, I would like to extend the scope of my study to the *ontological* experience which the exclusion of the nations entails. Particularly relevant in this context is the notion that the non-Jewish performance of many commandments, not least circumcision and *Torah* learning, is Halakhically and intrinsically *invalid*. In so far as the activity of the non-Jews, with reference to Jewish identity and to its *praxis*, is completely inconsequential and of no avail, the authors of our sources live and experience their Jewishness in an isolated world where the non-Jewish other does not count, where he does not belong. The *praxis* of Jewish identity—circumcision, *shabbat*, and *Torah* learning—is thus to our sources a fundamentally *solitary* experience.

---

mind (*ib.*); but so long as he is non-Jewish, he is not expected to be able to learn *Torah* in a systematic manner. Similarly, before his conversion he is told that Israel is a lowly and abject nation; only after his immersion can he be told that "the world was only created for Israel ... they are the sons of the Almighty ... they are dear to the Almighty" (*Gerim* 1,1; 1,5). See Shaye Cohen, 1990.

[117] See chapter IV.2.D.

This solitary experience may well be related, in broader terms, to a solipsistic world-view where the non-Jews are consistently ignored—an *Amora* could claim that never in his life had he looked at a non-Jew[118]—and their existence is virtually denied. Most significant is the verse: "all the nations are like nothing before Him . . ." (*Isaiah* 40:17), which is frequently quoted as evidence that the non-Jews *are nothing*—not only in God's eyes (as the verse indeed implies),[119] but also *absolutely*.[120]

Obviously, such a notion can only be considered true in *relative* or *restricted* terms, since rabbinic awareness that the non-Jews *do* exist is evident from the source material we have surveyed throughout this study.[121] But as I have explained in another chapter,[122] awareness can be either 'focal' or 'subsidiary', depending entirely on *context*. Thus our sources can entertain the nothingness of the non-Jews as a '*sensible* reality', provided this notion is confined to a specific context or frame of reference where solipsism acquires pragmatical veracity. Interestingly, the notion that the non-Jews are "dead" occurs in the context of a ruling that their prayers are *ineffective*;[123] that "the non-Jews are nothing" occurs in the context of a ruling that the light of a non-Jew is *unfit* for the ritual of *havdala*,[124] and elsewhere, implicitly, that the non-Jews are not subjected to the commandments.[125] This suggests that rabbinic solipsism acquires experiential veracity in the specific context of the *exclusion* of the nations from the *praxis* and ontological identity of Israel.

---

[118] *B.Meg.* 28a.

[119] *Num.R.* 4,2 (= *Tanh. Bamidbar* 20).

[120] *Y.Ber.* 9,1; *Lev.R.* 27,7 (= *Tanh. Emor* 11; *Pes.dRK* 9,6). More ambiguously: *T.Ber.* 7,18 (L: 6,18); *B.Sanh.* 39a–b; *Tanh. Vayyeshev* 3 (also, of Antoninus' legions); cf *Song R.* 7,3,3.

[121] Besides, empirical experience would suggest that *absolute* solipsism is in reality impossible. See Merleau-Ponty, *op.cit.* part II, ch. 4.

[122] See, at length, section III.5.

[123] See p. 203 and note 31.

[124] *Tanh. Vayyeshev* 3, quoted in p. 158.

[125] This may be inferred from a parallelism in *T.Ber.* and *Y.Ber.* (*ib.*), where one is told to bless the Almighty for not having made one a non-Jew, an ignoramus, or a woman: a non-Jew—because he is *nothing*; an ignoramus—because he has no fear of sin; a woman—because she has *no commandments* (on the parallelism between non-Jews and women, see further pp. 238 and 241).

A Comparison with schizophrenia

Exclusory solipsism can be in itself a strategy for the protection of self-identity. I would like to draw, for the sake of comparison, on R.D. Laing's phenomenological analysis of schizophrenia.[126] Schizophrenia, according to Laing, is a desperate and pathological attempt to prevent loss of identity among people suffering from acute 'ontological insecurity'. The schizophrenic person is unable to perceive himself as an autonomous, individuated self, and fears at all times that the outside world will 'engulf' him and take over his personal identity. Thus the other is intrinsically and existentially threatening to him:

> A firm sense of one's own autonomous identity is required in order that one may be related as one human being to another. Otherwise, any and every relationship threatens the individual with loss of identity. One form this takes can be called engulfment. In this the individual dreads relatedness as such, with anyone or anything or, indeed, even with himself, because his uncertainty about the stability of his autonomy lays him open to the dread lest in any relationship he will lose his autonomy and identity (p. 44).[127]

In this predicament the schizophrenic has no option but to 'bend backwards', as he continues:

> The main manoeuvre used to preserve identity under pressure from the dread of engulfment is isolation. Thus, instead of the polarities of separateness and relatedness based on individual autonomy, there is the antithesis between complete loss of being by absorbtion into the other person (engulfment), and complete aloneness (isolation) (*ib.*).[128]

Although this ultimately leads to the development, as a *façade*, of an external 'false self' and to severe pathological disorders, Laing stresses that the potential schizophrenic can live with this isolationist strategy for a long period without showing any signs, overt or covert, of incipient

---

[126] R.D. Laing, *The Divided Self: an existential study in sanity and madness*, London: Penguin Books, 1965.

[127] Laing draws much of his inspiration from the existentialist work of J.P. Sartre whom he repeatedly quotes (e.g. p. 47). In part 3 of *Being and Nothingness: an essay on phenomenological ontology*, trans. H. Barnes, London: Methuen, 1957, Sartre argues that the other, even just by *looking* at the self, turns the latter into an object and strips him of his autonomy and freedom: "I am no longer master of the situation" (p. 265). But I think that Laing goes further than Sartre, as he perceives that *the very presence* of the other—a stranger in my house, another person in the elevator— can be experienced by the self as ontologically intruding, impinging and *engulfing*, even without him looking at me or entering a subject-object, master-slave relationship.

[128] See also *ib.*, p. 53.

insanity. Others have also argued that the schizoid type of personality, introvert, withdrawn, absent-minded, 'difficult to get to know', is actually quite common in modern society;[129] schizoid traits are even considered as normal and perhaps as normative in contemporary Western culture.[130]

I will *not* suggest, in any sense, that the rabbis of Late Antiquity displayed schizophrenic tendencies: many aspects of the schizophrenic syndrome, even as described by Laing, clearly did not apply to them. It would be absurd to consider that they suffered from the mental, pathological disorders which characterize the schizophrenic condition.[131] All I will suggest is that their isolationist perception of Jewish identity may have been related to an experience of 'ontological insecurity', which is also found, albeit to a much greater degree, in the context of schizophrenia. As I have just mentioned, indeed, schizoid traits are not specific or exclusive to schizophrenics. Reference to R.D. Laing's study is valuable to us precisely because we may be able to sympathize with the existential experience which, in the course of his work, he so lucidly describes.

The non-Jews and the threat of 'engulfment'

Our sources suggest that their authors saw the non-Jewish other as potentially impinging on their own identity. Laing's metaphor of engulfment, indeed, is curiously echoed in the following passage:

---

[129] H. Guntrip (*op.cit.*) pp. 46ff.; 62f.

[130] G. Devereux, *Basic problems of Ethnopsychiatry*, Univ. of Chicago, 1980, ch. 10, arguing that schizophrenia, as a disorder, consists in taking these unhealthy social norms to their logical—though pathological—extremes.

[131] Turning to the *psychotic* developments of the schizoid condition, Laing observes that in his efforts to cut off his relatedness with others so as to protect his self against engulfment and loss of identity, the isolated 'inner self' becomes ironically (and sadly) unable "to preserve what precarious identity or aliveness it may already possess". This is because, Laing argues, "the self can be 'real' only in relation to real people and things"; therefore, "the withdrawal from reality results in the 'self's' own impoverishment". Moreover, "the sense of identity requires the existence of another by whom one is known; and a conjunction of this other person's recognition of one's self with self-recognition". Without this dialectical confirmation of the self by others, the 'inner', isolated self loses contact with its own reality; "its freedom operates in a vacuum. Its activity is without life. The self becomes desiccated and dead" (pp. 137–142). The case of the rabbis is obviously different, if only in so far as they did not withdraw from the whole of reality but only from part of it (the non-Jews), and only in relative terms; moreover, the rabbis were not disconnected, isolated individuals, but a collective, inter-relating group, within which, presumably, reciprocal self-confirmation could be amply achieved.

> If I leave Israel as they are, they will be *swallowed up* among the nations; let Me set my great Name among them, and they will survive.[132]

Elsewhere, the nations are compared to the sea in which Israel are *drowning* (but again, the Almighty comes and saves them);[133] or to a wave, which rises high against the beach (Israel) and threatens to *engulf* it.[134]

These passages do not necessarily refer to a physical threat of persecution and coercive assimilation. They may refer, I would suggest, to an existential threat of ontological engulfment. Such a threat is not necessarily related to violence or hostility, as Laing writes:

> Engulfment is felt as a risk in being understood (thus grasped, comprehended), in being loved, or even simply in being seen. To be hated may be feared for other reasons ... (p. 44).

The fear of engulfment may well account for the rabbinic exclusion of the nations from the *Torah* and its commandments. Indeed, the exposure of Jewish practices to non-Jewish outsiders may be perceived as potentially leading to being grasped, comprehended and understood. The non-Jewish gaze, in other words, might constitute an ontological threat to Jewish identity. This may explain why a non-Jew who observes *shabbat*, learns *Torah* and participates in the experience of 'being Israel' is described in rabbinic sources as a thief, or as committing an adulterous inroad into the ontological privacy of Israel's identity. The fear of engulfment is most apparent in the passages describing how the non-Jews (i.e. the Christians) have translated the written *Torah* and appropriated the identity of Israel, thus robbing it from the Jews and subsuming it.[135]

The solipsistic exclusion of the nations can thus be seen, similarly to Laing's 'isolationism', as manoeuvres to avert this ontological engulfment. Non-Jewish impingement is Halakhically forbidden so as to eliminate, in Laing's words, "any direct access from without to this 'inner' self" (*ib.* p. 139). Furthermore, non-Jewish impingement

---

[132] *Y.Taan.* 2,6.

[133] *Midrash Tehillim* 17,9, on *Psalms* 69:2–3.

[134] Invariably, however, the wave collapses helplessly on the sea-shore; so the nations threaten Israel but always to no avail: *Midrash Tehillim* 2,2.

[135] See pp. 49–50, 75. If however the non-Jew intends to convert, in other words, to become 'engulfed' himself into Israel, his approach to *Torah* is presumably no longer a threat. Nonetheless, his motives remain subject to rabbinic scrutiny. The exclusion of the nations may go a long way towards explaining the abiding mistrust which our sources show towards converts, even long after their conversion (see pp. 93–4).

is *neutralized and negated*, in that it is deemed Halakhically invalid and null and void. Consequently, our sources go as far as stating that the non-Jews themselves are "nothing". The existential threat of the other is thus averted; Jewish identity, now solitary and solipsistic, becomes ontologically secure.[136]

The secrecy of Jewish identity

Because of the perceived "risk in being understood (thus grasped, comprehended)", the schizophrenic resorts, according to Laing, to the "deliberate use of obscurity and complexity as a smoke-screen to hide behind", which is designed to

> preserve the secrecy, the privacy, of the self against intrusion (engulfment, implosion) . . . Any form of understanding threatens his whole defensive system (p. 163).[137]

This may be compared, again, with the remarkable secrecy which surrounds the experience of Jewish identity.[138] Indeed, inasmuch as the non-Jews are forbidden from discovering, through practising the commandments, 'what it is like' to be a Jew, they are prevented from *acquiring knowledge* of what Jewish identity consists of.

Many specific aspects of the *Torah* are shrouded, moreover, with secrecy.[139] Commonly quoted in our sources, in this context, is the verse:

---

[136] In this respect we return to the notion that the exclusion of the nations is a protective measure, though in a completely different sense from that of 'dissimilation in reverse'.

[137] Laing speaks of a schizoid patient who "had emerged from his infancy with his *'own self'* on the one hand, and 'what his mother wanted him to be', his 'personality', on the other; he . . . made it his aim and ideal to make the split between his own self (which only he knew) and what other people could see of him, as complete as possible . . . His ideal was, *never to give himself away to others*" (p. 71). See also Guntrip p. 236f.

[138] The *Talmud* praises Esther for not having revealed her identity as Jewish: *B.Meg.* 13a–b, on *Esther* 2:10 and 2:20.

[139] The 'secrets' (*siterei*) of *Torah* may not be revealed: *B.Pes.* 119a. A disciple was expelled from the house of study for having revealed some secrets: *B.Sanh.* 31a. The preparation of the shew-bread (and other elements of the Temple ritual), was kept secret lest it be diverted and used for *avoda zara* (*T.Kippurim* 2,5–8); likewise, the ineffable names of God (*B.Pes.* 50a; *B.Kid.* 71a). Early mystical sources refer to their esoteric knowledge as 'secrets'. A mystical-magical work of the Talmudic period is called *Sefer HaRazim*, the Book of Secrets: see Schürer vol. III.1, pp. 347–50. See also *Sefer haYetzira* (ed.Eisenstein) 6,15: Abraham was revealed the secret (*sod*) of the 22 letters of the Hebrew alphabet. On secrecy among the Essenes, see Josephus, *BJ* 2,141; on secrecy in the Qumran sect, see *IQS* 9,17.

Judeo-Christian sects, particularly the Gnostics, may have also emphasized the

The secret (*sod*) of the Lord is with those that fear him (*Psalms* 25:14).[140]

The *Talmudim* speak of "the secret of calendrical intercalation" (*sod haIbbur*),[141] which may not be revealed to the nations.[142] According to later *Midrashim*, the moon, i.e. the lunar calendar, is a secret (*sod*) which God transmitted exclusively to Israel.[143] Concerning the Passover celebrations, *Exodus Rabba* instructs: "let no other nation mix with (Israel) and know their secrets (*mistorav*)".[144] Ezekiah was punished with a wicked son (Menasseh) for having revealed to a non-Jew the Ark

---

importance of secrecy. Secrecy is also central to the pagan mystery cults of Antiquity: see W. Burkert, *Ancient Mystery Cults*, Cambridge Mass.: Harvard University Press, 1987, *passim* (on Gnosticism, see especially pp. 67–8). Jakob J. Petuchowski has argued that early rabbinic Judaism borrowed some of the *terminology* of contemporary mystery cults in order to rival them ("Judaism as "Mystery"—the Hidden Agenda?", in *HUCA*, 52, 1981, pp. 141–52), but he fails to prove that it borrowed their *features* or their *practices*. On the distinction between pagan mystery cults and Judaism and Christianity, see Burkert pp. 51–3 and 102.

[140] Quoted for instance in *Tanh. Hayye Sara* 4 and *Eliyahu R.* 18, p. 93. In Biblical Hebrew the term *sod* means either 'assembly' or 'counsel', the latter at times with a connotation of secrecy. However in rabbinic Hebrew it means—and is understood to mean—exclusively 'secret': thus the *Targumim* render it as *raz* (which has the unequivocal meaning, in Aramaic, of 'secret') even in passages where we would rather translate it as 'assembly': see *ad Gen.* 49:6; *Ezekiel* 13:9; *Psalms* 64:3; *ib.* 89:8; *ib.* 111:1; *Job* 19:19.

[141] *Y.RH* 2,6; *Y.Sanh.* 1,2; *B.RH* 20b; *B.Ket.* 112a. See Levine (1989) pp. 72–4, who rightly translates *sod* as 'secret' and not as 'assembly'—there is no evidence for the existence of a special assembly, distinct from the rabbinical courts, which would have dealt exclusively with calendrical decisions.

[142] *B.Ket.* 111a, according to ms.Munich, ms.Rome 113, ms.Leningrad (Firkovitch), Geniza fragments, and the parallel version in *Midrash Shir HaShirim* 3,5. However, ms.Rome 130 and printed editions (including of *Ein Ya'akov*) read that "the secret" (*tout court*) may not be revealed to the nations (see *B.Ket.*, ed. *Makhon HaTalmud HaYisre'eli*). This version is rather enigmatic, as it does not specify what this "secret" would relate to; but it seems to have been Rashi's reading (whereas *Tosafot* appear to have had the former version).

A parallel to the notion of a 'secret' (*tout court*) may be found in the inscription discovered at the En Gedi synagogue, which curses whoever reveals "the secret (*raza*) of the city to the nations"—again, without specifying what this secret relates to (for the various conjectures which have been made, see L.I. Levine (ed.), *Ancient Synagogues Revealed*, Jerusalem: Israel Exploration Society, 1981, pp. 140–5). Whatever the meaning of this curse, it seems that this Jewish community perceived itself as sharing a "secret" which could not be divulged to the non-Jews. This inscription is dated around the 6th century CE, by which time rabbinic influence had probably spread to most Jewish communities in Palestine.

[143] *Ex.R.* 15,27. This secret was known to Adam; it was transmitted from individual to individual, and eventually entrusted to the nation of Israel as a whole: *PdRE* 8. Similarly, the secret (*sod*) of redemption, which we are told is contained in the five 'final' letters (*mem, nun, tzadi, pe, khaf*), was transmitted to the Patriarchs and eventually to the elders of Israel in Egypt: *PdRE* 48.

[144] *Ex.R.* 19,6.

in the Temple and the secret (*sod*) of the worlds above.[145] A homily
explains the verse, "the glory of God is secrecy" (*Prov.* 25:2), as follows:

> why do you want to flaunt yourselves to the nations and slaughter your
> sacrifices outside the Temple? Take your sacrifices to the Temple, lest
> the nations see you and treat your offerings with contempt.[146]

Secrecy is thus specifically associated, in all these sources, with the
exclusion of the nations.[147] The latter passage suggests, in particular,
that secrecy is to Israel a source of *security*. Furthermore, the relationship
between secrecy and *Jewish identity* is indicated in the *Midrash Tanhuma*,
which refers to the most distinctive features of Jewish identity as being
"secrets": circumcision (*sod*),[148] and the *Mishna* (*mistorin*), cornerstone
of the Oral *Torah*, a secret of the Almighty which is only revealed
to Israel.[149]

   According to a *Midrash* which I have already referred to, the Israelites
were redeemed from Egypt through the merit of having kept these
four *mitzvot*: 1. they did not have forbidden relations; 2. they did not
inform against each other; 3. they did not change their names; 4.
they did not change their language.[150] I have argued that restraint
from items 1 (intermarriage), 3 and 4 (assimilation) are considered
to ensure the preservation of Israel's distinct identity. Item 2, according
to one later version, reads as follows: "they did not reveal their secret
(*mistorin*)"; which means, the same *Midrash* explains, that they did not
inform the Egyptians that they intended, before leaving Egypt, to despoil
them of their gold and silver utensils.[151] This may suggest, by analogy
with the other items, that the keeping of secrets was *itself* essential
for the preservation of the identity of Israel.

   Finally, I have mentioned that in rabbinic sources the non-Jews
are always depicted as calling the Jews *Yehudim* ('Jews'), but never
'Israel'. Moreover, although 'Israel' is the rabbis' main designation
of Jewish identity, when conversing with non-Jews they refer to
themselves as *Yehudim*.[152] This suggests that the term "Israel" is *deliberately*

---

[145] *Eliyahu R.* 9 (beginning).
[146] *Midrash Yelamdenu* (ed. Wertheimer) *Aharei*.
[147] Whereas we are told that God does not hide His secrets from Israel: *Midrash Tehillim* 111,1; *Eliyahu R.* 18, p. 93.
[148] *Tanh. Lekh* 19; *Tanh. Ḥayye Sara* 4.
[149] *Tanh. Vayyera* 5; *Tanh. Ki Tissa* 34; *Pes.R.* 5,1.
[150] *Lev.R.* 32,5, etc. See pp. 161, 192.
[151] *Num.R.* 20,22; *Tanh. Balak* 16. Cf *Lev.R.* 32,5; *Song R.* 4,12.
[152] See p. 10.

kept unknown from the non-Jews: No doubt, this usage *reflects* a historical reality, namely that *Ioudaioi* was the current Greek term for 'Jews'; but in the context of rabbinic writings it takes on a significance of its own: the nations are prevented from knowing the Jews, even from knowing their proper name. The term 'Israel' is out of reach of the nations, and hence completely secure.

Conclusion

I have argued that aside from enhancing Israel's distinction from the nations, the exclusion of the nations and the inaccessibility of Israel may proceed from an ontological urge to protect Jewish identity against the threat of non-Jewish impingement and engulfment. The strategy of 'isolationism' would lead to a solitary, secretive and solipsistic experience of being Israel. This may be related to the introvert, self-referential stance of early rabbinic writings with reference to the concept of 'Israel', which we have noted in many other contexts in this work.

2. TZENIUT: THE ONTOLOGY OF CONCEALMENT

"But with *tzenu'im* is wisdom"—*Proverbs* 11:2.

A. *The norms of tzeniut*

In the previous section, I have interpreted the secretive, exclusory solipcism of our sources in *functional* terms, as a means of protecting Jewish identity against the ontological threat of 'engulfment' which the non-Jews may represent. In this section I will adopt a more *phenomenological* approach, and study this introvert stance as a given fact, a plain, phenomenal reality of early rabbinic self-experience. I will argue that this stance characterizes not only their self-experience as Jews or as 'Israel', but indeed their self-experience in general, ontological terms. In this respect, secrecy need not be seen as a protective device against the threat of the non-Jews: to the authors of our sources, it may be no more than their ordinary, general 'way of being'.

Secrecy and introversion are especially related, I will argue, to the rabbinic virtue of 'self-concealment'. This virtue is referred to in rabbinic writings as *tzeniut* (or in its adjectival form, *tzanua/ tzenua*), derived from the verbal root TzN^c meaning 'to conceal'; this term is quite frequent in early rabbinic writings.[153] Although *tzeniut* means literally 'conceal-

---

[153] As can be judged from the concordances, it occurs with the same frequency

ment', it may often be translated as modesty, decency, discretion, chastity. Since it is a virtue of considerable importance—"nothing is dearer to the Almighty than *tzeniut*"[154]—it occasionally refers, by extension, to stringency or scrupulousness in the observance of all commandments.[155] Other notions, such as shame (*busha*) and humility (*anava* or *anvetanut*) are related to the virtue of *tzeniut*, and I shall refer to them occasionally in this chapter.

Bodily tzeniut

Bodily *tzeniut*—i.e. concealment of one's body—is primarily designed to regulate sexuality and to conceal it. Curiously, although this virtue is treated, implicitly, as an obligation, it is not circumscribed with well-defined Halakhic rulings. Body concealment was a widespread norm in the Late Antique Near East,[156] and it is perhaps not surprising, therefore, if it is largely taken for granted in our sources.

Norms of (bodily) *tzeniut* appear to be more stringent for women, because women are deemed more likely to arouse men by exposing their nudity.[157] Indeed, according to *Derekh Eretz Rabba*,

---

in the *Babylonian Talmud* as the virtues of *yir'a* (fear, of God, of sin, or of Heaven) and *ahava* (love, of God). E.E. Urbach chooses to devote a whole chapter in *The Sages* (1975) to the latter (ch. 14: "Love and Reverence", pp. 400–419), but omits entirely the virtue of *tzeniut*; a chapter on this topic would not have been unwarranted.

[154] *Pes.R.* 46,1, quoting *Micah* 6:8; cf *Tanh. Ki Tissa* 31. R. Yose b.R. Halafta praised R. Meir for being "a great man, a holy man, and a *tzanua* man": *Y.Ber.* 2,7; *Y.MK* 3,5.

[155] See *M.Demai* 6,6. It is probably because of its importance in rabbinic ethics that the virtue of *tzeniut* can take on this extended meaning. In *M.Kilayim* 9,5–6, the term *tzenu'im* is applied to those who are scrupulous not to wear wool and linen together (in accordance with the Biblical prohibition: *Deut.* 22:11; cf *Lev.* 19:19) even when it is permitted; in this passage, *tzeniut* refers not without some deliberate paradox to the virtue of *not concealing* one's body with certain types of clothing.

[156] Nakedness is anathema in the book of *Jubilees* (3:31; 7:20) and in the Qumran sect (see *IQS* 7,12; 7,14). The Greeks would marvel at the Persians who were white-skinned because they never went without clothes (Xenophon, *Hellenica* III,4,19). It has been argued that in this respect the Greeks were the exception, with their exclusive traditions of nudity in the gymnasia (for instance): see L. Bonfante, "Nudity as Costume in Classical Art", in *American Journal of Archaeology*, 93.4, 1989, pp. 543–70. According to the rabbinic sources quoted below, it is only the "barbarians" and "Mauritanians" who go naked in the market-place (but see *Jubilees* 3:31: "they should cover their shame, and should not uncover themselves as *the Gentiles* uncover themselves").

[157] See pp. 244–7, where the possible relevance of this gender distinction to Jewish identity will be discussed.

he who gazes at a woman eventually comes to sin; and he who looks upon a woman's heal will beget blemished children; and he who has no shamefullness (*boshet panim*) is easily led to sin. . . .[158]

The *Babylonian Talmud* rules that it is forbidden for a man to hear a woman's voice, or to look "even at her small finger";[159] her leg, voice, hair, and uncovered flesh are considered 'nakedness'.[160] Consequently, a woman is expected in our sources to be "cloaked like a mourner";[161] her face is veiled in public;[162] out of modesty she conceals one eye and paints the other black,[163] or (according to the *Palestinian Talmud*) she paints both eyes black, for even the worst of harlots (!) would not go out with an eye uncovered.[164]

It is taken for granted, however, that men must also keep their body concealed. According to *Derekh Eretz Rabba*, a man who stands naked, even only by candle-light or by moon-light, is putting his life at risk.[165] Elsewhere, we hear that

nothing is more repulsive and abominable to the Almighty than going about naked in the market-place, as the barbarians and Mauritanians do.[166]

Both men and women are expected to wear many layers of clothing,[167] including a head covering.[168] Concerning the Mishnaic case of a naked woman making a dough,[169] or of a naked man working in the field without even a girdle,[170] the *Tosefta* adds:

It is not praiseworthy for a person to stand naked, for when the Almighty creates him, He does not create him naked (but in the sac and placenta).

---

[158] *Derekh Eretz R.*, 1.
[159] *B.Kid.* 70a.
[160] *Erva*: *B.Ber.* 24a.
[161] *Lev.R.* 19,4; *B.Eruv.* 100b.
[162] See Daniel Sperber, *A Commentary on Derech Erez Zuta, ch. 5–8*, Ramat-Gan: Bar-Ilan University Press, 1990, p. 123.
[163] *B.Shab.* 80a.
[164] *Y.Shab.* 8,3.
[165] *Derekh Eretz R.* 11.
[166] *B.Yev.* 63b; *Sifre Deut.* 320.
[167] See *Gen.R.* 19,6.
[168] *B.Kid.* 31a; *Lev.R.* 19,4; cf also *B.Shab.* 118b; *B.Shab.* 156b; minor tractate *Kalla R.* 2 (note however *Gen.R.* 17,8, where men are described as bare-headed in contrast with women who cover it).
[169] *M.Hala* 2,3.
[170] *T.Ber.* 2,15 (L: 2,14).

Moral tzeniut

Tzeniut is also a *moral* virtue. It is a form of self-effacement and self-concealment, which is most readily translated as 'modesty'[171] and 'discretion'. We find in the *Babylonian Talmud* that the ineffable, 12-lettered name of God was only transmitted to priests who were *tzenu'im* (and could be trusted not to divulge it); likewise, the 42-lettered name could only be entrusted to a person who is first and foremost *tzanua* and humble (*anav*).[172] *Tzeniut* refers, more specifically, to discretion about *oneself*. Saul's reluctance to announce that Samuel had anointed him as king is described as *tzeniut*, and so, by implication, Esther's reluctance to reveal her Jewish identity to Ahasuerus.[173]

Significantly, bodily and moral *tzeniut* are not explicitly distinguished in our sources. In R. Abbahu's justification for not teaching the mysteries of the Chariot ('*merkava* mysticism'), both bodily and moral *tzeniut* merge: "words which are the furnace of the world should be kept hidden *under your garments*".[174] Thus our sources treat bodily and moral *tzeniut* as analogous means of self-concealment. *Tzeniut* cuts across the whole range of human experience; the experience of Jewish identity, I will now argue, is also imbued with the observance of this virtue.

B. *Tzeniut and Jewish identity*

"Israel are tzenu'im"

The relevance of *tzeniut* to Jewish identity lies in the fact that it is considered a distinctive quality of Israel. According to *Song Rabba*, Israel are compared to a dove, for the dove is *tzenua* and so Israel are *tzenu'im*.[175]

---

[171] Or 'moderation'; in *B.Yoma* 39a it is contrasted to gluttony.

[172] *B.Kid.* 71a.

[173] *B.Meg.* 13a–b. The association of the latter with *tzeniut* is implicit, I believe, from the otherwise unaccountable textual juxtaposition in this passage.

[174] *B.Hag.* 13a, my emphasis.

[175] *Song R.* 1,15,2; *ib.* 1,15,4; *ib.* 4,1,2. It is probably inherent *tzeniut* which leads the Jew to defecate by the side of the road, whereas the non-Jew does so right in the middle of it: *B.Sanh.* 104b, quoted in p. 79.

Curiously, the Persians are also praised for being distinctively *tzenu'im*, in their eating, in the toilet, and in marital intercourse (*B.Ber.* 8b), as well as for their modest behaviour (*B.Ber. ib.*, *Gen.R.* 74,2, *Eccl.R.* 7,23,1, *Tanh. Hukkat* 6: they kiss only hands) and their discretion (*ib.*: they conduct secret meetings out in the open fields, in order to detect eavesdroppers; cf also *B.Ber.* 46b: at dinner time they communicate, if necessary, through sign language). On the ambiguous status of the Persians as non-Jews, see my remarks in p. 6–7, note 33. It should be noted that although the virtue of *tzeniut* appears to be shared by Persians and Jews, they fulfil it in a different manner, and hence remain distinguished even in this respect. Thus, the Persians have marital

Shamefulness, likewise, is one of the three virtues which, according to a well-known tradition, are distinctive to Israel and identify them as true descendants of Abraham[176] or of those who stood at Mount Sinai.[177] This virtue is interpreted in later sources as moral, if not sexual, modesty and restraint: it prevents Israel from sinning.[178] Abraham was the first to display it as he had never even seen his wife Sarah and only realized her beauty when they were forced to flee to Egypt.[179]

Moreover, individual practices which are essential to Jewish identity are permeated with the ethos of modesty and concealment. The *Babylonian Talmud* states that whereas all the commandments were given to Israel in public (*be-pharhesia*), *shabbat* was given to them in private, *be-tzin'a*—a term derived from the same root as *tzeniut*.[180] The *tefillin* must be placed on the upper arm (as opposed to the hand), in order that "it shall be *to you* as a sign" (*Ex.* 13:9)—to you as a sign, and not to any other.[181] Some authorities in the *Mekhilta* argue on the same exegetical grounds that the Israelites in Egypt placed the Passover blood on the *inside* of their doorposts, for it was a sign to the Almighty and to Israel, and not to the others outside.[182] This identity-marker which distinguished and effectively formed the people of Israel, and which the *Mekhilta* and the *Targum* describe significantly as being blood from the Passover lamb as well as from their circumcision,[183] was thus similarly hidden.

---

intercourse wearing clothes in contrast with Israel who do so in the nude (*B.Ket.* 48a)—in spite of the requirement that intercourse should be performed with "shame" (*B.Ned.* 20a–b; cf below note 194).

[176] *Kalla R.* 10.

[177] The other two are mercy and good deeds; *bayshanim* ('shameful') is derived from *busha* (shame, timidity, or modesty), which is semantically related to *tzeniut. Y.Kid.* 4,1; *Midrash Tehillim* 1,2; cf *Deut.R.* 3,4; *Kalla R.* 10. Consequently, Gibeonite converts are not entitled to marry the Jewish-born, because they do not display these virtues: *Y.Sanh.* 6,7; *B.Yev.* 79a; *Num.R.* 8,4; *Midrash Tehillim* 17, end. This passage has been discussed in p. 31.

[178] *Num.R. ib.*

[179] *Kalla R. ib.*

[180] *B.Betza* 16a, quoted above in p. 208.

[181] *Sifre Deut.* 35; *B.Men.* 37b. The upper arm is less external, hence less visible, than the hand. Alternatively, as according to the *Shita mekubbetzet*, the upper arm is normally covered with clothing, and hence physically hidden.

[182] *Mekh. Bo* 6. The *Targum Yerushalmi* follows the dissenting view (*ad Ex.* 12:7 and 22).

[183] *Mekh. ib.*; *Targum Yerushalmi ad Ex.* 12:13.

Torah and tzeniut

Torah learning, another corner-stone of Jewish identity,[184] is frequently associated with *tzeniut* in its 'moral' sense, namely privacy and discretion. *Torah*, it is suggested, must be studied with *tzeniut*. If a person toils in his learning *be-tzin'a* (in private), his learning will not soon be forgotten.[185] A *Torah* scholar must be *tzanua*;[186] indeed, one of the merits of the person who occupies himself with *Torah* "for its own sake" is that he is *tzanua*.[187] Also of some relevance, perhaps, is the later *Midrash* whereby the first Tablets of the Law were broken because they were given in public and the Evil Eye took hold of them; so the second Tablets were given by God in private, "for there is nothing better than *tzeniut*".[188]

The following story, in the *Babylonian Talmud*, is particularly revealing. Rabbi once decreed that disciples should not be taught *Torah* in the market-place (just as, in the previous generation, R. Akiva had instructed his son not to sit and teach in prominent places in the city).[189] He argued that words of *Torah* are compared to a thigh (in *Song* 7:2), because in the same way as a thigh is *hidden* (*be-seter*), so are words of *Torah*. Moreover, he went on, since the *Torah* tells us to "go with *tzeniut*" (*hatzne'a lekhet*—*Micah* 6:8) with "things that are done in public (*be-pharhesia*)", *a fortiori* one should "go with *tzeniut*" with "things that are done in private".[190] R. Ḥiyya, defying this decree, went out and taught two of his nephews in the market-place; as a result, during the following thirty days he was virtually excommunicated. R. Ḥiyya attempted later on to justify his actions with Scriptural evidence. He was told, according to Rava, that *Torah* can only become manifest to the outside if one learns it *"from within"*.[191]

---

[184] But also of 'rabbinic' identity, in contrast with the ignorant *amei haAretz* (see section III.4.A). In this context, the identity of the rabbis as Jews and their identity as rabbis (*Torah* scholars) is difficult to distinguish, as we shall presently see.

[185] *Y.Ber.* 5,1, quoting as a source *Prov.* 11:2.

[186] *Song R.* 4,11; *Derekh Eretz Z.* 7,2.

[187] *Avot* 6 (= *Kinyan Torah*), 1. According to other readings (also in the gloss in *Kalla R.* 8 on the same passage), this person is *commanded* to be *tzanua*.

[188] *Tanh. Ki Tissa* 31.

[189] *B.Pes.* 112a.

[190] *Be-tzin'a*. It should be noted that Rabbi takes for granted that *Torah* is included in the category of "things done in private". Both these arguments are also found in *B.Suk.* 49b; cf *B.Mak.* 24a. There is no evidence that R. Akiva or Rabbi were worried about non-Jewish polemics or persecution, or that they feared that inappropriate people such as the *amei haAretz* would overhear.

[191] And that *Torah* can only be taught in public on days of general assembly (*de-kalla*): *B.MK* 16b.

The *tzeniut* with which *Torah* must be studied is associated in this passage with introversion ("learning from within"), privacy, as well as body concealment (of the thigh). Sexual modesty is also associated with the activity of studying *Torah*, which is called, as we have seen, the 'bride' of Israel.[192] We are told in *B.Pes.*, indeed, that "whoever occupies himself with *Torah* in front of an *am haAretz*, it is as though he is having intercourse with his bride in his presence".[193] It is forbidden, indeed, to have marital intercourse in the presence of other people.[194] *Torah* learning is thus an intimate, quasi-sexual act, to which the norms of bodily *tzeniut* are made to apply; the presence of an outsider such as an *am haAretz*[195] may be experienced as 'engulfing', as I have previously suggested,[196] but it is also a transgression of quasi-sexual norms. *Tzeniut* in *Torah* learning is thus a remarkably holistic experience.

The bearing of circumcision

I have argued on many occasions that circumcision is central to the experience of Jewish identity. It would appear, as I shall now elaborate, that the rabbis' attitude towards their circumcised penis, and their bearing and bodily experience of it, may be characterized by the ethos of *tzeniut* more than any other feature of Jewish identity.

We have seen in the second chapter that the *Midrash Tanḥuma* describes circumcision as splendour and beauty, as a soldier's weapon, even as a bodily representation of the Almighty's name.[197] This suggests that circumcision is to be born with pride. In some sources it is revered as a ritual object of considerable importance. Eliezer took his oath holding Abraham's circumcision.[198] When King David entered the baths and saw himself naked, he would worry at being bereft of any commandment (such as *tefillin* or the fringes); but then, he would remember his circumcision—according to another version, he would see it—and its abiding presence would reassure him.[199] And as one

---

[192] See p. 74.

[193] *B.Pes.* 49b, quoted in pp. 116–7.

[194] Or to have it during daytime or under candle light: *B.Nida* 17a; cf *B.Sanh.* 46a.

[195] The *am haAretz* is excluded from *Torah* learning: see p. 117.

[196] Section V.1.D.

[197] Pp. 65–6.

[198] *Gen.R.* 59,8. Circumcision may have been, at the time, the only ritual object at his disposal.

[199] *Sifre Deut.* 36 (he saw it); *Y.Ber.* end, and *B.Men.* 43b (he remembered it).

Midrash adds, such an experience can be shared, in fact, by all.[200]

Yet on the other hand, bodily *tzeniut* requires that the circumcised penis remain concealed. The *Babylonian Talmud* rules that even in the toilet—and even at night time—a man must be *tzanua*;[201] he may only uncover his parts whilst he is sitting,[202] by one handbreadth behind and two handbreadths in front.[203] The only exception to this rule applies to public bathing, where, as we have just seen, a person may uncover himself completely;[204] as R. Gamliel told Proclus at the baths of Aphrodite in Acco, "everyone is naked and urinating by the sewer".[205] It is questionable, however, whether bath attendance was a central feature of the rabbis' daily lives.[206] Moreover, a *modicum* of *tzeniut* is recommended for bathers too. They must undress in a specific order.[207] As he came out of the river where he was bathing, R. Abbahu would cover his penis with his hand; other rabbis would simply bend forwards.[208] Thus, the circumcised penis is almost permanently concealed.[209]

It might be argued, however, that it is not circumcision *as such* which needs to be concealed, but rather the penis. The primary purpose of bodily *tzeniut*, indeed, is to regulate sexuality and to conceal it.

---

[200] According to the variant version of *Midrash Tehillim* 6,1.

[201] *B.Ber.* 62a; *B.AZ* 47b.

[202] *B.Ber. ib.*; *Derekh Eretz R.* 7. Cf Josephus, *BJ* 2,148 (on the Essenes).

[203] *B.Ber.* 23b; a woman, on the other hand, may only uncover one handbreadth behind and nothing in front (on women see also *B.Bekh.* 44b). Similarly during sexual intercourse one must conduct oneself with shame (*busha*): *B.Ned.* 20a–b (in detail)— although intercourse should take place in the nude, in contrast with the Persians who have it wearing clothes (*B.Ket.* 48a; cf note 23).

[204] See *Derekh Eretz R.* 10. Because of this, and for reasons of *tzeniut*, one may not bathe together with one's teacher, although it is permitted to bathe with one's father, father-in-law, step-father, and sister's husband: *B.Pes.* 51a; minor tractate *Semahot* 12. Among the Essenes, on the other hand, a loin-cloth had to be worn by men whilst bathing, according to Josephus, *BJ* 2,161.

[205] *M.AZ* 3,4, quoted in p. 153. There, R. Gamliel's circumcision would have been much in evidence, not only to him but also to the non-Jewish bathers, not least to his interlocutor.

[206] If anything, because in the bath-house *Torah* words (*M.AZ ib.*) and even *Torah* thoughts (*B.AZ* 44b) are forbidden. See however p. 173 and n. 238.

[207] Specified in detail in *Derekh Eretz R.* 10.

[208] *B.Shab.* 41a.

[209] The 4th-century mosaic floor of the Ḥammat-Tiberias synagogue depicts, for the Zodiac sign of Libra and Gemini, a completely naked man (with naked penis). However, it is not evident that this man is circumcised: see on this Moshe Dothan, *Ḥammath Tiberias: Early synagogues and the Hellenistic and Roman remains*, Jerusalem: Israel Exploration Society, 1983, pp. 46–8. See also Levine (1981), pp. 63–9 and illustration p. 8.

Concealment of circumcision *per se*, on the other hand, is undesirable and forbidden. Inside the water (where nakedness is anyway concealed), a bather who covers his penis with his hand is said by the *Babylonian Talmud* to be rejecting the covenant of Abraham our Father (i.e. circumcision);[210] the rabbis take care, therefore, not to bend forwards as they enter the water but to remain fully upright.[211] In other words, if the penis is already hidden, circumcision does not require additional concealment.[212] But my point is only that in *practice*, and for obvious reasons, circumcision and penis are always both concealed.[213] Therefore the *Midrash Tanḥuma* refers to circumcision as a secret (*sod*);[214] it is buried, it says elsewhere, within the person's 'bosom'.[215]

This confirms the connection of Jewish identity with introversion and *tzeniut*, to which I have earlier referred. Moreover, the concealment of the penis suggests that 'identity-markers' such as circumcision are not necessarily directed towards the outside world, as public expressions of difference from the non-Jews. They can be primarily introvert and *inwardly* directed. Indeed, a Jew is only circumcised to himself; at most times, nobody else can see it. Circumcision is experienced as a *private* feature of his Jewish bodily constitution.

Interestingly, the circumcised penis is concealed not only from the outside world, but also from the Jewish person himself. A number of rabbis are praised in the *Talmudim* for never having even looked

---

[210] *B.Shab.* 41a (Rashi *ad loc.*: "it is as though he is embarrassed at being circumcised").

[211] *B.Shab. ib.*

[212] We may also note that the performance of circumcision is the occasion of an expensive, well-attended *public* ceremony, which is vividly described in *Eccl.R.* 3,2,3; cf also *Tanh. Tetzave* 1; *Tanh. Tazria* 5; *PdRE* 29.

[213] It would also be wrong to establish a complete dichotomy between the sexual function of the penis and its circumcision. Indeed, in a sense, circumcision is the foundation of Jewish male sexuality, at once moderating it (God sealed his name unto the circumcision of Israel so as to prevent them from sinning: *Tanh. Shemini* 8) and endowing it with holiness (Abraham circumcised after the birth of Ishmael and before the birth of Isaac, so that only the latter would issue from "holy" seed: *Gen.R.* 46,2). Rebecca was privileged at being the first woman who had intercourse with a man circumcised when eight days old (*Gen.R.* 60,5); by contrast, Orpah had intercourse with 100 "*prepuces*" of non-Jews after her departure from Naomi (*Ruth R.* 2,20, see above p. 24). Forbidden relations are associated with the prepuce (when Nebuchadnezzar attempted to have a homosexual relation with Zedekiah, his prepuce grew to the length of 300 cubits!—*B.Shab.* 149b) and with decircumcision (intercourse with a non-Jewish woman: see at length pp. 163–4). In so far as circumcision transforms Jewish sexuality and sanctifies it, the rules of *tzeniut* which dictate the privacy of sexuality and its concealment are relevant to circumcision too.

[214] *Tanh. Lekh* 19, quoted above in p. 222.

[215] *Heik*, a word which has no adequate translation; it connotes above all the bodily snugness of the parent's or the spouse's embrace: *Tanh. Tetze* 9.

at their own circumcised penis: these are R. Yosi, and R. Yehuda
the Patriarch, who earned thereby the title: "our holy Rabbi".[216] When
Antoninus converted and circumcised, he visited the latter and proudly
exclaimed: "Look at my circumcision!"; Rabbi replied that he had
never seen his own circumcision—now, Antoninus had shown him
his.[217] The penis is also concealed, so to speak, from the sense of
touch. It may not be touched;[218] it is forbidden to hold it even whilst
urinating, so as not to induce wasteful seminal emission.[219] Whereas
a woman is praised for repeatedly inspecting her genitals (for menstrual
impurity), a man who does so (for seminal impurity) is rebuked by
the *Mishna* in severest, albeit figurative terms: "let his hand be cut
off!".[220]

With a few exceptions, therefore, the authors of our sources avoid
direct or explicit perception of their own circumcision; though a personal
and embodied experience, circumcision remains in most cases *implicit*.
I would suggest that the implicitness and *tzeniut* with which they carry
this mark of Jewish identity induces a bodily self-centred and *intimate*
experience which, as I have argued, is characteristic of the general
experience of Jewish identity.

C. *Ontology and habitus*

Pudeur

The virtue of *tzeniut* could be assigned a similar *functional* role to that
which we assigned, in the previous section, to exclusion and secrecy:
namely, to resist the threat of alien incursion. In his interpretation
of "*pudeur*" (modesty), Merleau-Ponty argues that it cannot be treated
as an instinctive law of nature, but must be understood as bearing
what he calls a "metaphysical" significance:

> Usually man does not show his body, and, when he does, it is either
> with fear or with an intention to fascinate. He has the impression that
> the alien gaze which runs over his body is stealing it from him, or

---

[216] The *Babylonian Talmud* adds that the latter never slipped his hand below his
belt: *B.Shab.* 118b.

[217] *Y.Meg.* 1,11; *ib.* 3,2; *Y.Sanh.* 10,5; *Eccl.R.* 9,10,2. On the other hand, according
to *Sifre Deut.* 36, King David *looked* at this circumcision; cf also *Song R.* 7,6, which
explains that Elijah placed his face between his knees in prayer (*IKings* 18:42) in
order to allude that the merit of circumcision should prevail.

[218] *B.Shab.* 41a (except in special circumstances).

[219] *B.Nida* 13a; 43a; *B.Shab. ib.*

[220] *M.Nida* 2,1. Also quoted in *Pes.dRK* 12,15.

else, on the other hand, that the display of his body will deliver the other person up to him, defenceless, and that in this case the other will be reduced to servitude. *Pudeur* and *impudeur*, then, take their place in a dialectic of the self and the other, which is that of master and slave.[221]

Although voluntary exposure of the body can represent an aggressive attempt to fascinate and master the other, Merleau-Ponty remarks that this does carry the alternative risk of being 'stolen' by the other, and, in Laing's terms, of being 'depersonalised'.[222] This may be why "usually man does not show his body" (at least, in the Western and Near Eastern cultural *milieux* which we, and Merleau-Ponty, are accustomed to). The virtue of *tzeniut*, concealing as it does the essential features of Jewish identity, may thus be designed to protect the latter, circumcision and *Torah* learning, against the engulfing threat of the onlooking other.

Being-in-the-world

Yet unlike the material we studied on the exclusion of the nations or on the notion of secrecy, the virtue of *pudeur* or *tzeniut* occurs in our sources without reference to the non-Jews, or indeed to any other external threat which may need to be averted.[223] The significance of *tzeniut*, although an introvert withdrawal from the outside world, may require therefore a different explanation.

I would suggest that rather than being directed against external intrusion, the ethos of *tzeniut* may be designed on the contrary to prevent the self from intruding, as it were, into the outside world. In the *Babylonian Talmud*, following a statement by R. Yitzhak that whoever commits a transgression in secret is unwittingly squeezing (*dohek*) the feet of the Divine Presence (*Shekhina*), R. Yehoshua b. Levi is reported as saying that one may not walk (even a minimal distance of four cubits) with an upright posture, for "His Glory fills the earth"

---

[221] Merleau-Ponty, *op.cit.* pp. 166–7. I have slightly altered the translation to make it, in my opinion, more accurate.

[222] Laing, *op.cit.* 46ff.

[223] With the exception, perhaps, of the passage describing *shabbat* as having been given to Israel 'in private' (*be-tzin'a*—which is, etymologically at least, akin to the term *tzeniut*), so that—the Talmud specifies—the nations do not know about it (*B.Betza* 16a). We also hear that it was the nakedness of Adam and Eve and their public sexual intercourse which led the snake, taken by desire for Eve, to "pounce upon them" (*Gen.R.* 18,6); their subsequent clothing (after the sin) could be seen, therefore, as a measure to prevent future aggressions of this kind.

(*Isaiah* 6:3); and the Talmud adds that R. Huna b.R. Yehoshua would never walk (even a minimal distance of four cubits) with his head uncovered, because, he said, "the Divine Presence (*Shekhina*) is above my head".[224] It appears that in the early rabbinic world-view, man is crushed by the overwhelming Presence of the Almighty which "fills the earth"[225] and whose "feet" reach down to his immediate surroundings. Man must contain himself, therefore, within his apportioned boundaries. He must walk with downcast posture and with covered head—and, I would suggest by extension, with covered body—lest he outstretches himself and thereby "squeezes the feet of the *Shekhina*".[226]

In this perspective, *tzeniut* or self-effacement is no longer a defence mechanism against the threat of the engulfing other, but rather the appropriate manner of carrying one's body and being within the *plenum* of the *Shekhina* in the world; it is, to the authors of our sources, an existential or *ontological necessity*. In other words, *tzeniut* is a form of bodily and mental *'intentionality'*, and an essential characteristic of *'being-in-the-world'*.[227] Consequently, *tzeniut* affects all modes of being; as an important element of one's general ontological experience, 'being Jewish' or Jewish identity must also conform, appropriately, to this self-effacing 'way of being'.[228]

Hexis and habitus

I will now argue that the notion of *habitus*, developed by Pierre Bourdieu in his anthropological studies, can account for the virtue of *tzeniut* in a most insightful manner.[229] *Habitus* is described as a "system of cognitive and motivating structures"(p. 76) which "functions at every moment as a matrix of perceptions, appreciations, and actions"(p. 83), and has an "endless capacity to engender products—thoughts,

---

[224] *B.Kid.* 31a. See also *B.Shab.* 12b: "he who visits a sick person must cover his head . . . for the *Shekhina* is above the sick person's head".

[225] Cf *Pes.dRK* 1,2; *Ex.R.* 2,5; *Num.R.* 12,4: "no place on earth is devoid of Divine Presence".

[226] See *B.Sot.* 5a: "of the arrogant person, the Almighty says: 'I and he cannot live together in the world'" (in a similar passage in *Midrash Tehillim* 101,3, this expression is explained as meaning that this person cannot see the "face of the *Shekhina*"). Also *B.Sanh.* 88b: "who is destined for the world-to-come? He who is meek, humble, *stooping* on entering and *stooping* on going out . . . "

[227] Concepts developed by Merleau-Ponty (*op.cit.*, *passim*; I have referred to 'intentionality' in pp. 62–3).

[228] See also *B.Hul.* 89a: God favours Israel because unlike the nations, even in periods of greatness they "reduce" (*mema'atin*) themselves before Him.

[229] I refer to P. Bourdieu, *Outline of a Theory of Practice*, (trans. R. Nice), Cambridge: CUP, 1977.

perceptions, expression, actions"(p. 95). Defining it as a "system of dispositions", Bourdieu writes:

> The word *disposition* seems particularly suited to express what is covered by the concept of *habitus*. It expresses first the result of an organising action, with a meaning close to that of words such as structure; it also designates a way of being, a habitual state (especially of the body) and, in particular, a predisposition, tendency, propensity, or inclination (p. 214 n.1).

The *habitus* (plural) are moreover

> systems of durable, transposable dispositions, structured structures predisposed to function as structuring structures, that is, as principles of the generation and structuring of practices and representations which can be objectively "regulated" and "regular" without in any way being the product of obedience to rules, objectively applied to their goals without presupposing a conscious aiming at ends or an express mastery of the operations necessary to attain them and, being all this, collectively orchestrated without being the product of the orchestrating action of a conductor (p. 72).

Tzeniut corresponds on all accounts to a *habitus* of this kind. Firstly, it is not a rigid Halakhic ruling, but rather a "tendency", "a habitual state", a "system of dispositions". We have noted, concerning bodily *tzeniut* in particular, the absence of explicit, systematic Halakhic rulings.[230] On the other hand, *tzeniut* underpins implicitly the performance of all the commandments: in the words of *Derekh Eretz Zuta*, "the glory of a *mitzva* (commandment) is *tzeniut*"[231]—just as "the glory of man is his garb".[232] Although it lacks precise Halakhic definition, in the passages just quoted *tzeniut* is nevertheless prescribed; in some sense, therefore, it is a structured, "regulated" and "regular" predisposition.

Secondly, as a *habitus*, *tzeniut* is a "system of *durable and transposable* dispositions", which can affect the widest variety of experiences. This is evident, again, in Derekh Eretz Zuta:

> A *Torah* scholar must be *tzanua* in eating, drinking, bathing, anointing, shoe-wearing, in marital intercourse, and in walking; in his dress, his voice, his spitting, and his good deeds.[233]

---

[230] Section V.2.A.
[231] *Derekh Eretz Z.* 5. See D. Sperber, p. 41.
[232] *Ib.* 10.
[233] *Derekh Eretz Z.* 7.

Moreover, we have seen that *tzeniut* applies not only to bodily sexuality but also to *Torah* learning and to the general experience of 'being Israel'. Bourdieu notes in his study that the same *habitus* can characterize merriment as well as mourning;[234] similarly, in a passage we have seen, the verse "go with *tzeniut*" (*Micah* 6:8) is made to apply not only to "things that are done in private (*be-tzin'a*)" but also to those that are done in public, such as *funerals* ("taking the corpse out") and *weddings* ("bringing the bride into the canopy")[235]—to the private and the public, to the "taking out" and to the "bringing in". I will presently argue that *tzeniut* is similarly transposable from man to woman, thus effecting, with Jewish identity, a "collectively orchestrated" experience.

Thirdly *tzeniut*, as a *habitus*, is fully *embodied* so as to become, in Jackson's words, a "pattern of body use", or in Bourdieu's words, a "body *hexis*"—which is to say, "a pattern of postures . . . charged with a host of social meanings and values":[236]

> Bodily *hexis* is a political mythology realized, *em-bodied*, turned into a permanent disposition, a durable manner of standing, speaking, and thereby of *feeling* and *thinking* (pp. 93–4).

Bodily dispositions are 'mythologies' embodied which induce in turn, by reciprocal analogy, distinctive ways of feeling and thinking. Similarly, it would appear that the practices of bodily concealment and of 'moral' *tzeniut* complement, induce and generate each other, thus constituting a distinctly *holistic* experience.

The habitus of Israel

Bourdieu illustrates the latter point with specific reference to gender distinction in Kabyle society:

> The oppositions which mythico-ritual logic makes between the male and the female and which organize the whole system of values reappear, for example, in the gestures and movements of the body, in the form

---

[234] With reference to Kabyle society he notes "the presence of symbolically identical objects or acts in the rituals associated with such different events in the existence of man and the land as funerals, ploughing, harvesting, circumcision, or marriage . . . the partial coincidence of the ritual acts and symbols, whose polysemy is perfectly appropriate to the requirements of essentially "multi-functional" practices"—p. 143 and ff. See also M. Jackson (*op.cit.*) ch. 8., especially on male to female transpositions.

[235] *B.Suk.* 49b; *B.Mak.* 24a; cf *B.MK* 16b. (Quoted above).

[236] Bourdieu p. 87. On the embodiment of the *habitus*, see also *ib.* pp. 87–95. *Hexis* is basically the Greek equivalent of the Latin term *habitus*, both meaning literally 'way of holding oneself', hence 'bearing' and 'way of being'.

of the opposition between the straight and the bent, or between assurance and restraint. . . . The man of honour's pace is steady and determined . . . The manly man stands up straight . . . Conversely, a woman is expected to walk with a slight stoop, looking down . . . she must always be girdled . . . In short, the specifically feminine virtue, *lahia*, modesty, restraint, reserve, orients the whole female body downwards, towards the ground, the inside, the house, whereas male excellence, *nif*, is asserted in movement upwards, outwards, towards other men (p. 94).

Gender distinction of this kind can also be found in rabbinic sources; in the next section, I will show how women's *tzeniut* is distinctively more important and more pronounced than men's. Nonetheless, the ethos of Israel in global terms, men and women alike, is strikingly similar to this "specifically feminine virtue" which Bourdieu describes elsewhere as 'centripetal'.[237] Both men and women, in rabbinic sources, are expected to be fully clothed; as we have seen, they may not walk with an upright posture; their pace is neither steady nor assured, but restrained[238] and awed by the Divine Presence which surrounds them. This is why, we may venture, Israel is described in symbolic imagery as a female[239] and a bride.[240]

D. *Women, tzeniut, and Jewish identity*

"Daughters of Israel"
The identity of Jewish women constitutes an important problem which I have not yet addressed. On the one hand, they are included unequivocally within the Halakhic category of "Israel": they are called in the *Mishna* 'benot yisra'el', daughters of Israel.[241] Inasmuch as Jewish

---

[237] Whereas the male stance is 'centrifugal'—p. 92. Bourdieu would emphasize, however, that gender or ethnic culture is made up of a plethora of *habitus* (plural); thus, *tzeniut* can only be seen as *one* of the *habitus* (plural) of rabbinic culture.

[238] A hasty (*gassa*, lit.: large) step is forbidden (on *shabbat* as well as on weekdays: *B.Shab.* 113b) and harmful to one's eyesight: *B.Ber.* 43b; *B.Taan.* 10b. Interestingly, the expression *gilluy arayot* (lit. 'exposure of nudity') in *Ex*.20:23 is interpreted in *Mekh. Bahodesh* 11, end (= *Ex.R.* 30,2) as meaning a 'hasty step'. Cf also *Derekh Eretz Z.* 7 (above-quoted): "A *Torah* scholar must be *tzanua* in . . . walking . . .".

[239] In this world—and male in the world-to-come: *Song R.* 1,5 (s.v. *shehora*), 3.

[240] *Pes. dRK* 22,5; *Tanh. Ki Tissa* 18; *Pes.R.* 38,3. See p. 83.

[241] *M.Ned.* 9,10; *M.Yev.* 13,1; etc. J.R. Wegner (*Chattel or Person? The status of women in the Mishna*, Oxford: Oxford University Press, 1988) notes that this expression (instead of the possible *yisre'elit*, which is found in restricted contexts in *Tosefta*) demeans the woman's personhood, by implying that she is to be treated as a 'daughter', i.e. as a minor; moreover, her personal status is defined solely by reference to men (who are *yisra'el*, but never—in rabbinic sources—*benei yisra'el*); "the demeaning effect of being defined always and only as someone else's daughter is self-evident" (p. 167,

identity is matrilineally transmitted,[242] the mother appears to be the repository of Jewish identity, its source and its foundation. The *Talmud* states explicitly that the verse: "you are a holy people", includes both men and women.[243]

And yet, we find that women are excluded from a considerable number of commandments. In itself, this may be reminiscent of the exclusion of the nations.[244] Moreover, this exclusion entails, remarkably, that Jewish women have no share in much of the distinctive *praxis* of Israel, which we have argued is an essential constituent of Jewish identity.[245] I will first examine in more detail the exclusion of women from the commandments; then, I will discuss whether Jewish women can be said to be excluded from the rabbinic experience of being Israel.

Women and the commandments

The status of women *vis-à-vis* the commandments has been reviewed elsewhere.[246] Briefly, we find in the *Mishna* and *Talmudim* that three commandments are specifically incumbent on women: menstrual purity, *ḥala* (dough offering), and candle lighting (on Friday night).[247] Moreover, "scripture treats man and woman as equal before the law", in civil as well as in penal cases.[248] But Jewish women are exempt, and in this sense excluded, from a large number of commandments: according to the *Mishna*, from "all positive commandments which depend on a time factor".[249]

---

and nn. 258–60 on p. 243, with reference to sources). For our purposes, however, the term "daughters of Israel" indicates unequivocally the belonging of women to the Halakhic category of Israel.

[242] See pp. 87–8.

[243] *Y.Kid.* 1,7. Implicit in *B.Kid.* 35b.

[244] Section V.1.A–C.

[245] Sections II.2–3.

[246] The best work on this topic, although limited to Mishnaic sources, is J.R. Wegner, *op.cit.* 1988. On other sources, see now *id.*, "The Image and Status of Women in Classical Rabbinic Judaism", in J.R. Baskin (ed.), *Jewish Women in Historical Perspective*, Detroit: Wayne State University Press, 1991, pp. 68–93. Wegner also argues that Jewish women are excluded in our sources from the public domain; I shall return to this notion later in this chapter, but it is not my immediate concern.

[247] *Y.Shab.* 2,6, based on *M.Shab. ib.*; *Gen.R.* 17, end; *Tanh. Noah* 1.

[248] *B.BK* 15a.

[249] *M.Kid.* 1,7. This principle is subject however to numerous exceptions: for instance, women are exempt, additionally, from the prohibition of shaving the corner of one's hair (*ib.*), but obligated to eat *matza* on Passover and to rejoice on festivals (*B.Kid.* 34a). See also *M.Ber.* 3,3.

The exemption of women from the commandments leads, by and large, to their exclusion from the distinctive elements of the rabbinic experience of 'being Israel'. First and foremost, women do not share the experience of circumcision.[250] It is disputed whether women must wear fringes.[251] According to the *Mishna*, they are exempt from reciting *shema* and wearing *tefillin*.[252] *Targum Ps-Jonathan* goes further and *prohibits* fringes and *tefillin* to women.[253] On the other hand, more lenient opinions are quoted in the *Babylonian Talmud*, whereby women are either exempt, or even obligated, to wear *tefillin*.[254] The *Talmudim* disagree with each other as to whether Mikhal, King David's wife, wore *tefillin* with impunity,[255] or whether she was actually rebuked.[256]

Most striking, however, is their exclusion from another centrepiece of Jewish identity: *Torah* learning. The *Sifre* forbids a woman from being taught *Torah*,[257] but this ruling is subject to a Mishnaic dispute. According to one Mishnaic passage, it would appear that daughters may be taught scripture.[258] Elsewhere, however, the following is found:

> B. Azzai says, a man is obligated to teach his daughter *Torah*, so that if ever she drinks (the draught of the *sotah*'s ordeal), she will know that merit will hold back her punishment.
> R. Eliezer says, if he teaches his daughter *Torah*, he is teaching her obscenity (*tiflut*).
> R. Yehoshua adds, a woman prefers one measure (of food) with obscenity to nine measures with abstinence.[259]

---

[250] Even though the *Talmud* states that a woman is considered "as though she was circumcised": *B.AZ* 27a.

[251] *Y.Ber.* 3,3; *B.Men.* 43a.

[252] But she must pray, affix a *mezuza* on her door-posts, and say grace after meals: *M.Ber.* 3,3. On *shema* and Jewish identity, see pp. 252–3.

[253] *Ad Deut.* 22:5.

[254] R. Yose (exempt), R. Meir and R. Yehuda (obligated): *B.Eruv.* 96b.

[255] *B.Eruv.* 96a–b, which would support R. Yose's opinion.

[256] *Y.Eruv.* 10,1.

[257] *Sifre Deut.* 46; *B.Kid.* 29b.

[258] *M.Ned.* 4,3: if a man has taken a vow not to derive any benefit from his fellow, his fellow may nevertheless "teach his sons and daughters scripture".

[259] *M.Sot.* 3,4. According to Wegner, "what Ben 'Azzai and Eliezer mean by their reference to "the law" (*torah*) is not entirely clear. In context their comments almost certainly refer only to the law of the ordeal, which scripture calls *torat ha-qena'ot* ("the law of jealousy"). "*Torah*" in the *Mishna* generally has the limited connotation of a specific law or set of rules, as here, rather than denoting "the *Torah*" in the general sense that talmudic Hebrew later assigns to the term" (1988, p. 161). I must disagree with her, as I do not know that the term "*Torah*" has such a narrow meaning in Mishnaic Hebrew; her restricted interpretation of *M.Sot.* is therefore unwarranted.

The suggestion that *Torah* is obscenity to a woman reminds us of the claim that it is a "lethal poison" to the non-Jews. Consistent with her interpretation, Wegner

According to the *Palestinian Talmud*, a *matrona* once asked the same R. Eliezer why it was that not all the Israelites had been punished for the Golden Calf in the same manner (some died by the sword and others by pestilence, yet all had committed the same sin—a subtle allusion, perhaps, to the inequality of women?). He refused to answer, and told her that "a woman's wisdom is only at her spindle"; and he added, "let words of *Torah* be burnt rather than be transmitted to women".[260]

The *Sifre*'s and R. Eliezer's view, whereby a woman should not be taught *Torah*, appears to have prevailed in subsequent Talmudic literature.[261] Thus, the *Babylonian Talmud* states that the only merit a woman may derive from *Torah* learning is by sending her sons to learn *Torah* and by waiting patiently for her husband to come back from the houses of learning . . .[262]

It is puzzling that Beruria, a woman from a distinguished rabbinic family (as the daughter of R. Ḥanina b. Teradyon and wife of R. Meir)[263] is said in the *Talmud* to have learnt *Torah* from three hundred rabbis (directly, or by eavesdropping?), and that her learning is even treated as exemplary.[264] She is quoted for her ethical wisdom,[265] as well as for her Halakhic opinions with which other rabbis concurred.[266] The case of Beruria, however, is likely to have been considered exceptional.

The relative exclusion of Jewish women from the experience of circumcision, *Torah* learning, and other features of Jewish identity, must affect the nature of their identity as Israel. Not surprisingly, we

---

quotes Jastrow's explanation, as follows: "because the laws concerning sexual aberrations may excite her sensuality" (1988, p. 242, n. 247). Again, one may question the restrictiveness of such an interpretation.

[260] *Y.Sot.* 3,4; *B.Yoma* 66b (reading: "A wise woman asked R. Eliezer"). R. Eliezer was not merely dismissing her because he could not answer her question; indeed— according to *Y.Sot.*—he was able to answer the question, but only did so to his disciples.

[261] *B.Ḳid.* 29b; cf *ib.* 34a.

[262] *B.Sot.* 21a, as explained in *B.Ber.* 17a. The *Babylonian Talmud*, in the same passage (*B.Sot.* 21b), does mitigate R. Eliezer's opinion with the gloss (on the *Mishna*): "if he teaches his daughter *Torah*, *it is as though* he is teaching her obscenity"; it would seem, however, that it is the equation of *Torah* with obscenity, rather than the unfavourable status of women, which disturbs the *Talmud* and leads it to making this amendment.

[263] *B.AZ* 18a.

[264] *B.Pes.* 62b; there is no reference to the effect that she was ('only') a woman.

[265] *B.Ber.* 10a; *Midrash Mishlei* 31,1.

[266] *T.Kelim BK* 4,17 (in disagreement with her brother); *T.Kelim BM* 1,6 (with R. Tarfon and the Sages); in both cases R. Yehuda (*BK*: b.Bava) ruled in favour of her opinion. Cf *B.Eruv.* 53b–54a.

are told that unlike a man a Jewish woman is able to pretend that she is non-Jewish.[267] If she is excluded from the distinctive *praxis* of Israel as defined in rabbinic sources, what then is her Jewish identity, namely her experience of 'being Israel' (or "daughter of Israel") supposed to consist of?

Domesticity and ethnic identity

Before attempting to address this question—which, I emphasize, will have to remain to some extent unanswered—it is important to stress that I can only refer to an experience which *is ascribed* to women by our rabbinic sources. Since the latter were written by men and exclusively for male consumption (women were excluded, as we have seen, from the study of these texts), the actual experiences which women had of their identity can be no more than implicit. Reconstructing women's experiences on the sole basis of men's interpretations of them is a task which could be dismissed as self-defeating. It is possible, however, to unravel what our sources *thought* women experienced; and we may hope that this reflected, to some extent at least, the subjective reality of the women's experience of being Israel.[268]

The elusiveness of female Jewish identity may be related to the *domesticity* of Jewish women which Mishnaic and Talmudic sources appear to prescribe. Women are excluded from public worship,[269] as well as from many other public functions. They may not appear in courts as judges or witnesses.[270] They are discouraged, though not forbidden, from conducting their own business.[271] They are discouraged

---

[267] *Y.AZ* 2,1: maybe because she is not circumcised. Esther was so successful at concealing her identity that everyone believed she came from his own nation: *B.Meg.* 13a. We may contrast this passage with the Midrashic assumption that the young Moses could not have resembled an Egyptian, even though he had been brought up in Pharaoh's household: *Tanh. Shemot* 11 (quoted in p. 68, n. 133). We may also note an implicit parallelism between non-Jews and women in the daily blessing "that He (the Almighty) has not made me a non-Jew" which is followed with the blessing: "that He has not made me a woman": *T.Ber.* 7,18 (L: 6,18); *B.Men.* 43b (the third blessing is: "that He has not made me stupid (*bur*)").

[268] Jackson notes, in his chapter on (female) witchcraft, that "general *beliefs* about witchcraft and the particular *experiences* of self-confessed witches are seldom congruent" (*op.cit.* p. 96); nonetheless, he attempts "to glean, from the distorted discourse of the oppressor, fragmentary clues 'to the antonymies (*sic*) which speak for a rival consciousness'" (p. 94). The same may be attempted, *mutatis mutandis*, here.

[269] *Torah* reading: *T.Meg.* 4,11 (L: 3,11); *B.Meg.* 23a.

[270] *Y.Sanh.* 3,9; *B.Shevu.* 30a; *Sifre Deut.* 190.

[271] The suggestion that a woman may not run an independent business is discarded in *B.Git.* 12a. However, all that a woman acquires becomes automatically her husband's

from going out to the market-place, where they are deemed likely
to stumble and sin.[272] Among the curses of Eve, women were to be
"cloaked like mourners, excommunicated from all men, and detained
in prison";[273] or on a more positive note, the following verse is quoted:
"all glorious is the king's daughter *inside*" (*Psalms* 45:14).[274] Women
are thus *confined to the home* and to the privacy of the domestic domain.[275]

It may be suggested that although the "daughters of Israel" are
theoretically fully Jewish, their confinement to the domesticity of the
home and their limited exposure to the non-Jewish, outside world
means that they are less in need of 'identity markers' (such as
circumcision and *Torah* learning) to distinguish themselves from the
non-Jews; thus, they can be 'Israel' without them. It could even be
argued that in their confinement, the very experience of ethnic
difference loses much of its relevance, and thus fades into 'subsidiary
awareness'. In other words, in the case of women the very *experience*
of being 'Israel' can be allowed, itself, to subside.

Such an argument may be taken further. We find that elements
of non-Jewish culture, though anathema to men, may be permissible
and even desirable to women. Although it is forbidden to teach Greek
to one's son,[276] R. Abbahu allows one to teach it to one's daughter,
on the basis that it is to her an "ornament".[277] Epigraphic evidence
may corroborate this point: inscriptions discovered in catacomb 20
of Beth Shearim, where 'rabbis' mentioned in our sources appear
to have been buried,[278] suggest that whereas men's names and titles

---

property: *B.Git.* 77b; *B.Kid.* 23b; etc. Men are considered fit for business (*massa u-mattan*), whereas women are not: *B.BK* 15a.

[272] *Gen.R.* 8,12. Cf *Gen.R.* 18,1: "It is the way of a woman to stay at home, and of a man to go out to the market-place".

[273] *B.Eruv.* 100b.

[274] Quoted in *B.Shevu. ib.*; *B.Git.* 12a.

[275] Such is the general argument of Wegner (1988, ch. 6; 1991), who considers that the exclusion of women from *Torah* learning and the public domain resulted in their being deprived of "spiritual and intellectual fulfilment". J. Neusner's detailed study of the Mishnaic "order of Women" leads him to the conclusion that to the authors of the Mishna, the woman is an object, an outsider (excluded from Israel?), and above all an anomaly which needs to be regularised and controlled especially in its most threatening moments, namely the transitional stages of marriage, divorce, levirate, etc. This control is achieved through the erection of complex Halakhic systems (see *A History of the Mishnaic Law of Women: part 5*, Leiden: Brill, 1980).

[276] See section IV.2.B.

[277] *Takhshit: Y.Peah* 1,1; *Y.Sot.* 9,15; *Y.Shab.* 6,1, quoted and discussed in p. 181. Shimon b. Ba disagrees with R. Abbahu. It is unclear whether "Greek" refers exclusively to Greek language in this passage.

[278] The South Western Galilean burial site of Beth Shearim was used apparently

tended to be Hebrew, those of their wives and daughters were in many cases Roman or Greek.[279] The importance of names to the constitution of personal self-identity should not be underrated.[280] It is intriguing, therefore, that Greek names and the study of Greek should be considered suitable or 'ornamental' to women. Clearly this cannot be a women-led, 'feminist' rebellion against their exclusion from the identity of Israel, since female 'Greekness' is ostensibly sanctioned, in the *Palestinian Talmud* and in Beth Shearim, by leading (male) rabbinic figures. Likewise, there is no good reason to assume that the adoption of 'Greekness' by women was reluctantly tolerated by the rabbis, as a form of controlled emancipation. Far more likely is, as I have suggested, that in their domestic confinement Jewish identity was simply considered less important for women, so that the benefits of 'Greekness' could, in their case, outweigh any other consideration.[281]

---

till the mid 4th century CE (or later). The 'rabbis' mentioned in the inscriptions of catacombs 14 and 20 can be plausibly identified with 'rabbis' of early rabbinic writings; these inscriptions constitute therefore an unique source of 'external' evidence for the study of our sources. See N. Avigad, *Beth She'arim: report on the excavations during 1953–58—vol.III: the catacombs 12–23*, transl. P. Shagiv, New Brunswick: Rutgers Press, 1976.

[279] Men's names tend to be Hebrew in the whole site of Beth Shearim; but whereas in the rest of Beth Shearim the proportion of Hebrew inscriptions is considerably lower than that of Greek inscriptions, the reverse has been found in 'rabbinic' catacombs (14 and especially 20): this suggests that these rabbis distinguished themselves through a deliberate usage of the Hebrew language (cf pp. 192–4). Nonetheless, whilst men in catacomb 20 are given the Hebrew title *Rabbi*, their wives and daughters are referred to as *Kyra* ('lady', in Greek). Thus in catacomb 20 we have Atio, daughter of R. Gamliel b. Neḥemia, and Ation, daughter of R. Yehuda b.R. Gamliel (inscription 15—Atio and Ation are obviously foreign names, though their origin is unclear); Kyra Mega wife of R. Yehoshua b.Levi (24—the latter is the name of an important figure in the *Talmudim*); Kyra Domna (20). All four belong to rabbinic families (including the latter, it seems, as her name is inscribed on the same grave as the daughter of R. Yonathan). The daughter of R. Yonathan, Miriam (21), is the only woman with a Hebrew name (two other Hebrew inscriptions have been found in the catacomb, with the names Kyrilla—sarcophagus 17—and Kyra Sh . . .—inscription 19). These inscriptions are clearly insufficient to prove that among these rabbis, Hebrew names and titles were in some way exclusive to men; but they do show that in spite of the Hebrew orientation of these rabbis, many of their own wives and daughters *could* be given a Greek name and Greek title (on the earlier period, however, see T. Ilan, "Notes on the Distribution of Jewish Women's Names in Palestine in the Second Temple and Mishnaic Periods", in *JJS* 40(2), Autumn 1989, pp. 186–200; on the basis of available evidence she concludes that in the whole of Palestine, in that earlier period, there is no major gender distinction in the proportion of bearers of Hebrew and Greek names).

[280] See pp. 192–3.

[281] This case may be compared with the late 19th century Breton women who embraced 'Frenchness' as a symbol of sophistication, finesse and femininity: see

Tzeniut: the "way" of women
In the following pages, however, I would like to propose a different
approach: namely, that it is domesticity *itself* which constitutes, in the
rabbinic perspective, the female experience of being Israel. Domesticity
is closely related to the ethos of modesty, *tzeniut* and self-concealment:
this is implied, for instance, by the *Midrash Tanḥuma* which states that
a woman should stay at home and not go out wearing jewels, as
everyone would look at her and this would be to her a blemish.[282]
I will argue that *tzeniut*, which pertains more specifically to women
than it does to men, is treated in our sources as intrinsically constitutive
of the woman's identity as 'Israel'.

I have suggested earlier that norms of bodily *tzeniut* are generally
more *extensive* for women than they are to men.[283] Our sources imply,
moreover, that these norms are also more *binding* upon them. Breaches
of *tzeniut*, on the part of women, are severely punished. The *Mishna*
rules that if a married woman goes out with her hair uncovered, spins
in the market-place (thus exposing her naked arms to the public),[284]
talks to other men, or—according to R. Tarfon—is loud-voiced and
can be heard by her neighbours, her husband may divorce her without
a *ketuba* (namely with no financial obligations):[285] indeed, the *Midrash*
glosses, she has not been *tzenua*.[286] A daughter of R. Ḥanina b. Teradyon
(and sister of Beruria) once walked with an affected gait in front of
Roman officials; appropriately, as a Divine punishment, she was
eventually condemned by the Romans to prostitution.[287]

On the other hand, the observance of *tzeniut* brings to women
considerable rewards. A woman named Kimḥit had seven sons who
all held the office of High Priest in succession, because, she said, the
beams of her house had never seen the plaits of her hair (she was
rewarded for never uncovering her hair, even in the privacy of her

---

M. McDonald 'Brittany: Politics and Women in a Minority World', in R. Ridd &
H. Callaway (eds.), *Caught up in Conflict*, London: Macmillan 1986; also M. McDonald,
"We are not French!". *Language, culture and identity in Brittany*, London and New York:
Routledge, 1989, ch. 14, esp. pp. 245–9.
    [282] *Tanh. Vayyishlah* 5.
    [283] Pp. 224–5.
    [284] *B.Ket.* 72b.
    [285] *M.Ket.* 7,6. Cf *T.Sot.* 5,9: "if a woman goes out, uncovers her hair, is wanton
with her slaves and her neighbours, spins in the market-place, and bathes with other
people (men?), one is commanded to divorce her".
    [286] *Num.R.* 8,9.
    [287] She managed however to retain her chastity, and was eventually redeemed
by her brother-in-law R. Meir: *B.AZ* 18a.

own home).[288] A bride who is *tzenua* in her 'in-law's' house has the merit of begetting priests and prophets.[289] Or as later *Midrashim* put it, a woman who conceals (*matzna'at*) herself at home is fit to be married to a High Priest.[290]

Tzeniut, however, is a virtue which naturally pertains to women. Our sources suggest that women are so imbued with *tzeniut* that they are *embarrassed* to go with their head uncovered.[291] A man once uncovered a woman's head in the market-place, and was ordered to pay her 400 *zuz*—a considerable sum—for having put her to such shame.[292] Any form of public exposure is a "blemish" to women, which is why, as I have quoted, a woman should stay at home and not go out wearing jewels, for everyone would look at her and this would be to her a blemish.[293] The fact that women are (allegedly) embarrassed when being uncovered or exposed, and consider this to be a form of personal "blemish"—which is not found, in our sources, with reference to men—suggests that according to our sources, the *habitus* of domesticity and *tzeniut* is firmly rooted in women and an integral part of their ontological nature. Indeed, as other sources put it, it is "a woman's way" to stay at home;[294] it is "*her way*" to be *tzenua*.[295]

The *habitus* of *tzeniut* is, moreover, an essential part of their *ontogenetic* condition. *Genesis Rabba* tells us that Eve was created from a rib, a part of the body which remains concealed (*tzanua*)—"so that she should be *tzenua* and stay at home"[296]—and at every limb that God created, He told her: "be a *tzenua* woman, a *tzenua* woman".[297] Admittedly,

---

[288] *Y.Yoma* 1,1; *Y.Meg.* 1,10; *Y.Hor.* 3,2; *B.Yoma* 47a; *Lev.R.* 20,11; *Tanh. Aharei* 7; *Tanh.B. Aharei* 9.

[289] *B.Sot.* 10b.

[290] *Num.R.* 1,3; *Tanh. Vayyishlah* 6; *Tanh. Bamidbar* 3.

[291] *Gen.R.* 17,8. Embarrassment (*busha*), just as *tzeniut*, is a specifically female quality: an orphan girl should be married off before an orphan boy, because as a woman she is more embarrassed (to find a spouse) than the man: *T.Ket.* 6,8; *B.Ket.* 67b (similarly, a woman asks for intercourse in her heart, whereas a man asks for it in words: *B.Eruv.* 100b).

[292] *B.BK* 91a on the *Mishna*.

[293] *Tanh. Vayyishlah* 5.

[294] *Gen.R.* 18,1. Cf *Y.Yev.* 7,1; *B.Git.* 71a: "it is not a woman's *way* to go around law-courts"; *B.Ket.* 67a: "it is not a woman's *way* to go begging from door to door".

[295] *B.Shab.* 53b: a man married a woman with a stumped finger, but never noticed it until the day of her death. Said Rabbi: "See how *tzenu'a* was this woman, that her husband never noticed it!". R. Hiyya replied: "As to the woman, *this is her way* (i.e. *tzeniut* is natural to her and needs no praise); but how *tzanua* was the man, that he never noticed it!".

[296] A gloss in the version of *Tanh. Vayyeshev* 6.

[297] *Gen.R.* · 18,2.

the *Midrash* concludes with disappointment that women turned out
to be arrogant, inquisitive, eavesdroppers, jealous, thievish, run-
about,[298] and talkative[299]—the very opposite, in a sense, of the *tzeniut*
which had been planned. Yet in spite of these accidental shortcomings,
it remains that the woman's intrinsic, ontogenetic nature was fundamentally, by design, *tzeniut*.

Tzeniut and the identity of Israel

The laws of *tzeniut* in *M.Ket.* 7,6, quoted above, are referred to by
the *Mishna* as *dat Yehudit*, the 'law of a Jewess'; whereas other
commandments, namely tithes, menstrual purity, dough offering, and
oaths, are referred to by the same *mishna* as *dat Moshe*, the law of
Moses. The expression *dat Yehudit*, not found elsewhere in rabbinic
writings, is no doubt of highest significance. It implies, firstly, that
the virtue of *tzeniut* belongs not to women in general, but specifically
to *Jewish* women. Secondly, since the 'law of a Jewess' consists *specifically*
in being *tzanua* (as opposed to other commandments, which come
under the heading of 'law of Moses'), we *may* infer that *tzeniut* represents
the specific feature of a woman's identity *as Jewish*.

Various *Midrashim* present *tzeniut*, indeed, as exclusive to the "daughters of Israel". Non-Jewish women are generally considered even *less
tzanua* than Potiphar's infamous, adulterous wife.[300] By contrast, it is
"the way of the daughters of Israel" to cover their hair,[301] and again,
it is "their way" to be neither loud-voiced, nor high-paced, nor wanton[302]
with laughter.[303] The daughters of Israel are "worthy (*kesherot*) and
tzenuot".[304] This suggests, therefore, that in the rabbinic perspective
tzeniut could be experienced by Jewish women as *their way of 'being
Israel'*.[305]

---

[298] *Gen.R. ib.*

[299] *Tanh. ib.* See also *B.Kid.* 49b: "ten measures of talk came down to the world;
the women took nine, and the rest of the world took one".

[300] *Tanh. Vayyeshev* 6.

[301] In contrast with non-Jewish women: *Num.R.* 9,16 and 33. However in *B.Sanh.*
58b it is implied that non-Jewish women also cover their hair.

[302] *Perutzot*, often used as antonymous to *tzenuot*.

[303] *Num.R.* 9,12; *Tanh. Naso* 2. However, when Naomi converted Ruth, she warned
her that "it is not the way of the daughters of Israel to go to the theatres and circuses
of the non-Jews . . . to live in a dwelling with no *mezuza* . . . etc." (but without any
reference to *tzeniut*): *Ruth R.* 2,22.

[304] *Song R.* 2,15,2.

[305] This tentative suggestion should not be regarded as a merely apologetic response
to Wegner's feminist critique of the exclusion of Jewish women from the commandments
and the public domain. I would point out that 'spiritual fulfilment'—whatever this

Since men and women are firmly distinguished in *halakha* and rabbinic traditions, their experience of Jewish identity was bound to be substantially different. I am suggesting that according to our sources, the female experience of Jewish identity is grounded not in a distinctive *praxis*, as with the men's commandments, but rather in a *habitus* or *hexis*, which we have identified as *tzeniut*. But although in the main *praxis* is male and *habitus* is female, the *habitus* of *tzeniut* is also characteristic of men's experience of Jewish identity albeit, no doubt, to a lesser degree. Through the medium of a *habitus* which is to some extent "transposable" between both sexes, a *similar* experience of belonging to Israel can arise. *Tzeniut* facilitates therefore the emergence of what Bourdieu calls "collective orchestration": an intersubjective, commonly shared experience, which justifies the unequivocal inclusion of women among the peoplehood of Israel.

E. *Conclusion*

My aim in this section has been to argue that the solipsistic and centripetal stance of Jewish identity is not necessarily a protective strategy against an external threat, but is related to the general ontology and *habitus* of Jewish (male and, particularly female) experience. The *habitus* of *tzeniut* characterizes not only the *praxis* of Jewish identity, such as circumcision and *Torah* learning, but also the rabbinic general experience of *being*. There is thus a congruence between 'being Jewish' and simply 'being-in-the-world'. *Tzeniut*, introversion and self-effacement characterize the experience of being Israel as much as any other aspect of the rabbinic personal identity; they are, to the authors of our sources, the natural way of being.

3. TRANSCENDENCE: THE ALMIGHTY AND ISRAEL

"The Holy Blessed Be He, the *Torah*, and Israel, are One"—popular paraphrase of the *Zohar*, III, 73a.

The relationship between the Almighty and Israel is perhaps the most important feature of early rabbinic Jewish identity. As we have seen in the second chapter, the main constituents of Jewish identity are those commandments which enact Israel's covenantal relationship with the Almighty. This theme has been encountered in a number of ways throughout my work, as I have summed up at the beginning of this chapter. It is appropriate, therefore, that we conclude this study with a more detailed analysis of this crucial notion.

In a certain sense, the relationship between the Almighty and Israel completes and complements the ethos of *tzeniut* which we have just examined; in another sense, it succeeds in transcending it. On the one hand, indeed, we have encountered in the previous section the notion of the *Shekhina* (Divine Presence) as encompassing and overwhelming the person, to the extent that self-concealment becomes the only appropriate manner of being in its presence. In this sense, it is the relationship between Israel and the Divine which generates its ontologically 'centripetal' way of being. On the other hand, however, the presence of the *Shekhina* is considered not a burden to Israel but rather a privilege; to quote just one passage: "Israel are dear, for wherever they go into exile, the *Shekhina* goes together with them".[306] As I will argue in this section, the intimate bond between the Almighty and Israel does not stifle the authors of our sources into *tzeniut*, implosion and ultimate self-annihilation.[307] On the contrary, it provides them, simultaneously, with a transcendental experience which might prove to be just as crucial, in itself, to the constitution of the identity of Israel.

A. *Endearment to the Almighty*

The phrase "Israel are dear" (*havivim Tisrael*)[308]—meaning, in most cases, that Israel are dear to the Almighty[309]—is frequent in all our sources.[310] With the exception perhaps of one passage in *Avot*, where the phrase "Israel are dear" is correlated with the saying: "man (*adam*)

---

expression (Wegner's) is supposed to mean—can be achieved through alternative means (e.g. *tzeniut*) and not just through the male activities of public worship and *Torah* learning.

[306] *Mekh. dRShbT*, beginning; *B.Meg.* 29a.

[307] As, according to Laing, does the schizophrenic: see p. 218, note 131.

[308] As in the passage just quoted. For the sake of convenience, I have consistently translated the root *ḤVV* as 'dear' with all its English derivatives ('endear', etc.).

[309] As explicit in *Mekh. Vayyassa* 2, *Gen.R.* 80,7, *Lev.R.* 2,4, and *Pes.R.* 20,3. See also *Num.R.* 2,15: Israel are dear to the Almighty even if they sin. In some passages it is unclear to whom Israel are endeared, though it is probably, again, to the Almighty: "Israel are dear" because they are called 'priests' (*Sifre Num.* 119) or the Almighty's 'sons' (*M.Avot* 3,14; cf *Ex.R.* 27,9), because they have been given the *Torah* (*M.Avot ib.*; cf *Deut.R.* 8,7), because the Almighty encompassed them with the commandments of *tefillin, mezuza*, fringes (*Sifre Deut.* 36; *B.Men.* 43b), because the nations atone for them (*Mekh. Nezikin* 10).

[310] See J. Neusner (*op.cit.* 1989, e.g. p. 110), who claims that in the earlier sources, the notion of endearment reaches its richest expression in the *Palestinian Talmud* and in *Leviticus Rabba*.

is dear, for he was created in the image (of God)",[311] the nations are implicitly excluded from this endearement. Indeed, Israel are "dearer" than the nations,[312] "dearer" even than the angels.[313]

Endearment can also take the form of friendship, possession, and even kinship with the Almighty, which I will now describe on the basis of a wide range of early rabbinic sources.

Friendship, betrothal

Israel are always friends of the Almighty;[314] they are close to Him,[315] whereas the nations are alien to Him.[316] Israel are the Almighty's bride; they were betrothed by Him at Mount Sinai.[317] In ten scriptural passages they are called a "bride", corresponding to which the Almighty puts on ten different garments.[318]

Possession

Israel are a possession of the Almighty,[319] His inheritance,[320] His find,[321] His people.[322] "Israel are Mine", He says;[323] and conversely, in the liturgy, Israel is referred to as "Your people".[324] They are His slaves,[325] and may not be enslaved to any other slave (i.e. to each other).[326] The Almighty is to them as a shepherd to his flock, a guardian to his orchard.[327]

In some respects, however, Israel and the Almighty are in *reciprocal* possession of each other, for the passage just quoted also says: "He

---

[311] *M.Avot* 3,14. But as to whether non-Jews enter the category of *adam*, see section I.4.B (beginning).

[312] *Targum Onkelos ad Ex.*19:5; *Song R.* 1, s.v. *ki tovim*, end; *Tanh. Ki Tissa* 8.

[313] *Sifre Deut.* 306; *B.Hul.* 91b.

[314] *Y.Ber.* 9,1; *Sifre Deut.* 19. Cf *Ex.R.* 27,9; *ib.* 52,1; *Num.R.* 13,2; *Deut.R.* 3,11.

[315] *Y.Ber.* 9,1.

[316] *Est.R.* 7,13.

[317] *Tanh. Ekev* 11. Cf *Mekh. Bahodesh* 3.

[318] *Pes.dRK* 22,2; *Deut.R.* 2,37; *Song R.* 4,10.

[319] *Avot* 6 (= *Kinyan Torah*),10; *Sifre Deut.* 309; *Mekh. Shira* 9; *B.Pes.* 87b.

[320] *Mekh. Shira* 10.

[321] *Gen.R.* 29,3.

[322] *B.Yoma* 84a.

[323] *Sifre Num.* 92; *Ex.R.* 30,1; *Ruth R., pet.*1. Especially when they are holy: *Mekh. Nezikin* 20; *Tanh. Beha'alotekha* 11.

[324] *M.Ber.* 4,4; *T.Ber.* 3,7. The nations, on the other hand, do not belong to God but to the treasury chest of Gehenna: *Pes.R.* 10,5.

[325] *B.BB* 10a; *Num.R.* 16,27; *ib.* 23,11.

[326] *B.BM* 10a.

[327] *Song R.* 2,16,1, s.v. *dodi*; cf *Midrash Tehillim* 23,1.

is my God and I am His people".[328] Similarly, the Almighty is not the 'God of the nations', but specifically the 'God of Israel'.[329]

Kinship

Israel and the Almighty are akin to each other, most frequently as *sons and Father*: "Israel are dear, for they are called the sons (or children) of the Almighty".[330] Because He loves them, the Almighty calls them "my son, my first-born" (*Ex.*4:22);[331] Israel are His only son.[332] R. Yehuda holds that Israel are only called "sons" if they behave like sons; but R. Meir maintains that this title is unconditional: "in either case, you are called 'sons'".[333]

The Almighty, in turn, is "their Father in Heaven".[334] R. Akiva addressed Him in prayer as "our Father, our King".[335]

Israel are also *brothers* of the Almighty,[336] which is why, again, they are dear to Him.[337] They are always His brothers, His friends.[338]

Even more daringly, the *Midrashim* suggest that Israel are a *mother* to the Almighty: thus "'"His mother"—this is Israel".[339] R. Eliezer b.R. Yose said in the name of his father that the Almighty, who loved Israel excessively (*yoter mi-day*), originally called Israel 'daughter'; He

---

[328] *Song R.ib.*

[329] *Ruth R.ib.* According to *Num.R.* 9,7 this depends on Israel remaining holy and restrained from adultery. On the Almighty as the "God of Israel", see Samuel S. Cohon, "The Name of God. A Study in Rabbinic Theology", in *HUCA* 23(1), 1950–1, p. 602 (unfortunately Cohon provides no references, and the list of expressions he discusses is clearly not exhaustive).

[330] *Avot* 3,14; *Sifre Deut.* 15; *ib.* 96; *Y.RH* 1,3; *B.Shab.* 31a; *B.BB* 10a; minor tractate *Gerim* 1,5; *Ex.R.* 34,3; *ib.* 46,4; *Est.R.* 7,13; *Song R.* 2,16,1, s.v. *dodi*; *Eccl.R.* 4,8; *Tanh. Yitro* 5; *Midrash Tehillim* 23,1; etc.

[331] *B.Shab.* 31a.

[332] *Lev.R.* 2,5, drawing on the reference to the Israelites, in the Bible, as "sons (children) of Israel".

[333] *Sifre Deut.* 96; *B.Kid.* 36a; cf *B.BB* 10a. The Father-son metaphor is already common in the Bible: in the *Sifre* this dispute is presented as a comment on *Deut.* 14:1 ("You are sons of the Lord . . ."), whilst four other verses are adduced in *B.Kid.*

[334] *T.Shab.* 14,5; *B.Shab.* 116a; *Sifra Kedoshim* 10,8; *Song R.* 7,11; etc. See also *Ex.R.* 30,5; *Num.R.* 17,1; *Tanh. Shelah* 14: "'father' is the Almighty; 'son' are Israel".

[335] *B.Taan.* 25b.

[336] Cf *Midrash Tehillim* 23,1.

[337] *Sifre Deut.* 15; *Eccl.R.* 4,8; *Tanh. Yitro* 5.

[338] *Y.Ber.* 9,1; *Sifre Deut.* 15.

[339] *Sifra Shemini* 1,15, based on *Song* 3:11 (where 'King Solomon' is interpreted as the Almighty and His 'crown' as the Tabernacle). In this *Midrash*, Israel are called simultaneously God's 'daughters' and His 'mother'; the usage of such divergent kinship metaphors is apparently not considered problematic. The same occurs in the following passage.

went on loving them until He called them 'sister'; He went on loving them until He finally called them 'My mother'. When R. Shimon b. Yoḥai heard this, he stood up and kissed R. Eliezer on his head, exclaiming: "if only for hearing this homily from your mouth, it would have been worth my coming!".[340]

B. 'Chosenness' and reciprocity

"He chooses Israel"

On the one hand, the relationship between Israel and the Almighty is initiated entirely by Him: He created and "chose" them,[341] hence the liturgical phrase: "He who chooses Israel".[342] Of all the nations that He has created, He loves only Israel;[343] He cannot exchange them for another nation.[344] "He has conferred His Name upon Israel above all".[345] According to *Pirkei deRabbi Eliezer*, whereas each nation came under the tutelage of an angel, Israel came under the direct tutelage of the Almighty Himself.[346]

Israel enjoy preferential treatment from Him, which according to the *Babylonian Talmud*, the angels themselves have questioned as unfair.[347] *Song Rabba* presents Israel as the younger sister of the nations; just as the youngest of the family is forgiven for her wrongdoings, so Israel are forgiven on the Day of Atonement—even if, the *Midrash* specifies, they worship *avoda zara* in the same way as the nations.[348] Elsewhere, we hear that even though Israel are just as sinful as the nations, the Almighty does not wage his anger against them, for they are the "younger sister".[349] In all these passages, therefore, it is clearly the

---

[340] *Song R.* 3, end; *Ex.R.* 52,5; *Num.R.* 12,8.

[341] *Lev.R.* 27,5; cf *Num.R.* 14,9.

[342] *Haboḥer be-Yisrael*: *Y.Yoma* 7,1; *Y.Sot.* 7,6.

[343] *Deut.R.* 5,7. The *Sifre* (*Deut.* 24) dismisses emphatically the suggestion that Almighty could possibly hate Israel: it is only they who (occasionally) hate Him. Cf *Tanḥ. Ki Tissa* 8: "the Almighty desires to mention Israel at all times".

[344] *Ruth R.*, *pet.*3.

[345] *Mekh. Nezikin* 20; cf *Ex.R.* 29,4; *Num.R.* 5,6. According to *Num.R.* 9,7 this depends on Israel remaining holy and restrained from adultery.

[346] *PdRE* 24. Cf *Deut.R.* 2,34.

[347] *B.Ber.* 20b.

[348] *Song R.* 8,8.

[349] *Num.R.* 2,16. J. Heinemann, *op.cit.*, pp. 175–9, shows how a Palestinian *Midrash* depicting God's preferential love for Israel during the crossing of the Red Sea is radically re-formulated in *B.Meg.* 10b in such a way as to depict, on the contrary, God's mercy towards the Egyptians, as follows:

Almighty who initiates and maintains his preference for Israel, even in cases where they go astray from Him.

Reciprocity

On the other hand, the relationship between the Almighty and Israel is initiated on a remarkably reciprocal basis. We have already noted this reciprocity in terms of their mutual possession and of their parallel ties of kinship (as brothers, or as father and mother to each other). This reciprocity is further explicitated in many *Midrashim*. It may account for the quasi-divine nature of Israel which, we have seen, some passages hyperbolically suggest.[350] To some extent, indeed, reciprocity suggests that the Almighty and Israel are on equal standing.

Thus, God chooses Jacob, and Jacob chooses God.[351] Israel's only share (*ḥelek*) is the Almighty, and the Almighty's only share is Israel.[352] The Almighty sanctifies Israel, and Israel sanctify Him.[353] They were at Mount Sinai each other's guarantors.[354] Israel are compared to the olive and the Almighty to the lamp—hence, they produce light in conjunction, as the Almighty says: "since My light is your light and your light is Mine, let us go and bring light to Zion".[355]

Reciprocity is most vividly depicted in the context of prayer and liturgy. According to the *Sifre*, indeed, the prayers of Israel are echoed by those of the Almighty. Israel say the verse, "There is none like God", and in reply the Holy Spirit continues it, "like God is *Yeshurun* (i.e. Israel)".[356] They say the verse, "Who is like You, Lord?" (*Ex.* 15:11) and He answers with the verse, "Happy are you, Israel, who is like you?" (*Deut.* 33:29); Israel say, in the *shema*, "Hear Israel, the

---

The ministering angels wanted to chant a hymn; but the Almighty said: 'the work of my hands is being drowned in the sea, and you shall chant a hymn?' However, it is impossible to draw from this isolated case a general distinction between Palestinian and Babylonian sources on the topic of the Almighty's preference for Israel, particularly as Heinemann himself argues that this particular case of re-formulation by the *Babylonian Talmud* is largely due to the specific context of tractate *Meg.*

[350] See pp. 41–2.
[351] *Sifre Deut.* 312.
[352] *Midrash Tehillim* 28,1.
[353] *Ex.R.* 15,24.
[354] *Ex.R.* 27,9. According to *Num.R.* 15,18, God's throne is "as it were" securely based only when Israel form a united whole.
[355] *Pes.dRK* 21,4.
[356] *Deut.* 33:26. The verse actually reads: "There is none like God, *Yeshurun*" (or perhaps: "there is none like the God of *Yeshurun*").

Lord our God the Lord is *one*",[357] and He answers, "Who is like Israel, Your people, a *single* nation on earth?".[358]

Similarly, the *Babylonian Talmud* conceives of the Almighty as wearing *tefillin*; whereas the *tefillin* of Israel contain the text of the *shema*, the *tefillin* of the Almighty contain the reciprocal verse just quoted.[359] Moreover, the injunction to love God in the second verse of the *shema* (*Deut.* 4:7) is implicitly reciprocated in the morning and evening services, where the recitation of the *shema* is preceded with a blessing entitled: "A great love" (or "An everlasting love"),[360] which apparently invokes the reciprocal love of God for Israel.[361]

Thus the daily recitation of the *shema* and the wearing of *tefillin* represent not only Israel's profession of the monotheistic faith, but also, by implication, the Almighty's reciprocal profession of the singularity of the Jewish people. The relevance of the saying of *shema* to the identity and singularity of Israel also finds expression, perhaps, in the following *Midrash*:

> No nation in the world is like Israel: as soon as they wake up they recite *shema* and proclaim the kingdom of the Almighty.[362]

C. *Concreteness and transcendence*

To achieve a state of reciprocal endearment with the Almighty may be of eminent importance to our sources, but what this experience actually consists of—'what it is like', in pragmatic, experiential terms, to be reciprocally endeared to Him—is difficult for us to gage. A phenomenological analysis of this experience may be called for at this stage. Although transcendental, this experience is not merely 'abstract' or theoretical; as we have seen, it is predicated on the bodily observance of commandments such as *tefillin*, and thus constitutes a *concrete* reality in the rabbis' day-to-day existence. This transcendental

---

[357] *Deut.* 6:4. The *shema*, a centrepiece of the liturgy, is recited twice a day: cf *M.Ber.* 1–3 *passim*.

[358] I*Chron.* 17:21—*Sifre Deut.* 355. Cf *Mekh. Shira* 3.

[359] *B.Ber.* 6a. The *Talmud* adds, to the *Sifre*, the following verses: "For what great nation is there . . . and what great nation is there etc." (*Deut.* 4:7–8); "Happy are you, Israel, who is like you? etc." (*Deut.* 33:29); "Or has God tried etc." (*Deut.* 4:34); and "To make you high above all nations" (*Deut.* 26:19). Cf *Mekh. Shira* 3.

[360] *B.Ber.* 11b.

[361] As explicit in later, mediaeval liturgical sources, and implicit already in *B.Ber.* (*ib.*) which quotes in this context a verse where it is God who tells Israel: "I have loved you with everlasting love" (*Jer.* 31:2).

[362] *Tanh. Balak* 14.

experience may be defined, possibly, as self-surpassing yet in a holistic manner: the whole person, body and soul, may be experienced as 'going beyond' their natural confines towards their encounter with the Almighty.[363]

A medium which, in our sources, invests this experience with further concreteness is the metaphor. The purpose of the metaphors we have listed in this section is not merely descriptive: by referring to *concrete* images such as betrothal, slavery or kinship, they generate in themselves—at least in the perception of our sources—a feeling that this transcendental relationship is concretely real.[364] For instance, the metaphor of the olive (i.e. Israel) and the lamp (i.e. the Almighty) suggests with much immediacy that Israel dwell, *concretely*, inside the Almighty: for as the same *Midrash* stresses, "it is usual for oil to be put inside the lamp".[365] The notion that Israel are physically immersed inside the Almighty is also suggested in the following *mishna*:

> In the same way as a pool of water (*mikve*) purifies the impure, so the Almighty purifies Israel.[366]

Conversely, the notion that the Almighty is "the heart of Israel"[367] implies that the Almighty, in turn, dwells inside the body or bodily intimacy of Israel.

A number of such metaphors are based, in this context, on the theme of clothing, which conjures up again an experience of considerable bodily potency. For instance:

---

[363] Transcendence should not be confused, as it often is, with disembodiment or abstraction. Whereas 'abstract' means, according to the *Shorter Oxford Dictionary*, "*separated from matter, practice, or particulars*", transcendence implies no more than a notion of 'surpassing', 'excelling', or in its etymological sense, '*going beyond*'. Although the experience of being related to the Almighty 'goes beyond' the immediate experience of human existence, this does not entail that it is 'disembodied' or divorced from bodily *praxis*.

[364] See M. Black, *Models and Metaphors: Studies in Language and Philosophy*, Ithaca: Cornell University Press, 1962. Black argues that a metaphor (M), which has a 'literal meaning' (L), is not based on a pre-existing similarity between them (M and L) but quite on the contrary creates it. Metaphors are not merely substitutional figures of speech: they generate a novel interaction between M and L in such as way as to produce considerable shifts of meaning (in L as well as in M). Metaphors are thus a unique mode of cognition, which cannot be replaced with direct references to the 'literal meaning' alone. In our case, I am arguing that they implicitly induce a 'concrete' perception of Israel's relationship with the Almighty.

[365] *Pes.dRK* 21,4, above quoted.

[366] *M.Yoma* 8,9.

[367] As a gloss on the verse: "I (Israel) am asleep, but my heart is awaken" (*Song* 5:2): *Pes.R.* 15,6; *Pes.dRK* 5,6; *Song R.* 5,2,1; *Tanh.B. Toldot* 18.

Every day, the upper worlds crown the Almighty with three 'holies'[368]
... the Almighty places two of them on the heads of Israel.[369]
Israel are clothed with the Almighty's clothes—which are might ... the
Almighty gave them to Israel.[370]

Reciprocally, Israel are themselves the clothing which the Almighty
wears:

Israel are the (royal) purple cloak, through which the Almighty is
glorified.[371]

According to *Leviticus Rabba*, the Almighty is comparable to a king
who told his slave (i.e. Moses) to take special care of his purple cloak
(i.e. Israel), to fold it and to shake it out; the slave asked why this
garment, of all garments, deserved such special treatment; he answered,
"because I wore it on the day I was made king". Alternatively, the
Midrash goes on, Israel are like the King's shirt, which he instructed
his slave to fold and to shake out; the slave inquired, and he replied:
"because I wear it *against my body*".[372] Nothing could adhere closer
to the 'body' of the Almighty than His clothing; but it is the emphasis
on *physical* contact (in the last passage) which I find particularly striking.
Similarly, the daily, *physical* act of donning clothes is associated in
the *Babylonian Talmud* with the transcendental relationship between
the Almighty and Israel:

When a person fastens his girdle, he should say: "Blessed is He who
girds Israel with might".
When he spreads his turban over his head, he should say: "Blessed
is He who crowns Israel with glory".[373]

A phenomenological approach to early rabbinic experience is limited
by the evidence at our disposal; our sources cannot be more than
suggestive. It is difficult to grasp the experiential significance of
statements such as, "the Almighty purifies Israel",[374] "the Almighty
keeps guard on them outside",[375] or "the Almighty waits upon them".[376]

---

[368] *Kedushot*: a reference to *Isaiah* 6:3.
[369] *Lev.R.* 24,8.
[370] *Ex.R.* 8,1.
[371] *Est.R.* 7,10. Cf *Ex.R.* 21,4: "the Almighty crowns himself with the prayers of
Israel".
[372] *Lev.R.* 2,4: lit. "I stick it against my body".
[373] *B.Ber.* 60b.
[374] *M.Yoma* 8,9, quoted above; *Midrash Mishlei* 20,9.
[375] *B.AZ* 11a.
[376] "*Yisrael mishtameshim bo*", i.e. Israel are waited upon by Him: *Ex.R.* 38,4.

Clearly, however, it is the *concreteness* of these phrases which gives Israel's relationship with the Almighty its vividness and reality, and which contributes, perhaps, towards its experiential veracity.[377]

D. *Solipsism and transcendence*

The security of transcendence

If we now turn to the *function* which the transcendental relationship of Israel with the Almighty may serve, a comparison with R.D. Laing's study may again prove useful. According to Laing, the experience of transcendence is *functionally* similar, in the case of schizophrenia, to that of isolation and solipsism.[378] Indeed, the schizophrenic commonly attempts to transcend his body and person so as to overcome the threat of 'engulfment' and loss of identity. His self becomes disembodied, "detached", "never revealed directly in the individual's expressions and actions . . . (his) relationship to the other is always at one remove" (p. 80). Transcendent, he fancies that he is out of danger and free (p. 86, and generally ch. 5).[379]

Likewise, we find the notion in our sources that Israel's transcendental relationship with the Almighty leads to ontological security. It is this relationship, indeed, which saves Israel from 'engulfment':

> If I leave Israel as they are, they will be swallowed up among the nations;
> let Me set my great Name among them, and they will survive.[380]

Their transcendent relationship with the Almighty itself cannot be challenged, for

> if all the nations gathered together to abolish the love which is between
> the Almighty and Israel, they would not succeed.[381]

---

[377] Cf *B.Sanh.* 58b (quoted in p. 41): "if a non-Jew slaps the jaw of a Jew, it is as though he slapped the jaw of the Divine Presence".

[378] See pp. 217–20, quoting R.D. Laing *op.cit.*

[379] According to Laing (quoted in p. 218, note 131), in the case of schizophrenia these strategies lead to a sense of emptiness, desiccation and death. The quasi-concreteness, in rabbinic sources, of the transcendental relationship between the Almighty and Israel (see above) may be crucial in turning 'transcendentalism' into an experience which is ontologically viable, as opposed to the pathological experience of transcendental disembodiment described by Laing.

[380] *Y.Taan.* 2,6. Cf *Midrash Tehillim* 17,9: the Almighty saves Israel from drowning in the sea of the nations. Quoted in p. 219.

[381] *Ex.R.* 49,1; *Num.R.* 2,16. The nations have been warned by the Almighty that Israel are His: *Ex.R.* 30,1.

On a transcendental plane, Israel are out of reach from the nations and completely impregnable.

Exclusion and solipsism

Transcendence over the nations is thus functionally similar to the solipsistic negation of their existence, which I have discussed in the first section of this chapter. As strategies against the threat of ontological engulfment, transcendence and solipsism are often difficult, in fact, to distinguish.[382] In some respects, the transcendental relationship of Israel with the Almighty is itself, simultaneously, solipsistic. The nations, indeed, are *excluded* from Israel's relationship with the Almighty. For instance, according to the *Babylonian Talmud*, Moses asked that the *Shekhina* (the Divine Presence) should rest only on Israel and not upon the nations, and this request was granted.[383] In an allegorical interpretation of the *Song of Songs*, R. Akiva depicts the nations as asking Israel why they are so in love with the Almighty (*Song* 5:9) and why they do not assimilate with them; when Israel tell them some of His praises (in *Song* 5:10–16), the nations decide instead to assimilate with Israel (*Song* 6:1); whereupon Israel reply:

> you have no share (*helek*) in Him, for "My Beloved is to me, and I am to Him" (*Song* 2:16), "I am to my Beloved, and my Beloved is to me" (*Song* 6:3).[384]

We have also seen, finally, how the exclusion of the nations from the observance of *shabbat* is depicted as an exclusion from Israel's intimate 'conversation' with the Almighty.[385]

Underlying this exclusion may lie an implicit perception that Israel are *alone* in the world with the Almighty. We have seen how the *shema* and *tefillin* express at the same time the oneness of God and that of Israel, "a *single* nation on earth"; and as the *Babylonian Talmud* adds in the same passage, the Almighty has said to Israel: "since you have made Me a single entity[386] in the world, I will make you a single

---

[382] It should be noted that in Laing's analysis of schizophrenia, the strategies of transcendence and of solipsism are largely conflated.

[383] *B.Ber.* 7a. The last verse of the Song of Songs is read as a similar request: "'Escape, my beloved'—from the nations, and adhere to Israel": *Song R.*, end.

[384] *Mekh. Shira* 3; *Sifre Deut.* 343. See also *Eliyahu R.* 7, paraphrasing Song 1:4: "The Almighty has led me into His innermost chambers, but He has not done so to any kingdom or nation".

[385] See pp. 207–8.

[386] 'Entity': *hativa* in the *Babylonian Talmud* (see also *Targum Onkelos ad Deut.* 26:17–8);

entity in the world".[387] Monotheism (God is one) is thus mirrored with '*monoethnism*' (Israel are one), which suggests somehow that the nations (just as alien, pagan gods) do not exist. In a later *Midrash*, indeed, God is depicted as saying:

> "It was My intention that I and you should be in the world, for I am a father and you are My sons—how could I insert other nations between us?".[388]

In this respect, Israel's relationship with the Almighty is itself, just as the general experience of being Israel, a solitary and solipsistic experience.

E. *Conclusion: Israel and covenantal transcendence*

Israel's relationship with the Almighty cannot be restricted, however, to the *function* of ensconcing their identity and rendering it, in their perspective, impregnable. As I have argued with *tzeniut*, an ontological experience such as this cannot be described exclusively in terms of a 'function' or of a 'strategy'. Transcendence must be seen, primarily, as a fundamental experience which is characteristic and *constitutive* of the identity of Israel. This experience is related to the notion, discussed above in the second chapter, that Jewish identity consists essentially of practices with an explicit *covenantal* connotation, such as circumcision, *shabbat*, and *Torah* learning,[389] which embody a covenant between the Almighty and Israel. According to *Pes.dRK*, it was a reciprocal covenant with the Almighty which formed the basis of their election at Mount Sinai, and which turned them into a "whole nation"[390] and gave them the distinctive name of 'Israel'.[391] The embodied but transcendental and solipsistic experience of the Almighty, which I have attempted to describe in this section, constitutes therefore the *ontogenetic* essence of the identity of Israel.

   This said, we should not lose sight of the fact that from the perspective of our sources, adhering to the Almighty constitutes a goal in its own

---

imra in *Mekh*. The meaning of these terms is unclear.

[387] *B.Ber*. 6a (cf *B.Hag*. 3a); *Mekh. Shira* 3; *Tanh. Tavo* 2.

[388] *Tanh. Mishpatim* 17.

[389] As well as *shema* and *tefillin*, as we have seen in this section, although their covenantal nature is not explicit in the scriptures and only expounded in rabbinic writings.

[390] *Pes. dRK* 1,2.

[391] *Pes. dRK* 12, 23 and *Tanh.B. Va'era* 1 ("My people"); *ib. Yitro* 15 ("Israel"); all quoted in p. 74.

right; it is not seen, in first instance, as a means to constitute the identity of 'Israel'. In spite of what has been found in this study, the pursuit of Jewish identity remains, in our sources, a matter of secondary importance.[392] On that basis, our proposition could be, if anything, reversed: namely, that Jewish identity or 'being Israel' could itself be perceived, by the authors of our sources, as a means towards achieving greater proximity to the Almighty. Indeed, in so far as it is ontogenetically related to the Almighty, the notion of 'Israel' may represent in itself a powerful, concrete embodiment of Divine transcendence.

---

[392] See my remarks in the introduction (pp. xiv–xv). I have also shown in chapter IV how dissociation and dissimilation from the non-Jews are presented in our sources more often as means of averting *avoda zara*, than as strategies of resistance against non-Jewish assimilation.

BIBLIOGRAPHY

ALON Gedalia, review article on S. Lieberman, *Greek in Jewish Palestine*, in *Kirjath Sepher* 20, 1943–4, pp. 76–95 (Hebrew).

ALON Gedalia, *Jews, Judaism and the Classical World*, (trans. I. Abrahams), Jerusalem: Hebrew University, 1977, pp. 146–189.

AVIGAD Nahman, *Beth She'arim: report on the excavations during 1953–58—vol. III: the catacombs 12–23*, transl. P. Shagiv, New Brunswick: Rutgers Press, 1976.

AVISHOR Y., *"Darkhe haEmori"* (Hebrew), in H. Rabin *et al.* (eds.), *Studies in the Bible and the Hebrew Language offered to Meir Wallenstein*, Jerusalem: Kiryat Sepher, 1979, pp. 17–47.

BAMBERGER B.J., *Proselytism in the Talmudic period*, New York: Ktav, 1968 (1939).

BARTH Fredrik (ed.), *Ethnic Groups and Boundaries*, Bergen/Oslo/London, 1969.

BARTHES Roland, *Image, Music, Text*, (ed. and transl. S. Heath), Glasgow: Fontana 1977.

BATAILLE George, *L'Eroticisme*, Paris: Editions de Minuit, 1957.

BEER M., "Notes on three edicts", in S. Shaked (ed.), *Irano-Judaica* vol. 1, Jerusalem: Yad Ben-Zvi, 1982, (Hebrew).

BLACK M., *Models and Metaphors: Studies in Language and Philosophy*, Ithaca: Cornell University Press, 1962.

BLACKING J. (ed.), *The Anthropology of the Body*, London: Academic Press, 1977.

BONFANTE L., "Nudity as costume in Classical art", in *American Journal of Archaeology*, 93.4, 1989, pp. 543–70.

BOURDIEU Pierre, *Outline of a Theory of Practice*, (trans. R. Nice), Cambridge: Cambridge University Press, 1977.

BRAUDE W.G. & KAPSTEIN I.J., *Tanna Debe Eliyyahu*, Jewish Publication Society of America, 1981.

BRODY Robert, "Judaism in the Sassanian Empire: a case study in religious coexistence", in S. Shaked & A. Netzer (eds.), *Irano-Judaica II*, Jerusalem: Ben-Zvi Institute, 1990.

BURKERT W., *Ancient Mystery Cults*, Cambridge Mass.: Harvard University Press, 1987.

CHAJES Z.H., *The Student's Guide through the Talmud*, J. Shachter transl., London: East and West Library, 1952.

COHEN Abner, *Custom and Politics in Urban Africa*, London: Routledge, 1969.

COHEN N.G., "Jewish names as cultural indicators in Antiquity", in *JSJ* 7, 1976, pp. 97–128.

COHEN Shaye J.D., "The significance of Yavneh: Pharisees, Rabbis, and the end of Jewish sectarianism", in *HUCA* 55, 1984, pp. 27–53.

COHEN Shaye J.D., "The origins of the matrilineal principle in Rabbinic law", in *AJS Review*, 10, 1985, pp. 19–53.

COHEN Shaye J.D., "The matrilineal principle in historical perspective", in *Judaism* 34, 1985, pp. 5–13.

COHEN Shaye J.D., "The Rabbinic conversion ceremony", in *JJS* 41:2, Autumn 1990, pp. 177–203.

COHEN Y., "The attitude to the Gentile in the Halakhah and in reality in the Tannaitic period", in *Immanuel* 9, 1979, pp. 32–41.

COHON Samuel S., "The name of God. A study in Rabbinic theology", in *HUCA* 23(1), 1950–1.

DAUBE David, "Rabbinic methods of interpretation and Hellenistic rhetoric", in *HUCA* 22, 1949, pp. 239–62.

De Ste CROIX G.E.M., *The Class Struggle in the Ancient Greek World*, London: Duckworth, 1981.

DEVEREUX George, "Ethnic identity: its logical foundations and its dysfunctions", in G. De Vos & L. Romanucci-Ross (eds.), *Ethnic Identity, Cultural Continuity and Change*, Palo Alto, 1975, pp. 42–70.

DEVEREUX George, *Basic problems of Ethnopsychiatry*, Univ. of Chicago, 1980.

DEXINGER F., "Limits of tolerance in Judaism: the Samaritan example", in E.P. Sanders et al., *Jewish and Christian self-definition*, vol. II (1981), pp. 88–114.

DOTHAN Moshe, *Hammath Tiberias: Early synagogues and the Hellenistic and Roman remains*, Jerusalem: Israel Exploration Society, 1983.

DUMONT Louis, *Homo Hierarchicus*, London: Weidenfeld & Nicholson, 1970.

DUMONT Louis, "The individual as impediment to sociological comparison and Indian history", in *Religion, Politics and History in India: Collected Papers in Indian Society*, The Hague: Mouton, 1970.

EILBERG-SCHWARTZ Howard (ed.), *People of the Body. Jews and Judaism from an embodied perspective*, New York: SUNY Press, 1992.

EISENMENGER Johann Andreas, *Entdecktes Judenthum*, Koenigsberg 1711, 2 vols.

Encyclopedia Talmudit, S.Y. Zevin (ed.), Jerusalem, vol. 6, 1954 (s.v. *Ger* & *Ger toshav*); vol. 15, 1976 (s.v. *Hokhmot hitzoniot*).

EPSTEIN J.N., *Mavo leNusah haMishna*, Jerusalem: Magnes Press, 1964 (2 vols.).

FALK Z.W., "On the historical background of the Talmudic laws regarding Gentiles", in *Immanuel* 14, 1982, pp. 106–109.

FEINTUCH Israel Z., *Mesorot veNus'haot baTalmud*, Ramat-Gan: Bar-Ilan University Press, 1985.

FELDMAN Louis H., "How much Hellenism in Jewish Palestine?", in *HUCA* 57, 1986, pp. 83–111.

FELDMAN Louis H., "Some observations on Rabbinic reactions to Roman rule in third century Palestine", in *HUCA* 1992, pp. 39–81.

FELDMAN Louis H., *Jew and Gentile in the Ancient World*, Princeton, NJ: Princeton Univ. Press, 1993.

FINKELSTEIN Louis (ed.), *Siphre ad Deut.*, New York: Jewish Theological Seminary, 1969.

FLESHER Paul V.M., *Oxen, Women or Citizens? Slaves in the System of the Mishnah*, Atlanta: Scholars Press, 1988 (n.v.).

FRIEDLANDER Gerald (trans.), *Pirke de Rabbi Eliezer*, New York: Sepher Hermon, 1981 (1916).

GARNSEY Peter, *Social Status and Legal Privilege in the Roman Empire*, Oxford Univ. Press, 1970.

GILAT Y.D., *R. Eliezer ben Hyrcanus. A scholar outcast*, Ramat-Gan: Bar-Ilan University Press, 1984.

GOLDSTEIN J.A., "Jewish acceptance and rejection of Hellenism", in E.P. Sanders et al. (eds.), *Jewish and Christian Self-Definition*, vol. 2 (1981), pp. 64–87.

GOODENOUGH Erwin R., *Jewish Symbols in the Graeco-Roman Period*, (13 vols.), New York: Bollingen, 1953–68.

GOODMAN Martin D., *State and Society in Roman Galilee AD132–212*, New Jersey: Rowman and Allanheld, 1983.

GOODMAN Martin D., "Proselytising in Rabbinic Judaism", in *JJS* 40:2, Autumn 1989, pp. 175–85.

GOODMAN Martin D., "Identity and Authority in Ancient Judaism", in *Judaism* 39(2), Spring 1990, pp. 192–201.

Greek Anthology (The), transl. W.R. Paton, London: Loeb, 1926, vol. 5.

GRUNFELD I., introduction to the English edition of S.R. Hirsch, *The Pentateuch*, Gateshead: Judaica Press, 1982 (1963).

GRYNBAUM Y., *Otzar haMalbim: Sefer haKarmel*, Jerusalem: Hamesorah, 1982, vol. II (Hebrew).

GUNTRIP Harry, *Schizoid Phenomena, Object-Relations and the Self*, London: Hogarth Press, 1968.

HADAS-LEBEL Mireille, "Le paganisme à travers les sources rabbiniques des IIe et IIIe siècles. Contribution à l'étude du syncrétisme dans l'empire romain", in *Aufstieg und Niedergang der Römischen Welt*, vol. II.19.2, Berlin and New York: Walter de Gruyter, 1979, pp. 397–485.

HADAS-LEBEL Mireille, "La fiscalité romaine dans la littérature rabbinique jusqu'à la fin du IIIème siecle", in *Revue des études juives* 143, 1984, pp. 5–29.

HADAS-LEBEL Mireille, "Jacob et Esaü ou Israel et Rome dans le Talmud et le Midrash", in *Revue de l'histoire des religions* 201, 1984, pp. 369–392.

HADAS-LEBEL Mireille, *Jérusalem contre Rome*, Paris: Cerf, 1990 (*n.v.*).

HALL Edith, *Inventing the Barbarian: Greek self-definition through tragedy*, Oxford: Oxford University Press, 1989.

HALLEWY E.E., "Concerning the ban on Greek wisdom", in *Tarbiz* 41, 1971–2, pp. 269–74.

HAMEL G., *Poverty and Charity in Roman Palestine, first three centuries CE*, Berkeley and LA: Univ. of California Press, 1990.

HARTOG François, *Le Miroir d'Hérodote. Essai sur la représentation de l'autre*, NRF Gallimard, 1980.

HEINEMANN Joseph, *Aggadot veToledotehen*, Jerusalem: Keter, 1974.

HEINEMANN Yitzhak, *Darkhey Ha-Aggadah*, Jerusalem: Magnes Press, 1954.

HENGEL Martin, *Judaism and Hellenism* (trans. J. Bowden), 2 vols., Philadelphia: Fortress Press, 1974.

HENGEL Martin, *The Zealots* (trans. D. Smith), Edinburgh: T & T Clark, 1989.

HERR Moshe David, "Anti-semitism in the Roman Empire as seen in Rabbinic literature" (Hebrew), in E.Z. Melamed (ed.), *Sefer Zikaron le-Binyamin De-Fries*, Jerusalem: Univ. of Tel Aviv Press, 1968–9, pp. 149–59.

HERR Moshe David, "The historical significance of the dialogues between Jewish sages and Roman dignitaries", in *Scripta Hierosolymitana* 22, Jerusalem: Magnes Press, 1971.

HERR Moshe David, in *Encyclopedia Judaica*, s.v. *Midrash*, vol. 11, pp. 1511–2.

HIRSHMAN M., "The preacher and his public in third century Palestine", in *JJS* 42(1), Spring 1991, pp. 108–114.

HOPKINS Keith, *Conquerors and Slaves*, Cambridge: Cambridge University Press, 1978.

ILAN Tal, "Notes on the distribution of Jewish women's names in Palestine in the Second Temple and Mishnaic periods", in *JJS* 40(2), Autumn 1989, pp. 186–200.

ISAAC Benjamin, *Limits of Empire: the Roman army in the East*, Oxford: Clarendon Press, 1990.

JACKSON Michael, *Paths towards a Clearing: radical empiricism and ethnographic inquiry*, Bloomington and Indianapolis: Indiana University Press, 1989.

JACOBS Louis, "How much of the Babylonian Talmud is pseudepigraphic?", in *JJS* 28, 1977, pp. 46–59.

JAMES William, *Pragmatism*, Indianapolis: Hackett Publishing Company, 1981 (1907).

JANKELEWITZ R., "The Gentiles' struggle for land ownership in Eretz-Israel", in A. Kasher, A. Oppenheimer, U. Rappaport (eds.), *Man and Law in Eretz-Israel in Antiquity*, Jerusalem: Yad Ben-Zvi, 1986, pp. 117–127 (Hebrew).

JASTROW Marcus, *A Dictionary of the Targumim, the Talmud Babli and Yerushalmi, and the Midrashic Literature*, New York: Judaica Press, 1971.

JONES A.H.M., *The Later Roman Empire—AD 285–602*, Oxford: Blackwell, 1964 (3 vols.).

KAPFERER Bruce, *Legends of People, Myths of State: violence, intolerance and political culture in Sri Lanka and Australia*, Washington & London: Smithsonian Institution Press, 1988.

KASHER Menahem M., *Torah Shelemah*, vol. 9 (tome 10: *Va'era*), New York: American Biblical Encyclopedia Society, 1945, (Hebrew).

KASSOVSKY H.J., *Otzar Leshon haMishna*, Frankfurt a.M. 1927, vol. 1.

KATZ Jacob, *Exclusiveness and Tolerance. Studies in Jewish-Gentile relations in Medieval and Modern times*, London: OUP, 1961.

KATZ Jacob, "*Af al pi she-hata, Yisrael hu*", reprinted in *Halakha veKabbala*, Jerusalem: Magnes Press, 1984.

KIMELMAN R., "*Birkat Ḥa-Minim* and the lack of evidence for an anti-Christian Jewish prayer", in E.P. Sanders et al., *Jewish and Christian self-definition*, vol. II (1981), pp. 226–44.

KLAGSBALD V., "La symbolique dans l'art juif", in *Revue des études juives* 144, 1985, pp. 408–38.

KNOHL Israel, "The acceptance of sacrifices from Gentiles", in *Tarbiz* 48, 1978-9, pp. 341–5, (Hebrew).

KRAEMER D., "On the reliability of attributions in the Babylonian Talmud", in *HUCA* 60, 1989, pp. 175–190.

KRAUSS Samuel, *Griechische und Lateinische Lehnwörter im Talmud, Midrash und Targum*, vol. 2, Berlin: Calvary & co., 1899.

KRAUSS Samuel, *Antoninus und Rabbi*, Vienna 1910.

KRISTEVA Julia, *Pouvoirs de l'Horreur—essai sur l'abjection*, Paris: Editions du seuil, 1980.

LAING R.D, *The Divided Self: an existential study in sanity and madness*, London: Penguin Books, 1965.

LEVINE Lee I., *Caesarea under Roman Rule*, Leiden:Brill, 1975.

LEVINE Lee I. (ed.), *Ancient Synagogues Revealed*, Jerusalem: Israel Exploration Society, 1981.

LEVINE Lee I., *The Rabbinic Class of Roman Palestine in Late Antiquity*, New York & Jerusalem: Jewish Theological Seminary, 1989.

LICHTENSTEIN Hans, "Die Fastenrolle", in *HUCA* 8–9, 1931-2, pp. 257–51.

LIEBERMAN Saul, *Greek in Jewish Palestine*, New York: Jewish Theological Seminary, 1942 (2nd ed. 1965).

LIEBERMAN Saul, *Hellenism in Jewish Palestine*, New York: Jewish Theological Seminary, 1950 (2nd ed. 1962).

LIEBERMAN Saul, *Tosefta Ki-feshuta—Zera'im vol. II*, New York: Jewish Theological Seminary, 1955.

LIEBERMAN Saul, 'How much Greek in Jewish Palestine?', in A. Altmann (ed.), *Biblical and Other Studies*, Cambridge Mass.: Harvard Univ. Press, 1963, pp. 123–41.

LIEBESCHUETZ J.H.G.W., "Epigraphic evidence on the Christianisation of Syria", in J. Fitz (ed.), *Limes: Akten des 11 Internationalen Limeskongresses, Szekesfehervar*, Budapest 1978, pp. 485–505.

LIEBESCHUETZ J.H.G.W., "Problems arising from the Conversion of Syria", in D. Baker (ed.), *The Church in Town and Countryside*, 1979.

LIENHARDT G., "Self: public, private. Some African representations", in M. Carrithers, S. Collins, S. Lukes (eds.), *The Category of the Person*, Cambridge: Cambridge University Press, 1985.

LINDER A., *The Jews in Roman Imperial Legislation*, Detroit: Wayne State Univ. Press and Jerusalem: Israel Academy of Sciences and Humanities, 1987.

LUZ Menahem, "Oenomaus and Talmudic anecdote", in *JSJ* 23, 1992, pp. 42–80.

MacMULLEN Ramsay, "Judicial savagery in the Roman Empire", in *Chiron*, 16, 1986, pp. 147–66.

McDONALD Maryon, "Britanny: politics and women in a minority world", in R. Ridd & H. Callaway (eds.), *Caught up in Conflict*, London: Macmillan 1986.

McDONALD Maryon, "*We are not French!*". *Language, culture and identity in Brittany*, London and New York: Routledge, 1989.

MAIMONIDES Moses, *Code of Law: the Book of Torts*, H. Klein (trans.), New Haven: Yale University Press, 1954.

MAIMONIDES Moses, *Code of Law: the Book of Judges*, A.M. Hershman (trans.), New Haven: Yale University Press, 1949.

MARMORSTEIN A., *Studies in Jewish Theology*, London: OUP, 1950.

MAUSS Marcel, "A category of the human mind: the notion of person, the notion of self" (1935, rev.1950), in M. Carrithers, S. Collins, S. Lukes (eds.), *The Category of the Person*, Cambridge: Cambridge University Press, 1985.

MERLEAU-PONTY Maurice, *Phenomenology of Perception*, trans. C. Smith, London: Routledge & Kegan Paul, 1962.

MILIKOWSKI Chaim, "Gehenna and the "Sinners of Israel" in the light of *Seder Olam*", in *Tarbiz* 55, 1985–6, (Hebrew).

MILIKOWSKY Chaim, "The *status quaestionis* of research in Rabbinic literature", in *JJS* 39(2), 1988, pp. 201–211.

NEEDHAM Rodney, *Primordial Characters*, Charlottesville, 1978.

NEUSNER Jacob, *The Idea of Purity in Ancient Judaism*, Leiden: Brill, 1973.

NEUSNER Jacob, *Talmudic Judaism in Sassanian Babylonia*, Leiden: Brill, 1976.

NEUSNER Jacob, *A History of the Mishnaic Law of Women: part 5*, Leiden: Brill, 1980.

NEUSNER Jacob, *Judaism: the evidence of the Mishna*, Univ. of Chicago Press: Chicago, 1981.

NEUSNER Jacob, *A History of the Mishnaic Law of Damages—part 2, Baba Mesia: translation and explanation*, Leiden: Brill, 1983.

NEUSNER Jacob, *Judaism and its Social Metaphors: Israel in the history of Jewish thought*, Cambridge: Cambridge University Press, 1989.

NOVAK D., *The Image of the Non-Jew in Judaism*, Toronto Studies in Theology 14, 1983.

OPPENHEIMER Aharon, *The 'Am Ha-Aretz*, Leiden: Brill, 1977.

PETUCHOWSKI Jakob J., "The Mumar. A study of Rabbinic psychology", in *HUCA* 30, 1959, pp. 179–90.

PETUCHOWSKI Jakob J., "Judaism as "mystery"—the hidden agenda?', in *HUCA*, 52, 1981, pp. 141–52.

POLL Solomon, *The Hasidic Community of Williamsburg*, New York: Schocken, 1969 (1962).

PORTON Gary G., "Forbidden transactions: prohibited commerce with Gentiles in earliest Rabbinism", in J. Neusner & E. Frerichs (eds.), *"To see ourselves as others see us"*, Atlanta: Scholars Press, 1985, pp. 317–335.

PORTON Gary G., *Goyim: Gentiles and Israelites in Mishnah-Tosefta*, Atlanta: Scholars Press, 1988.

POSTGATE J.N. & POWELL M.A. (eds.), *Bulletin on Sumerian Agriculture*, vol. II, Cambridge U.K.: Faculty of Oriental Studies, 1985, pp. 39–66, 153–8.

REICH R., "The hot bath-house (*balneum*), the *miqweh* and the Jewish community in the Second Temple period", in *JJS* 39(1), Spring 1988, pp. 102–7.

REICH R., "The Warm Bath and the Jewish Community in the Early Roman Period (2nd Jewish Commonwealth", in A. Kasher, V. Rappaport, G. Fuks (eds.), *Greece and Rome in Eretz Israel* (Hebrew), Jerusalem: Yad Ben-Zvi and IES, 1989, pp. 207–11.

REYNOLDS J. & TANNENBAUM R., *Jews and Godfearers at Aphrodisias*, Proceedings of the Cambridge Philological Society Suppl. 12, 1987.

ROSENTHAL David, *Mishna Aboda Zara—a critical edition with introduction* (Doct. Diss.), Jerusalem: Hebrew University, 1980 (2 vols.).

ROYCE Anya P., *Ethnic Identity: Strategies of Diversity*, Bloomington and Indianapolis: Indiana University Press, 1982.

RUBIN Jody P., "Celsus' decircumcision operation: medical and historical implications", in *Urology* July 1980, XVI:1, pp. 121–124.

RUBIN Nissan, "On drawing down the prepuce and incision of the foreskin", in *Zion* 54, 1989, pp. 105–17, (Hebrew).

SAFRAI S., "The avoidance of public office in papyrus Oxy.1477 and in Talmudic sources", in *JJS* 14, 1963, pp. 67–70.

SAFRAI Z., "Fairs in the land of Israel in the Mishna and Talmud period", in *Zion* 49, 1984, pp. 139–58, (Hebrew).

SANDERS E.P., *Judaism: Practice and Belief. 63BCE–66CE*, London: SCM Press & Philadelphia: Trinity Press Int., 1992.

SANDERS E.P., BAUMGARTEN A.I., & MENDELSON A. (eds.), *Jewish and Christian Self-Definition, vol. II: Aspects of Judaism in the Graeco-Roman Period*, Philadelphia: Fortress Press and London: SCM Press, 1981.

SANDMEL S., *Judaism and Christian Beginnings*, New York: Oxford University Press, 1978.

SARFATTI G.B., "The Table of the Covenant as a symbol of Judaism", in *Tarbiz* 29(4), July 1960, pp. 370–393.

SARTRE Jean-Paul, *Being and Nothingness: an essay on phenomenological ontology*, trans. H. Barnes, London: Methuen, 1957.

SCHÄFER Peter, "Research into Rabbinic literature: an attempt to define the *status quaestionis*", in *JJS* 37(2), 1986, pp. 139–152.

SCHÄFER Peter, "Once again the *status quaestionis* of research in Rabbinic literature: an answer to Chaim Milikowsky", in *JJS* 40(1), 1989, pp. 89–94.

SCHIFFMAN Lawrence H., "The Samaritans in Tannaitic Halacha", in *JQR* 75:4, 1985, pp. 323–350.

SCHIFFMAN Lawrence H., "Jewish identity and Jewish descent", in *Judaism* 34, 1985, pp. 78–84.

SCHIFFMAN Lawrence H., *Who was a Jew?*, Ktav: New Jersey, 1985.

SCHOCHET E.J., *Animal life in Jewish tradition*, New York: Ktav, 1984.

SCHOLEM Gershom, "The Star of David: history of a symbol", in id., *The Messianic Idea in Judaism*, London: Allen and Unwin, 1971.

SCHÜRER Emil, *The History of the Jewish People in the Age of Jesus Christ (175 B.C.–A.D. 135)*, revised and edited by G. Vermes and F. Millar (and M. Black (vols. I–II), M. Goodman (vols. III.1–2)), 4 vols., Edinburgh: T. & T. Clark, 1973–87.

SEPTIMUS B., "Better under Edom than under Ishmael: the history of a saying", in *Zion*, 47, 1982 (Hebrew).

SHAHID I., *Byzantium and the Arabs in the Fourth Century*, Washington 1984.

SHIMOFF S.R., "Hellenisation among the Rabbis, some evidence from early Aggadot concerning David and Solomon", in *JSJ* 18.2, 1987, pp. 168–87.

SMITH Anthony D., *The Ethnic Revival*, Cambridge: Cambridge University Press, 1981.

SMITH Jonathan Z., *Map is not Territory*, Leiden: Brill, 1978.

SMITH Morton, "On the Shape of God and the Humanity of Gentiles", in J. Neusner (ed.), *Religions in Antiquity. Essays in memory of E.R. Goodenough*, Leiden: Brill, 1968.

SOKOLOFF M., *A Dictionary of Jewish Palestinian Aramaic of the Byzantine Period*, Ramat-Gan: Bar-Ilan Univ. Press, 1990.

SPERBER Daniel, *A Commentary on Derech Erez Zuta, ch. 5–8*, Ramat-Gan: Bar-Ilan University Press, 1990.

STERN Sacha, "The Death of Idolatry?", in *Le'ela*, April 1993, pp. 26–8.

STERN Sacha, "Attribution and Authorship in the Babylonian Talmud", in *JJS* 45.1, Spring 1994, pp. 28–51.

STRACK H.L., *Introduction to the Talmud and Midrash*, Philadelphia: Jewish Publishing Society, 1931.

STRACK H.L. & STEMBERGER G., *Introduction to the Talmud and Midrash*, Edinburgh: T. & T. Clark, 1991.

SUSSMANN J., *Sugyot to the orders Zera'im and Tohorot* (Hebrew), Doct. Diss., Jerusalem: Hebrew University, 1969.

SUSSMAN J., "'An Halachic inscription from the Beth-Shean valley'", in *Tarbiz* 43, 1974, pp. 88–158, cf pp. 127 & 135 (Hebrew).
SUSSMAN J., "The History of Halakha and the Dead Sea Scrolls", in *Tarbiz* 59, 1989–90, pp. 11–76 (Hebrew).
TEIXIDOR Javier, "Interpretations and misinterpretations of the East in Hellenistic times", in Per BILDE, Troels Engber-Pedersen, Lise Hannestad, and Jan Zahle (eds), *Religion and Religious Practice in the Seleucid Kingdom*, Aarhus University Press, 1990, pp. 66–78.
URBACH Ephraim E., "Homilies of the Rabbis on the prophets of the nations and the Balaam stories", in *Tarbiz* 25, 1955–6, pp. 272–89, (Hebrew).
URBACH Ephraim E., "The Rabbinic laws of idolatry in the second and third centuries in the light of archaeological and historical facts', in *Israel Exploration Journal* 9, 1959.
URBACH Ephraim E., "Halakhot regarding slaves as a source for the social history of the 2nd Temple and the Talmudic period", in *Zion* 25, 1960, pp. 141–189, esp. 162–6 (Hebrew).
URBACH Ephraim E., *The Sages, their Concepts and Beliefs*, (trans. I. Abrahams), Cambridge (Mass.): Harvard Univ. Press, 1975.
VERMES Geza, *Post-Biblical Jewish Studies*, Leiden: Brill, 1975.
VERMES Geza, "*Leviticus* 18:21 in ancient Jewish Bible Exegesis", in *Studies in Aggadah, Targum and Jewish Liturgy in Memory of Joseph Heinemann*, Jerusalem: Magnes Press, 1981.
WASSERSTEIN A., "Rabban Gamliel and Proclus the philosopher", in *Zion* 45, 1980, pp. 257–67 (Hebrew).
WEGNER Judith R., *Chattel or Person? The status of women in the Mishna*, Oxford: Oxford University Press, 1988.
WEGNER Judith R., "The image and status of women in Classical Rabbinic Judaism", in J.R. Baskin (ed.), *Jewish Women in Historical Perspective*, Detroit: Wayne State University Press, 1991, pp. 68–93.
WOLFSON Elliot R., "Circumcision and the Divine Name: a study in the transmission of esoteric doctrine", in *JQR* 78, 1987, pp. 77–85.
ZALCMAN Lawrence, "Christians, Noṣrim, and Nebuchadnezzar's daughter", in *JQR* 81 (3–4), 1991, pp. 411–26.
ZEITLIN Solomon, "The names Hebrew, Jew and Israel", in *JQR* 43, 1952–3, pp. 365–79.
ZOHAR Dana, *The Quantum Self*, London: Bloomsbury, 1990.

INDEX

ARBEITEN ZUR GESCHICHTE
DES ANTIKEN JUDENTUMS UND DES URCHRISTENTUMS

———

MARTIN HENGEL *Tübingen* · PETER SCHÄFER *Berlin*
PIETER W. VAN DER HORST *Utrecht* · MARTIN GOODMAN *Oxford*
DANIËL R.SCHWARTZ *Jerusalem*

———

1 M. Hengel. *Die Zeloten.* Untersuchungen zur jüdischen Freiheitsbewegung in der Zeit von Herodes I. bis 70 n.Chr. 2. verbesserte und erweiterte Auflage. 1976. ISBN 9004043276

2 O. Betz. *Der Paraklet.* Fürsprecher im häretischen Spätjudentum, im Johannes-Evangelium und in neu gefundenen gnostischen Schriften. 1963. ISBN 9004001093

5 O. Betz. *Abraham unser Vater.* Juden und Christen im Gespräch über die Bibel. Festschrift für Otto Michel zum 60. Geburtstag. Herausgegeben von O. Betz, M. Hengel, P. Schmidt. 1963. ISBN 9004001107

6 A. Böhlig. *Mysterion und Wahrheit.* Gesammelte Beiträge zur spätantiken Religionsgeschichte. 1968. ISBN 9004001115

7 B.J. Malina. *The Palestinian Manna Tradition.* The Manna Tradition in the Palestinian Targums and its Relationship to the New Testament Writings. 1968. ISBN 9004001123

8 J. Becker. *Untersuchungen zur Entstehungsgeschichte der Testamente der zwölf Patriarchen.* 1970. ISBN 9004001131

9 E. Bickerman. *Studies in Jewish and Christian History.*
   1. 1976. ISBN 9004043969
   2. 1980. ISBN 9004060154
   3. 1986. ISBN 9004074805

11 Z.W. Falk. *Introduction to Jewish Law of the Second Commonwealth.*
   1. 1972. ISBN 9004035370
   2. 1978. ISBN 9004052496

12 H. Lindner. *Die Geschichtsauffassung des Flavius Josephus im Bellum Judaicum.* Gleichzeitig ein Beitrag zur Quellenfrage. 1972. ISBN 9004035028

13 P. Kuhn. *Gottes Trauer und Klage in der rabbinischen Überlieferung.* Talmud und Midrasch. 1978. ISBN 9004056998

14 I. Gruenwald. *Apocalyptic and Merkavah Mysticism.* 1980. ISBN 9004059598

15 P. Schäfer. *Studien zur Geschichte und Theologie des rabbinischen Judentums.* 1978. ISBN 9004058389

16 M. Niehoff. *The Figure of Joseph in Post-Biblical Jewish Literature.* 1992. ISBN 900409556X

17 W.C. van Unnik. *Das Selbstverständnis der jüdischen Diaspora in der hellenistisch-römischen Zeit.* Aus dem Nachlaß herausgegeben und bearbeitet von P. W. van der Horst. 1993. ISBN 9004096930

18 A. D. Clarke. *Secular and Christian Leadership in Corinth*. A Socio-Historical and Exegetical Study of 1 Corinthians 1-6. 1993. ISBN 9004098623

19 D. R. Lindsay. *Josephus and Faith*. Πίστις and πιστεύειν as Faith Terminology in the Writings of Flavius Josephus and in the New Testament. 1993. ISBN 9004098585

20 D. M. Stec (ed.). *The Text of the Targum of Job*. An Introduction and Critical Edition. 1994. ISBN 9004098747

21 J. W. van Henten & P. W. van der Horst (eds.). *Studies in Early Jewish Epigraphy*. 1994. ISBN 9004099166

22 B. S. Rosner. *Paul, Scripture and Ethics*. A Study of 1 Corinthians 5-7. 1994. ISBN 9004100652

23 S. Stern. *Jewish Identity in Early Rabbinic Writings*. 1994. ISBN 9004100121